American Paintings from the Manoogian Collection

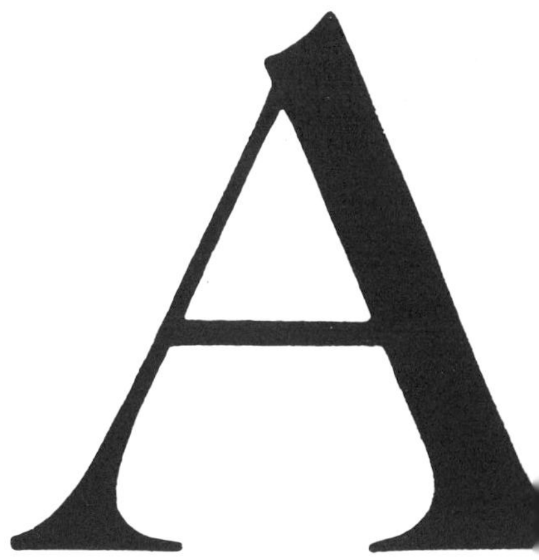

National Gallery of Art, Washington / Detroit Institute of Arts

Paintings from • the Manoogian Collection

merican

The exhibition is made possible by United Technologies Corporation

The exhibition was organized by the Detroit Institute of Arts and the National Gallery of Art, Washington

Exhibition dates:
National Gallery of Art, Washington: 4 June 1989–4 September 1989
Fine Arts Museums of San Francisco: 23 September 1989–26 November 1989
The Metropolitan Museum of Art, New York: 18 December 1989–25 February 1990
Detroit Institute of Arts: 27 March 1990–27 May 1990

This book was produced by the editors office, National Gallery of Art
Editor-in-Chief, Frances P. Smyth

Designed by Derek Birdsall RDI
Color photographs by Dirk Bakker
Edited by Jane Sweeney
Typeset in Monotype Van Dijck
Printed in England by Balding + Mansell International Limited
on Parilux cream 150 gsm
Dimensions are given in inches, followed by centimeters in parentheses

Cover: Detail, William Merritt Chase, *The Nursery* 1890 (cat. 51)

Library of Congress Cataloging-in-Publication-Data

American paintings from the Manoogian Collection.
p. cm.
Catalogue of an exhibition organized by the Detroit Institute of Arts and the National Gallery of Art, Washington, held at the National Gallery, June 4–Sept. 4, 1989, and at three other museums.
Bibliography: p.
Includes index.
ISBN 0-89468-130-3
1. Painting, American—Exhibitions. 2. Painting, Modern—19th century—United States—Exhibitions. 3. Manoogian, Richard—Art Collections—Exhibitions. 4. Painting—Private collections—Michigan—Detroit—Exhibitions. I. Manoogian, Richard. II. National Gallery of Art (U.S.) III. Detroit Institute of Arts.
ND210.A72829 1989
759.13'074'73—dc20 89-3337
CIP

Contents

Foreword

Often anonymous and always generous, Richard Manoogian has been a lender to exhibitions of American art for many years. Indeed, no important American exhibition would be complete without something from his extraordinary comprehensive collection. Here, for the first time, *American Paintings from the Manoogian Collection* presents to the public an entire exhibition drawn solely from this great private collection. Those visitors who are taken with the range and quality of these paintings are reminded that this show includes only a part of the Manoogian holdings, which are so extensive that to show them in their entirety is not feasible. Curators at the National Gallery of Art and the Detroit Institute of Arts chose the works in this exhibition to reflect the keenness of Richard Manoogian's eye, the splendid diversity of his taste, and, what we are sure he is most proud of, the greatness of American art. That, above all, is what this project celebrates with enthusiasm and conviction.

As museum directors we are keenly aware that long before the advent of public museums in which American art could be seen, there existed in the United States a remarkable succession of private collectors. Although few in number, they undertook to support and champion the art of their own country with unswerving dedication and commendable farsightedness. Richard Manoogian belongs to this proud tradition of private collecting. We are particularly pleased that by hosting *American Paintings from the Manoogian Collection* our institutions are able to recognize the public importance of private collecting.

The organization of this exhibition was the joint responsibility of Nancy Rivard Shaw, curator of American art at the Detroit Institute of Arts, Nicolai Cikovsky, Jr., curator of American art at the National Gallery, and Franklin Kelly, formerly a curator in the department of American art at the National Gallery, and now curator of collections at the Corcoran Gallery of Art. They shared the responsibilities for the scholarly editing of the exhibition catalogue and also contributed their own catalogue entries. Larry Curry, curator of the Manoogian collection, deserves particular mention and special thanks. We are grateful not only to them but also to the many individuals, including the authors of the catalogue, who worked with such efficiency and grace to make this exhibition a reality. Their names and contributions are detailed in the acknowledgments and list below.

We offer our special thanks to United Technologies Corporation and its chairman, Robert F. Daniell, for so generously supporting the exhibition and its catalogue. Above all, of course, our deepest and ultimate debt of gratitude is reserved for Richard Manoogian.

J. Carter Brown
Director
National Gallery of Art

Samuel Sachs II
Director
Detroit Institute of Arts

Richard Manoogian A Conversation on Collecting

(In response to questions from Nicolai Cikovsky, Jr., Samuel Sachs II, and Nancy Rivard Shaw)

I began collecting seriously for several different reasons. In the early 1970s I became a trustee of the Detroit Institute of Arts, and I was also appointed to the White House Preservation Committee and the Fine Arts Committee at the State Department. Since I was devoting time to the arts from a civic standpoint, I decided that I might as well get more personally involved, and began collecting. I'm sure that collecting also served as a diversion from my busy work schedule. My work regularly took me to New York and other major cities where I often had opportunities to take an hour or two to visit galleries or museums, which reinforced my interest in art.

Initially, I was interested in contemporary art. My first acquisitions included Pollock, Stella, Kline, and David Smith. I even bought two paintings at the original Scull auction in the early 1970s. Unfortunately, my home had limited wall space, which made collecting large contemporary paintings difficult. At that time, there were a number of collectors in the Detroit area who had a great love of nineteenth-century American art. I think some of their excitement rubbed off on me, which started my collecting in that direction.

I really began putting the major part of my collection together in the late 1970s. It was then that Larry Curry joined me as curator. Larry had been a curator of American art at several museums and I had a great deal of confidence in his "eye" and judgment. Although we have not always agreed on every painting, our tastes are very similar and Larry's knowledge of the history of American art and his museum background have played a major role in building the collection.

My wife, Janie, has also had a major influence on my collecting. Her support and tolerance of all the time and energy that goes into collecting have been invaluable. She has a natural instinct for judging the quality of paintings and I have come to regret the few times I did not act upon her advice.

I started collecting abstract paintings because of my liking for color and form. However, I also love trompe l'oeil still lifes, several of which are included in the exhibition. I admire their precision and detail and the extra amount of work that an artist puts into a trompe l'oeil painting. Maybe that comes from my manufacturing background and the appreciation it fosters in the physical effort that goes into making a successful, quality product. I hope that the same appreciation for quality is reflected in all the paintings in the exhibition.

I have always admired the great nineteenth-century landscapes because they were painted when our country was still young and growing. They expressed the uniqueness of America, as opposed to portraits, whose style might have been copied from other times and places. Another area I have always loved is genre, because these paintings show American life as it was and as it has evolved. Although many collectors think genre is too pictorial, I find that it captures the essence of a way of life we would have otherwise had difficulty visualizing. I have also loved impressionist works from my earliest days as a collector.

I'm often asked, if the house is burning down, which of your paintings would you grab? Forgetting value for the moment, it would be quite a few; I'd probably try to grab all of them. If I had to identify my personal favorites in the collection I would probably end up identifying twenty, thirty, or forty pictures.

My collection is probably broader and much larger than most American private collections. I don't know if that's good or bad or just an obsession. It depends on your viewpoint. In retrospect, I think there are areas in which I might have been more selective, but a lot of that was a learning process. Sometimes one grows to love a painting whether or not it is the best work by that artist. The reasons for loving it may have to do with the painting itself, or what went into acquiring it. Every collection goes through a pruning process, but looking back, I regret letting go of only a few pictures. That's one of the advantages of having a large collection.

Some collectors know exactly what they are looking for—a Bierstadt of 1860 or 1862, or whatever it might be—and there's nothing wrong with that. Other collectors just love certain things, regardless of the year, or the period, or the artist. If they love it, they want it in their collection. I probably fall somewhere between these two types of collectors. I am trying to build a comprehensive collection, but for me passion probably plays a bigger role than seeking out particular artists and periods. Anyway, I'm not sure in collecting you can pick exactly what you want. The passion of collecting is simply restricted by what is available.

One of the most frustrating aspects of collecting is trying to cover certain areas that are relatively rare. One would love to have important works by major artists—Homer, Whistler, or Eakins—but very few are available. The search goes on, of course, but the facts are that only so many paintings exist, and many are already in other permanent collections. I have never collected with the idea of having something by everyone or of being encyclopedic. I have found it very enjoyable to locate a terrific painting by a lesser-known artist—a work of high quality by somebody of whom no one ever heard or really appreciated. I love to find a hidden treasure by an unknown artist or an unusual work by a well-known artist that would surprise most people. I think that is as exciting, or more exciting, than finding major works by more recognized artists.

It is also a challenge to find paintings that are dirty or in need of restoration and to try to visualize how they might look when cleaned and restored and reframed. Such works may have been overlooked by others, and yet turn out to be wonderful works of art.

In short, for me nothing surpasses the search and intrigue of collecting. I think all collectors get special satisfaction from locating objects that are difficult to find.

My greatest regret has been not paying a little bit more for something that was just wonderful, or taking the advice of experts who said something was not important enough to be in the collection even though my heart told me otherwise. Listening to your own feelings can lead you into trouble once in a while, but as long as you enjoy something, even if other people don't agree, you are still getting satisfaction out of owning it. It is surprising that if you really love something you tend not to change your opinion about it. On the other hand, if you are talked into acquiring something because it is important, you will often decide later that it is not something you are really all that excited about. If a collector really loves something at first sight, that reaction tends not to go away. The missing of the object that aroused that feeling may be a painful thing he has to live with all of his life.

It is crucial for a collector to become knowledgeable enough to be able to make his own judgments. When a collector cannot learn everything he needs to know, he should seek out the best information and guidance available. He must be free to make his own choices, and sometimes to disregard the advice he has been given. For example, you may have been told that this is not the period that you want of this artist, or this is not an artist of sufficient importance to have in your collection. Yet, you just love the work anyway. That's what personal collections are all about.

Consciously or unconsciously, collecting American paintings is important to me in a special way. Those from an ethnic background like mine often have a great appreciation for America because of the opportunity this country has created for their families. The result is a deep love for one's country and a particular appreciation for the period in which the country grew and expanded. A love for one's country also instills a desire to give something back to it. I have lent paintings to many exhibitions. To some extent my collecting has been driven by wanting to share my paintings with others as a way of giving something back to the country that has been so good for our family.

Although I enjoy collecting and sharing the collection with others, I am a very private person. In fact, it is because of the personal publicity that inevitably results from an exhibition that I have been reluctant to have one before now. Yet, I believe strongly that it is important for people to appreciate the unique character, diversity, and quality of American art. I hope that the present exhibition will encourage others to both appreciate and collect American art.

Detroit
1989

Acknowledgments

The exhibition and catalogue would not have been possible without the support and cooperation of numerous individuals. Warm thanks are due to our catalogue designer Derek Birdsall and to Frances Smyth, Jane Sweeney, and Mary Yakush of the editors office of the National Gallery. At the Detroit Institute of Arts, Dirk Bakker produced the superb photographs, assisted by Robert Hensleigh, Timothy Thayer, and Marianne Letasi. Staff at participating institutions, Sally Mills and Marc Simpson of the Fine Arts Museums of San Francisco and John K. Howat and Lewis Sharp of The Metropolitan Museum of Art, contributed in various ways to the selection of the exhibition and the writing of its catalogue.

Particular thanks are due to Joan Barnes, registrar of the Manoogian Collection, for her careful compilation of the vital statistics of the collection, and to Carl Anderson of Masco Corporation, who assisted in handling and shipping several works to Detroit. At the National Gallery, Mary Suzor, registrar, D. Dodge Thompson, chief of exhibition programs, and Deborah Shepherd, exhibition officer, worked with Judith Dressel, head of registration and exhibitions at the Detroit Institute of Arts, handling myriad details with the appearance of ease. Thanks are due to Elizabeth A. C. Weil, the National Gallery's corporate relations officer, assisted by Karen Ward, for arranging the funding of the exhibition.

At the Detroit Institute of Arts, Barbara Heller and her conservation staff, particularly Alfred Ackerman and Kenneth Katz, performed such treatment of the collection as was necessary for the exhibition, and James W. Tottis in the department of American art coordinated the photography and conservation of the paintings and assisted with numerous administrative and organizational details; Anita Calvert, departmental secretary, performed a variety of clerical tasks with timeliness and care, and Sheila Michael, a departmental intern in the early stages of research, gathered materials for catalogue entries. Others who have been unusually helpful are Kyra Curtis and Carla Reczek of the Art Research Library, and Jeanne Zanke of the Archives of American Art. At the National Gallery, Patricia Burda and Michael Godfrey did research for catalogue entries and biographies, and Rosemary O'Reilly efficiently and patiently handled all the necessary correspondence, countless telephone calls, and endless lists.

Nicolai Cikovsky, Jr.
Franklin Kelly
Nancy Rivard Shaw

Contributors to the Catalogue

Henry Adams
Nancy Anderson
Linda Ayres
Patricia Burda
Warder H. Cadbury
Gerald L. Carr
Sarah Cash
Deborah Chotner
Nicolai Cikovsky, Jr.
Carol Clark
Sarah Towne Hufford
Franklin Kelly
Sally Mills
Gwendolyn Owens
Ronald G. Pisano
Jules D. Prown
Debora Rindge
Richard H. Saunders
Nancy Rivard Shaw
Marc Simpson
D. Dodge Thompson
James W. Tottis
John Wilmerding
Christopher Kent Wilson

I

Jasper Francis Cropsey (1823–1900)
The Backwoods of America 1858
oil on canvas, 42 x 70¼ (106.7 x 178.4)

In 1858, when Cropsey painted this ambitious view of the American wilderness, he had been living in London for two years. It was a time of creative genius, financial success, and critical acclaim. This was Cropsey's second European trip (he had traveled extensively on the continent from May 1847 to July 1849), and he seems to have settled in London because he correctly believed there was a market for his pastoral landscapes with English clients and traveling Americans.

During these years he painted a number of English subjects, but the majority of his works capitalized on his ability to capture the wild and rugged beauty of the American landscape. *The Backwoods of America* was among his largest works to that date and he must certainly have considered it a major achievement. As it was exhibited at the Royal Academy (in 1858), he most likely painted it with this exhibition in mind. His time and effort were quickly rewarded. On 10 March 1859 he recorded in his account book that the painting had been sold through W. B. Huggins in Glasgow for $725, his third most lucrative sale to that date.[1]

The subject of *The Backwoods of America* is one that fascinated Americans and Europeans alike. The painting, which was among Cropsey's London works *which attracted the greatest attention*,[2] depicts a hearty pioneer family in solitary isolation. It is in many ways symbolic of the indomitable American spirit, and typifies a lifestyle confronted by countless families throughout much of the rural countryside from Maine to Minnesota. It was the kind of image that through literature, music, and paint was becoming engraved on the consciousness of the American and European mind.

The setting is an early morning in late summer. Ripening corn, cabbages, and pumpkins herald the impending harvest. Light of the sun, which is just beginning to rise over the mountain peaks, strikes the floor of the valley. A beam cuts through the trees to the right and highlights a lone pioneer who, accompanied by his dog, sets out on a long day of felling trees. He carries over his shoulder an American long-handled broadax. This improved tool was developed about 1740 for felling trees and building log cabins.[3]

The cabin he has just departed sits on a knoll and faces east, a site preferred by some builders to benefit from the warmth of the morning sun.[4] Other family members have also begun their daily activities: the pioneer's wife stands in the doorway overseeing a small child on the stoop, while two more children play nearby. Further from the house a cow is being milked and a boat launched.

The pioneer family was a self-contained unit, entirely self-sufficient, and above all determined to succeed. De Tocqueville, who met many log cabin dwellers during his stay in America, eloquently described the male pioneer type represented by Cropsey's ax-wielding foreground figure: *His angular muscles and thin limbs make one recognize at first glance the inhabitant of New England. This man has not been born in the solitude where he lives. His temperament alone makes that clear. His first years were passed in a society used to thought and argument. It is the strength of his will that has taken him to do work in the wilds to which he seems little adapted. But if his physical powers seem too slight for this undertaking, his features lined by the cares of life bespeak a practical intelligence and a cold, persevering energy that strike one at first sight. His movements are slow and stiff, his words measured and his appearance austere.*[5] In the lean-to attached to the house, a scythe, symbolic of the fields yet to come, hangs on a hook. An animal skin drying on the cabin wall is a further reminder of the degree of dependence on the forest for food and clothing.

A number of elements in the composition suggest that it is this pioneer family's first year in the wilderness. Their rudimentary garden has been sited on recently cleared ground and their cabin seems to have been hastily constructed. The roof is composed of long wide boards. Eventually these would most likely be replaced with shingles or "shakes" held down with weight timbers. But all this required additional skills, riving tools, and time. Even the cabin itself was considered a first and temporary dwelling that most settlers believed would be superseded in a few years by more commodious frame houses.[6]

The figure of a woodsman, ax in hand, literally carving his existence in the seemingly endless virgin forests that covered so much of North America, was both myth and reality. Despite the lifestyle of many Americans that was the complete opposite of what Cropsey chose to depict here, this was the vision that symbolized the American experience. It is not surprising that Cropsey chose to paint such a scene. It was simply the way both Americans and Europeans chose to characterize the North American experience. In a similar fashion Cropsey selected ancient castles and picturesque coastal subjects, rather than less idyllic but more accurate urban subjects, when he chose to paint English or Scottish landscapes.

The subject of the pioneer family alone in the wilderness was one that had occupied Cropsey's interest at least since 1847 when he painted *Retired Life* (Mrs. John C. Newington). Presumably, Cropsey's enthusiasm for the subject had been whetted by Thomas Cole, who during the 1830s and 1840s set the precedent for depicting this subject. In both composition and size Cropsey's work most directly recalls Cole's *The Hunter's Return* (fig. 1), painted in 1845 and exhibited in 1848 at the American Art-Union memorial exhibition for the artist. Cropsey revived all the essential elements assembled by his predecessor: the isolated rustic cabin, the supportive family, as well as the residue of frontier life (felled trees, rudimentary garden, livestock, and the ever-burning hearth).

The specific inspiration for Cropsey's painting was his August 1849 sketching trip to New Hampshire's White Mountains. Like Cole twenty-two years before him, Cropsey traveled to this area of northern New Hampshire to see the tallest range of mountain peaks in New England and visit sites such as Franconia Notch, Crawford Notch, and the Old Man of the Mountain. This trip enabled Cropsey to collect firsthand the raw material for more ambitious treatments of American wilderness subjects. Throughout this trip Cropsey recorded, in an unpublished notebook, detailed observations of flora and climatic conditions.

Traveling by coach from Crawford Notch to Franconia on 15 August 1849, Cropsey vividly described the images that ultimately became the basis for *The Backwoods of America*. As he wound along the Amnonoosuc River below *a particularly fine peak of mountain* he observed: *now come some log houses, some garden patches about them sunflower, and morning glory, and pumpkin vines were growing and creeping around—our place of the description not very far from the above named place [Fabyan] had much of the picturesque about it.*[7] To complement his notes on this journey Cropsey drew several small sketches of log cabins and their setting (figs. 2, 3). An undated compositional sketch (fig. 4) for the painting also survives and was presumably made in the 1850s.

Although Cropsey had employed the cabin motif as early as 1847, it was not until two years after his European trip that the first highly developed use of the cabin appeared in a painting (*Sunset, Eagle Cliff*, Museum of Fine Arts, Boston). A handful of other works survive that suggest the cabin had become a staple element of his landscape vocabulary.[8]

Despite the relative success Cropsey had with these log cabin subjects, after 1858 he is known to have done only two further versions. In later paintings of White Mountain subjects, such as *Sunset: Eagle Cliff, Franconia Notch, New Hampshire* (1867, Peter W. Fosburgh), he seems to have abandoned the log cabin motif. This development is, perhaps, a reflection of the increasing settlement evident in the area and a realization that, while still majestic, the White Mountains were no longer the untamed wilderness on the frontier of America. Further suggestive of this is that in his major paintings of the 1860s, such as *Valley of Wyoming* (1865, The Metropolitan Museum of Art, New York), which is similar in size and conception to *The Backwoods of America*, the log cabin has been succeeded by a two-story house with porches and a barn. In the foreground picnickers recline in a open field reflective of the tamed landscape.

After the artist's sale of *The Backwoods of America*, it remained in a private collection in Glasgow until 1932, when it was sold by Williams & Such, London, to William H. Abott, of London, Ontario, Canada. It was eventually acquired by the University of Western Ontario, London, where it remained until 1981.[9] *Richard H. Saunders*

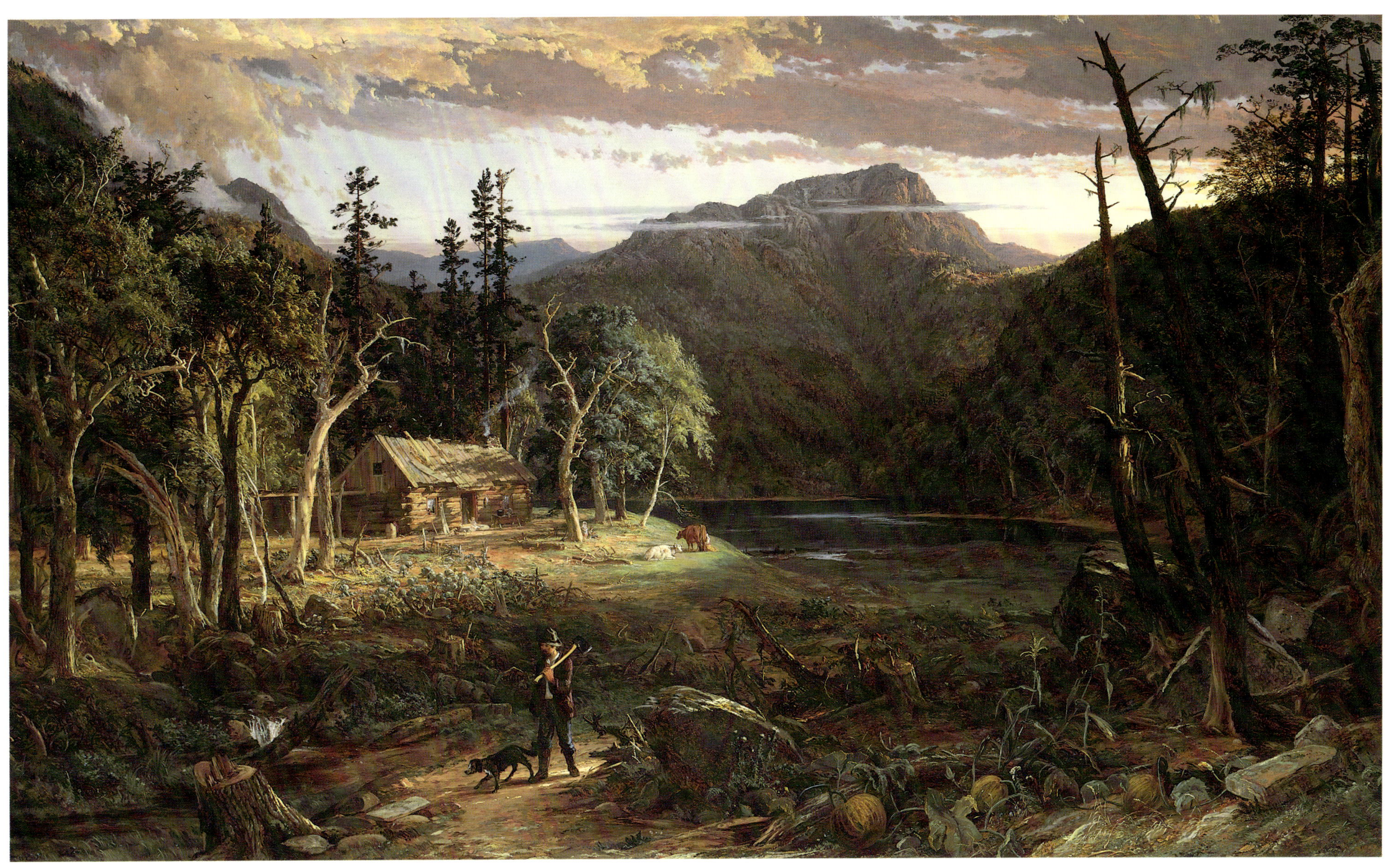

1. William S. Talbot, *Jasper F. Cropsey 1823–1900* (New York, 1977), 318.
2. Henry Tuckerman, *The Book of the Artists* (New York, 1867), 536.
3. C. A. Weslager, *The Log Cabin in America* (New Brunswick, New Jersey, 1969), 11.
4. Weslager, *Log Cabin*, 12–13.
5. Alexis de Tocqueville, *Journey to America*, *Log Cabin*, trans. George Lawrence, ed. J. P. Mayer (New Haven, 1960), 334, as quoted in Weslager, *Log Cabin*, 22–23.
6. Weslager, *Log Cabin*, 15, 21.
7. "White Mountain Excursion [1849]," notebook, manuscript collection, Newington-Cropsey Foundation, Hastings-on-Hudson, New York.
8. At least five pictures with related compositions survive: *Eagle Cliff, New Hampshire*, 1850, 23 x 40 inches (Saint Louis Art Museum); *Eagle Cliff, Franconia Notch, New Hampshire*, 1858, 24 x 39 inches (North Carolina Museum of Art, Raleigh); *Eagle Cliff (Pioneer's House)*, 1859, 18 x 29 inches (Hirschl & Adler, New York, 1975); *Sunset after a Storm in the Catskills*, 1861, 20 x 32 inches; and *Fishing*, 1868 10 x 15 inches (Columbus Museum of Art, Ohio).
9. *American 18th Century, 19th Century & Western Paintings, Drawings, Watercolors & Sculpture*, Sotheby Parke Bernet, Inc., Sale 4583M, 23 April 1981, lot 18.

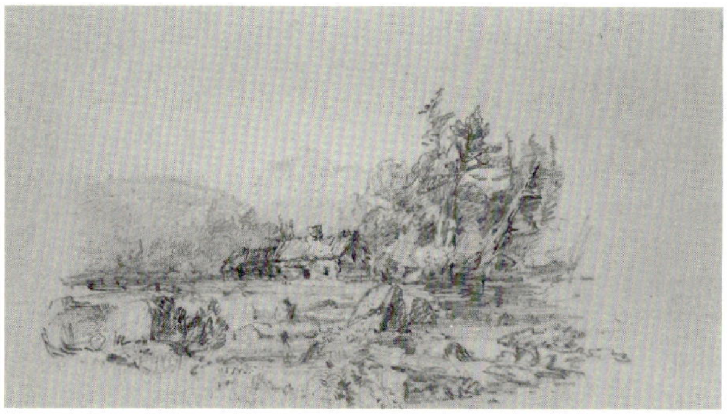

Fig. 2
Jasper Francis Cropsey, "White Mountain Excursion," 1849, Newington-Cropsey Foundation [David M. Hayes Photography]

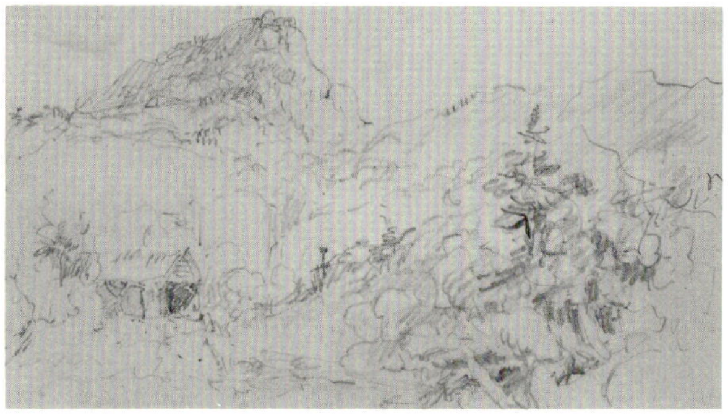

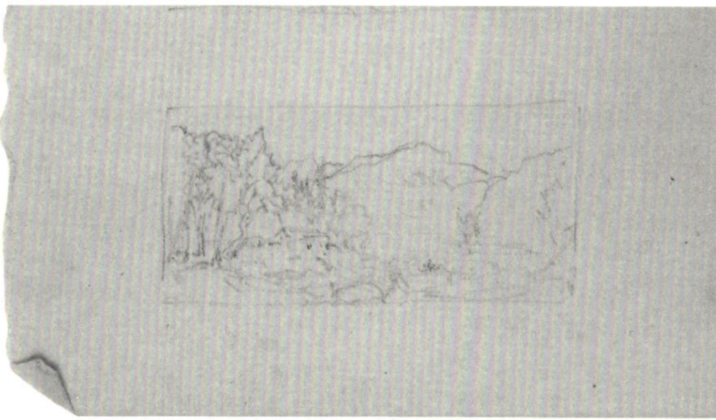

Fig. 3
Jasper Francis Cropsey, "White Mountain Excursion," 1849, Newington-Cropsey Foundation [David M. Hayes Photography]

Fig. 4
Jasper Francis Cropsey, "White Mountain Excursion," 1849, Newington-Cropsey Foundation [David M. Hayes Photography]

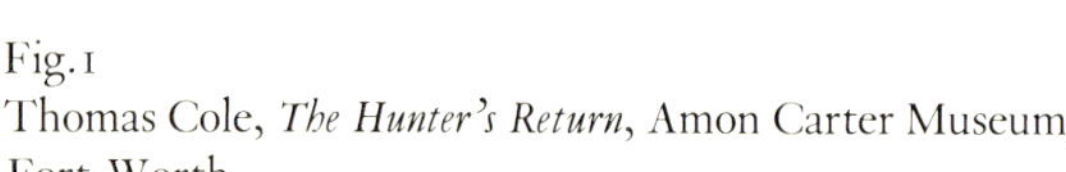

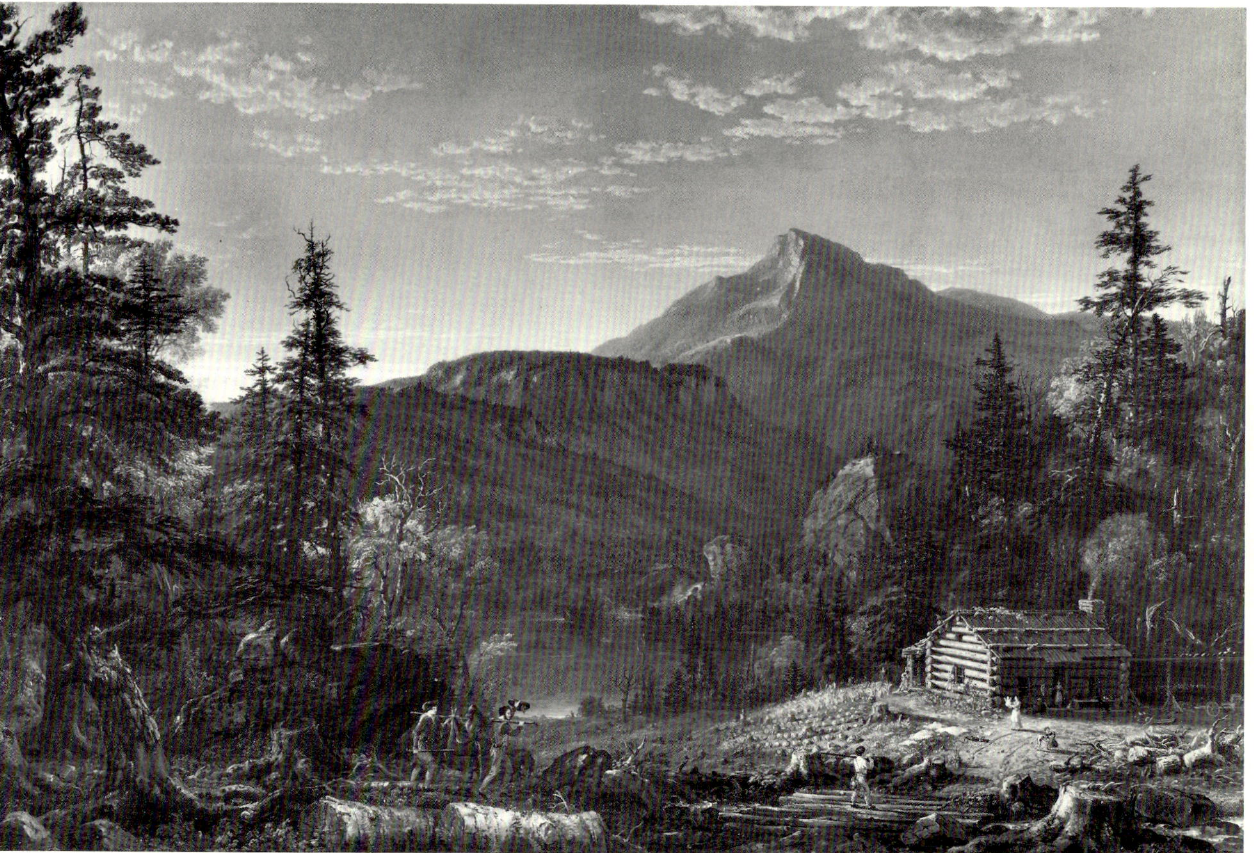

Fig. 1
Thomas Cole, *The Hunter's Return*, Amon Carter Museum, Fort Worth

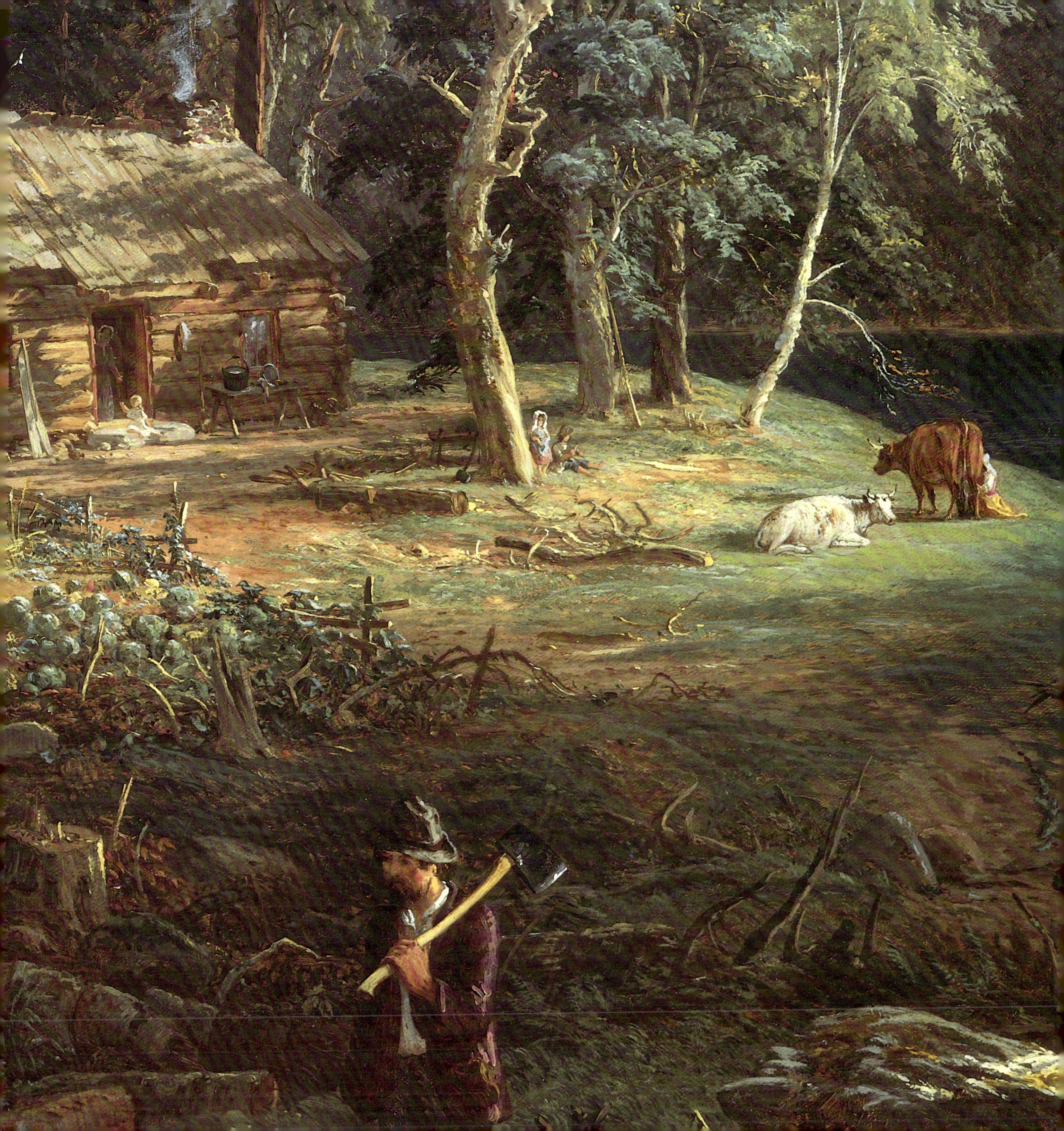

Thomas Cole (1801–1848)
Schroon Lake c. 1835–1838
oil on canvas, 34⅛ x 46⅛ (86.7 x 117.2)

Thomas Cole first visited Schroon Lake in the Adirondacks in the fall of 1835, on *an excursion in search of the picturesque towards the head-waters of the Hudson. The lake*, he noted in his journal on 7 October, closely describing the subject of this painting, *I found to be a beautiful sheet of water, shadowed by sloping hills clothed with heavy forests . . . . in the distance mountains of remarkable beauty bound the vision. Two summits in particular attracted my attention: one of a serrated outline, and the other* [Schroon Mountain] *like a lofty pyramid. It is my intention*, he added, *to visit this region at a more favourable season.*[1] However, it was not until June of 1837, with the landscape painter Asher B. Durand and his wife, that he visited Schroon Lake again. Of this visit he wrote in his journal, *Here we felt the sublimity of untamed wildness, and the majesty of the eternal mountains.*[2]

Schroon Lake was painted, though we do not know at precisely what time, during an unusually active and thoughtful period of Cole's life, when, on one hand, he completed the first and most ambitious of his historical series, the five-part *Course of Empire* (1836, New-York Historical Society), and on the other, he composed his most complete and disciplined statement on national landscape and landscape art, the *Essay on American Scenery* of 1835[3]—at a time when he was intensively applying himself to the formal development and theoretical articulation of the two principal, yet very different, parts of his art.

For all its exceptional beauty, both of nature and of art, *Schroon Lake* is also something more. Like such contemporary paintings of Cole's as *The Oxbow* (1836, The Metropolitan Museum of Art, New York) and *Schroon Mountain* (1838, Cleveland Museum of Art), it is an emblematically national landscape. Several years after Cole's death in 1848 its subject was described as *peculiarly American in its character, being both wild and picturesque . . .*,[4] and this was exactly what Cole himself found at Schroon Lake, the picturesquely *beautiful sheet of water, shadowed by sloping hills clothed with heavy forests*, and *the sublimity of untamed wildness*. The subject also contained what were, Cole wrote in his *Essay on American Scenery*, not only the two most important elements of landscape, but ones that, in America, had a distinctive character: mountains and water. In *Schroon Lake* the mountain was a specially American one that, unlike "mostly bare" European mountains, was *clothed to the summit by dense forests*. And the water was of a special purity and transparency that *contributes greatly to the beauty of landscape; for the reflections of surrounding objects, trees, mountains, sky, are most perfect in the clearest water; and the most perfect is the most beautiful.*[5]

Schroon Lake is not an exact transcription of its subject. The trees in the foreground are a common compositional artifice for framing and setting off distant space. But their broken and twisted forms are also tokens of natural wildness, and by completing that "peculiarly American" formula of picturesque beauty and dramatically expressive sublimity, they interpret and explain the subject's specially and specifically national meaning.[6]

The clarity of that meaning, and the pictorial devices that conveyed it, may have influenced another great national painting. Cole kept *Schroon Lake* after it was painted, and his wife owned it for a number of years after his death. It was surely available to Frederic Edwin Church when he became Cole's pupil in 1844. And Church's intimate knowledge of the painting, preserved as an experience of *those pleasant days [that] ever occupy a large place in the memory of the pupil*,[7] might have served as a model when, in 1860, he painted his own very similarly conceived national icon, *Twilight in the Wilderness*.[8]

Nicolai Cikovsky, Jr.

1. Quoted in Louis L. Noble, *The Life and Works of Thomas Cole* [first edition 1853] (Cambridge, Massachusetts, 1964), 151–152.
2. Noble, *Cole*, 179.
3. In 1835 also he composed "a kind of dramatic poem, in twelve parts, called The Spirits of the wilderness." (Noble, *Cole*, 154). No poem of that title is known, but it suggests a lengthy and disciplined consideration of the meaning of American nature on Cole's part comparable to *The Essay on American Scenery* of the same year.
4. *The Home Book of the Picturesque* (New York, 1852), 165. The text was accompanied by a vignette engraving of the painting.
5. Thomas Cole, "Essay on American Scenery," in John W. McCoubrey, *American Art 1700–1960: Sources and Documents* (Englewood Cliffs, New Jersey, 1965), 102–103.
6. A preparatory drawing (M. & M. Karolik Collection, Museum of Fine Arts, Boston) includes a figure of an Indian among the trees at the right, shooting at the deer in the center foreground. Perhaps Cole felt it added narrative interest or—more obviously than the way he finally did so—reinforced the painting's nationality.
7. Noble, *Cole*, 272.
8. In the mid-1850s Church helped sell one of Mrs. Cole's paintings after her husband's death. (See Franklin Kelly, *Frederic Edwin Church and the National Landscape* [Washington, 1988], 83, 153 n. 20). It is suggestive that William Earl Dodge, Jr., who purchased *Schroon Lake* from Mrs. Cole, also commissioned Church's *Morning in the Tropics* (National Gallery of Art, Washington) in 1877.

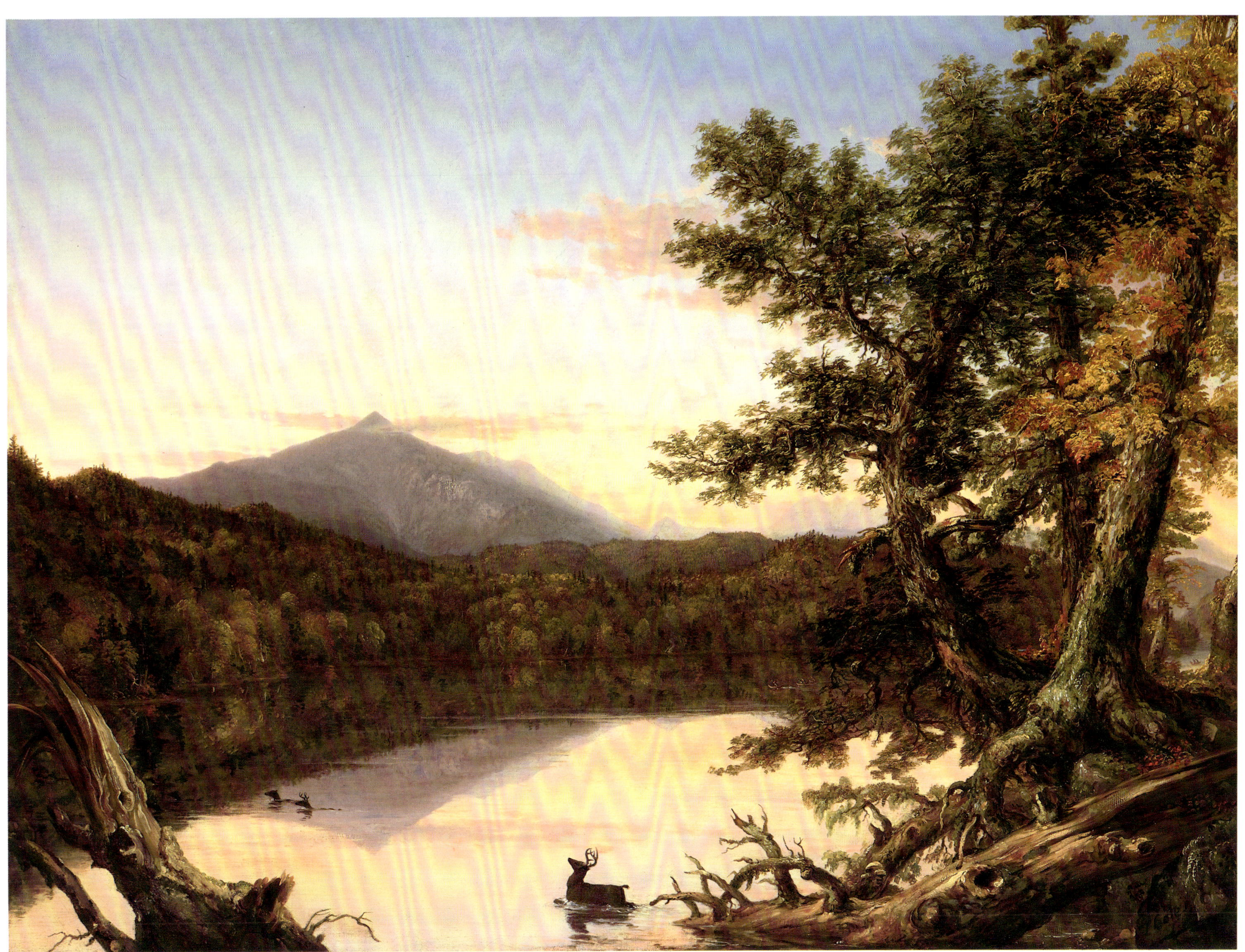

3

Frederic Edwin Church (1826–1900)
July Sunset 1847
oil on canvas, 29 x 40$\frac{3}{8}$ (73.7 x 102.6)

Church's early works, especially those of 1845–1847, were strongly influenced by the paintings of his teacher, Thomas Cole, and this was recognized by his contemporaries. As one wrote of *July Sunset: The first glance at this picture impresses one with the idea that it must be one of Cole's.*[1] Comparison of *July Sunset* to a work by Cole such as *Schroon Lake* (cat. 2) reveals that the similarities are indeed pronounced. Both works employ the same compositional scheme, with large framing trees, a body of water leading from the foreground to the middle distance, ranges of hills beyond, and a radiant sunset sky above, and their colors are also generally similar. Church's painting, however, is a more matter-of-fact vision of nature than Cole's *Schroon Lake*, with details of trees, plants, rocks, and clouds portrayed in meticulous detail. From the first Church strove for a more realistic depiction of the world than did his teacher, and although he would occasionally be criticized for having *sacrificed general resemblance to detail*, he would increasingly be praised for his *appreciation of the fine qualities of nature.*[2]

July Sunset depicts a scene along Catskill Creek, a picturesque stream on the west bank of the Hudson River that Church had come to know well during his two years of study with Cole in the village of Catskill.[3] Church roamed the surrounding countryside, often with Cole, or sometimes with Cole's young son Theodore, making careful sketches of both broad vistas and small details of scenery.[4] Once established in his own studio, Church drew inspiration from his student sketches for many of his first paintings. A drawing for the present composition exists (Cooper-Hewitt Museum, Smithsonian Institution, New York), but Church may also have used one of his sketches of Hartford's famous Charter Oak (for example, *Charter Oak, Hartford, Connecticut*, Olana State Historic Site, Hudson, New York) when working out the details of the intricately painted foreground tree.

July Sunset was one of two paintings Church sent for exhibition at the National Academy of Design in the spring of 1847. The other, a large and dramatic picture entitled *Christian on the Borders of the "Valley of the Shadow of Death," Pilgrim's Progress* (1847, Olana State Historic Site, Hudson, New York), also reflected the profound influence Cole had on the young artist, for it was clearly indebted to his allegorical and moralizing works. *Franklin Kelly*

1. "The Fine Arts. Exhibition at the National Academy. Second Saloon," *The Literary World*, 5 June 1847, 419.
2. "The Fine Arts," 419.
3. See Franklin Kelly and Gerald L. Carr, *The Early Landscapes of Frederic Edwin Church, 1845–1854* (Fort Worth, 1987), 43, 85, 89, 94–95.
4. The young child at the lower left of the painting is probably Theodore Cole, who appears wearing a similar smock and hat in several of Church's drawings of this period; see Kelly and Carr, *Early Landscapes*, 85.

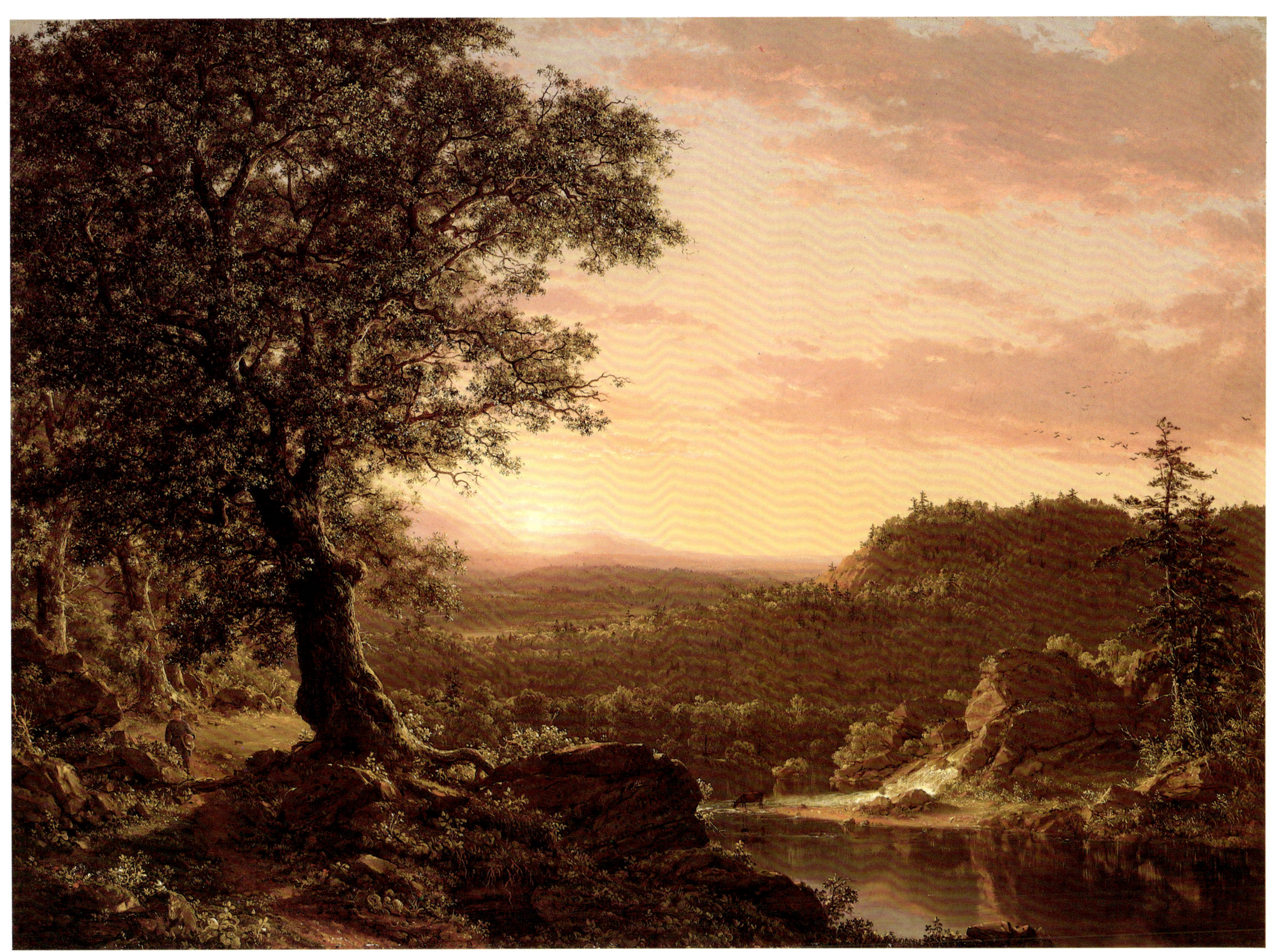

4

John Frederick Kensett (1816–1872)
Landscape (A Reminiscence of the White Mountains) 1852
oil on canvas, 35½ x 50 (90.2 x 127)

Although clearly one of Kensett's most accomplished works of the early 1850s, this painting has not previously been identified as one he is known to have exhibited at either the National Academy of Design or the American Art-Union. Nor has there been any certainty as to whether or not it depicts a specific site, although Lake George in New York state, Camel's Hump Mountain in Vermont, and Mount Chocorua in New Hampshire have been suggested.[1] However, an extensive discussion in the *New-York Tribune* of Kensett's works at the 1852 exhibition of the National Academy includes the following description of a work entitled *A Reminiscence of the White Mountains: In the distance of this picture rises a characteristic mountain peak. In the upper right a mass of storm-clouds recoil* [sic], *and on the left, serene bars of summer vapor float in the sky. A broad, still stream bends out to the front from the blue mistiness of the mountain shadow. Upon the right foreground is a lower hillside, receding from the stream, and dotted with fine trees, and directly in the left corner of the foreground lies a mass of shrubby rock, steeply rising from the water.*[2] No other known Kensett of 1852 so closely fits this description as does *Landscape*, making it likely that it is the work that the *Tribune* critic considered *one of the three finest landscapes in the exhibition.*[3]

When Kensett had returned to America late in 1847 after more than seven years of travel and study in Europe, he had found a thriving group of landscape painters centered in New York City. Inspired by the examples of Thomas Cole and Asher B. Durand, such younger painters as Frederic Church, Jasper Cropsey, and Sanford Gifford were vigorously exploring the scenery of the northeastern United States. The paintings they created from the sketches gathered on these trips found increasing favor with wealthy patrons and with institutions such as the National Academy and the Art-Union. Encouraged by these circumstances, Kensett quickly moved to establish his own reputation, and was soon considered one of the country's leading landscape painters.

Through the early 1850s Kensett remained very much under the influence of both Cole and Durand. From Cole he derived a love of dramatic scenery and active, expressive compositions, and from Durand he developed a preference for meticulous brushwork and for cool greens, blues, and grays that were less assertive than the vivid reds and yellows favored by Cole. *Landscape* shows these two poles of influence on Kensett quite clearly. On the one hand, its wilderness subject and its composition, with a sharply peaked mountain at the center of a circular, swirling movement formed by trees, rocks, and clouds, strongly recall such works by Cole as *Landscape with Tree Trunks* (1828, Museum of Art, Rhode Island School of Design, Providence) and *Schroon Mountain* (1838, The Cleveland Museum of Art). On the other, the intricately painted rocks and trees, the still water, and cool blue tones of the mountains and sky are reminiscent of Durand. Yet like his contemporary Church, who was similarly influenced by Cole and Durand, Kensett was able to use these influences as the foundation for his own vision of the American scene, which was both factual in its grasp of the reality of nature and expressive of the less tangible but powerful associations Americans at mid-century found in the pristine scenery of the young nation. *Franklin Kelly*

1. Theodore E. Stebbins, Jr., in "Luminism in Context: A New View," in John Wilmerding, ed., *American Light: The Luminist Movement, 1850–1875* [exh. cat., National Gallery of Art] (Washington, 1980), 227, proposed that the painting depicts Lake George based on its similarity to the topography seen in a *Lake George* of 1858 (collection of Jo Ann and Julian Ganz, Jr.). However, there is no known evidence that Kensett visited Lake George before 1853. John Paul Driscoll, an authority on the artist, noted in a letter to the author of 3 August 1988 that the background mountain resembles Camel's Hump as it appears in several of Kensett's drawings and paintings of the 1850s and Mount Chocorua as it appears in others, but did not feel that the site could be identified with certainty.
2. [George William Curtis], "The Fine Arts; Exhibition of the National Academy; II," *New-York Tribune*, 1 May 1852, 3.
3. Curtis, *Exhibition*. Curtis considered *Norwegian Forests* (location unknown) by the Düsseldorf-trained Norwegian artist Herman August Cappelen (1827–1852) and Kensett's *Early Autumn in the Franconia Mountains* (location unknown) the other landscapes worthy of this distinction.

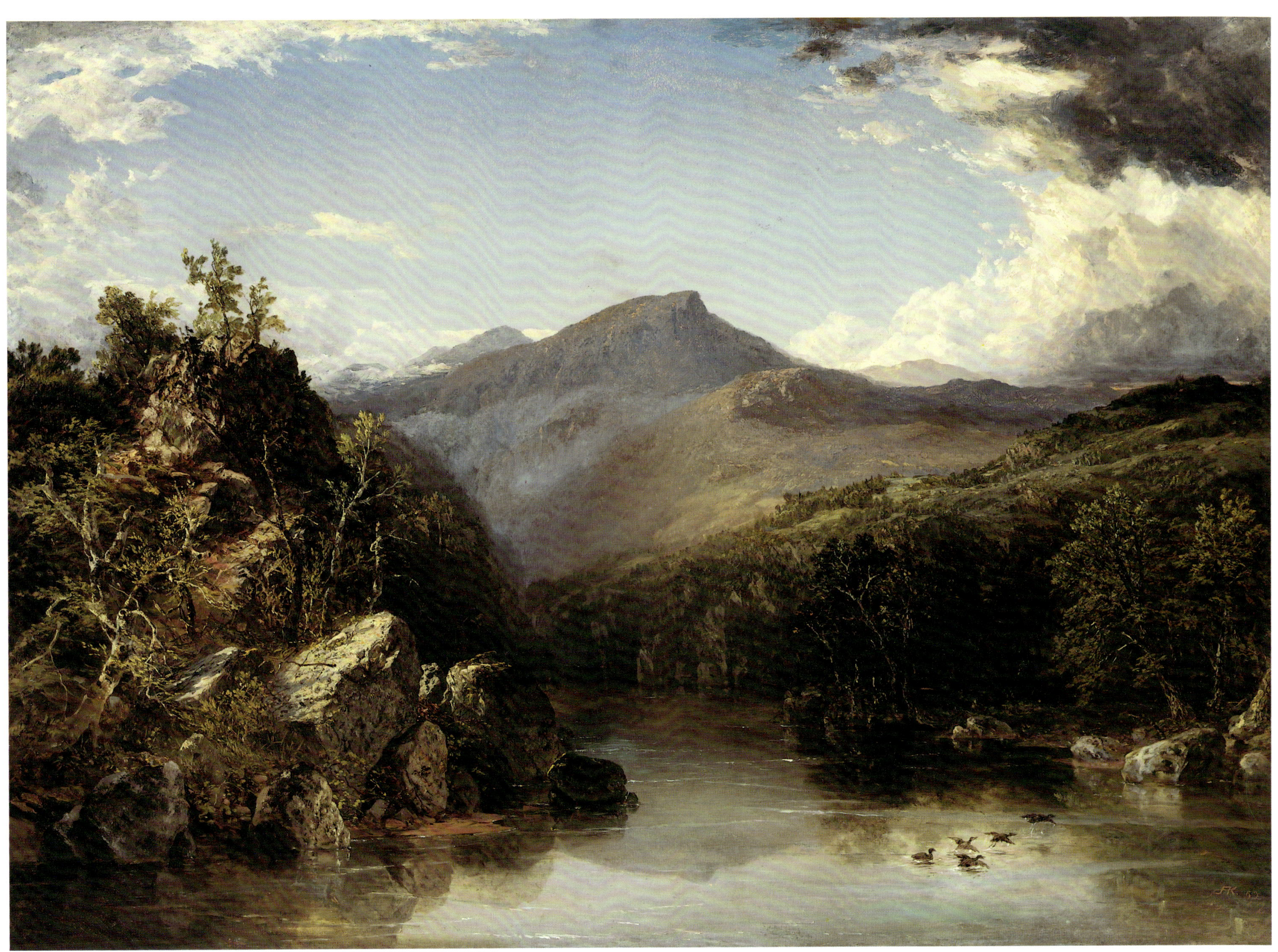

5

Asher Brown Durand (1796–1886)
June Shower 1854
oil on canvas, 33⅛ x 48⅛ (84.2 x 122.2)

Asher B. Durand is usually thought of as the archetypal Hudson River School painter, creator of gentle pictures of pastoral fields and mountains or still woodland interiors. The tranquility of such familiar works as *In the Woods* (1855, The Metropolitan Museum of Art, New York) is far removed from the mood of *June Shower*, which is one of his most dramatically charged landscapes. Although Durand often included passing showers in his paintings, as in *Clearing Up*, also of 1854 (private collection), they usually appeared in the role of refreshing and cleansing the landscape. Only rarely did he portray the full fury of a thunderstorm as it broke, and in no other pure landscape did he do so as effectively as in *June Shower*. Critics who saw the painting at the National Academy of Design in the spring of 1854 generally admired it as a faithful representation of a summer storm, with one writer in particular praising *the lurid and watery clouds, and the peculiar tints lent for the moment to the foliage.*[1] However, another, although admitting the picture was *suggestive*, concluded that *compared with the emotional intensity of the real storm, it is an ineffectual as a candle at noon-day.*[2]

During the early 1850s several important American artists tried their hand at painting major storm pictures. In 1851 Jasper Cropsey's *The Cove* (now known as *Storm in the Wilderness*, The Cleveland Museum of Art) and Frederic Church's *The Deluge* (unlocated) had dominated the first room of the annual exhibition of the National Academy. Both works were highly dramatic, large, and included lightning; both owed much to the example of Thomas Cole's earlier storm pictures; both were much discussed by critics. Durand himself the following year exhibited at the Academy *God's Judgement on Gog* (The Chrysler Museum, Norfolk), which included a divinely inspired thunderstorm complete with roiling black clouds and flashing lightning. Durand had only rarely before attempted imaginary works and his *Gog* was not, in fact, well received by the critics.[3] Perhaps unwilling to subject his reputation to such reprobation again, Durand never again attempted an imaginary work with highly charged atmospheric effects. But he obviously felt no reluctance two years after the failure of *God's Judgement on Gog* to infuse his pastoral style of portraying the American scene with a similar heightened sense of drama and tension, as *June Shower* attests. Although he especially loved *Sunshine* [as] *the joyous expression of Nature*, he also could be thrilled by *dark rain-clouds, agitated and convulsed with awful threatenings. . . .*[4] *June Shower*, with its alternating zones of light and dark, and sharp contrast between the pastoral landscape and dramatic storm, managed to convey both sides of nature's character. Most of his contemporaries recognized that the result was a singular success, for as Henry T. Tuckerman noted in his *Book of the Artists* of 1867, *It is a masterly work; in breadth, freedom, and vital truth, equal to the artist's best efforts.*[5] *Franklin Kelly*

1. "Fine Arts. National Academy of Design (Second Notice)," *The Albion*, 15 April 1854, 177.
2. "The Fine Arts. Exhibition of the National Academy (Second Article)," *New-York Tribune*, 22 April 1854, 177.
3. An angry exchange of letters between Durand's supporters and George William Curtis, art critic for the *Tribune* until 1852, appeared in the *Tribune* and *The Home Journal* debating the merits of the picture and of the artist himself. John Durand, the artist's son, mentioned the controversy in his biography, *The Life and Times of Asher B. Durand* (New York, 1894), 174–175, and admitted *the picture was not a success*. He considered *June Shower*, however, *among the best works that left my father's studio.*
4. Durand, "Letters on Landscape Painting," nos. VI and VIII, *The Crayon* 1 (1855), 209, 355.
5. (New York, 1867), 189.

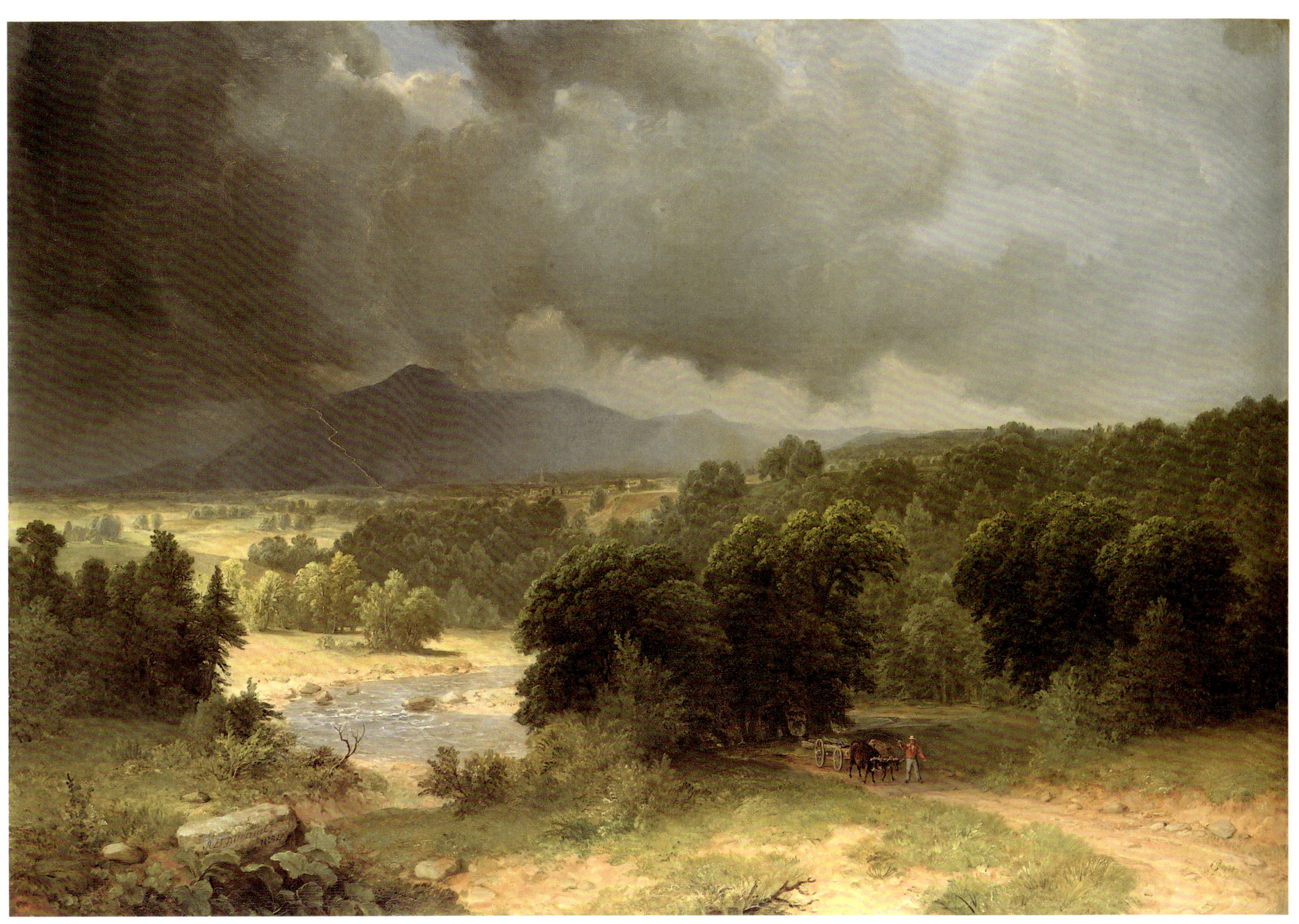

6

Robert S. Duncanson (1821–1872)
Arcadian Landscape 1867
oil on canvas, 28⅝ x 52⅛ (72.7 x 132.4)

Arcadian Landscape belongs to a body of Duncanson's work known as his literary landscapes.[1] By adding narrative content to landscape, Duncanson was emulating the historical landscapes of Claude and Turner. Of more immediate inspiration were Thomas Cole's allegorical series and William Sonntag's four paintings, *The Progress of Civilization*, 1847.[2] In 1852, Duncanson painted his first literary landscape, *The Garden of Eden*.[3]

Arcadian Landscape is the third and most important of Duncanson's paintings inspired by Thomas Moore's 1817 romance, *Lalla Rookh*. The subject was suggested to Duncanson at the Cincinnati Sketch Club in 1863. His resulting oil sketch formed the basis of the composition and motifs for two subsequent versions of the theme.

Lalla Rookh is the story of a Persian princess' journey to the Vale of Kashmir to be married. Duncanson based his conception of all three paintings on a poem recited to the princess that describes an idyllic valley with temples, grottoes, and fountains. The bridal party is depicted on the shore of the lake. *The Vale of Kashmir*, 1864 (private collection), the second of the three paintings, contains more pictorial references to the literary source than does *Arcadian Landscape*, his third and final restatement of the scene, in which Duncanson has subordinated narrative detail to the landscape, making it the primary means of re-creating Moore's vision of paradise.[5]

Compared to that of the 1864 *Vale of Kashmir*, *Arcadian Landscape*'s composition has a greater sense of order. The more detailed vegetation and the more emphatic presence of the mountains[6] are among the other refinements that make *Arcadian Landscape* one of the finest examples of Duncanson's unique blend of European and American landscape traditions. *Sarah Towne Hufford*

1. Joseph D. Ketner II, "Robert S. Duncanson (1821–1872): The Late Literary Landscape Paintings," *The American Art Journal* 15 (winter 1983).
2. Thomas Cole's two series, *The Course of Empire*, 1833–1836, and *The Voyage of Life*, 1839–1840, influenced both Duncanson and Sonntag. Cole's replica of *The Voyage of Life* of 1842 was sold to a Cincinnati collector in 1846 and was exhibited by the Western Art Union in 1848. Paul Schwitzer, "The Voyage of Life: A Chronology," in *The Voyage of Life by Thomas Cole, Paintings, Drawings and Prints* [exh. cat., Museum of Art, Munson-Williams-Proctor Institute, Utica, New York] (Utica, 1985), 45, 48.
3. Joseph D. Ketner II has generously shared this information from his monograph on Duncanson, which is to be published by Cambridge University Press in 1989.
4. Ketner, monograph on Duncanson to be published in 1989.
5. Ketner, "The Late Literary Landscape Paintings," 40–42.
6. Duncanson's original inspiration for the exotic plant life and the fanciful temples probably was from *Youth* in Cole's *The Voyage of Life*. Although the mood of *Arcadian Landscape* remains pastoral as in Cole's work, the more prominent mountains may have been influenced by Frederic E. Church's paintings.

   Church's *Heart of the Andes*, 1859, was exhibited in Cincinnati and mentioned in a contemporary review as having similarities to Duncanson's *Land of the Lotus Eaters*. See Guy McElroy, "Robert S. Duncanson (1821–1872): A Study of the Artist's Life and Work," in *Robert S. Duncanson: A Centennial Exhibition* [exh. cat., Cincinnati Art Museum] (Cincinnati, 1972), 13.

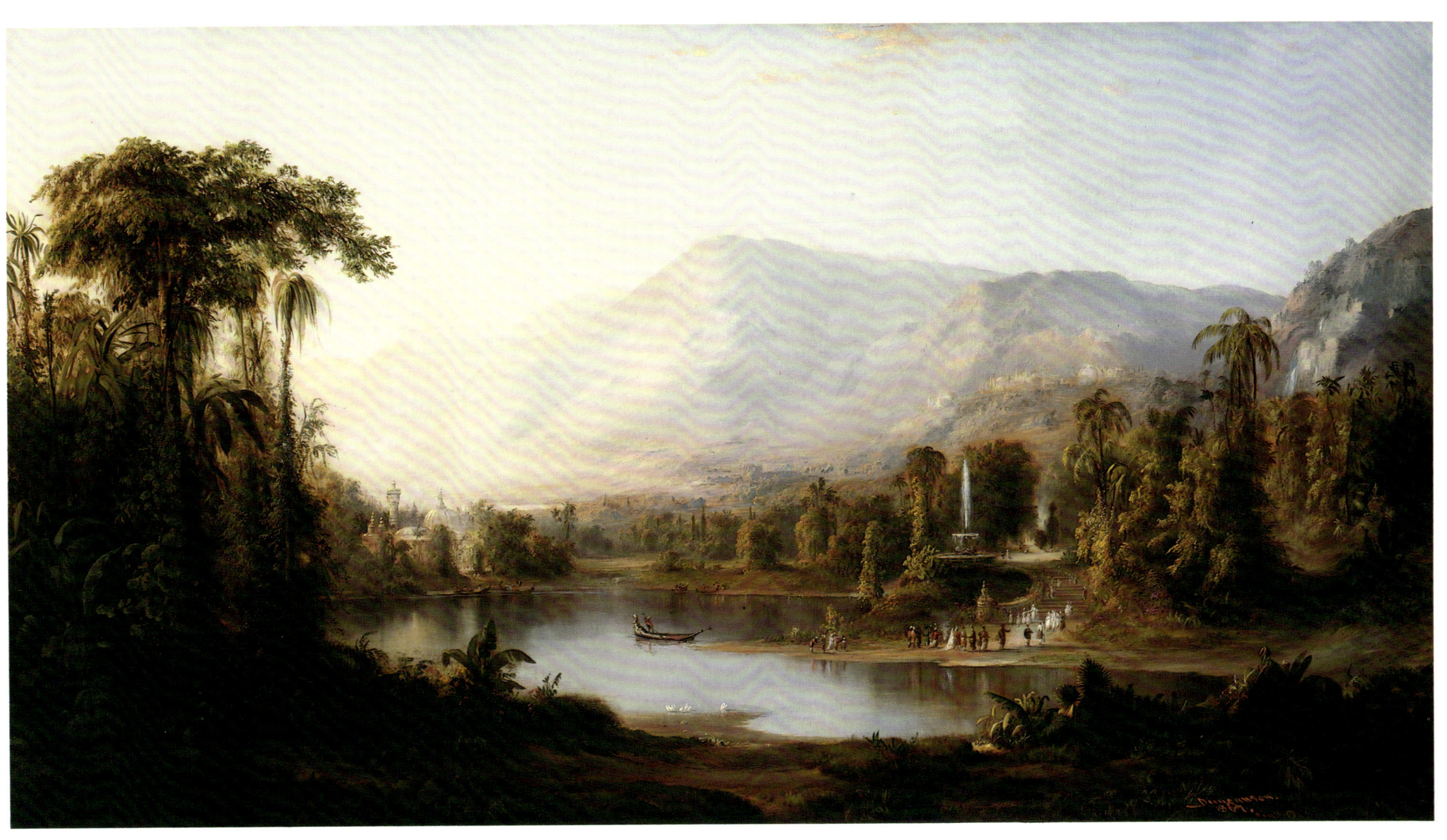

7

Thomas Worthington Whittredge (1820–1910)
Twilight on the Shawangunk Mountains 1865
oil on canvas, 45 x 68 (114.3 x 172.7)

Twilight on the Shawangunk Mountains was deemed by a contemporary art critic *one of the noblest landscapes* in the National Academy of Design's annual exhibition of 1865, *one of those true and strong representations of nature that do honor to the American school and keep it healthful.*[1] Whittredge himself was congratulated for being *direct and manly in his work* and capable of *truth to nature and solemnity of sentiment beyond the reach of some of our ablest and most popular painters.*[2] This was high praise indeed, especially when one considers that the same exhibition included major paintings by some of Whittredge's most talented colleagues in the Hudson River School. Among them were Jasper Cropsey's *The Valley of Wyoming* (1865, The Metropolitan Museum of Art, New York), John F. Kensett's *Hudson River* (possibly the painting known as *View on the Hudson*, 1865, Baltimore Museum of Art), and Frederic Church's *Twilight* (*Mount Desert Island*, 1865, Washington University Art Gallery, Saint Louis). Whittredge's close friend Sanford Gifford was represented by his own Shawangunk subject, *Shawangunk Mountains* (30 x 48 inches, location unknown), which was judged *an example of consummate art.*[3] That Whittredge's painting could be accorded a place of honor among such distinguished company was clear testimony to its superb quality and heroic force, which are easily recognizable today. But it also suggests that he had, with particular saliency, addressed a number of key issues about landscape art and American nature and the national identity at a moment of changing tastes and attitudes. *Twilight on the Shawangunk Mountains* was, in fact, a veritable summation of the tradition of American wilderness paintings that had begun with Thomas Cole's works of the mid-1820s and been brought to a high pitch with Church's great *Twilight in the Wilderness* of 1860.

Whittredge's first attempts to portray the American wilderness, such as *Scene Near Hawk's Nest, West Virginia* (1845, Cincinnati Art Museum), date from the mid-1840s. These works, although little more than provincial reflections of contemporary developments in New York (in particular the work of Asher B. Durand), gave indication of considerable talent.[4] In 1849 supportive patrons in Cincinnati provided the young artist with money to finance study in Europe, where he would remain for the next ten years. Whittredge's time in Europe was important, of course, for his artistic development, because while there he received excellent technical training, made the acquaintance of leading landscape painters, and had ample opportunity to study the great collections of Old Masters in Germany and Italy. But his absence from America during virtually all of the 1850s also played a role in forming his artistic personality, for he missed firsthand experience of one of the most energetic periods in this country's political, social, and cultural history. Whittredge was not part of the New York art world in the years immediately following Cole's death in 1848, and it was then that Durand, Cropsey, Church, and others were establishing the basic tenets of Hudson River School painting.

When he did return to New York in 1859, Whittredge found he would have to move quickly to find his own artistic identity, for other landscape painters already had secure reputations with the city's critics and patrons. Although he had learned a great deal in Europe, Whittredge realized that he had missed a great deal too. As he wrote in his *Autobiography*, *My previous acquaintance with New York was slight indeed*, and he admitted he *may have been a little nervous* when he went first to the New-York Historical Society to study the works of Cole and Durand.[5] He found Cole's *Voyage of Life* and *The Course of Empire* unrelated to the American landscape and too allegorical, but Durand's works impressed him as *so delicate and refined* and *faithful* that tears came to his eyes.[6] Deciding to settle in New York, Whittredge rented a studio in the new Tenth Street Studio Building, where Church, Gifford, and other leading painters were already in residence. Whittredge managed to have four of his European paintings accepted for the National Academy of Design's exhibition in the spring of 1860, but he realized that to succeed he would need to *produce something new and which might claim to be inspired by my home surroundings.*[7] He had recognized that the success of the Hudson River School was due largely to the way its native subject matter gave pictorial expression to strong currents of American nationalism and pride. And he knew, too, that his own art was still so much under the spell of Europe that he needed an aesthetic jolt of fresh inspiration. So, like Thomas Cole thirty-five years before him, Whittredge went to *the first available outdoor place* he could find, the Catskills.[8]

The scenery Whittredge found in the Catskills surprised him greatly: *But how different was the scene before me from anything I had been looking at for many years! The forest was a mass of decaying logs and tangled brush wood, no peasants to pick up every vestige of fallen sticks to burn in their miserable huts, no well-ordered forests, nothing but the primitive woods with their solemn silence reigning everywhere. I think I can say that I was not the first or by any means the only painter of our country who has returned after a long visit abroad and not encountered the same difficulties in tackling home subjects.*[9] Gradually, Whittredge came to terms with his new subject, while still maintaining a firm grasp on the painting techniques he had learned in Europe. He started sending American scenes to the Academy exhibitions, and in 1864 his *Old Hunting Ground* (Reynolda House Museum of American Art, Winston-Salem, North Carolina), a radiant, still view of a forest interior, received high praise. Although obviously inspired by such works by Durand as the famous *In the Woods* of 1855 (The Metropolitan Museum of Art, New York), Whittredge had still managed to express his own vision, because *The Old Hunting Ground* is both meticulous in its delineation of the intricate forms of the forest and remarkably assured in its fluent brushwork. Whittredge's years of study in Europe (especially in Düsseldorf) had taught him that the actual appearance of nature could be portrayed through means other than the literal, precise brushwork so often favored by his colleagues. He knew that sometimes more could be achieved by suggesting, rather than simply mimicking, the facts of external reality. Four years later, in 1868, Whittredge perfected the painting of forest interiors with his *Woods of Ashokan* (fig. 1), where the autumnal woods are virtually dissolved by shimmering light. Not even Durand could surpass this seemingly flawless evocation of the material facts of American nature and the immaterial sensations involved in perceptual experience. Whereas Durand, and others, by the mid-1860s were increasingly considered repetitive and even old-fashioned, Whittredge had managed to bring a new vitality to American landscape. None of his contemporaries would be so successful in melding the sophisticated lessons of European painting with the nationalist aspirations and religious associations that had become endowed in the American landscape itself.[10]

Although it is uncertain when Whittredge first visited the Shawangunk Mountains, he had certainly done so by 1863, when he painted a *Twilight on the Shawangunk River* (fig. 2). The Shawangunks lie in southern New York State, and though not as well known as the neighboring Catskills, they include some of the most dramatically rugged scenery of the entire area.[11] The mountains are generally wild and rocky, with steep slopes and dangerous precipices. Much of the land in the area had been cleared for farming by the early nineteenth century, but at mid-century some of the more difficult terrain, especially along the mountain ridges, had returned to wild growth.[12] Given their proximity to New York City, it was not long before the Shawangunks were attracting tourists and sportsmen, many of whom were drawn to Lake Mohunk, where a ten-room tavern was in operation by 1859.[13] For many artists and travelers the scenery in the vicinity of Lake Mohunk, with *enormous masses of granite*, intricate thickets of *laurel and evergreen trees*, and *magnificent views of the Wallkill and Hudson River valleys on the east, and the Warwarsing valley and the Catskills on the west* surpassed even that of the famous Catskill Mountain House further to the north.[14]

When Whittredge first sketched the site that would be the basis for *Twilight on the Shawangunk Mountains* he may well have been with Sanford Gifford, who recorded the same scene in a sketchbook dated 1864 (collection of Sanford Gifford, M.D.).[15] The view, looking south-southwest from the base of Eagle Cliff toward the escarpments known as the Trapps and the Near Trapps, is one of the most dramatic in the Shawangunks. Whittredge's painting accurately captures the piled masses of granite, dense undergrowth, and sharp drop-offs the area was known for, but also manages to transcend purely local associations to become a statement about the American wilderness in general. Like Church's *Twilight in*

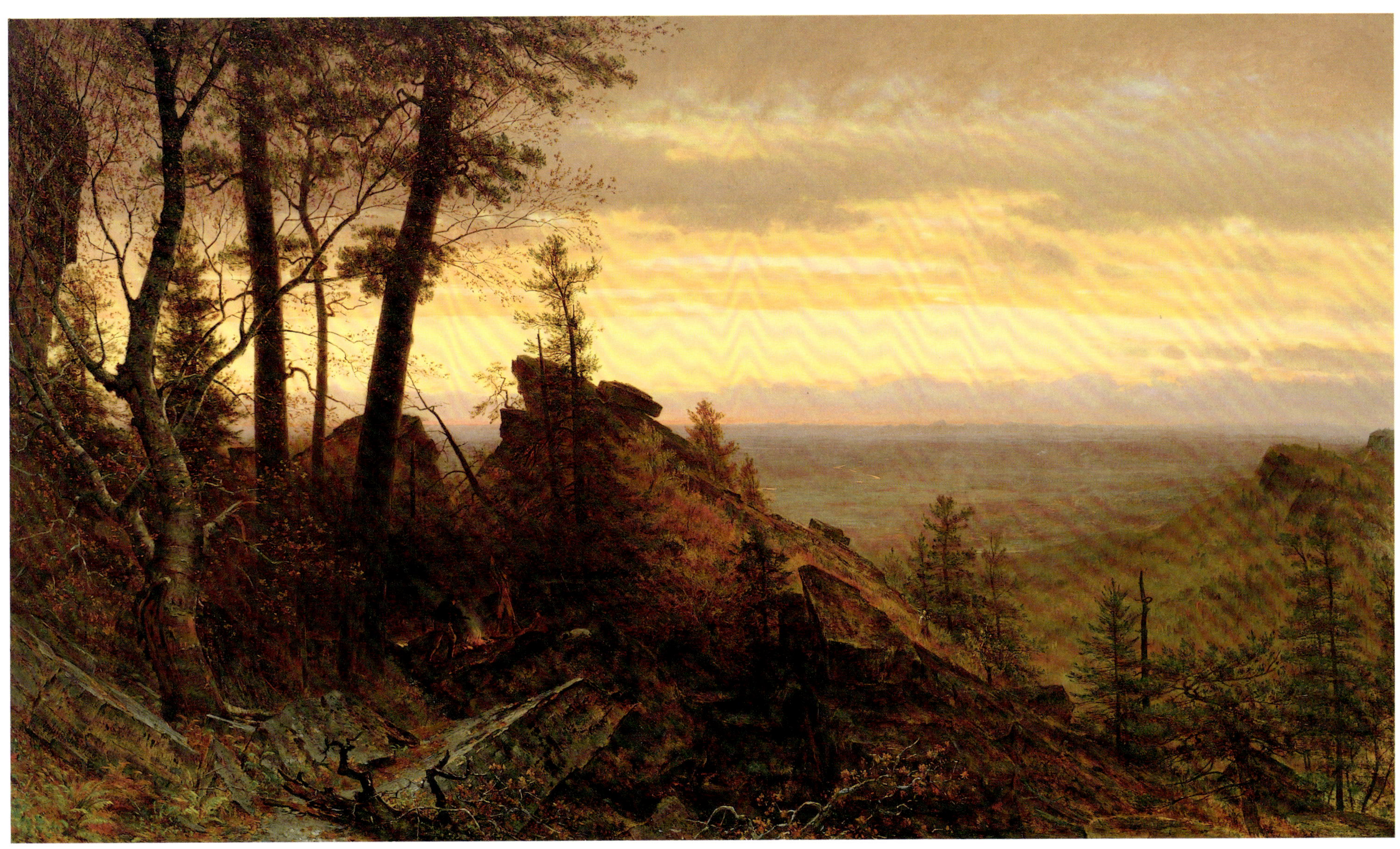

Fig. 1
Thomas Worthington Whittredge, *The Woods of Ashokan*, 1868, 57¼ x 40¾ (146 x 103.5), The Chrysler Museum, Norfolk, Gift of Mr. Edward J. Brickhouse

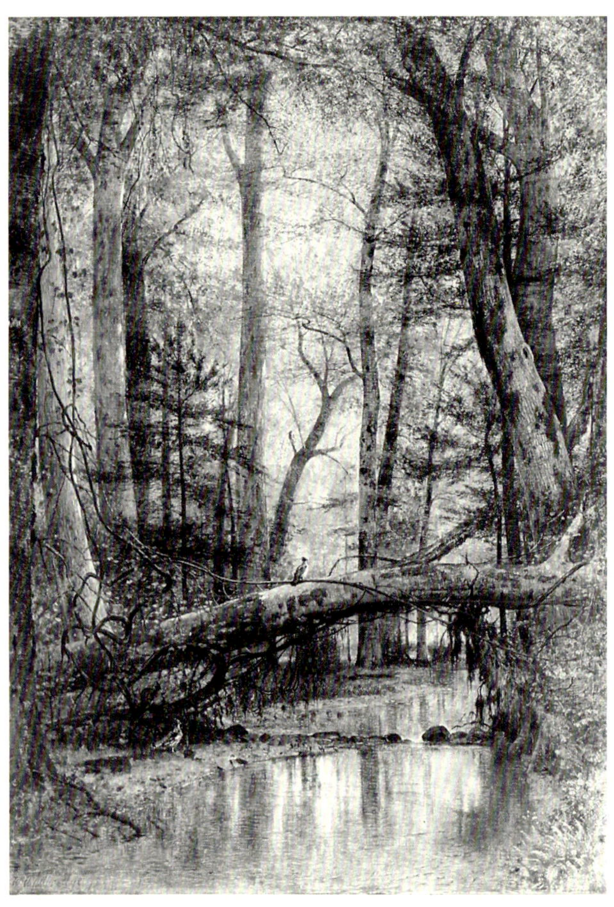

the Wilderness, *Twilight on the Shawangunk Mountains* portrays an unspoiled landscape at a moment of high natural drama as daylight fades and night approaches. But whereas Church deliberately excluded all evidence of man from his landscape, Whittredge included three hunters and their dogs around a campfire and a fourth hunter walking the face of the ridge at the right. The presence of these figures, and the low vantage point and implied pathway into the picture from the lower left, make *Twilight on the Shawangunk Mountains* more directly involving for the viewer than Church's *Twilight in the Wilderness*. In the latter the viewer seems to float at some undefined point above the landscape, able to enjoy the scene and ponder its implications, but still remaining somewhat psychologically distanced from it. Church intended this effect, for *Twilight in the Wilderness* was meant ultimately to be an image of national implications rather than personal associations. Five years later Whittredge apparently sensed that the Hudson River School mode could no longer speak to Americans with the same authority it had before the Civil War. Americans' faith in their political and social institutions had been sorely shaken, and they were no longer prepared to find in the landscape—and painted representations of it—clear confirmations of the sanctity of the nation's destiny. *Twilight on the Shawangunk Mountains* offered something else; it confirmed that American nature endured and remained a place where man could find solace and escape from troubles of his own creating. It was subtly evocative and soothing where Church's painting had been assertive and challenging in its implications; like George Inness's *Peace and Plenty* of the same year (fig. 3), *Twilight on the Shawangunk Mountains* encouraged a more suggestive, even meditative approach to the experience of American nature.[16]

Whittredge's painting thus successfully reformed and updated the Hudson River School convention of the wilderness panorama. With its archetypal subject matter and its sweeping portrayal of American space the painting was clearly a legitimate descendant of the works of Cole, Durand, and Church. But Whittredge's fluid, flickering brushstroke, visible in the foreground, and the broad confidence evident in the way he painted the twilight sky, were equally testaments to his European training. Before the Civil War such indications of foreign influence might have been undesirable (as they were with George Inness), but in 1865 they spoke of a talent that was not hostage to what were becoming viewed as insular and outmoded values.[17] Just as in his *The Old Hunting Ground* of the previous year, Whittredge had managed to breathe new life into the Hudson River genre just when it seemed on the verge of expiring. He had taken the essential message of the Hudson River School and expressed it with a new but perfectly intelligible aesthetic language. Some painters, such as Albert Bierstadt and Thomas Moran, would keep the Hudson River mode alive a few years longer by introducing the new and dramatic scenery of the American West, and one painter, Inness, would gradually forge a completely new style of landscape. But for a few years in the 1860s Whittredge was arguably the finest landscape painter of the day and perhaps the only one capable of a truly fresh statement. *Twilight on the Shawangunk Mountains* was the greatest and most profound evidence of that achievement, a work that continues to this day to *do honor to the American school. Franklin Kelly*

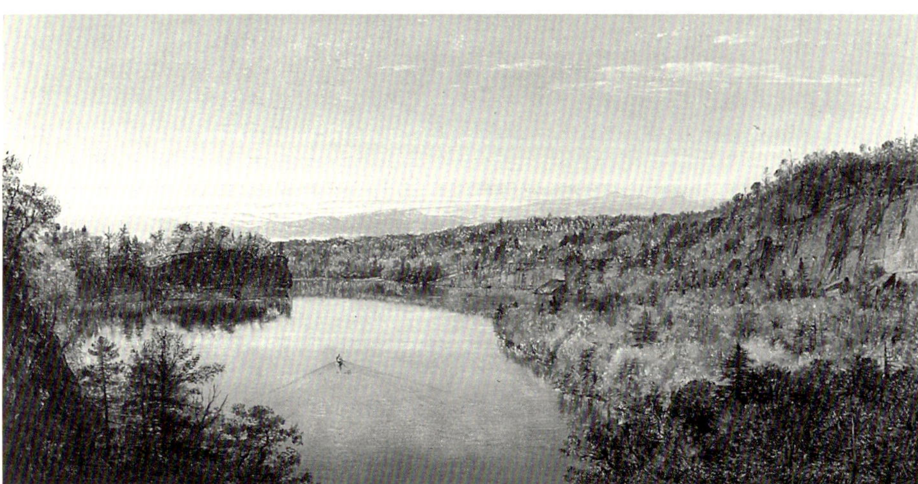

Fig. 2
Thomas Worthington Whittredge, *Twilight on the Shawangunk River*, 1863, 12⅞ x 24¾ (32.7 x 62.9), Indianapolis Museum of Art, Gift of Newhouse Galleries

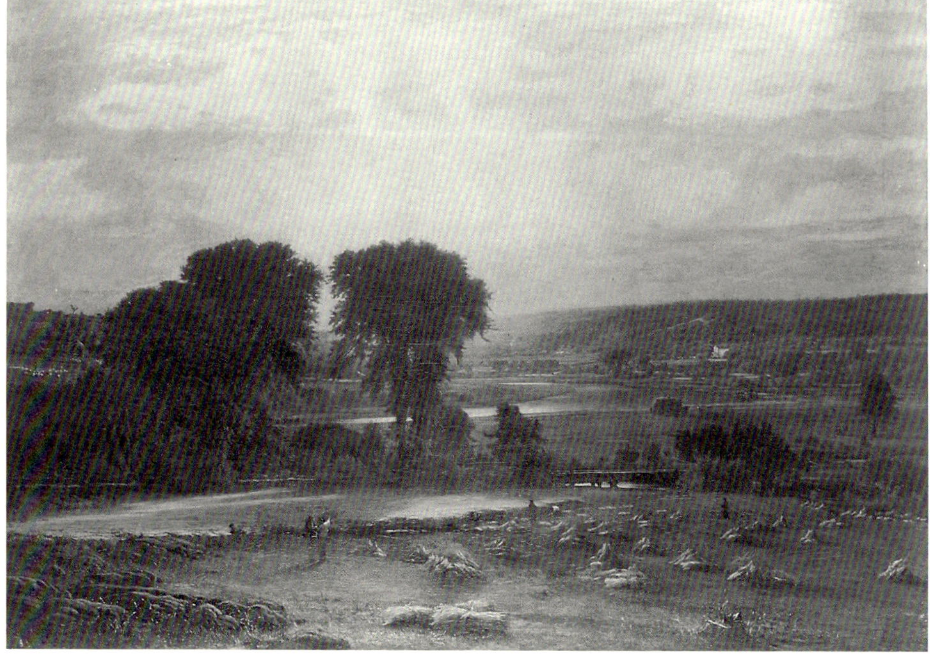

Fig. 3
George Inness, *Peace and Plenty*, 1865, 77⅝ x 112⅜ (197.2 x 285.5), The Metropolitan Museum of Art, New York, Gift of George A. Hearn, 1894

1. Sordello [pseud.], "National Academy of Design. Fortieth Annual Exhibition; Third Article," *Evening Post* (New York), 22 May 1865, 1.
2. Sordello, "National Academy," 1.
3. Sordello, "National Academy," 1.
4. Whittredge's *View on the Kanawha, Morning*, exhibited at the academy in 1846, apparently impressed Durand, because he sent the young painter a complimentary note about it; see "The Autobiography of Worthington Whittredge, 1820–1910," John I. H. Baur, ed., *Brooklyn Museum Journal* (1942), 16.
5. "Autobiography," 40.
6. "Autobiography," 41.
7. "Autobiography," 42.
8. "Autobiography," 42.
9. "Autobiography," 42.
10. Henry T. Tuckerman, in his *Book of the Artists* (New York, 1866), 518, considered Whittredge both "a progressive artist" and one who achieved "fidelity to the simple verities of nature. . . ."
11. See Philip H. Smith, *Legends of the Shawangunk (Shon-Gum) and Its Environs* (Syracuse, 1965) and Bradley Snyder, *The Shawangunk Mountains* (New Paltz, New York, 1981).
12. Snyder, *The Shawangunk*, 27.
13. Snyder, *The Shawangunk*, 27.
14. "Lake Mohunk, (Paltz Point), A New and Delightful Summer Resort," anonymous pamphlet, quoted in Snyder, *The Shawangunk*, 29. Mohunk is often spelled "Mohonk."
15. Ila Weiss, *Poetic Landscape: The Art and Experience of Sanford R. Gifford* (Newark, Delaware, 1987), 302. The composition of *Twilight on the Shawangunk Mountains* strongly recalls Gifford's work in general; compare his *Mount Mansfield* (cat. 15). I am grateful to John D. Cooper of the Mohonk Mountain House for his expert assistance in identifying the site depicted by Gifford and Whittredge.
16. In 1866 both Church's *Twilight in the Wilderness* and Whittredge's *Twilight on the Shawangunk Mountains* were on view at Samuel P. Avery's gallery in New York, and both were singled out for special praise; see "Fine Arts," *Evening Post* (New York), 6 January 1866, 2; "Avery's Gallery," *Evening Post*, 12 January 1866, 2; and "Art Notes," *The Round Table*, 27 January 1866, 55.
17. On the general issue of the Hudson River School and changing tastes in the 1860s and 1870s see Doreen Bolger Burke and Catharine Hoover Voorsanger, "The Hudson River School in Eclipse," *American Paradise: The World of the Hudson River School* [exh. cat., The Metropolitan Museum of Art] (New York, 1987), 71–90, where, however, Whittredge is not specifically discussed.

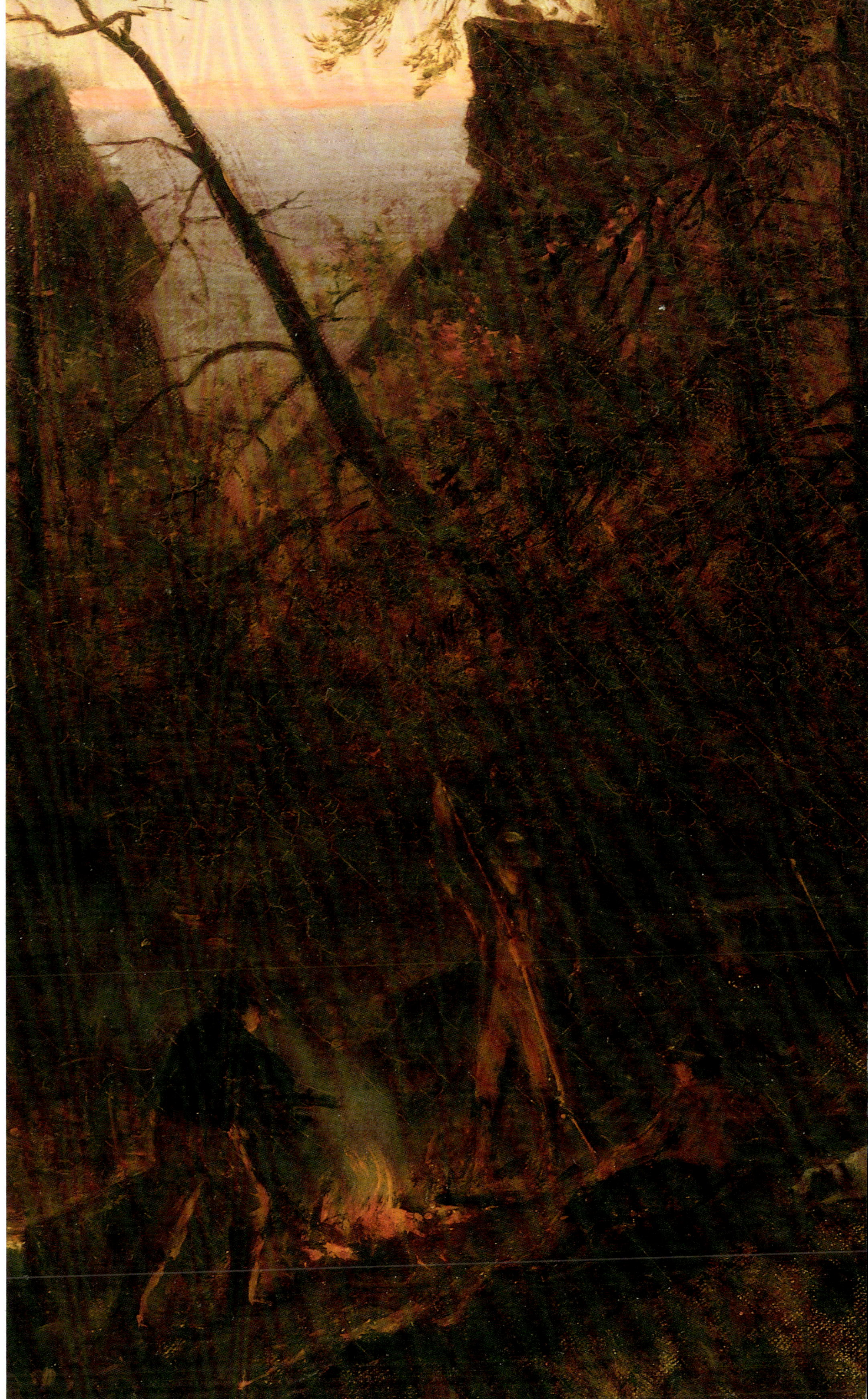

8

Thomas Moran (1837–1926)
Under the Trees 1865
oil on canvas, 40 x 34¼ (101.6 x 87)

Although known best for panoramic landscapes of the American West, Thomas Moran did not see Yellowstone, the landscape that changed the course of his career, until 1871, fifteen years after he had left his position as an engraver's apprentice to become a painter. During that fifteen-year period Moran served, in effect, a second apprenticeship.

Working in the studio of his older brother, Edward, he benefited from the advice of James Hamilton, a Philadelphia marine painter and Edward's teacher. Sometimes called *the American Turner*, Hamilton was English-born and an enthusiastic champion of J. M. W. Turner. If Moran had not already discovered the writings of John Ruskin, Turner's great defender, by the time he entered Edward's studio, Hamilton surely corrected the oversight. Moran's early and continued admiration for Turner is well known and, in fact, evident in his own paintings dating from the 1860s onward. It was, however, Ruskin's other cause célèbre, the Pre-Raphaelites, that seems to have had the greatest impact on the young artist during the early and mid-1860s.

In 1858, when an exhibition of English paintings opened in Philadelphia, Moran had the opportunity to see and study original works by the Pre-Raphaelites. Three years later he traveled to England where he spent months studying the works of Turner and contemporary English artists, including the Pre-Raphaelites. Thoroughly steeped in English painting, he returned to Philadelphia in 1862. At the time, the American Pre-Raphaelites were only months away from formal organization as the Association for the Advancement of Truth in Art.[1] *Under the Trees* suggests that Moran, though never an official member of the American Pre-Raphaelite group, had strong sympathy for the "truth to nature" tenets of their philosophy.

Long a subscriber to Ruskin's doctrine that detailed outdoor studies were the raw material of painting, Moran had frequently taken sketching trips in rural Pennsylvania in the late 1850s and early 1860s. In 1864 he continued the practice, traveling to the Allegheny Mountains. Sketches made on that trip may have served as the immediate stimulus for *Under the Trees* (Opus 17).[2] While the compositional format and vivid autumnal colors of *Under the Trees* suggest American sources (first-generation Hudson River School painters), the jewellike rendering of foreground foliage and the near scientific concern for the specific character of rocks and trees testify to Moran's early admiration of Pre-Raphaelite painting.

As much an admirer of English romantic poetry as of British painting, Moran created, in his secluded forest interior, a natural sanctuary perfectly suited to the solitary pursuits of the Byronic figure reclining in the foreground. *Nancy Anderson*

1. The Association for the Advancement of Truth in Art was formally organized in January 1863. In 1985 *Under the Trees* was included in an exhibition and catalogue devoted to this group. See Linda S. Ferber and William H. Gerdts, *The New Path: Ruskin and the American Pre-Raphaelites* [exh. cat., The Brooklyn Museum] (Brooklyn, 1985), 274.
2. In 1863 Moran began numbering his major paintings with the designation "Opus" and a numeral. He discontinued the practice five years later, with the final painting identified as "Opus 42."

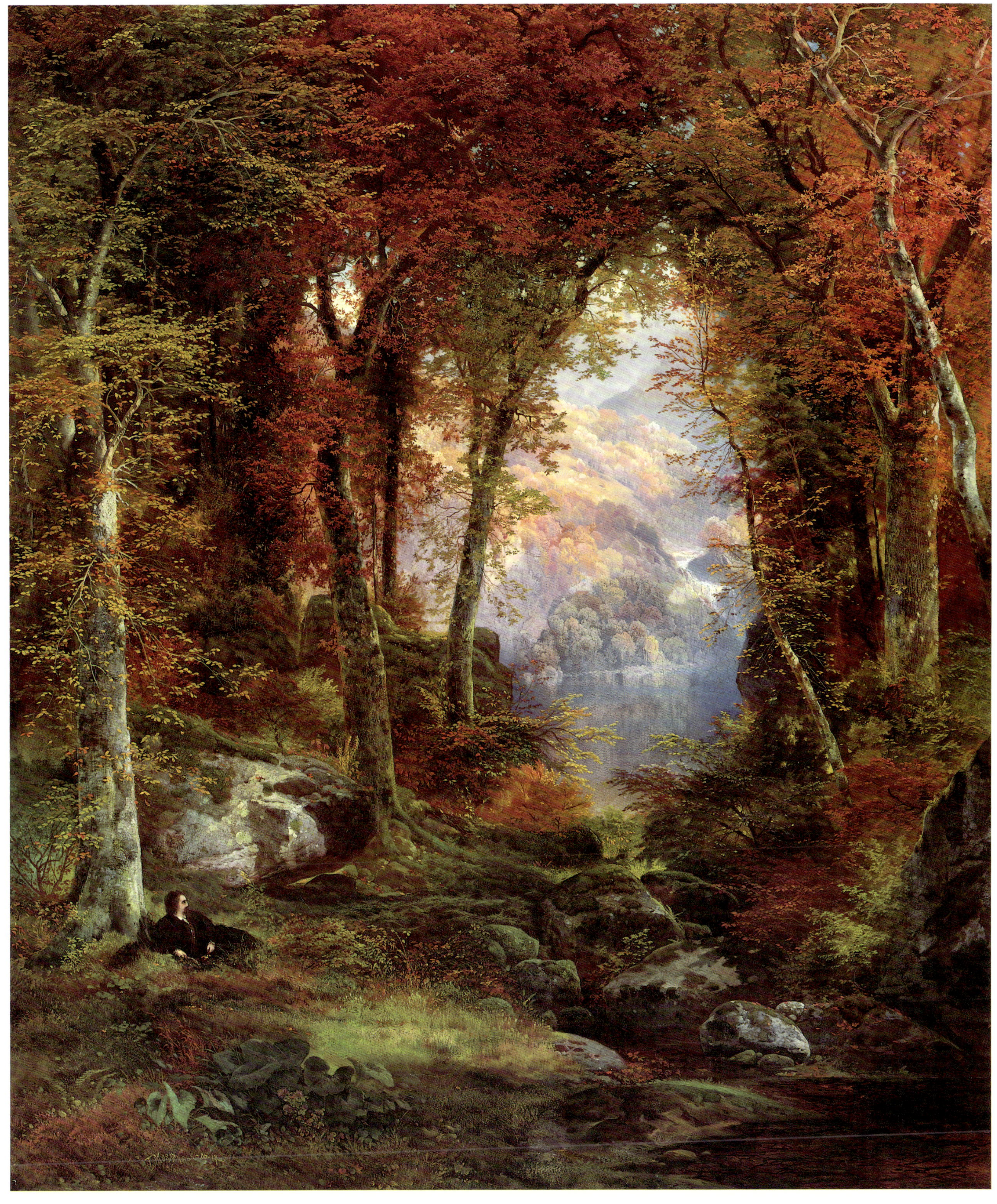

9

Thomas Moran (1837–1926)
A Miracle of Nature 1913
oil on canvas, 20⅛ x 30⅛ (51.1 x 76.5)

Thomas Moran stood above the Grand Canyon[1] of the Colorado River in northwest Arizona for the first time in 1873. He had come as the guest of John Wesley Powell, whose harrowing but triumphant descent of the river four years earlier had made him a national hero. Powell, who was competing with such able colleagues as Ferdinand Hayden, Clarence King, and George Wheeler for government funding, had seen Moran's Yellowstone paintings (completed following a trip with Hayden in 1871) and was aware of the decisive role they had played in the quick passage of the Yellowstone Park bill in 1872. Hoping to enlist the persuasive power of Moran's art for his own cause, Powell invited the artist to join his survey party in the Southwest during the summer of 1872. Prior commitments kept Moran from accepting the invitation until the following summer, when he journeyed to the Grand Canyon and stood on the north rim, stunned by the beauty of the chasm's multicolored walls. Later he described the moment: *On reaching the brink the whole gorge for miles lay beneath us and it was by far the most awfully grand and impressive scene that I have ever yet seen.*[2]

Powell's confidence in the power of Moran's art was well placed, for shortly after the artist's return east, he began work on a 7 by 12 foot painting of the Grand Canyon intended as a pendant to *The Grand Canyon of the Yellowstone* (1872, U.S. Department of the Interior, on loan to the National Museum of American Art, Smithsonian Institution, Washington), which had been purchased by the government the previous year. Completed in the spring of 1874, *The Chasm of the Colorado* (U.S. Department of the Interior, on loan to the National Museum of American Art, Smithsonian Institution, Washington) was also purchased by the government.

Although he confessed early in his career that he felt his artistic skills inadequate when faced with the challenge of the Grand Canyon, Moran returned to the site repeatedly over a forty-seven-year period. *A Miracle of Nature* was completed following one of his late trips to the Southwest. Less interested in topography than the emotional impact of the site, Moran felt no obligation to reproduce exactly what he saw. Instead he composed his paintings from numerous sketches and photographs, attempting to duplicate for the viewer the astonishment he felt rather than the precise geography he sketched while standing above the canyon. *Nancy Anderson*

1. An enormous gorge, 217 miles long, 4 to 18 miles wide rim to rim, and a mile deep, the Grand Canyon offers one of the most remarkable displays of geologic history in the world.
2. Fritiof Fryxell, *Home-Thoughts, from Afar: Letters of Thomas Moran to Mary Nimmo Moran* (East Hampton, 1967), 39.

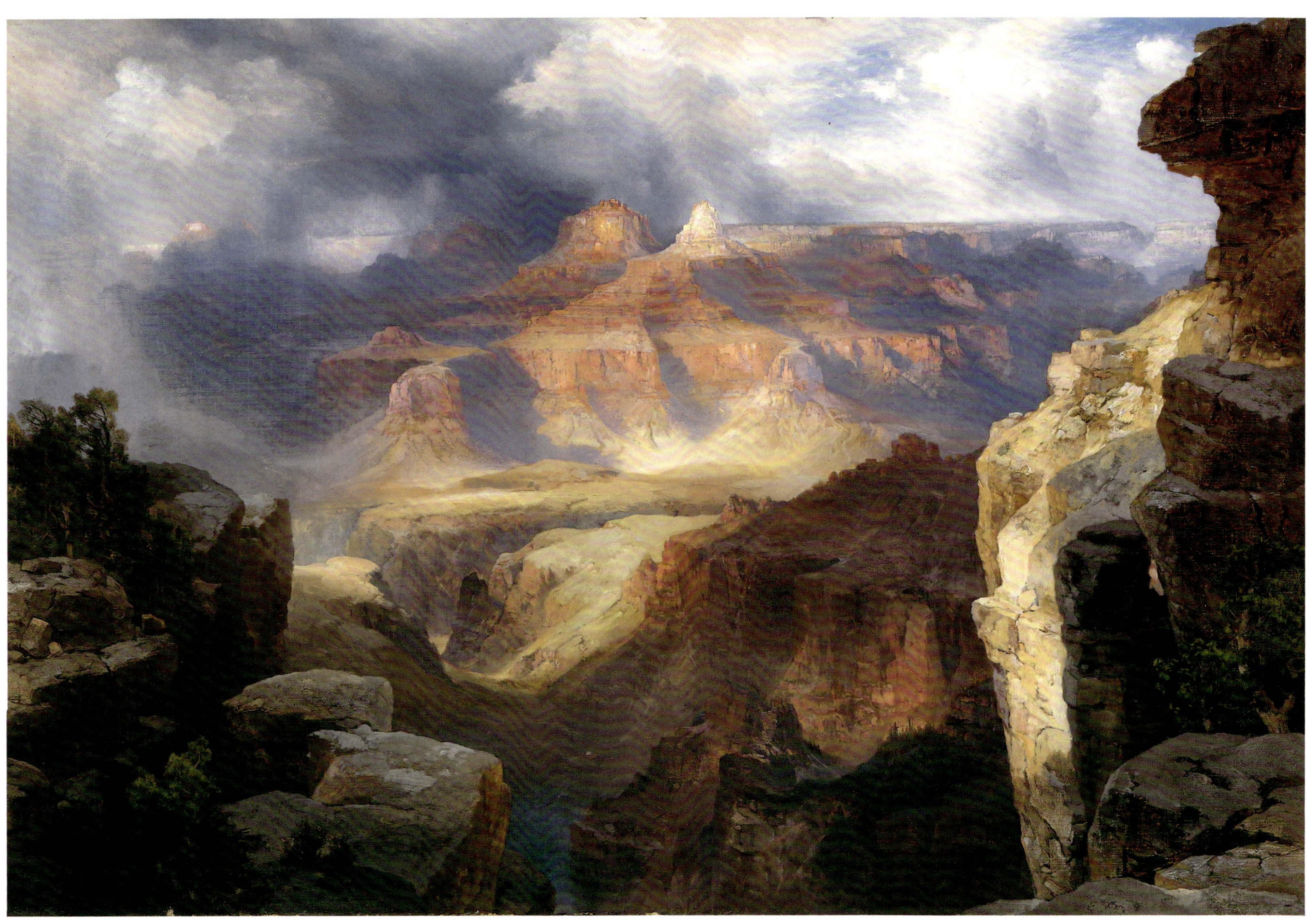

10

Thomas Moran (1837–1926)
Green River, Wyoming 1896
oil on canvas, 20⅛ x 30¼ (51.1 x 76.8)

When Thomas Moran stepped from the train that brought him west for the first time in 1871 and gazed across the horizon at the towering, multicolored buttes through which Wyoming's Green River had cut its path, he saw a landscape that had already staked a lasting claim on the American imagination.[1] Once the site of the fur trappers' annual rendezvous and later of Captain Bonneville's first fort, the Green River had most recently captured public attention as the starting point of John Wesley Powell's celebrated descent of the Colorado River to the Grand Canyon.[2]

Despite numerous attempts by able writers including Washington Irving, the Green River's sandstone cliffs with their azure, lavender, and orange striations had defied adequate verbal description.[3] Thus it was a gift of fate that Thomas Moran, whose love of color was born of J. M. W. Turner, emerged as the first artist to bring superior technical skills to the challenge posed by the Green River landscape.

Moran's earliest sketches of the site are topographical, and reflect the artist's attempt to capture the chief geologic features of what one traveler described as *scenery for Hades*.[4] The early studio paintings that followed offer clear evidence that Moran reveled in the juxtapositions of blue, green, lavender, yellow, and orange that the landscape itself dictated. In later paintings Moran took the subject one step further, transforming, through the addition of mounted Indians, a landscape already verging on the phantasmagoric into something resembling a mirage.

Green River, Wyoming, a painting completed twenty-five years after Moran first sketched the site, unites these elements. In the distance, through the shimmer of palpable western heat, distinctive sandstone buttes rise above the languid Green River. In the foreground a caravan of Indians, so loosely painted that individual figures dissolve into one another, moves toward the river. Though colorfully clad, they are no match for the intense blue and green of the tree-lined river, or the hot gold and orange of Castle Rock in the middle distance. The product of imagination rather than observation, Moran's Indians serve as an appropriate measure of scale for the landscape that towers above them.

In his Green River paintings Moran coupled a known landscape, startling in its beauty, with evocative images of Indians that literally vanish to produce a compositional formula that met the nostalgic call, already strong in the 1870s, for a mythic West. So successful was the combination that Moran's Green River paintings became his "best-sellers." *Nancy Anderson*

1. The Green River rises near Fremont Peak in the Wind River Range and flows south a distance of 730 miles through Wyoming, Colorado, and Utah, to join the Colorado River (of which it is the largest tributary) near Moab, Utah.
2. In 1869 John Wesley Powell led an expedition of ten men 1,000 miles down the churning and uncharted waters of the Colorado River. Powell's subsequent account of the journey constitutes one of the great adventure stories of western exploration.
3. See Irving's *The Adventures of Captain Bonneville* (New York, 1837).
4. Ernest Ingersoll, *The Crest of the Continent* (Chicago, 1885), 307.

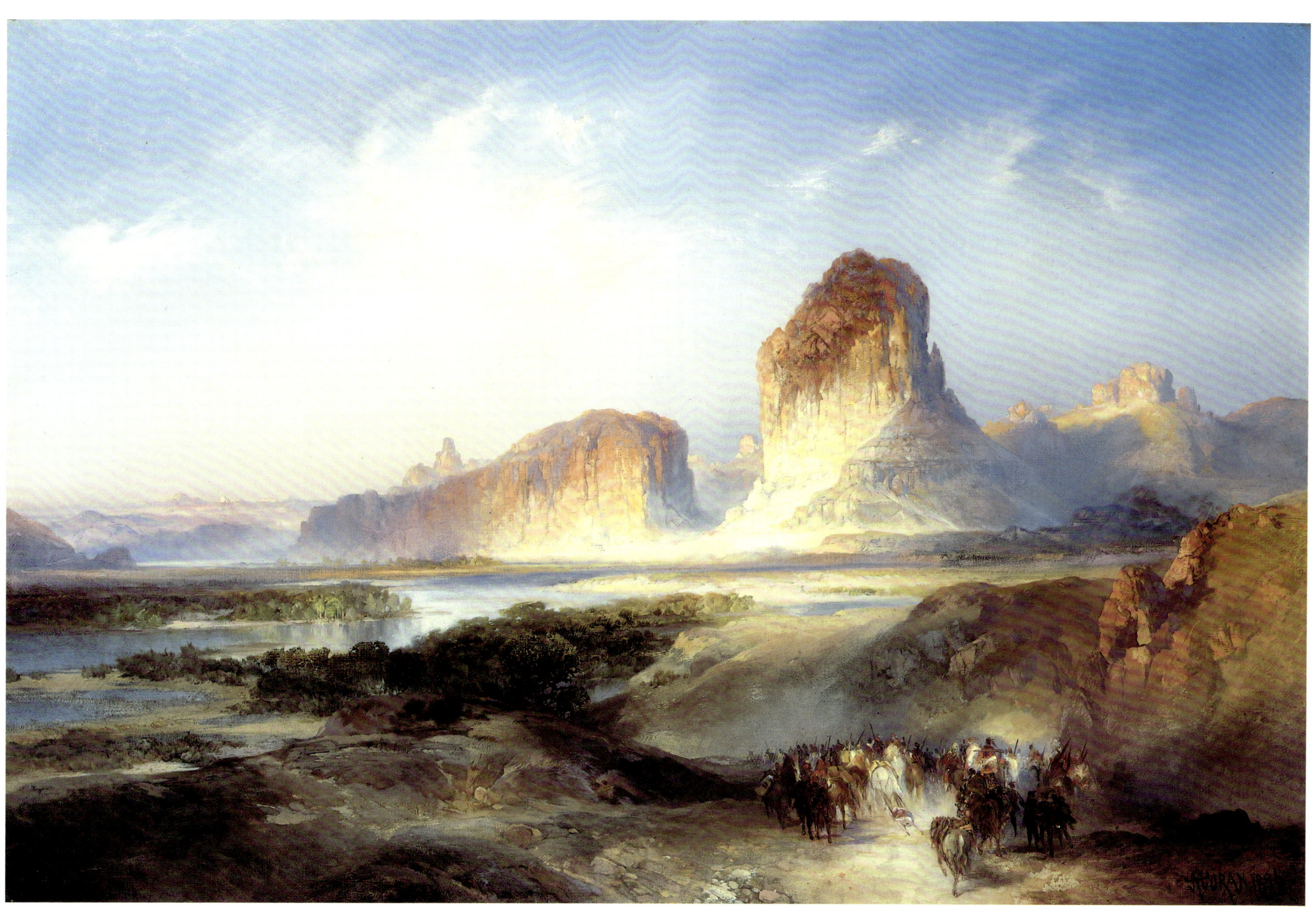

11

Thomas Moran (1837–1926)
Landscape 1898
oil on canvas, 20¼ x 30⅛ (51.4 x 76.5)

Few artists are linked as closely with a single geographic site as Thomas Moran is with Yellowstone National Park. The partnership began in 1870, before Moran actually saw the canyons and colors of Yellowstone. In the summer of that year, a party of nine men entered Yellowstone attempting to verify tantalizing rumors of geysers, hot springs, and mud pots. Far from disappointed, they emerged from "Coulter's Hell" with wondrous tales to tell. One member of the group, Nathaniel Langford, described what he had seen in two articles published by *Scribner's Monthly*.[1] Accompanying Langford's manuscript were several drawings, which an editor at *Scribner's* asked Thomas Moran to rework for publication. His interest piqued by the drawings and Langford's report, Moran arranged to join Ferdinand Hayden's survey party bound for Yellowstone the following summer. Although not an experienced horseman and so anatomically spare that he required a pillow on his saddle, Moran quickly adapted to camp life, and during a two-month period gathered the sketches and watercolors that launched his career.

Returning East, he recast his Yellowstone sketches into magazine illustrations, chromolithographs, and paintings. In addition, he loaned a group of watercolors to Ferdinand Hayden, who used them to help promote passage of a bill designed to make Yellowstone the nation's first national park. Approved in record time, thanks in part to the persuasive power of Moran's paintings, the bill was signed by President Grant on 1 March, 1872. Less than three months later, Congress appropriated $10,000 to purchase, for the Senate lobby, the most ambitious painting to result from Moran's first trip west, *The Grand Canyon of the Yellowstone* (1872, U.S. Department of the Interior, on loan to the National Museum of American Art, Smithsonian Institution, Washington).

Although Moran and Yellowstone became inextricably linked (the artist even altered his signature to include a "Y" for Yellowstone), Moran did not return to the park until 1892, when commissions from the Santa Fe Railroad and the State of Wyoming provided an opportunity to study afresh the landscape he had claimed as his own twenty-one years earlier.

Landscape, a dramatically composed view of the canyon and falls, dates from the period following Moran's 1892 trip. The painting depicts the Lower Falls and Grand Canyon of the Yellowstone River, which rises in the Absaroka Range in northwest Wyoming, flows north through Yellowstone National Park, east through Montana, and eventually joins the Missouri River. This late painting, although still panoramic in scope, is strikingly different in point of view than Moran's earlier renderings of the site. Gone is the safe "platform" from which the viewer could scan the distant falls, coursing river, and multicolored canyon walls. Instead Moran suspends the viewer between two narrow outcroppings midway down one side of the chasm. A rugged lava tower, bathed in light and faceted with colors that confirm the artist's long-standing debt to J. M. W. Turner, dominates the center of the canvas. Mist, spray, and low sweeping clouds move in counterpoint through passages of rock alternately threatening and resplendent. *Nancy Anderson*

1. "The Wonders of the Yellowstone," *Scribner's Monthly* (May, June 1871).

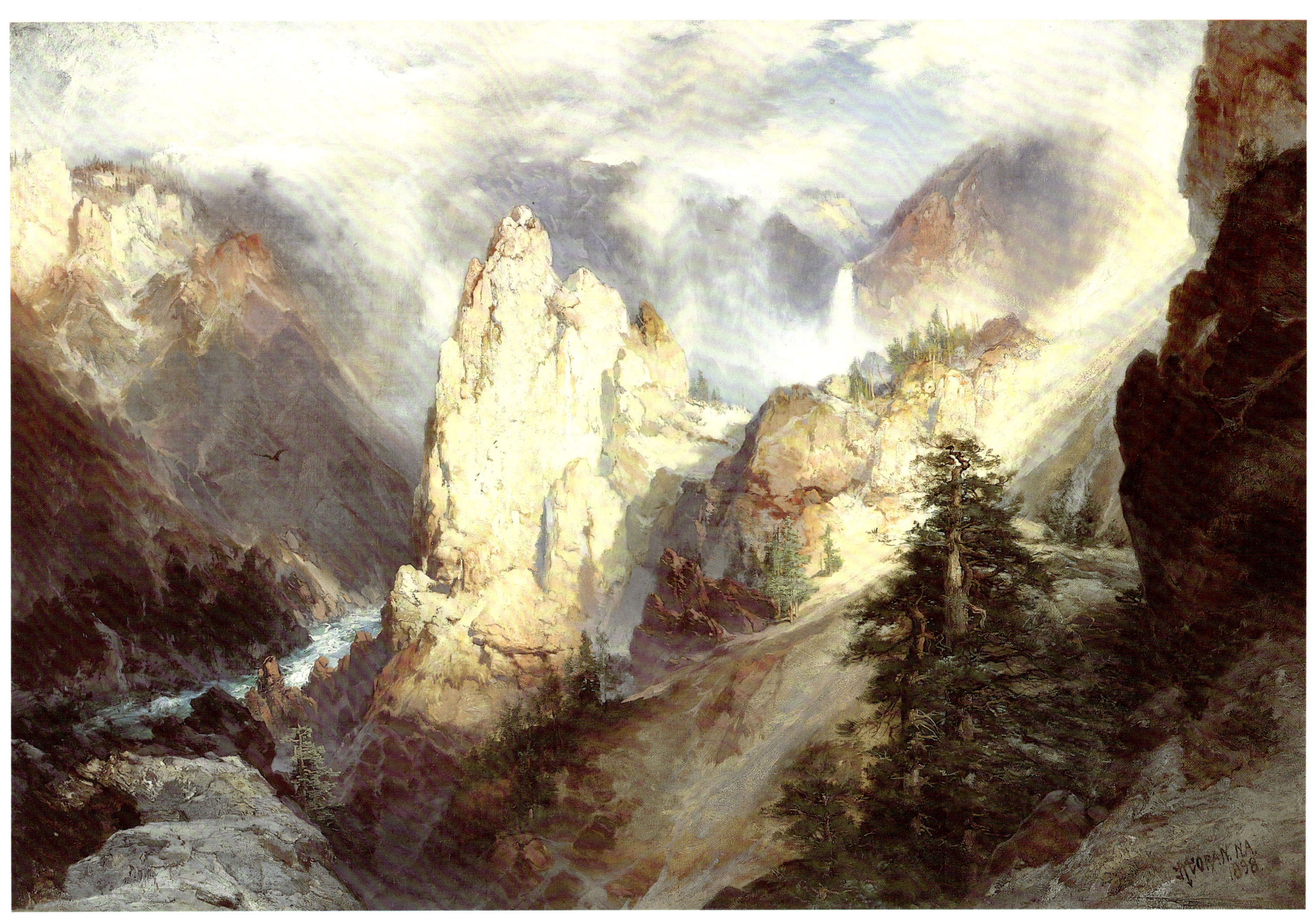
MORAN. N.A.
1898.

12

George Inness (1825–1894)
Overlook Mountain in the Catskills 1868
oil on canvas, 20¼ x 30 (51.4 x 76.2)

The Catskill Mountains of New York were sacred territory for American landscape painters of the first half of the nineteenth century, the place where, to a remarkable extent, the conceptual and stylistic canons of a national landscape were formulated, chiefly by Thomas Cole (see cat. 2). Although he was born nearby, in Newburgh, New York, George Inness' vision was formed elsewhere—in Italy and, most of all, in France—and was very far from canonical. By the 1860s his landscape style was unmistakably and deliberately different in appearance and intention from the practices and principles of "official" American landscape painting. *Mr. Inness . . . has long held the opinion*, it was said in 1863, *that . . . the highest beauty and truest value of the landscape painting are in the sentiment and feeling which flow from the mind and heart of the artist.*[1] The primary visible vehicle of Inness' subjective, self-expressive landscape—which, as a sympathetic critic put it, *uses nature's forms simply as language to express thought*[2]—was active and suggestive brushwork: *rough* and *rugged* handling, *grand, hasty strokes of the brush*, *nervous force of execution*, and *great sprawling marks of the brush*.[3] *Overlook Mountain in the Catskills* is, in its quality and clarity of purpose, a particularly fine example of Inness' interpretive landscape style, the projection upon natural fact of the *fiery energy* and *sensitive nervous organization* of his personality.[4]

Inness disdained mere resemblance, *what is called the real . . . that is to say, the local and particular.*[5] Once, when asked where a picture had been painted, he replied, *Nowhere in particular; do you suppose I illustrate guide-books? That's a picture.*[6] In 1868, the year he painted *Overlook Mountain*, Inness and his family summered at Leeds, on one of his several campaigns in the Catskills in the 1860s.[7] He may, therefore, have painted it from nature. But if *Overlook Mountain* is the *landscape, already finished . . . a scene near Leeds, partly a composition* that a reporter saw in Inness' New York studio in May 1868 and in which, as it was described, *Catskill Creek winds from the middle to the left foreground. In the left background are the Catskills*,[8] then, composed from sketches and memory, it was painted a month or two before that summer's trip and was to that extent an enactment of the artist's disinterest in *the local and particular.* *Nicolai Cikovsky, Jr.*

1. *The Sign of Promise* (New York, 1863), unpaginated.
2. *The Sign of Promise.*
3. "Art Gossip," *Cosmopolitan Art Journal* 4 (December 1860), 183; *New York Evening Post*, 30 March 1866; *New York Commercial Advertiser*, 22 May 1862; H., "When is an Artist True to Himself?," *Boston Evening Transcript*, 19 February 1862.
4. Mrs. Conant, "George Innis," *The Independent* 27 (27 December 1860).
5. *The Sign of Promise.*
6. Quoted in Reginald Coxe, "George Inness," *Scribner's Monthly* 44 (October 1908), 511.
7. Letters to Thomas B. Carroll, July 1866, New-York Historical Society.
8. *New York Evening Post*, 21 September 1868.

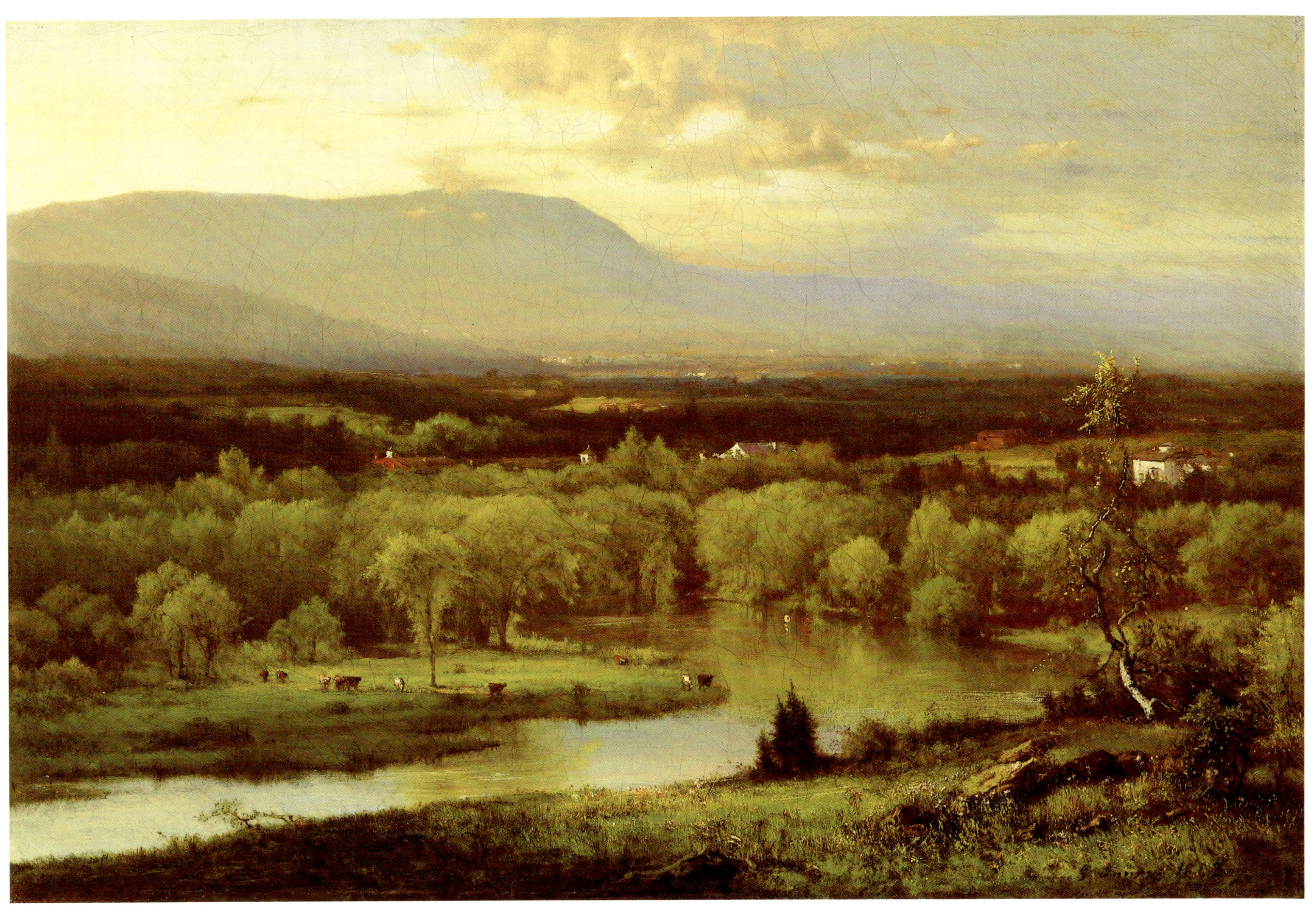

13

George Inness (1825–1894)
A Breezy Autumn 1887
oil on canvas, 30⅛ x 50 (76.5 x 127)

At about the time he painted *A Breezy Autumn*, people began referring to the synthetic quality of Inness' paintings. By that they meant that Inness' paintings were more completely—more wholly and artificially—synthesized from the formal resources of art than analyzed from direct and particular experiences of nature, and that they were more manifestly *made*, that Inness himself was chiefly responsible for their form: the design of their structure, the choice of their color, the manipulation of their surface. At the end of Inness' life a critic described one of his works as *more of a painting than a picture*.[1] As one of his students put it, his late works were *painted within the four walls of a room, away from and without reference to any particular nature; for he himself was nature*.[2] He reconstituted a convincingly natural experience composed of recognizable things and familiar effects—such as the fresh breeziness of an autumn day with patches of blue sky and flashes of sunlight bursting through scudding clouds—from his memory and from the formal instruments of art. *My forms are at my finger tips*, he said, *as the alphabet is on the tongue of a schoolboy*.[3]

At his death in 1894 Inness was universally regarded as one of America's greatest artists, his only serious rival being Winslow Homer. It was upon paintings like this, ones he began making during the last decade of his life, that his reputation was founded. He had always received critical attention, and he had for some time been a major influence on American landscape painting. But only in the 1880s did he begin to achieve commensurate fame and fortune. In 1886 a writer in the *Boston Transcript* spoke of *the heavy boom that is being sounded for George Inness. Orders*, he said, *are flowing in upon him from the highest sources; and the amount he realizes on them is something of the Aladdin stamp. Mr. Inness is so crowded with orders that, to use his own expression, made recently to a friend, 'pictures grow from his fingers' ends*.[4]

A Breezy Autumn was purchased from the artist the year it was painted by the important New York collector Richard H. Halsted. *Nicolai Cikovsky, Jr.*

1. "Some Living American Painters. Critical Conversations by Howe and Torrey," *Art Interchange* 32 (April 1894), 102.
2. Elliott Daingerfield, "George Inness," *The Century* 95 (1917), 71.
3. George Calvert, "George Inness: Painter and Personality," *Bulletin of the Art Association of Indianapolis. The John Herron Institute* 12 (November 1926), 49.
4. "Art and Artists," *Boston Evening Transcript* (22 April 1886).

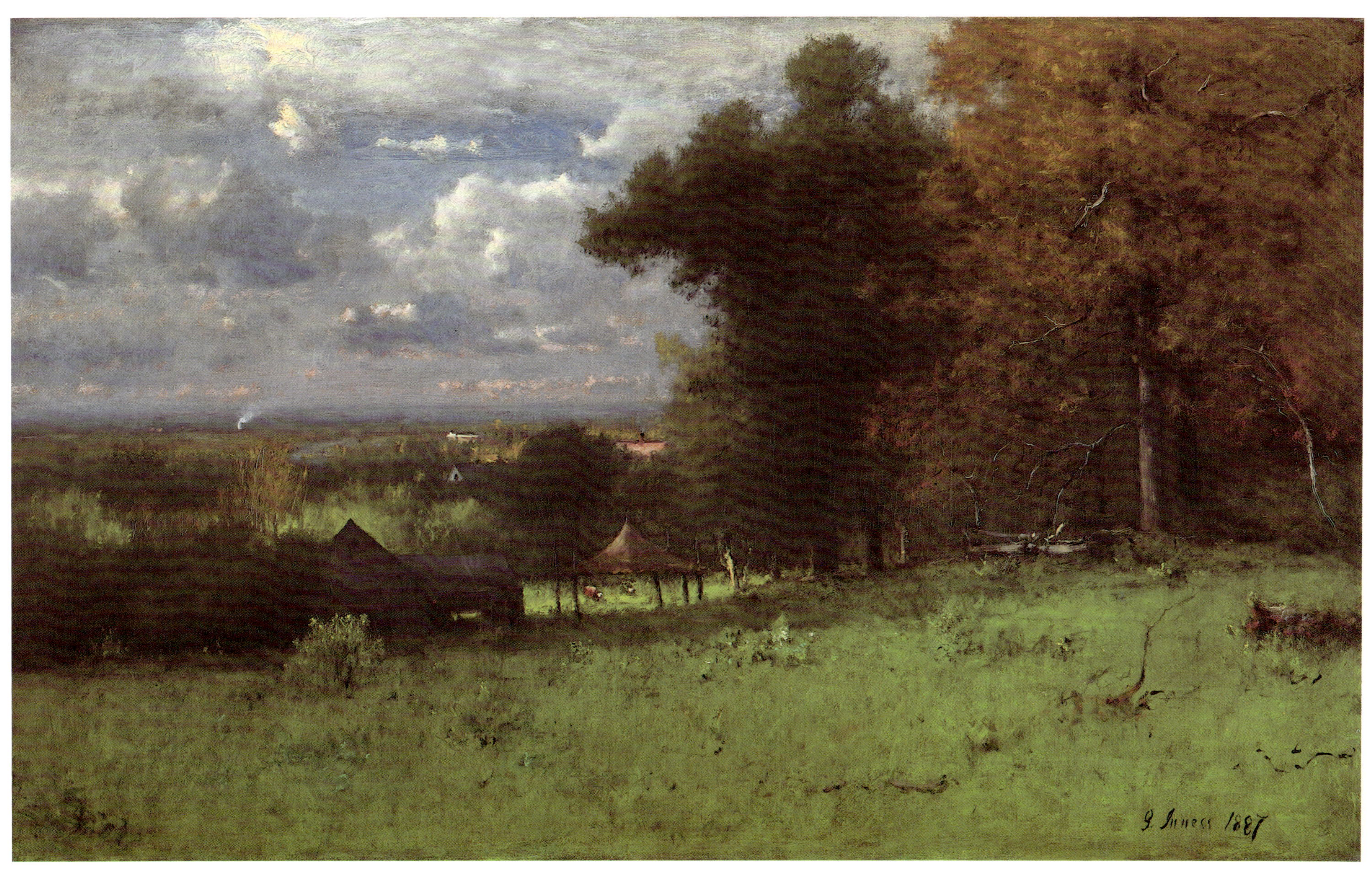
G. Inness 1887

14

Alfred Thompson Bricher (1837–1908)
View on the Providence River 1877
oil on canvas, 25⅛ x 50⅛ (63.8 x 127.3)

Alfred T. Bricher was very much a creature of artistic habit. In a career of more than thirty years he seldom forsook his favorite subjects or tried and true pictorial conventions. Coast scenes with a bit of beach and a mass of rocks at right or left with a view to open sea, painted from sea level and on a format twice as wide as high—these occur again and again in his art. Bricher was an acute observer and had a refined sense of color, light, and composition, all of which relieved and redeemed what might otherwise be an unbearably repetitious pictorial formula. In *View on the Providence River*, however, with its wonderful range of textures, the dramatic flash of light on the water, its subtly cadenced accents, and almost oriental compositional balance, that formula is varied in unusually beautiful and subtle ways.

View on the Providence River was painted from drawings that Bricher made six years earlier on a visit to Narragansett Bay in the summer of 1871. What is more, it was assembled from drawings made at two geographically separated places.[1] Effects of light and atmosphere that seem so directly seen, and a subject so intensely specific in its features, therefore, are in fact largely the products of practiced visual memory and accomplished pictorical artifice. *Nicolai Cikovsky, Jr.*

1. See Robert G. Workman, *The Eden of America: Rhode Island Landscapes, 1820–1920* [exh. cat., Museum of Art, Rhode Island School of Design] (Providence, 1986), 57, entry 31. Jeffry Brown has very kindly shared his unrivaled knowledge of Bricher with me and given free access to his extensive files on the painting. This painting has also been titled *Looking Seaward at Beverly*. Robert R. Perron, Marine Curator, The Beverly Historical Society, believes that the painting could have been made at Beverly, *executed from a location on the westerly side of Curtis Point, in Beverly, at about 10 a.m., looking SSE toward Marblehead Neck and Peaches' Point*. The day beacon on Haste Rock is still there, though in a different form, and a lighthouse has long been located on Marblehead Neck; the sandy beach is now severely eroded. But if the painting does indeed depict Beverly, Bricher used considerable artistic license, deleting islands and changing the perspective. (Letter to the author, 22 December 1988, which is most gratefully acknowledged).

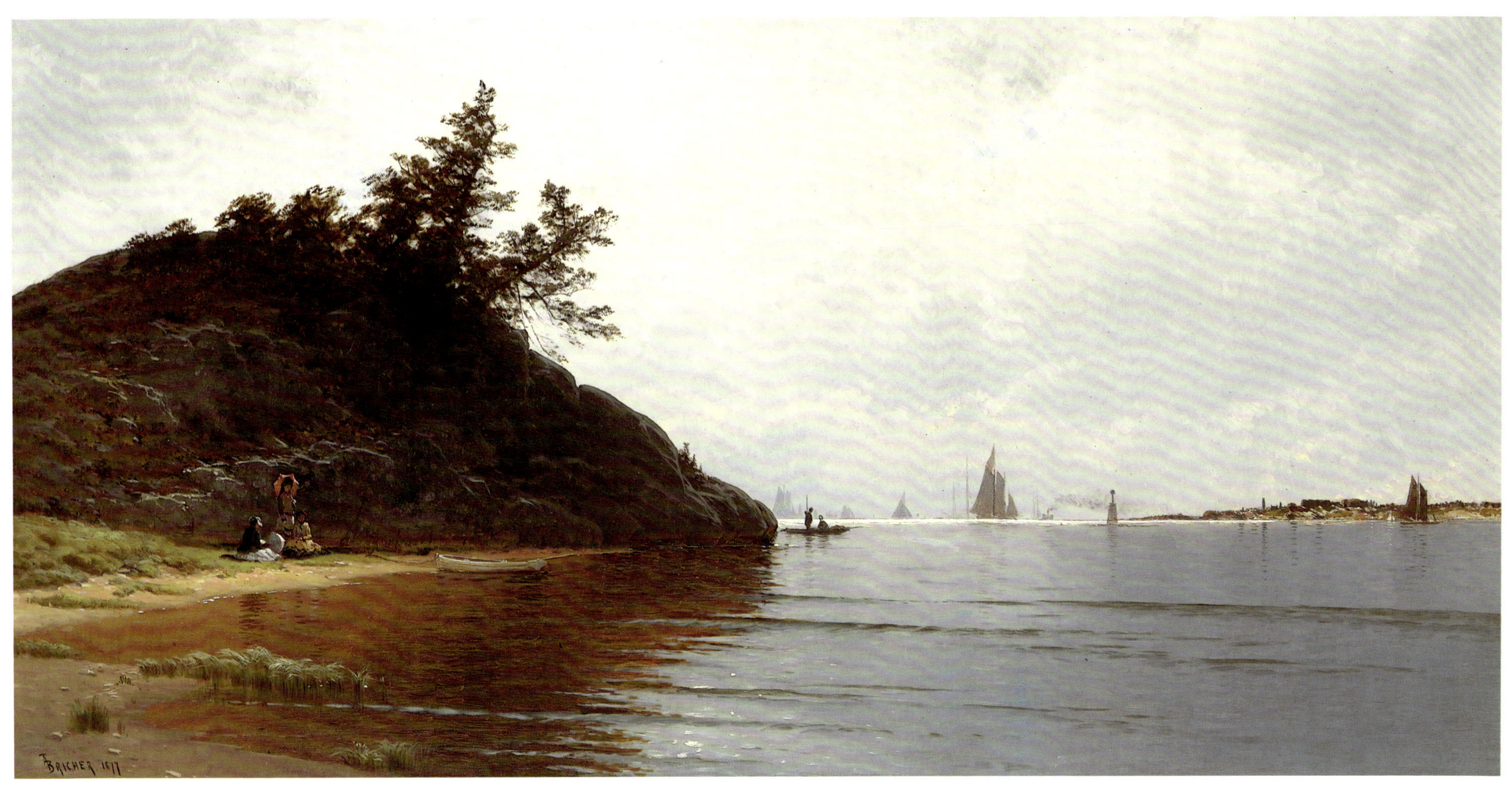
BRICHER 1877

15

Sanford Robinson Gifford (1823–1880)
Mount Mansfield 1858
oil on canvas, 30½ x 60¼ (77.5 x 153)

In early summer 1858, Sanford Gifford embarked on his first American sketching tour since returning from a two-year sojourn in Europe. During July, Gifford and his friend and fellow artist Richard Hubbard traveled through the Erie region of Pennsylvania and back across New York State toward the Green Mountains of Vermont.[1] In August they climbed Mount Mansfield, Vermont's largest mountain twenty miles east of Lake Champlain, and made a series of sketches. From these studies Gifford created a large oil painting, *Mount Mansfield.* He sold it to the prominent Philadelphia collector Joseph Harrison, Jr., who exhibited it at the 1859 exhibition of the National Academy of Design.[2] Prior to the exhibition, a critic for *The Crayon* enthusiastically described the painting as it neared completion in the artist's Tenth Street studio: *The picture is a vast panorama of hill country, stretching away from the foot of the mountain to Lake Champlain; a rocky span of the mountain intercepts the view on the right, while on the left, in the foreground, we have massive rocks with figures; a charm is thrown over the scene by placing it before us in the sunlight of a sultry summer afternoon.*[3] Another critic, viewing the work at the academy exhibition, extolled its design and atmospheric effects: *The aerial perspective is admirable; the mist is a palpable, floating mist, the two or three figures standing on the brink of a chasm are gazing down into a deep abyss, over which the spectator looks through the vaporous atmosphere so well given, to mountains beyond mountains. The bold, black rocks on the left aid in giving this great depth to the picture.*[4]

Mount Mansfield was Gifford's first major American oil painting following his return from Europe. Its success at the academy and its sale to a prominent collector reaffirmed Gifford's reputation as one of America's leading landscape painters. Years later the artist acknowledged its importance when he described the painting as one of his *chief pictures.*[5]

Mount Mansfield comprises of a series of peaks and ridges which, when viewed from a distance, suggest the shape of a human face.[6] In Gifford's painting, a camping party of four has just scaled the nose of the mountain. As two men prepare a fire, a third completes his climb, while a fourth turns to enjoy the panoramic view of the mountain and valley. To the right is the celebrated Chin with its lofty elevation of 4,393 feet. The Champlain Valley, framed by the rocky summits of the Nose and Chin, is bathed in the light of a setting sun that shines on the silvery waters of Lake Champlain and shrouds the mighty Adirondacks beyond.

Gifford's selection of Mount Mansfield as the site for such an important painting is somewhat unusual in light of the mountain's rather limited reputation. For example, in his 1836 essay on American scenery, Thomas Cole described the mountains, lakes, and valleys of the Northeast but never discussed Vermont.[7] In the early 1850s *Harper's New Monthly Magazine* ran a series of illustrated articles on American scenery but never mentioned Mount Mansfield.[8] If the Green Mountains were not well known, then why did Gifford travel there in 1858? Although we have no documentary evidence, it seems likely that one of Gifford's fellow artists in the Tenth Street Studio Building, Edward West Nichols, may have recommended Mount Mansfield as a possible site. During the 1850s Nichols made several trips to the Green Mountains and exhibited a number of Vermont landscapes at the National Academy, including two views of Mount Mansfield in 1857 and a view of the Champlain Valley in 1858.[9]

Nichols' artistic interest in Mount Mansfield and its surrounding scenery reflects a growing popularity of the Green Mountains during the late 1850s. With the development of a state railroad system, improved roads, and new hotels, tourists throughout New England began to explore Vermont's rolling hills and cultivated valleys.[10] Not surprisingly, Mount Mansfield was one of the chief attractions. For example, in his 1854 *Northern Guide*, Zadock Thompson praised the *exceedingly fine* view from the summit of Mount Mansfield: *On the west the whole valley of Lake Champlain appears spread out as a map, bounded by the lofty and picturesque Adirondacks on the south-west, and opening in the north-west into the valley of the St. Lawrence to the city of Montreal.*[11] In 1856, to accommodate sightseers, a carriage toll road was constructed halfway up the east side of the mountain along with a small house and stable. Two years later, the two-story Summit House was constructed between the Nose and Chin, which greatly enhanced tourist traffic. *It is truly astonishing to come upon so large and snug looking a house, when we remember that all its finishing and furnishings came up on horse backs, or on rudely-constructed drags. There is a sitting-room, bar-room, dining-room, kitchen and several bedrooms on the lower floor, and the whole upper story is finished off into cozy bedrooms, making accommodations for fifty people. The house is neatly furnished throughout, and the unceasing wonder in the visitor's mind is, "how* did *these things all get up here?"*[12]

In July 1864, W. Allan Gay (1821–1910), a popular landscape painter of the White Mountains, traveled to Vermont to explore and evaluate the "new" mountain. *Next morning we drove some miles up Mt. Mansfield to the bridle path. Here, taking horses, we were an hour ascending by a rocky path to the summit which reminded me of the Swiss ascents. A fine sunset set off the beauty of this summit peak, other peaks of the Green Mts. rolling off into delicate distance on one side while on the other gentle slopes of rich farming lands swept away to Lake Champlain which lay towards the west like a silver sheet gleaming in the sun. . . . It is a fine mountain view, I should judge of perhaps more beauty than that from Mt. Washington.*[13]

The exhibition of Gifford's painting in 1859 at the National Academy certainly enhanced Mount Mansfield's growing reputation. Gifford's painting, however, was not the only view of the mountain at the 1859 exhibition. For in the same gallery, Jerome B. Thompson exhibited an even larger painting of the same scene (fig. 1.).[14] There is no evidence that either artist was aware of the other's work prior to the exhibition. Although these competing views are painted from almost the same spot, they present very different interpretations of the mountain and man's relationship to nature. For example, Gifford depicted four outdoorsmen camping on the mountain.[15] In contrast, Thompson portrayed a party of sightseers who have spent the afternoon on the rocky ledge of the Nose, but who have no intention of spending the night. As the sun sets over the Adirondacks, a man in the foreground holds up his pocket watch to remind the party of the belated hour and to summon their departure.

With the construction of the Summit House in 1858, Mount Mansfield was being transformed from a place of solitude to one of social gatherings. In a July 1858 article from the Burlington *Free Press*, the summit is described as *a place to which ladies and gentlemen are daily resorting.*[16] Gifford's painting then is an intentionally nostalgic view of the mountain, focusing upon its past rather than its future.

In April 1860, Gifford's interpretation of Mount Mansfield was curiously reinforced by an anonymous article in *The Knickerbocker* entitled "Adventures on a Mountain-Top."[17] The article, which describes a camping trip by four men (two friends and two guides) on Mount Mansfield, begins: *During the summer of 1858 I ascended* [Mount Mansfield] *of the Green Mountain ranges, which until within a few years has been comparatively little visited,* [and] *is still unknown to the majority of summer tourists, but from which can be had a view of scenery, for variety, extent and grandeur, scarcely excelled on this continent. A good portion of the sentiment of travelling is lost even amid the utmost magnificence of Nature, as soon as the path begins to be beaten, and the crowd rushes in.*[18]

The author does not provide any clue to his identity except to say that he had received his walking stick as a gift from the descendants of Resolved Hubbard, who was presumably a real or fictitious ancestor of Gifford's sketching partner Richard Hubbard.[19] With the aid of that walking stick, the author climbed to the top of Mount Mansfield and described Lake Champlain at sunset. *There I beheld the orb of day go down gorgeously on a serene night . . .* [the] *lingering reflections upon the floating clouds, the long streaks of light, the appearance of islands, all bathed with lustre, and the reluctant dying out of day in the west exceeded all which I had conceived of Italian skies.*[20]

As the campers descended the mountain and arrived at the halfway house, there was a great bustle of noise and activity. *Preparations were making for a party of ladies to ascend on the next week. There were several stout fellows with axes going to clear the obstructed path, so that the fair cavalcade might advance and the Dryads and Hamadryads peep out from the leafy coves to salute the new-come wood-nymphs. Then should these last interrupt the solemnity of the sacred grove with shouts and laughter, while the rocks, which for centuries untold had been invaded only by the winds, or felt the fall of the snow-flake, should be strewed all over with the crumbs and fragments of a pic-nic.*[21]

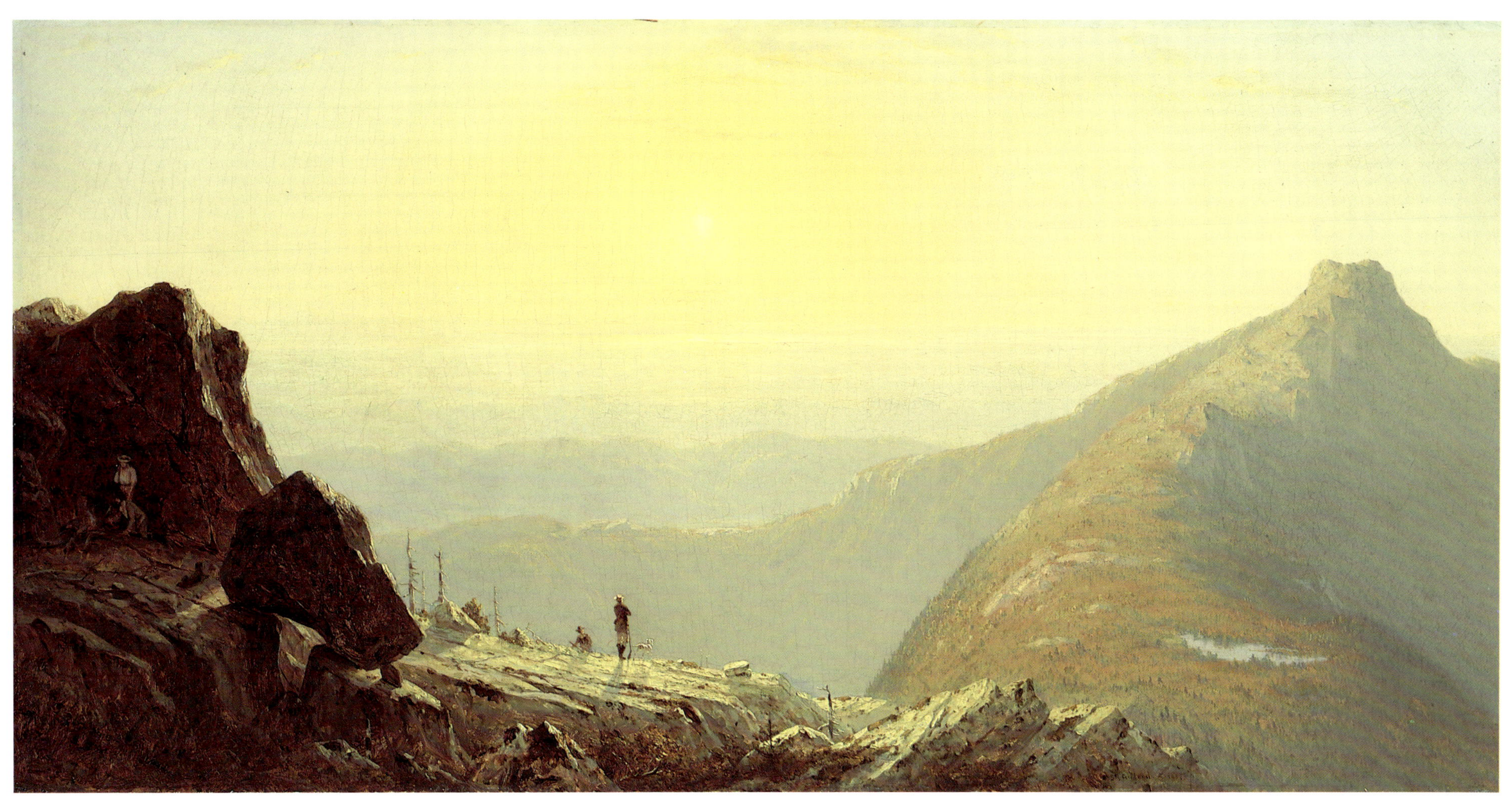

This pejorative description certainly recalls Jerome Thompson's painting of the previous spring with its windswept picnickers some of whom assume poses reminiscent of Raphael's woodland nymphs (and later those of Manet). The unknown author concludes his Mount Mansfield article proclaiming, *Ere long the tide of travel will set in this direction, bringing much which is vapid with it. But I will promise those who come at once, that they will not be disappointed in their expectations.*[22]

Unfortunately, this promise could not be fulfilled, for in the summer of 1860, thousands of tourists visited the mountain and transformed its summit into a fashionable resort.[23] However, Gifford's painting stands as a visual fulfillment of the unknown writer's promise. For in his painting of Mount Mansfield, Gifford created an arrested moment that forever celebrates the joy and beauty of the natural world. The painting is also imbued with a more somber theme, for just as it celebrates the American wilderness, it simultaneously reminds us of its passing.

Christopher Kent Wilson

Fig. 1
Jerome Thompson, *The Belated Party on Mansfield Mountain*, 1858, oil on canvas, 38 x 63⅛ (96.5 x 160.3), The Metropolitan Museum of Art, New York, Rogers Fund, 1969

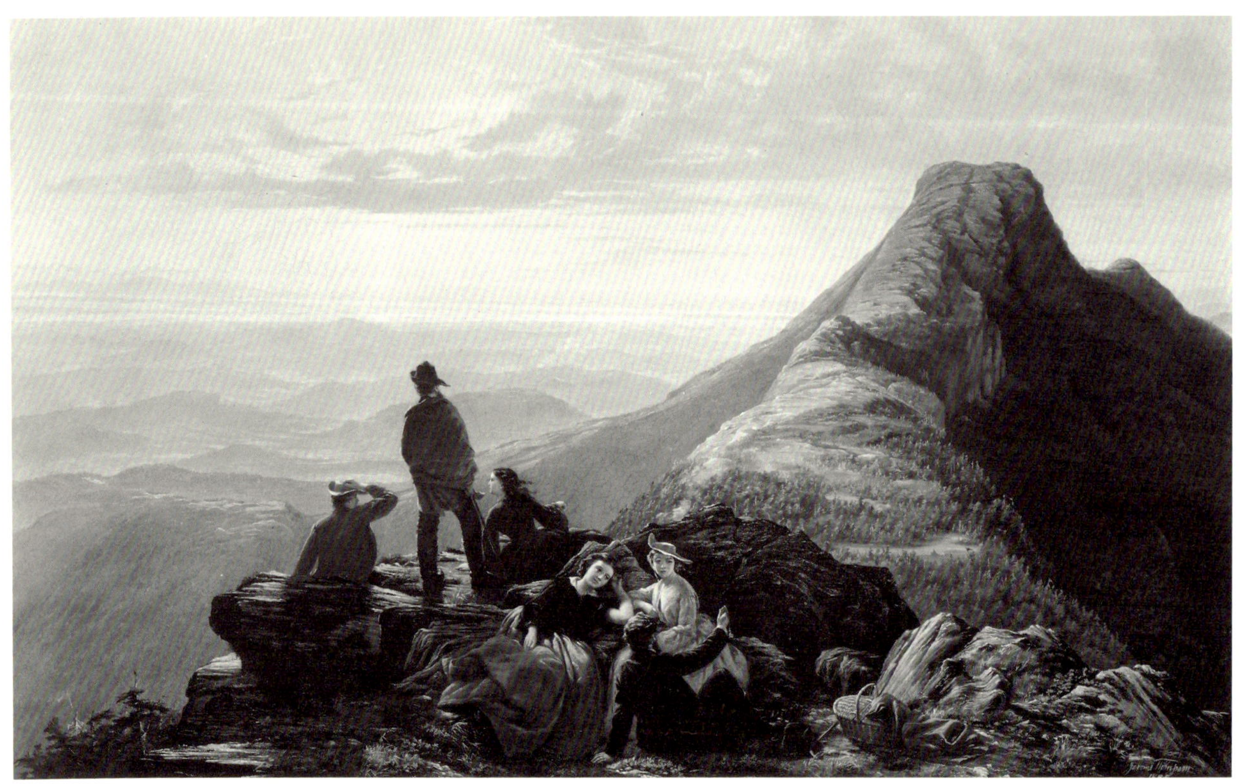

1. "Sketchings," *The Crayon* 5 (August 1858), 238.
2. Mary B. Cowdrey, *National Academy of Design Exhibition Record, 1826–1860*, 2 vols. (New York, 1943), 1:182. During the twentieth century, the painting's location was unknown until it was discovered in the basement of a New Jersey home in 1985. Ila and Steven Weiss, *Sanford R. Gifford* [exh. cat., Alexander Gallery] (New York, 1986).
3. *The Crayon* 6 (March 1859), 91.
4. "Exhibition at the Academy of Design," *New York Semi-Weekly Tribune* (17 May 1859).
5. Letter, 6 November 1874, Gifford to Octavius Brooks Frothingham as quoted by Ila Weiss, *Poetic Landscape: The Art and Experience of Sanford R. Gifford* (Newark, Delaware, 1987), 327.
6. The Abnaki Indians perceived the mountain in a different way, calling it "Moze-o-de-be-Wadso" or "the mountain with a head like a moose." Llew Evans, "Capstone of Vermont," *Appalachia*, New Series 10, no. 7 (June 1944), 41.
7. Thomas Cole, "Essay on American Scenery," *The American Monthly Magazine*, New Series, 1 (January 1836), 1–12.
8. William M'Leod, "The Summer Tourist—Scenery of The Franconia Mountains, New Hampshire," *Harper's New Monthly Magazine* 5, no. 25 (June 1852), 4–11; T. Addison Richards, "Lake George," *Harper's New Monthly Magazine* 7, no. 36 (July 1853), 161–170; Anon., "Niagara," *Harper's New Monthly Magazine* 7, no. 39 (August 1853), 289–305; and T. Addison Richards, "The Valley of the Connecticut," *Harper's New Monthly Magazine* 8, no. 75 (August 1856), 289–302. Mount Mansfield's limited reputation is also reflected in a contemporary review of Gifford's painting. The critic for *The Crayon*, who described the painting in Gifford's studio before its Academy exhibition, referred to it not as *Mount Mansfield* but as *View of Mansfield Mountain, Vermont*. *The Crayon* 6 (March 1859), 91.
9. Cowdrey, *Academy Exhibition Record*, 2:51.
10. Louise B. Roomet, "Vermont as a Resort Area in the Nineteenth Century," *Vermont History* 44, no. 1 (winter 1976), 1–13; and Andrea Rebek, "The Selling of Vermont: From Agriculture to Tourism, 1860–1910," *Vermont History* 44, no. 1 (winter 1976), 14–27.
11. Zadock Thompson, *Northern Guide* (Burlington, Vermont, 1854), 34–35.
12. Mattie Whiting Baker, "A Day on Mt. Mansfield in 1866," *The Vermonter* (May 1945), 247. See also *Mount Mansfield and its Environs* (Concord, New Hampshire, 1861).
13. Letter, July 17, 1864. W. Allan Gay, "An Artist Describes His Vist to Mt. Mansfield in 1864," *Vermont History* 39, no. 1 (winter 1971), 53–54. For another comparison of mounts Washington and Mansfield, see "The View from Mansfield," Burlington *Free Press* (28 July 1858), as originally quoted by Boston *Atlas and Bee*, "We have tried both, and if we could see but one, should choose the view from Mansfield."
14. Cowdrey 1943, 2:158. See also *Catalogue of the Thirty-Fourth Annual Exhibition of the National Academy of Design, 1859* (New York, 1859), 46. For an excellent analysis of Thompson's painting, see Kevin J. Avery, "*The Belated Party on Mansfield Mountain.*" *American Paradise* (New York, 1987), 146–147.
15. During the late 1850s and early 1860s, Gifford painted several smaller pictures of Mount Mansfield. The depiction of four outdoorsmen camping on the Nose was a common theme among these works. For some examples, see Weiss, *Poetic Landscape*, 208.
16. "The Bostwick House and Mount Mansfield," Burlington *Free Press* (23 July 1858).
17. Anonymous, "Adventures on a Mountain-Top," *The Knickerbocker* 55, no. 4 (April 1860), 353–363.
18. "Adventures," *The Knickerbocker*, 353.
19. "Adventures," *The Knickerbocker*, 355.
20. "Adventures," *The Knickerbocker*, 363.
21. "Adventures," *The Knickerbocker*, 362.
22. "Adventures," *The Knickerbocker*, 363. The *Knickerbocker* article not only supported Gifford's view of Mount Mansfield, but also served to introduce another large painting of the mountain by Richard Hubbard, exhibited just a few weeks later at the National Academy. See Cowdrey, *Academy Exhibition Record*, 1:242.
23. For a description of the mountain top and its tourists, see Albert D. Hager, *Report on the Geology of Vermont*, 2 vols. (Claremont, New Hampshire, 1861), 2:879.

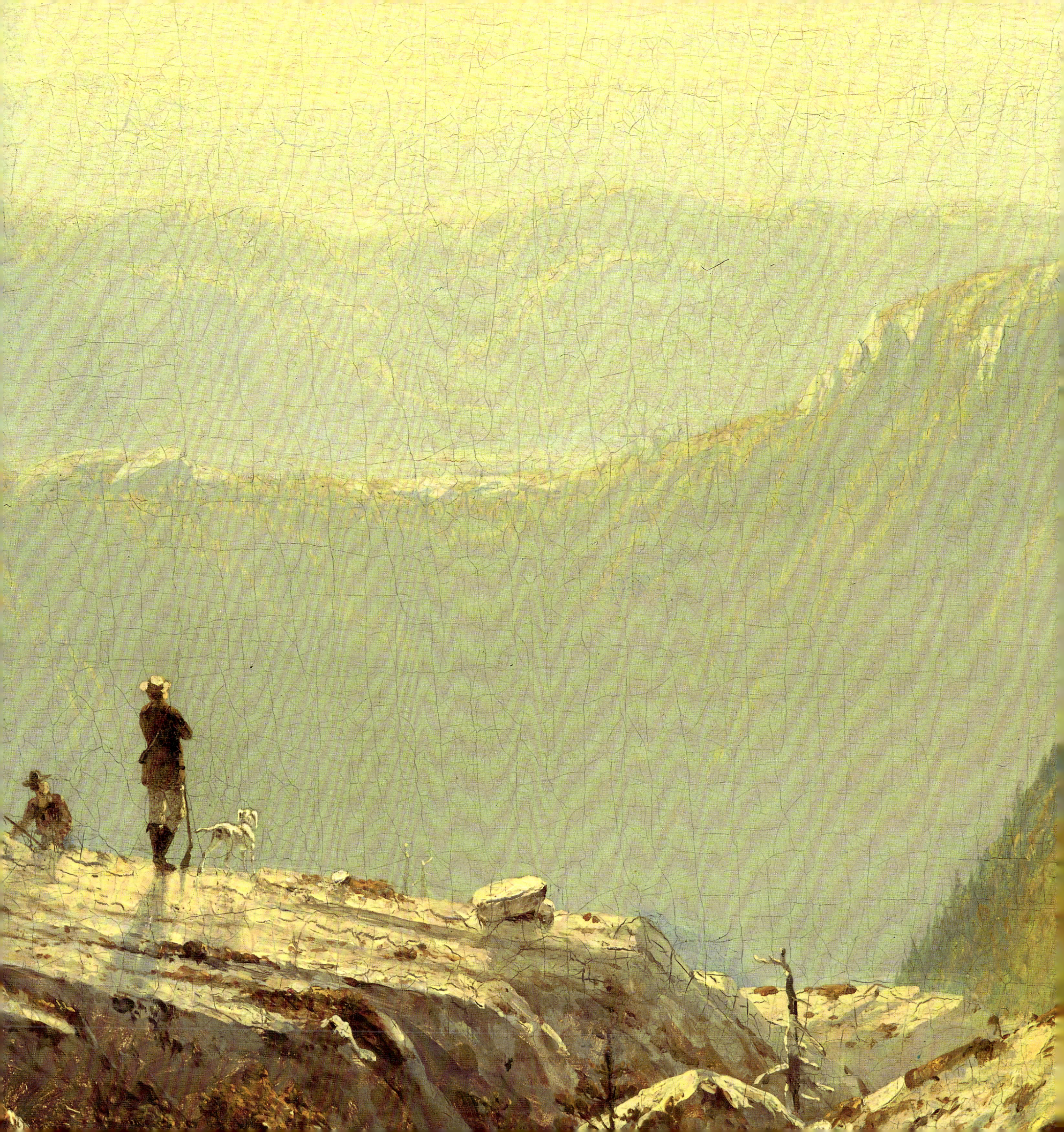

16

Francis Augustus Silva (1835–1886)
The Schooner "Progress" Wrecked at Coney Island, July 4th, 1874 1875
oil on canvas, 20⅛ x 38⅛ (51.1 x 96.8)

The Schooner "Progress" is one of two paintings Silva made of this particular shipwreck, which he meticulously recorded in four watercolor sketches made on 11 July, 28 July (two), and 15 August (Peabody Museum, Salem, Massachusetts); *Approaching Storm* (n.d., 20 x 38, private collection) is virtually identical, save for a few details.[1] In its balanced composition, polished handling, and carefully studied effects of light and atmosphere, the dated canvas represents Silva at the height of his skill as a marine painter. It is undoubtedly the painting Silva exhibited in the November 1875 exhibition of the Brooklyn Art Association.[2]

Silva surely was drawn to shipwrecks as a subject not only because they were common along the New York coastline he so often painted, but also because the theme fulfilled his expressive needs. Late in his life he wrote that *a picture must be more than a skillfully painted canvas,—it must tell something*... and derided artists who *never paint from memory or feeling*... [and in whose works] *the subject must convey no sentiment—call up no emotion, awaken no interest.*[3] His treatment of the subject spanned his entire career, but was intermittent; among the few known paintings are *Old Wreck* (unlocated), his first work shown at the Brooklyn Art Association (in 1869), and *Old Wreck at Long Branch* (private collection), which undoubtedly dates from the last years of his life.[4]

How Silva learned of the destruction of the *Progress* is unknown; though he carefully identified and dated the event on his first sketch,[5] it is not documented in the major New York and Brooklyn newspapers of the time, nor in official shipping registers.[6] Whatever the circumstances, the four sketches and two oils he produced confirm Silva's avid interest in this particular wreck and allow rare insight into his working methods.

Silva based *The Schooner "Progress"* on his last surviving sketch of the wreck, made on 15 August 1874.[7] Placing the ship's broken hull at the left of the composition, Silva retained its appearance and angle in the sand from the sketch, but added more remains of the ship at the lower left. He lowered the horizon from the study and filled in details of beach, surf, and sky, which are absent from it; the long, cresting wave was undoubtedly copied from the 28 July sketch. In addition to contrasting rough surf against smooth sand, and rushing diagonals against the expansive horizon, Silva also provided a symbolic foil for the broken ship: the most prominent of the ships dotting the horizon is a schooner in full sail, whose presence casts an elegiac tone over the tranquil scene. *Sarah Cash*

1. Reproduced in *Antiques* 101 (June 1972), 944. Its composition is identical to that of *The Schooner "Progress,"* though *Approaching Storm* was composed from different sketches (the 11 July sketch and one of the 28 July sketches). A third Silva seascape, *Coney Island Beach* (20 x 36", n.d., reproduced as lot 40 in the catalogue for Sotheby's New York sale 4704M, 20 October 1981), though it does not include a shipwreck, is almost identical in composition to the two wreck scenes and features a similar placement of both the rolling wave and the prominent ship on the horizon.

   The only other extant image of this wreck is a photograph taken by George Brainerd on 3 November 1874 (Brooklyn Collection, Brooklyn Public Library, Brainerd no. 76, reproduced reversed in Ronald G. Pisano, *Long Island Landscape Painting 1820–1920* [Boston, 1985], 72).
2. As *A Wreck on Coney Island Beach*, no. 368. *Approaching Storm* most likely was the painting Silva exhibited as *The Wreck* in the November 1874 Brooklyn Art Association exhibition (no. 237).
3. Francis A. Silva, "American vs. Foreign-American Art," *The Art Union* 1 (June–July 1884), 130–131; quoted in John I. H. Baur, "Francis A. Silva: Beyond Luminism," *Antiques* 118 (November 1980), 1018.
4. *Old Wreck at Long Branch* is reproduced in the catalogue for Sotheby's New York sale "5436 SPRING," 29 May 1986, lot 11. Two other wreck scenes are *Coastal Sunset* of 1874 (reproduced *Antiques* [August 1988], 217), and *Old and Abandoned*, dated 1883 (reproduced in the catalogue for Christie's New York sale "Raymond–6274," 2 December 1988, lot 78).
5. The 11 July sketch is inscribed at the lower left *Sch. PROGRESS wrecked at Coney Island, July 4th 1874*, and dated at the lower right.
6. Despite the lack of documentation on the wreck, newspapers did report that very stormy weather occurred in New York on 4 July 1874; the 6 July 1874 *Brooklyn Daily Eagle* (2. col. 4) noted that [T]*he storms of Saturday* [4 July] *were widespread and of destructive force.*

   The schooner *Progress* in the painting may very well be the one by that name built at Rondout, New York, in 1851, which measured 52.91 tons. According to a handwritten note on its Port of New York Enrollment (No. 117, 14 September 1872, Bureau of Marine Inspection and Navigation Record Group 41, National Archives), the schooner was surrendered in New York 19 December 1877 because it was *lost on shore of Long Island Sound in 1875*. However, early records of this type vary in accuracy and the vessel could well have been wrecked in 1874.
7. The watercolor and pencil sketch measures 6¼ x 4 inches, and is found in sketchbook no. M8871–1 in the Peabody collection. It is inscribed at the lower left *Coney Island Aug 15 74*.

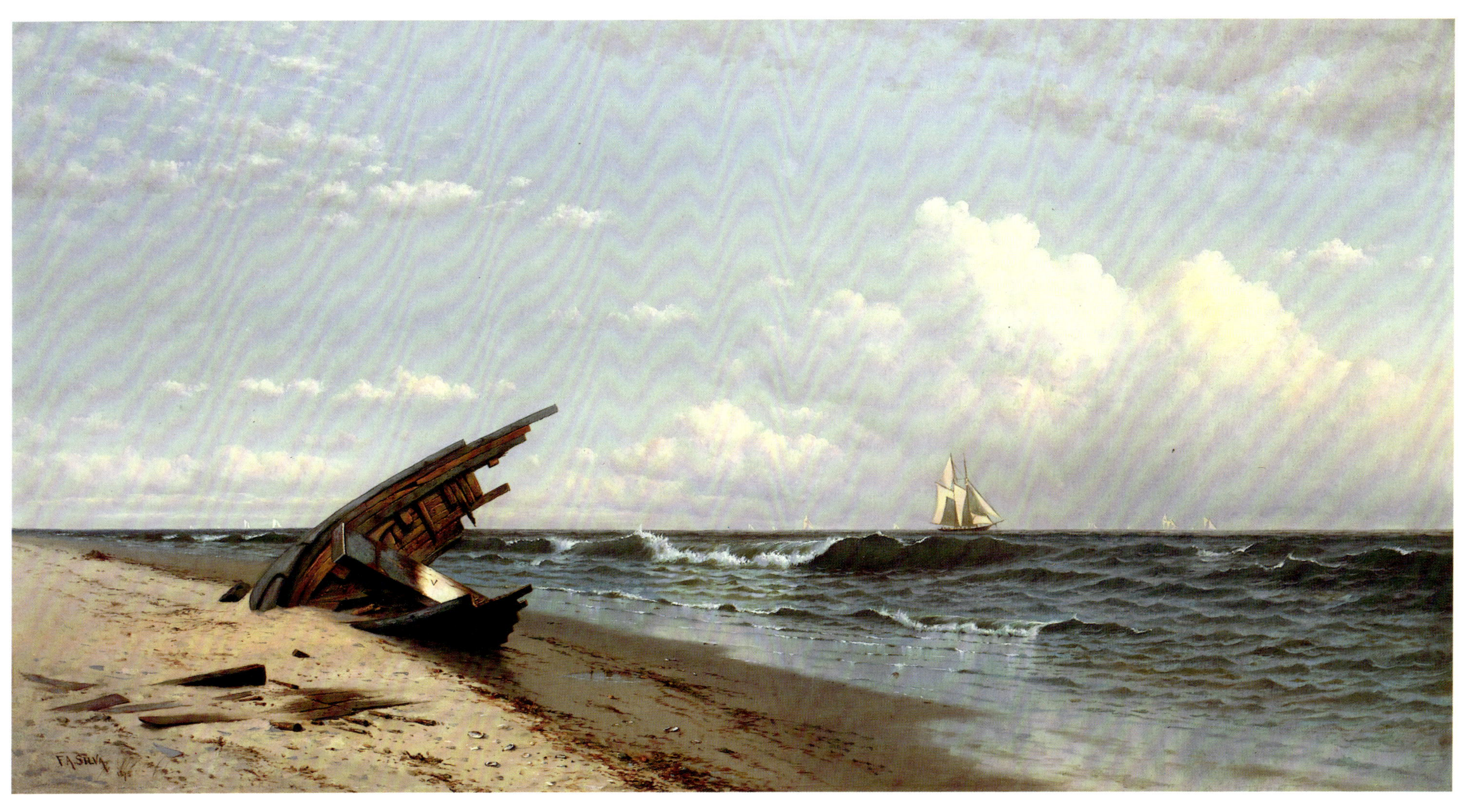
FASILVA

17

William Bradford (1823–1892)
Whalers Trapped in Arctic Ice c. 1870–1880
oil on canvas, 28 x 44 (71.1 x 111.8)

William Bradford first visited the Far North in the spring of 1861, but his fascination with the Arctic had actually begun some years earlier. In 1856 he read Elisha Kent Kane's popular book *Arctic Explorations in the Years 1853, '54, '55* and carefully studied the accompanying illustrations by the marine painter James Hamilton.[1] From such sources Bradford formed a vivid impression of the natural drama of the landscape of the Arctic and the human drama faced by the men who explored it. His own experiences during the 1861 visit and several subsequent trips would serve as inspiration for his most memorable works, which capture both its mysterious beauty and its ever-present danger.

Bradford's most important trip to the Arctic took place in the summer of 1869, when he sailed with a group that included the scientist-explorer Isaac I. Hayes and several photographers aboard the whaling steamer *Panther*.[2] In both sketches and photographs Bradford carefully recorded the sights, later using his material as the basis for a lavish book entitled *The Arctic Regions*.[3] Bradford was particularly fascinated by the men who earned their livings from the harsh arctic environment, and paid special attention to the parties of sealers and whalers he encountered during his trip.

Although undated, the present painting most likely postdates Bradford's 1869 visit, and may well have been composed using sketches, studies, and photographs gathered then.[4] Bradford often reused details and basic compositional schemes in a number of paintings, so it is difficult to identify many works with certainty. However, *Whalers Trapped in Arctic Ice* does conform to the description of a work entitled *Crushed in the Ice* he exhibited in London in 1872, and which represented . . . *the wreck of one of the numerous whaling fleet that annually fishes these waters. She has been caught between the masses of ice, and is heaved up on a pile of blocks, whereby her bulwarks are destroyed, and her timbers crushed in so far below the water-line as to show the impossibility of repair. Her bowsprit and all her upper rigging are gone, and much of the lower cordage has disappeared. Some of the boats have been saved, and the crew are actively engaged in preserving whatever they can from the wreck. The ill-fated ship lies near a lofty iceberg, which not only rises perpendicularly to a great height above sea-level, but may have grounded at a depth of hundreds of feet below the surface*.[5] Whether or not the present painting is *Crushed in the Ice*, it is certainly one of Bradford's most striking mid-size canvases, with the dramatic composition and kaleidoscopic effects of light and color that characterize his finest works. *Franklin Kelly*

1. John Wilmerding, *William Bradford, 1823–1892* [exh. cat., DeCordova Museum] (Lincoln, Massachusetts, 1969), 14–15.
2. Wilmerding, *Bradford*, 16–22.
3. Published in London in 1873 and limited to three hundred copies, each of which included one hundred twenty-five original photographs hand tipped into the text.
4. Although Bradford apparently did not paint works based directly on photographs, he admitted that he *could not paint without them*; "The Paintings of Mr. William Bradford of New York," *Philadelphia Photographer* 31 (January 1884), 7–8, quoted in Frank Horch, "Photographs and Paintings by William Bradford," *The American Art Journal* 5 (November 1973), 61, 63.
5. "Arctic Scenery," *The Art-Journal* (London) 11 (1872), 241; quoted in Wilmerding, *Bradford*, 41. It has also been suggested that a painting sold at Sotheby's in New York on 25 October 1979 (no. 38, 28 x 44¼ in.) might be the *Crushed in Ice* exhibition in London in 1872, because it, too, is similar to the description.

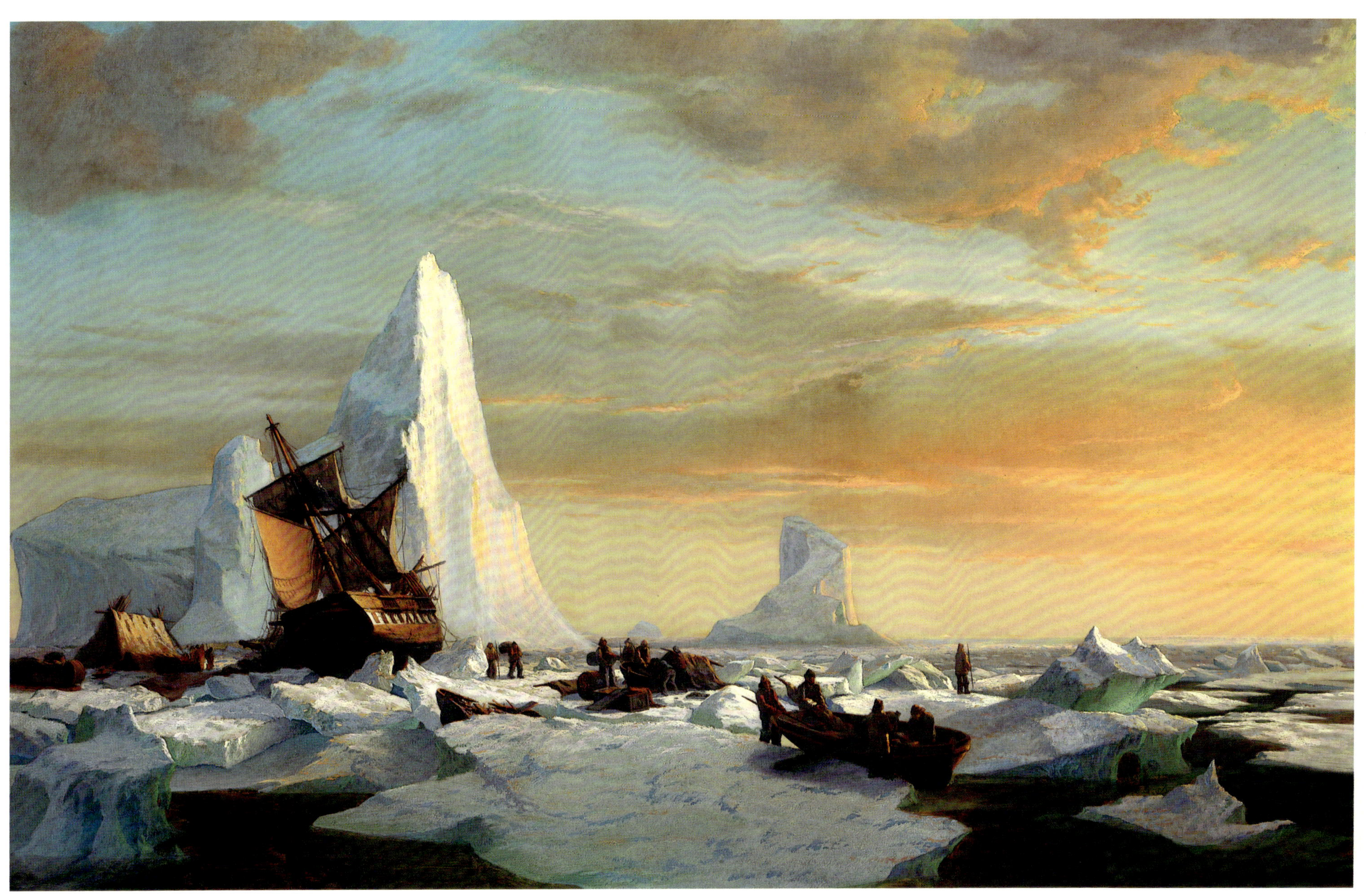

18

Albert Bierstadt (1830–1902)
The Shore of the Turquoise Sea 1878
oil on canvas, 42½ x 64½ (108 x 163.8)

The Shore of the Turquoise Sea is Bierstadt's most important marine painting. Exhibited unfinished in January 1878, and shown as a completed work one month later and in 1880, the picture was a product of a journey by the artist and his wife in the spring of 1877 to the Bahamas, the first in a series of excursions they took to that region to ease her failing health. In the mid-1880s and again in 1900 he painted two large variants of the composition, both of which were publicly exhibited.

The Bierstadts' initial visit to the Bahamas, which included a stopover in Florida, lasted *a couple of months* during the spring of 1877.[1] A flourishing British colony, the Bahamas were a popular winter refuge for wealthy Americans and for invalids from both Europe and the Americas. On that trip the couple probably stayed at Government House in Nassau, although they also must have acquainted themselves with the nearby Royal Victoria Hotel, reputedly the *best-kept hotel in the West Indies*, which provided luxurious accommodations (priced at $3 per day), a focus for social life, and access to the scenic beauty of neighboring islands.[2] On subsequent journeys to the islands, they invariably resided at the Royal Victoria. By early June 1877 they had returned to New York, the artist bringing with him *some pretty sketches of the places visited*.[3] Evidently the Bierstadts embarked almost immediately thereafter on a tour of Egypt and the Near East.[4] Perhaps the delicacy of Mrs. Bierstadt's health, and more surely a pressing engagement, the commission of an eight-foot canvas of Estes Park (1878, Denver Public Library) by the Irish Lord Dunraven, induced them to cancel a return visit to Nassau planned for the following fall.[5]

Bierstadt threw himself into his work. By December Lord Dunraven's painting was sufficiently advanced to permit the artist to display it at both the Century Association and the Union League Club in New York.[6] Meantime, he sent *King's River Canyon, California* and *Sunset on the Western Plains* to the Century Association and Union League Club, respectively, in November, and *Sentinel Rock, Yosemite Valley* to the Brooklyn Art Association in December.[7] Visitors to his studio also saw pictures in progress of an Indian on horseback hunting a buffalo, one of Kern River, California (possibly that now in the Virginia Museum of Fine Arts, Richmond), a luminous *View of Nassau Light*, and *some fine color sketches of Bermuda* [sic] *seaside scenery, made during his recent trip to that island. . . . Notable among these is one of a rising storm on the coralline coast, a fine effect of a huge wave of that peculiar emerald one only sees in the tropics*.[8]

The artist began a large painting of the "rising storm" during this period, as well. The work must have progressed rapidly, since he exhibited the still-incomplete picture in January 1878 at the monthly meeting of the Union League Club. A reporter for the *New York Herald* noticed it there: . . . *The largest canvas in the room, a view looking seaward from a beach near Nassau, Bahamas, by Albert Bierstadt, hung on this* [the east] *wall. The motive, a difficult one of an immense emerald wave rolling on to the beach past the coral-line rock and lifted by the turn of the wind as the storm draws off is very admirably rendered*.[9]

Two days later, the paper printed a lengthy, appreciative description: *Albert Bierstadt has nearly finished on* [sic] *a large canvas "On the Coast Near Nassau, Bahamas." It represents a huge wave, with a storm tossed crest lifted up by the turn of the wind, dashing grandly past coral rocks on a smooth sandy beach, on which its predecessor has cast a derelict spar. A heavy storm is drawing off, and the second line of dark blue wave laps fiercely on, exceedingly well given to the right. On the left hand the storm is clearing away, allowing glimpses of a purer sky, under which two sails—one a brigantine not far out, and the other seen on the horizon—are riding bravely along, having weathered the storm. Seaweed lies on the foamy forewater between us and the great wave, and on the beach are a few conch shells. The general effect of the picture is very excellent, and it will be much appreciated by those who in those latitudes have seen just such a scene as this. The varying tints of the water giving it in certain lights that peculiar emerald green only there seen are well rendered, as is the water breaking up on the beach. On the whole a successful treatment of a difficult* motif.[10]

As the inscription on the stretcher of the picture indicates,[11] the scene is set in New Providence, one of the Bahama Islands. The subject is a "beachcomber," a huge wave generated by the storm passing away in the distance at right. Breaking from right to left, the wave is punctured toward upper left by the broken mast and crow's nest of a sailing vessel. Another portion of the mast lies prostrate on the beach at near right as a small wave rolls over it. The mood of the scene is unabashedly romantic. As the wave rises, a ray of sunshine lances through it from behind, producing a startling turquoise tint, which in turn is fragmentarily reflected from the near surfaces of the water and from facets of the sharp-edged coral outcropping in the left foreground. The arching wave, reduced to paper thinness and blown into spray at its apex, is virtually transparent, the strands of foam and seaweed on the inner surface defined like veins on a leaf.[12]

The work's thematic and stylistic origins can be traced to marine paintings by artists of the Düsseldorf school, in particular Andreas Achenbach (1815–1910). Achenbach's *Storm off the Coast of Sicily* (1847, Walters Art Gallery, Baltimore) had astonished viewers who saw it at the Düsseldorf Gallery in New York in 1849.[13] As a young painter, Bierstadt occasionally delved into marine subjects, notably with *The Marina Piccola, Capri* (1859, Albright-Knox Art Gallery, Buffalo). A large canvas he completed eleven years later, *Puget Sound, on the Pacific Coast* (private collection),[14] signaled his increased commitment to the genre. During the 1870s he painted several scenes of seals frolicking among tall waves in the Farallon Islands near San Francisco. In the first and largest of those, painted around 1872 and eventually purchased by the department store magnate Alexander T. Stewart,[15] a large wave, covered with a netting of surface foam and illuminated from behind, arches from right to left. In another smaller canvas (New Britain Museum of Art, New Britain, Connecticut) of the subject, a massive wave of similar character arches from left to right, as in the present work. With *Wave with Sailors* (1874, private collection), a small picture by Bierstadt acquired by Lord Dunraven, a rowboat rides the crest of a translucent wave in the open sea.[16]

Everything considered, *The Shore of the Turquoise Sea* exceeds those predecessors in conception and execution. The grandeur of the principal wave, the vibrant effects of color and light, the strong chiaroscuro, the diverting details of the mast, trompe l'oeil shells and turtle, and distant ships combine with the firm yet energetic brushwork to produce one of Bierstadt's most successful images.

He unveiled the finished canvas in Boston in February 1878. Ironically, its arrival there was delayed by a massive storm that blanketed the Northeast with snow and generated "wild waves" along the Atlantic coast causing severe property damage and the deaths of five children at Coney Island.[17] At Brainard's Gallery in Boston, where its display overlapped that of the artist's *View of Estes Park* painted for Lord Dunraven, *Bierstadt's gorgeous painting* was well received. One reviewer praised the *splendid example of the versatile genius of the artist, who rarely selects this class of subjects*, and another assessed *the spirit of the picture* as *strong and vivacious*.[18] The *Boston Transcript* published the longest notice. After mentioning that the scene was located *near the town of Nassau, New Providence*, their reporter described the work at length and termed it *one of the most powerful and satisfactory pictures Mr. Bierstadt has painted in many years*.[19] The writer added that the painting was destined for the Paris International Exposition of 1878, but in fact it was not shown there.[20]

Instead it resurfaced in New York two years later. To the monthly meeting of the Union League Club in January 1880, Bierstadt contributed a small picture titled *Near Nassau, Bahamas*, doubtless as a preview for the larger one.[21] One month later he sent the full-size canvas to the club.[22] At the end of March he placed the large work on display at the National Academy of Design, under the title *The Shore of the Torquoise* [sic] *Sea*. There, according to a reporter for the *New-York Tribune*, it *afford*[ed] *subject matter for a great deal of talk among visitors to the* [south] *gallery*.[23] Yet most critics were unimpressed, and at both showings they subjected the painting to hostile criticism that occasionally turned self-consciously picturesque. The writer for the *Tribune*, for example, declared that the scene could only have occurred in *fairyland*, and that *the wave is as much out of place as a real peacock with his tail spread would be in a Quaker meeting house*, while the *New York Evening Mail's* critic claimed that the water was *made of sugar candy, and a*

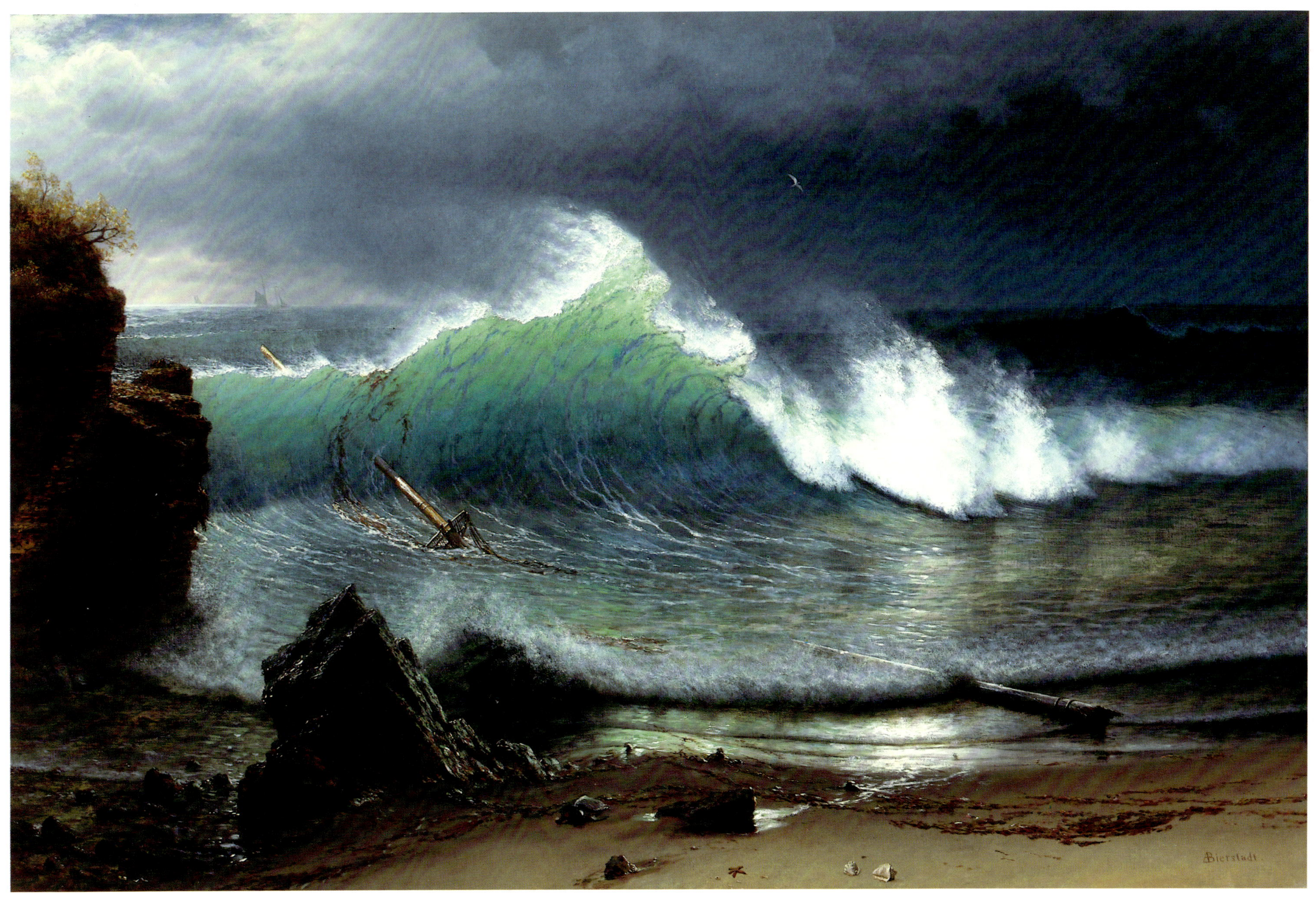
Bierstadt

confectioner, with some pistache, could probably produce its counterpart.[24] Only a few reviewers—presumably those who had traveled in the south Atlantic, or who had personally interviewed the artist—remarked on the truthfulness of the turquoise wave, and fewer still expressed overall satisfaction with the painting.

Today, however, it is much easier to sympathize with Bierstadt and his wave conceived as majestically as a mountain precipice. The painterly handling and the artifice of the scene as a whole are evidence of a strong artistic presence. Despite the criticisms, Bierstadt regarded the picture with lasting pride. By the spring of 1886, he completed a somewhat larger variant, *A Wave Breaking on the Bahamas Coast* (fig. 1) in time for the Colonial and Indian Exhibition in London.[25] As the focal image in the West Indian gallery of the exhibition, that painting symbolized the discovery of the New World, British colonialism at the height of Empire, and the climatic benefits of the Gulf Stream for Great Britain. One year later Bierstadt sent the same work, renamed *After a Norther (Bahamas)*, to the American Exhibition in London. In 1900 he produced yet another version of the composition with different topographical associations, *The Golden Gate* (private collection), for his brother Edward.[26] That work was exhibited in 1901 at the Worcester Art Museum in Worcester, Massachusetts, one year before the artist's death. *Gerald L. Carr*

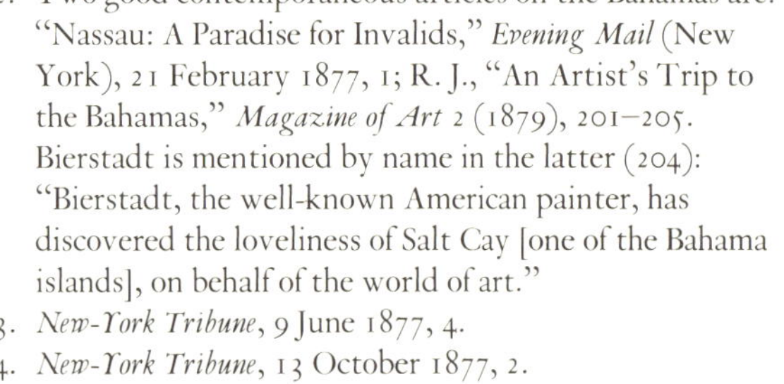

1. *New-York Tribune*, 9 June 1877, 4.
2. Two good contemporaneous articles on the Bahamas are: "Nassau: A Paradise for Invalids," *Evening Mail* (New York), 21 February 1877, 1; R. J., "An Artist's Trip to the Bahamas," *Magazine of Art* 2 (1879), 201–205. Bierstadt is mentioned by name in the latter (204): "Bierstadt, the well-known American painter, has discovered the loveliness of Salt Cay [one of the Bahama islands], on behalf of the world of art."
3. *New-York Tribune*, 9 June 1877, 4.
4. *New-York Tribune*, 13 October 1877, 2.
5. *Daily Evening Transcript* (Boston), 5 October 1877, 6; *New-York Tribune*, 13 October 1877, 2; *New-York Tribune*, 17 November 1877, 2.
6. *The Herald* (New York), 2 December 1877, 6; *The Herald* (New York), 14 December 1877, 6.
7. *The Herald* (New York), 4 November 1877, 14; *The Herald* (New York), 9 November 1877, 3; *The Herald* (New York), 2 December 1877, 6; *New-York Tribune*, 4 December 1877, 5.
8. *The Herald* (New York), 28 October 1877, 12; *The Herald* (New York), 21 October 1877, 5; *The Herald* (New York), 3 December 1877, 6; *The Herald* (New York), 8 October 1877, 6. The quotation is from the last-named source.
9. *The Herald* (New York), 11 January 1878, 10.
10. *The Herald* (New York), 13 January 1878, 6; excerpted in Gerald L. Carr, *Albert Bierstadt* [exh. cat., Alexander Gallery] (New York, 1983), 1.
11. The inscription reads: *A. Bierstadt/1155 Broadway corner 27 Street/Off the Island of New Providence/one of the Bahamas—a little west of San Salvadore.*
12. The fullest modern discussion of the painting is in Carr, *Albert Bierstadt*, no. 21.
13. *The Albion* (New York), 12 May 1849, 225; *Morning Courier and New-York Enquirer*, 13 July 1849, 2; William R. Johnson, *The Nineteenth Century Paintings in the Walters Art Gallery* (Baltimore, 1982), 164.
14. Bierstadt's *Puget Sound* is probably identifiable as the painting entitled *The Storm*, in Gordon Hendricks, *Albert Bierstadt* (New York, 1974), 192. See descriptions of *Puget Sound* in *The Evening Mail* (New York), 24 October 1870, 1; *Anglo-American Times* (London), 31 December 1870, 12.
15. This painting is presumably the one described in an article on the Ladies Fair, San Francisco, published by the *San Francisco Daily Evening Bulletin*, 3 April 1872, 3. I thank Alfred C. Harrison, Jr., for this reference. See also *New-York Times*, 17 April 1887, 6.
16. Carr, *Albert Bierstadt*, no. 19.
17. The paintings's delayed shipment to Boston was mentioned in the *Boston Herald*, 3 February 1878, 4. The storm and its aftermath were widely reported in Boston. The phrase "wild waves" appeared in an article in the *Boston Post*, 2 February 1878, 2.
18. *Boston Morning Journal*, 9 February 1878, 4; *Boston Herald*, 10 February 1878, 6.
19. *Daily Evening Transcript* (Boston), 9 February 1878, 6. I thank Alfred C. Harrison, Jr., and Merl M. Moore, Jr., for this reference.
20. Bierstadt undoubtedly expected to participate in the Paris exposition, but in the end he did not do so, perhaps because his works were refused by the American selection jury. See the report of the advisory committee, stating that *many of the paintings offered by artists were not up to the standard required by the committee, and were therefore rejected*, in the *New-York Tribune*, 16 March 1878, 3. I thank Eleanor Alexander for assistance on this point.
21. *The Evening Mail* (New York), 9 January 1880, 4. The picture is perhaps identifiable as *Study for the Shore of the Turquoise Sea*, ill. and discussed in Carr, *Albert Bierstadt*, no. 20.
22. *The Herald* (New York), 13 February 1880, 4; *New-York Times*, 13 February 1880, 5; *New-York Tribune*, 13 February 1880, 1; *Evening Mail* (New York), 14 February 1880, 1.
23. *New-York Tribune*, 18 April 1880, 7.
24. *New-York Tribune*, 18 April 1880, 7; *New York Evening Mail*, 14 February 1880, 1. The picture's display at the National Academy of Design also was discussed in the following sources: *Daily Evening Transcript* (Boston), 27 March 1880, 6; 5 May 1880, 6; *New York Evening Express* (New York), 27 March 1880, 1; 8 May 1880, 1; *The Sun* (New York), 28 March 1880, 5; *The Herald* (New York), 30 March 1880, 12; *The Independent* (New York), 8 April 1880, 6; S. G. W. Benjamin in *The American Art Review* (1880), 350, excerpted in Hendricks, *Albert Bierstadt*, 262.
25. For this work, see Hendricks, *Albert Bierstadt*, 259; Gerald L. Carr, "Albert Bierstadt, Big Trees and the British: A Log of Many Anglo-American Ties," *Arts Magazine* 60 (summer 1986), 67–69.
26. Sotheby's sale, New York, 5 December 1985, no. 77.

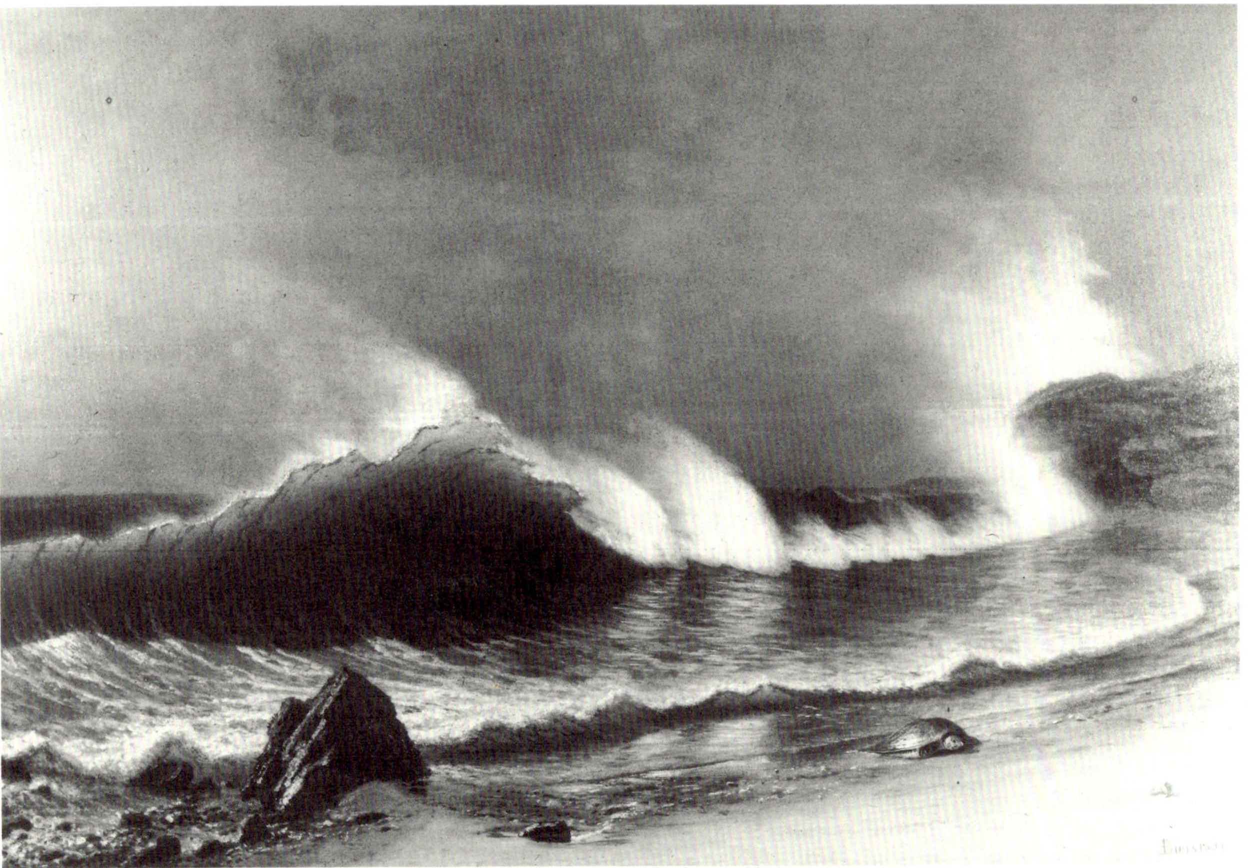

Fig. 1
Albert Bierstadt, *A Wave Breaking on the Bahamas Coast*, c. 1885–1886, oil on canvas, $53\frac{5}{8}$ x $83\frac{3}{4}$ (137.5 x 214.7), The Haggin Museum, Stockton, California

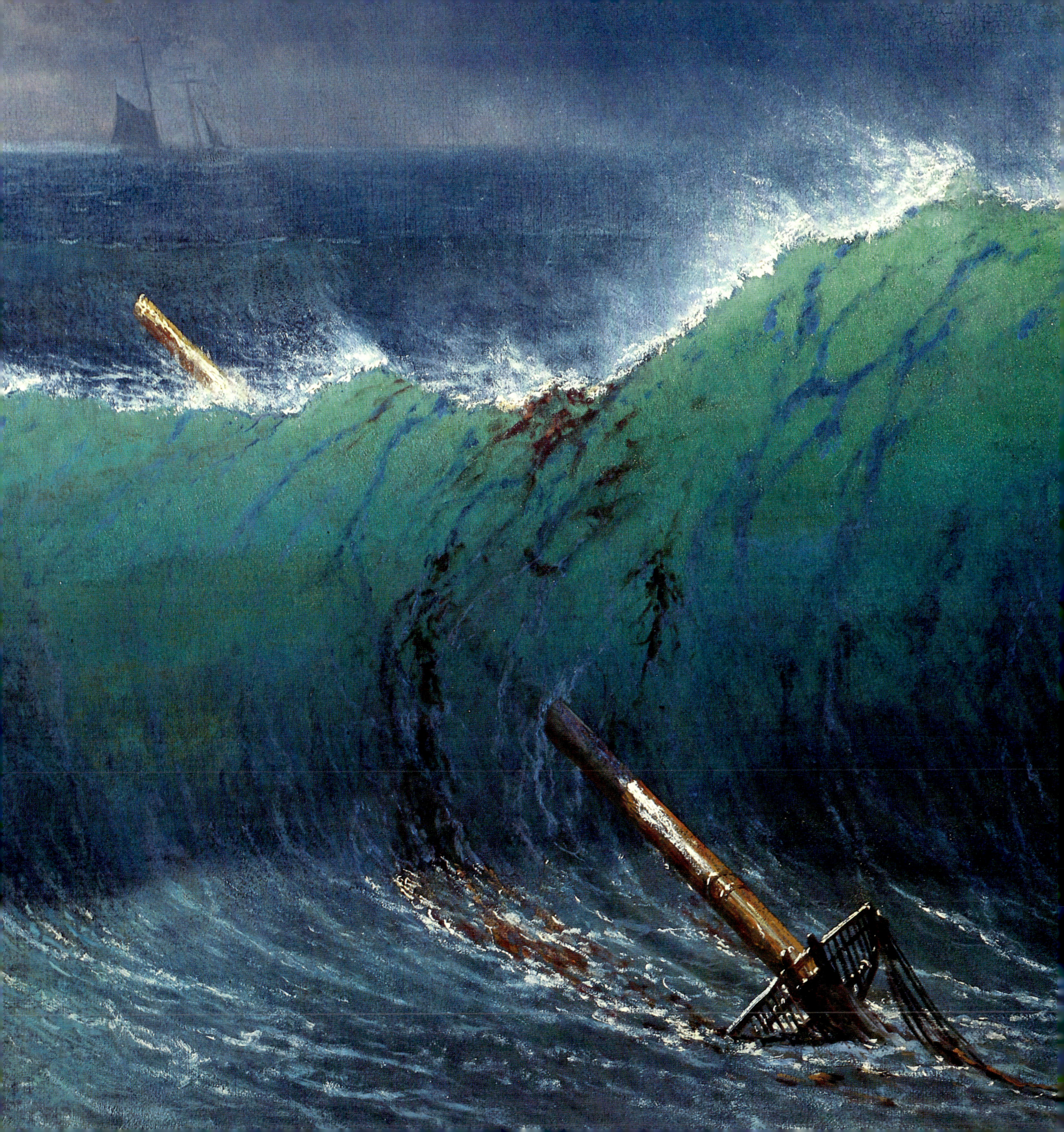

Frederic Edwin Church (1826–1900)
View on the Magdalena River 1857
oil on canvas, 24 x 36 (61 x 91.4)

View on the Magdalena River was one of three important paintings Church exhibited at the National Academy of Design in New York in the spring of 1857, immediately following his sensational triumph with *Niagara* (1857, Corcoran Gallery of Art, Washington) and just prior to leaving on his second trip to South America.[1] Church had first visited South America in 1853, traveling with his friend Cyrus Field through hundreds of miles of spectacular scenery in Colombia, much of it seen from the Magdalena River. Once back in New York, Church used sketches and his superb visual memory to create finished paintings of South America that were unlike anything Americans had ever seen. Four of these, including a river view called *La Magdalena* (1854, National Academy of Design, New York), created a sensation when they appeared at the National Academy in the spring of 1855.[2] Church showed another South American landscape at the academy the following year, but spent much of late 1856 and early 1857 working on *Niagara*. There are only a few important South American paintings that can be securely dated to the period just before his departure for the tropics in May 1857. In addition to *View on the Magdalena River*, there is a *View of Cotopaxi* (1857, The Art Institute of Chicago) and a small *South American Landscape* (1857, Manufacturers Hanover Trust, New York). Both of the latter, however, depict more rugged landscapes than the lush, pastoral world seen in the present work.

The scenery in *View on the Magdalena River* resembles that found in many of Church's drawings from his 1853 trip (for example, *Magdalena River, New Granada*, 1853, National Gallery of Art, Washington); the thatch-roofed chapel and bell tower were derived from a sketch of a church at Naré, a village on the Magdalena.[3] In a number of respects *View on the Magdalena River* looks back to the 1854 *La Magdalena*, in which Church also balanced masses of intricately painted jungle foliage against the quiet waters of the river and included a vista to a snow-capped mountain. *View on the Magdalena River* is particularly successful in its juxtaposition of lowland atmosphere with luminous mountain air, creating, as one of Church's contemporaries observed, an *unexpected change of tone from sultry warmth to clear coolness. . . .*[4] A similar transition from one zone of scenery to another, with a corresponding change of climate, and a similar balancing of elaborate foreground detail with a vista to a distant mountain would provide the basic structure for Church's masterpiece of two years later, *The Heart of the Andes* (1859, The Metropolitan Museum of Art, New York). *Franklin Kelly*

1. *Catalogue of the Thirty-second Annual Exhibition of the National Academy of Design* (New York, 1857), 3.
2. The other works were *The Cordilleras: Sunrise* (1854, Collection of Jo Ann and Julian Ganz, Jr.), *Tamaca Palms* (also known as *Scenery of the Magdalena River*, 1854, The Corcoran Gallery of Art, Washington); and *Tequendama Falls, near Bogotá, New Granada* (1855, Cincinnati Art Museum).
3. In the collection of the Cooper-Hewitt Museum, New York (1917–4–778). I am grateful to Gerald L. Carr for telling me about this drawing and to Daphne Saalman of the Cooper-Hewitt for assisting me in locating it.
4. "Topics Astir. National Academy of Design," *The Home Journal*, 13 June 1857, 2.

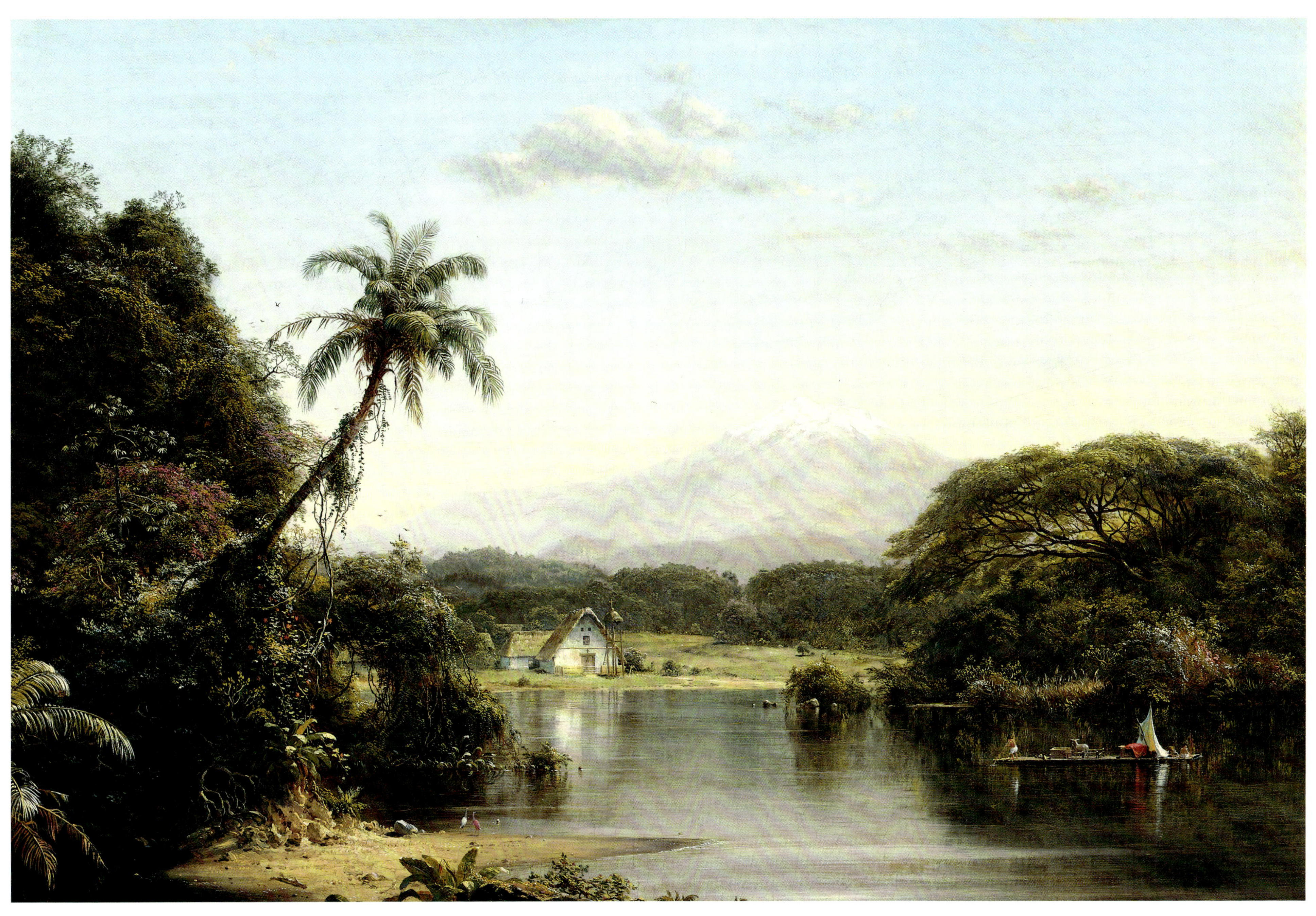

Martin Johnson Heade (1819–1904)
View from Fern-Tree Walk, Jamaica c. 1870
oil on canvas, 53 x 90 (134.6 x 228.6)

Although dated 1887 at the lower left, *View from Fern-Tree Walk* is almost certainly the work entitled simply *Jamaica* that Heade exhibited in America and abroad in 1870–1873.[1] He first visited the island in February and March of 1870 when returning from his third trip to South America, and while there filled most of a thirty-eight-page sketchbook (private collection) with drawings made in the vicinity of Kingston and Fort George.[2] It is likely that Heade was encouraged to see Jamaica by his friend Frederic Church, who had been there in 1865 and had found the scenery among the finest and most inspiring he had ever sketched. Church's finished paintings of the island, including *The Vale of Saint Thomas, Jamaica* (1867, Wadsworth Atheneum, Hartford, Connecticut), must have inspired Heade to try his hand at similarly grand pictures. Once back in New York he created two major Jamaican paintings, *Mountains of Jamaica* (unlocated) and the present work, which is his second-largest known painting and may well have been intended as a friendly challenge to Church's reputation as the master of large tropical panoramas.[3] Still, *View from Fern-Tree Walk* is unmistakably Heade's creation, for its composition and handling are more closely related to his own orchid and hummingbird paintings of the mid-1870s (for example, *Two Fighting Hummingbirds with Two Orchids*, 1875, private collection) than they are to any of Church's works.

Jamaica was well known for the *unrivalled magnificence of its vegetable growth*,[4] and a number of its more dramatic sites were popular with visitors to the island. One of these, Fern Gully, a four-mile-long valley of a former river that was covered with fern trees, is depicted in Heade's painting.[5] He was able to create a work of captivating beauty by juxtaposing the dense jungle foreground with a view of a quiet bay and distant ranges of hills. As in many of his paintings of American salt marshes, dark rain clouds are passing overhead; pools of sunlight illuminate some areas of the foreground, while deep shadow remains in others. The intricate detail of each plant and tree of the foreground recalls Church's tropical works, but *View from Fern-Tree Walk* is more subdued in coloring, with subtly varying shades of green predominating. For this reason, at least one of Heade's contemporaries found his works more truthful than those of Church.[6] Heade also managed to convey a vivid sense of the natural balance of growth and decay at work in the tropical landscape, showing the viewer both vibrant, living trees and rotting stumps, lush green fern fronds and dead branches wrapped in choking vines. *Franklin Kelly*

1. Theodore E. Stebbins, Jr., *The Life and Works of Martin Johnson Heade* (New Haven and London, 1975), 94, 162. Stebbins suggests that the 1887 date was added by Heade to the picture when it was purchased in that year by his patron Henry Morrison Flagler of Saint Augustine, Florida. Stebbins' proposal has been accepted by other scholars; see, for example, *American Paradise: The World of the Hudson River School* [exh. cat., The Metropolitan Museum of Art] (New York, 1987), 174.
2. Stebbins, *Heade*, 93.
3. Only the *Great Florida Sunset* of 1877 (private collection) is larger than *View from Fern-Tree Walk.*
4. A.M.R., "Natural Scenery in Jamaica," *The Crayon* 1 (June 1855), 397.
5. *American Paradise*, 174, Stebbins, *Heade*, 192. Another famous "fern gully," near Melbourne, Australia, was the subject of a painting by Eugene von Guerard (1811–1901), a German-born artist who emigrated to Australia in 1852 (*Ferntree Gully in the Dandenong Ranges*, 1857, Australian National Gallery, Canberra). There is little possibility Heade would have known of it; Church was a more likely influence, for he had sketched Fern Gully during his own visit to Jamaica.
6. See the comments of an anonymous critic quoted in Robert G. McIntyre, *Martin Johnson Heade* (New York, 1948), 37.

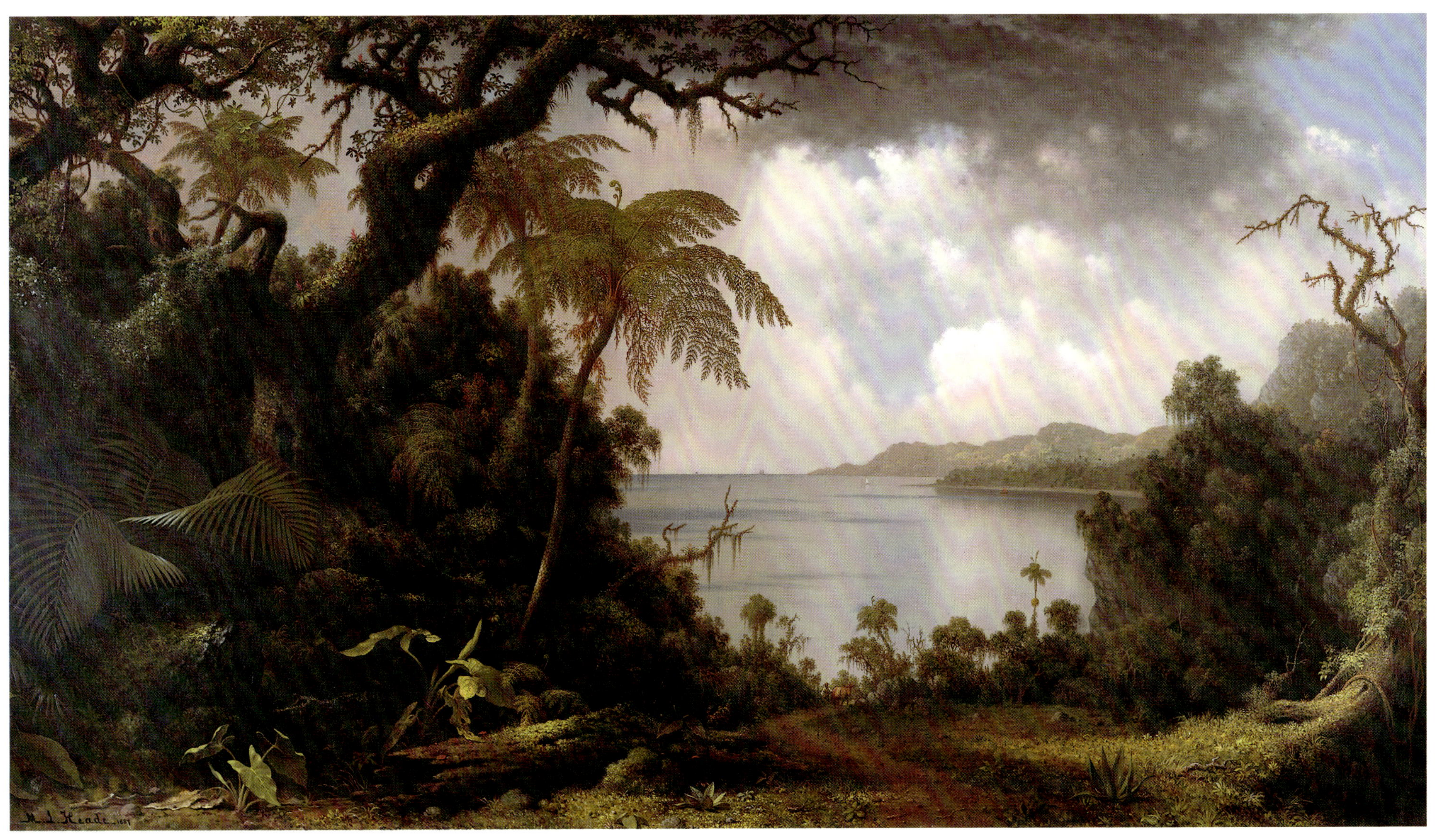

21

Martin Johnson Heade (1819–1904)
Sunset on the Marshes 1867
oil on canvas, 27 x 53 (68.6 x 134.6)

Among the great variety of subjects available to American landscape painters of the nineteenth century, perhaps none was seemingly as unpromising artistically as the salt marsh. Certainly none of Martin Johnson Heade's contemporaries in the New York art world took any particular notice of these low-lying border zones between land and sea, for such places were totally devoid of the features (majestic trees, mountains, and waterfalls) that had, by the 1860s, become standard elements in Hudson River School paintings. The marshes that fascinated Heade were anonymous places punctuated with a few shrubby trees and winding tidal streams and populated only by waterfowl, muskrats, mosquitoes, and an occasional cow.[1] The people who knew them best were fishermen and hunters and the farmers who annually harvested the free bounty of salt hay and formed it into great stacks. Still, Heade clearly found the marshes a compelling theme. He created more paintings of them than he did of any other subject, and many are among his most satisfying works.

Heade began painting marshes in the early 1860s and is generally thought to have created his greatest examples in the later years of the decade.[2] Most of the marsh scenes are small in size, usually 13 x 26 or 15 x 30 inches, but a very few are more grand in scale.[3] *Sunset on the Marshes*, one of the largest of the series, includes virtually all of the standard elements of Heade's marsh pictures: a gently curving stream winding through a flat expanse of marsh grass, tall haystacks receding into the distance, low hills and scrub vegetation bordering the marsh, and men at work cutting and raking salt hay. In many examples Heade portrayed the scene in broad daylight or with the passing clouds of a summer thundershower, while in others he set the time at sunset, as here. Thus, whether through atmospheric or temporal change, the artist infused his paintings with a sense of transition that complemented the mutable nature of the salt marsh itself, which changed with each rise and fall of the tide.[4] Often, too, there are hints of an even greater passage of time, as in the decayed fence standing near the water's edge at the lower left.

The popularity of Heade's marsh pictures with collectors in the last third of the nineteenth century indicates that there were more than a few others who shared his fondness for such scenes. Indeed, it has recently been suggested that New Englanders had a particular love of the *tints, lights, and shadows, and movements of* [the] *salt-marsh*, finding in it a microcosm of the larger, ever-changing world.[5] *Franklin Kelly*

1. Theodore E. Stebbins, Jr., *The Life and Works of Martin Johnson Heade* (New Haven and London, 1975), 42–53.
2. Stebbins, *Heade*, 53.
3. For example, *Sunset on the Newbury Marshes*, 1862, 25 1/16 x 50 in. (Walters Art Gallery, Baltimore), *Sunrise on the Marshes*, 1863, 26 x 50 1/4 in. (Flint Institute of Arts, Flint, Michigan), and *Duck Hunters in the Marshes*, 1866, 30 x 60 in. (private collection).
4. Carol Troyen, *The Boston Tradition* [exh. cat., Museum of Fine Arts] (Boston, 1980), 124.
5. Walter L. Creese, *The Crowning of the American Landscape: Eight Great Spaces and Their Buildings* (Princeton, 1985), 175.

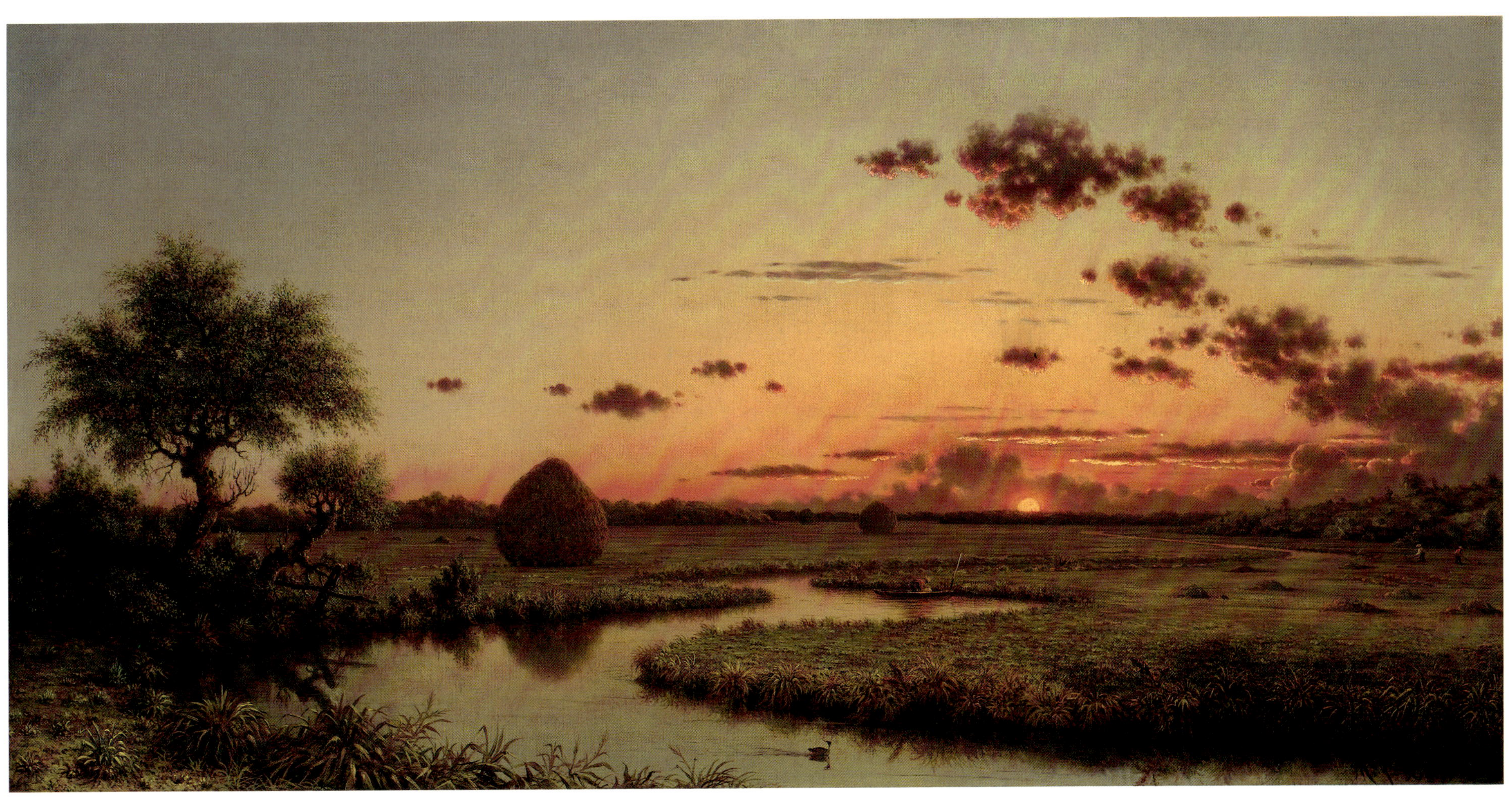

22

William Rimmer (1816–1879)
Sunset 1876
oil on canvas, 28 x 42⅛ (71.1 x 107)

William Rimmer believed *there should be an element of mystery in every picture.*[1] *Sunset* contains such an element. The shadowy quality of the scene, somewhat enhanced by the darkening of bitumen, creates the mysterious ambiance Rimmer desired. A sense of tranquility has been established, yet at the same time a feeling of anxiety. By placing the figures in the long shadows of dusk or behind a thin veil of water, he has provided the juxtaposition of emotions that give *Sunset* a spark of excitement. However, the overall mood of the picture is created not by the subject matter, but by the tonal qualities of the pigment.

The painting's atmosphere is not unusual for Rimmer, but the subject is. As day ends, the sun is retiring below the horizon as do the characters of the static play. This Italianate scene is assembled as if it consisted of props for a stage production. Although Rimmer never visited Italy, he would have been familiar with the subject through literature and the work of artists such as Washington Allston. Rimmer's choice of subject and the large size of the canvas indicate that this painting was probably a commissioned work.[2]

Whether Rimmer was influenced by the luminists is speculative. However, like the twentieth-century surrealists, he has created a world that exists in dreams, where images are formed in shadows and the uncertainty of what lies beyond provides the duality of tranquility and anxiety. Rimmer believed that *above all, remember atmosphere, that impalpable something which we feel but do not see, which softens every defect, and throws over every thing a thin, transparent veil.*[3] *James W. Tottis*

1. *Providence Daily Journal*, "Dr. Rimmer's Twelfth Lecture," 9 March 1873, 2.
2. Jeffrey Weidman, *William Rimmer: A Yankee Michaelangelo* (Hanover and London, New Hampshire, 1985), 76.
3. Truman H. Bartlett, *The Art Life of William Rimmer* (Cambridge, Massachusetts, 1890), 147.

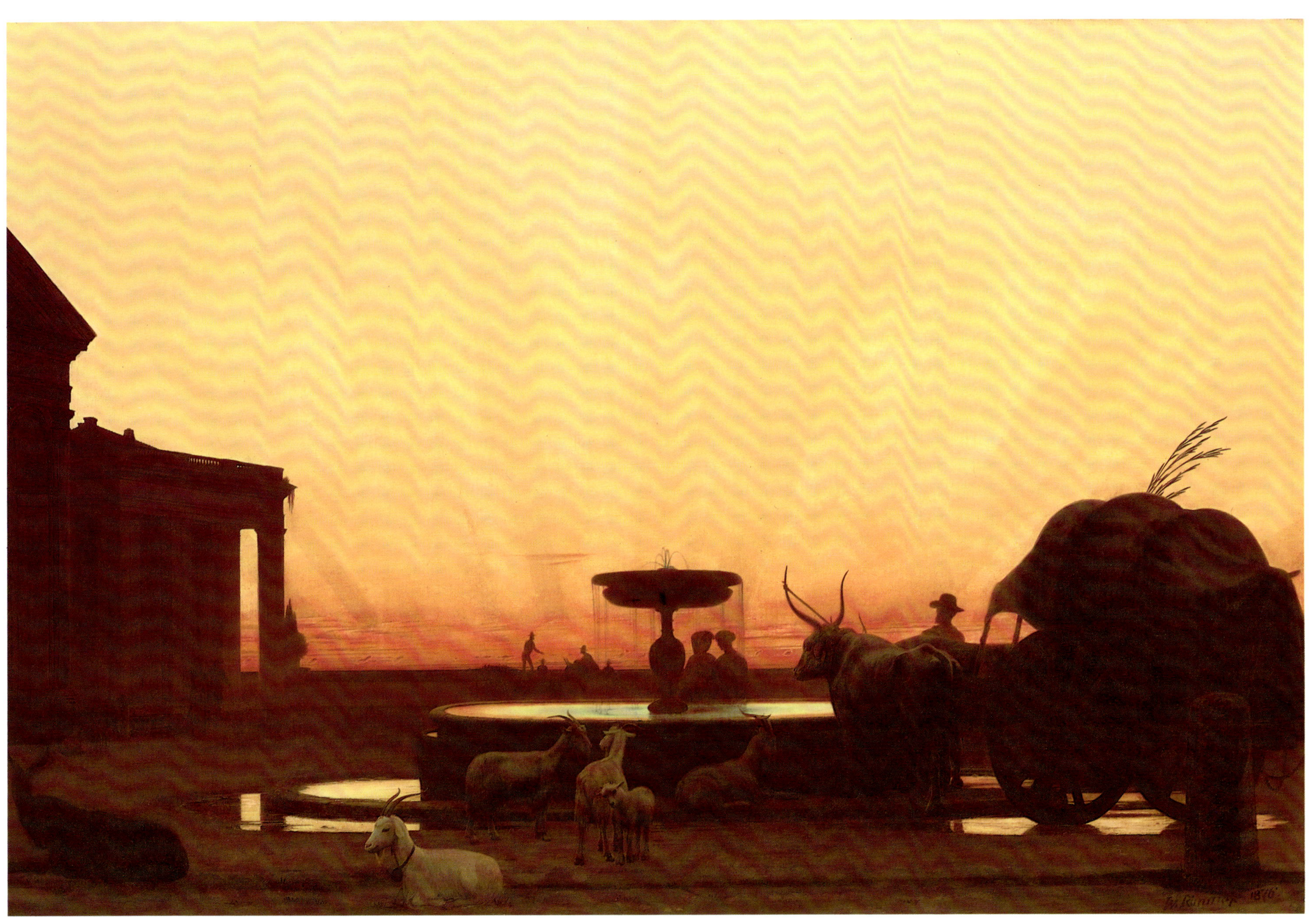

23

George Caleb Bingham (1811–1879)
The Jolly Flatboatmen 1846
oil on canvas, 38 x 48½ (96.5 x 123.2)

Bingham most often presented his subjects enjoying their leisure by singing and dancing, telling stories, smoking, or playing cards. In *The Jolly Flatboatmen*, he showed such a moment of relaxation: a man dances on a flatboat while a fiddler plays and a crewmate keeps time on a frying pan. Five other men lounge on the deck and watch. A coonskin tacked to the side of the boat informs us that the scene is taking place out west, for Davy Crockett's coonskin hat was already famous as an emblem of the frontier.[1] A turkey poking his head out from the crate that the dancer stomps on tells us the name of the tune being played, "Turkey in the Straw."

The work exhibited was the third river scene Bingham submitted to the American Art-Union. That organization purchased it on 8 October 1846. After it was awarded in their lottery to Benjamin van Schaick, a New York grocer, it dropped out of sight for more than a century. Not until 1954 was it again exhibited at the Saint Louis Art Museum, having just been rediscovered in the collection of the Pell family of New York.

The Jolly Flatboatmen remained Bingham's most popular image throughout the nineteenth century despite the disappearance of the original, for by means of prints its composition was widely circulated. In 1847 it was one of two paintings selected by the Art-Union to be reproduced in a large color mezzotint distributed to the members. The printmaker, Thomas Doney, worked for fourteen months on the plate for roughly ten times what Bingham was paid for the painting, and produced about ten thousand impressions. Many other reproductions of the design were circulated. Doney himself produced a small engraving of the canvas that the Art-Union published in its transactions, and a wood engraving was made in the same year for *Howit's Journal of Literature and Popular Progress*. Currier & Ives produced two lithographs, in 1866 and 1870, which were probably based on the Doney mezzotint, repeating the composition with only slight alterations. In addition, the Saint Louis artist Charles Wimar painted a scene of *Jolly Flatboatmen by Moonlight* in Düsseldorf in 1854.

The numerous reproductions of *The Jolly Flatboatman* attest to its popularity. But thanks to this very popularity, the aesthetic merit of the painting almost immediately came under attack. At the 1846 annual meeting of the Art-Union, William J. Hoppin introduced a resolution that it was the duty of the association *to elevate and purify public taste*. Presumably his remarks included some discussion of *The Jolly Flatboatmen*, for shortly afterward, when his campaign was picked up by the *Literary World*, Bingham's painting was singled out for attack.

Declaring that *the very name . . . gives a death blow to all one's preconceived notions of* "*HIGH ART*," the magazine characterized *The Jolly Flatboatmen* as *a vulgar subject, vulgarly treated*, commented that *the drawing was faulty and the composition artificial*, and lamented that the picture had ever been chosen to be engraved: *We should feel great commiseration for the members, that to the possibility of drawing* [in the lottery] *some of the bad pictures was added the certainty of getting a print of so low a character*.

The writer then went on to summarize the quality of Bingham's canvases: *In color they are disagreeable, a monotonous, dull, dirty pink pervades every part; and in texture there is the same monotony. Flesh, logs, and earthen jug have the same quality of substance, the same want of handling. We think this must be produced by going over the colors when wet with a "softener," in order to avoid hardness; but we would rather see the figures as hard as statues than see light, shade, color, and texture swept thus into a mass of soft confusion. In composition, Mr. B. should be aware that the regularity of the pyramid is only suitable to scenes of the utmost beauty and repose; that when motion and action are to be represented, where expression and picturesqueness are objects sought for, proportionate departures must be made from this formal symmetry. A little study of the compositions of any of the great men of old, would do much towards correcting the artist's faults in this respect.*[2]

At the beginning of their association, Bingham's relations with the Art-Union remained cordial despite the critical attacks. On 19 July 1849, for example, Andrew Warner, secretary of the American Art-Union, wrote to a friend in Saint Louis: *We have a Missouri friend here on a visit, Mr. Bingham the painter of the Jolly Flatboatmen. We like him quite as well as a man as we do as a painter*. He added that he was pleased to have Bingham's latest *clever picture, Raftsmen on the Ohio*.[3]

By the 1850s, however, Bingham's relationship with the Art-Union began to grow strained. The Art-Union declined several of his pictures, and he discovered that they paid other artists higher prices than they paid him. For example, they awarded Henry Peters Gray $2,000 for his *Wages of War* and *Apple of Discord*, while he netted only $350 for *Shooting for Beef*. In 1851 Bingham complained to a friend that the Art-Union displayed favoritism in their choices of pictures, and vowed to bargain more forcefully thereafter.[4] He offered the organization two paintings for $200 each, but the Art-Union declined his offer. He had to settle for a mere $125 each, including the frames.

In December of that year the bulletin of the Art-Union carried an article that compared his work unfavorably with that of William Sidney Mount. It concluded, *Bingham has made some good studies of western character, but so entirely undisciplined yet mannered, and often mean in subject, and showing much want of earnestness in the repetitions of the same faces, that they are hardly entitled to rank*.[5]

On 31 January 1852, Bingham demanded that *the Columns of the Bulletin* be placed at his disposal for a rejoinder to the damaging remarks they had published, and he was offered space in the April issue for his reply. Bingham's anger, however, had only increased in the intervening time. He threatened instead to sue the Art-Union for damages. No more is known of the suit, and the court order dissolving the Art-Union probably left Bingham with no case.

Despite their conflicts, the American Art-Union had created a market for Bingham's genre paintings. The liquidation of the organization virtually ended Bingham's career as a genre painter, even though in the years after its demise he made two copies of *The Jolly Flatboatmen*, the painting which had made him famous, to revive his failing career.

In 1857 while living in Düsseldorf, he painted a second, more elaborate version of the composition, titled *Jolly Flatboatmen in Port*. The figures on the boat repeat those in the previous version with one exception. However, this painting contains twenty-one figures, as opposed to the first painting, which contains eight. In 1860 Bingham submitted this second canvas to two exhibitions, one at the Pennsylvania Academy of the Fine Arts in Philadelphia, and the other the first show of the Western Academy of Art in Saint Louis, but it was not purchased until 1865.

Bingham painted a third and final version of the composition the year before he died. It was smaller in scale and had fewer figures than even the first version. As with *The Jolly Flatboatmen in Port*, however, the artist had difficulty finding a buyer. The painting was not sold until Bingham's wife died in 1893. *Henry Adams*

1. Russell Nye, *The Unembarrassed Muse: The Popular Arts in America* (New York, 1970), 146–148, 282.
2. *Literary World* 2 (23 October 1847), 277. The episode is discussed by John Francis McDermott, *George Caleb Bingham, River Portraitist* (Norman, Oklahama, 1959), 172–173.
3. McDermott, *Bingham*, 71.
4. C. B. Rollins, ed, "Letters of George Caleb Bingham to James S. Rollins," *The Missouri Historical Review* 33 (1937–1939), 21.
5. American Art-Union, "Development of Nationality in American Art," *Bulletin*, New Series, December 1850, 157.

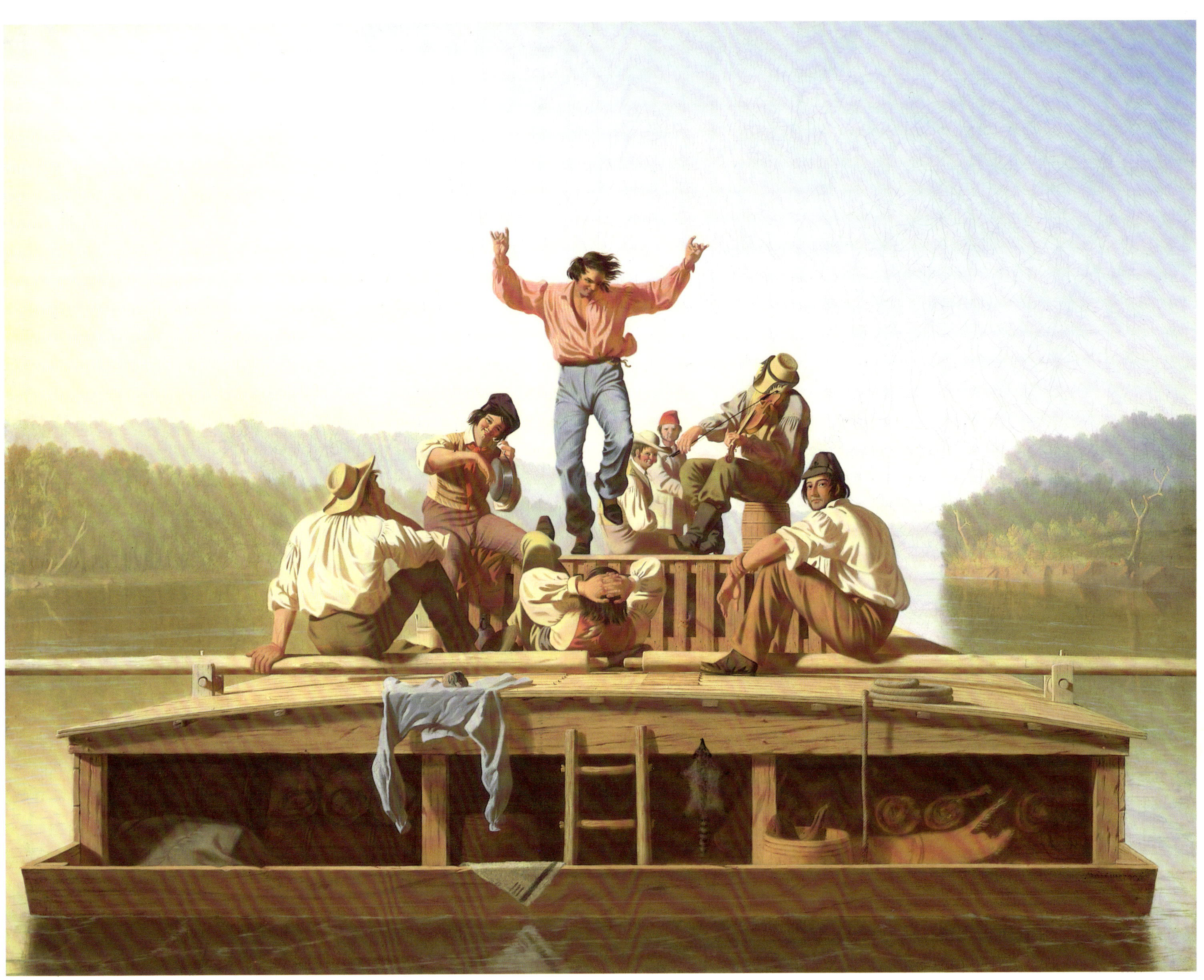

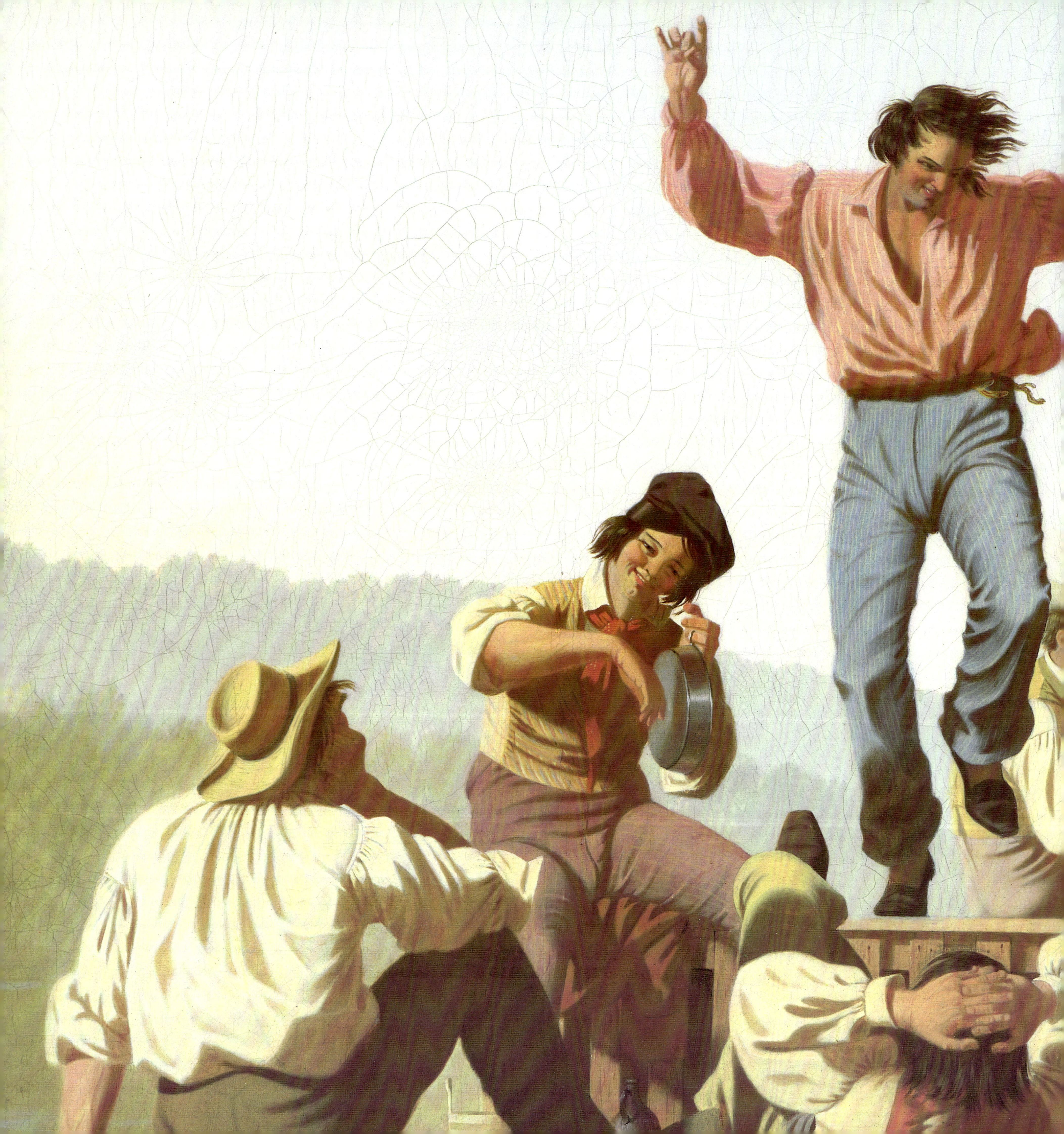

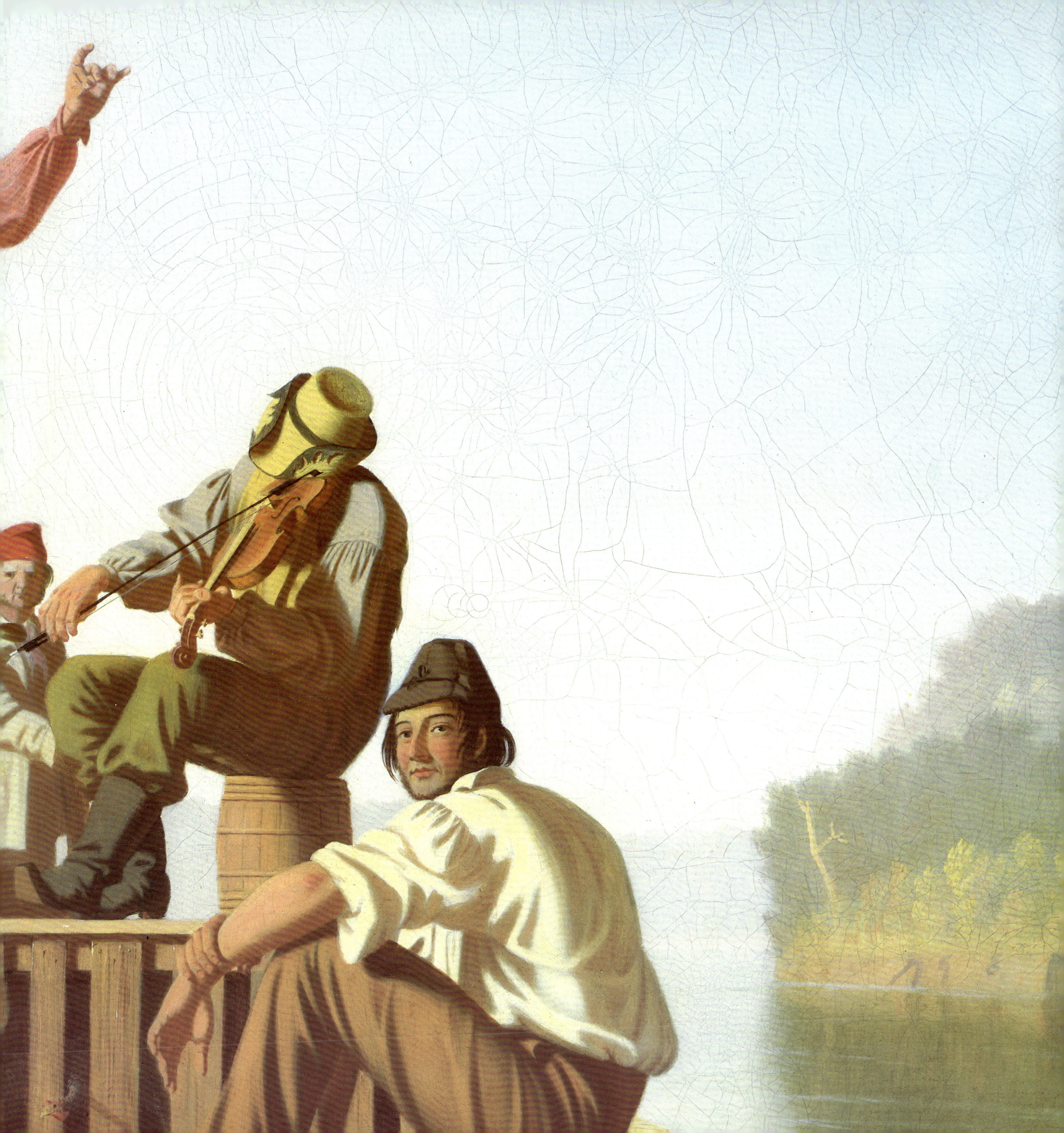

24

William Tylee Ranney (1813–1857)
The Sleigh Ride 1852
oil on canvas, 30⅛ x 40⅛ (76.5 x 101.9)

During his brief career as a painter in the 1840s and 1850s, William Ranney was best known for scenes of American frontier life and for hunting and sporting pictures. As Henry Tuckerman wrote in his *Book of the Artists*, *He had caught the spirit of border adventure, and was enamored of the picturesque in scenery and character outside the range of civilization. . . .*[1] Today Ranney is still most often considered in the same light, but he did create a small number of eastern subjects where the emphasis was not on heroic deeds or dramatic action, but on more commonplace, everyday themes.[2]

Like his contemporaries William Sidney Mount and James G. Clonney, Ranney found the carefree activities of children, especially young boys, particularly appealing subjects. Depictions of boys in mid-nineteenth-century American genre paintings cover the full range of boyhood pursuits, from the mischievous (as in Mount's *The Truant Gambler*, 1835, New-York Historical Society), to the resourceful (as in Clonney's *The Trappers*, cat.30), to the merely lazy (as in Mount's *Boys Caught Napping in a Field*, 1848, Brooklyn Museum). Ranney's *The Sleigh Ride* is a particularly lively depiction of schoolboys who have just been released from school on a winter's afternoon and are eagerly crowding onto an ox-drawn sleigh for a ride. In the distance a one-room schoolhouse is visible, and on a curving path leading downhill from it other children are sledding. One boy has ridden his sled right up to the back of the sleigh, apparently causing another boy to tumble into the snow. Yet another has tied his sled to the right runner of the sleigh, obviously intending to get a free tow. Using a simple pyramidal composition for the main group of figures, Ranney managed to crowd thirteen children onto the sleigh itself, most with their faces turned toward the viewer so that their expressions are clearly visible.[3] Several of the boys have snowballs in their hands, and one, at the center of the composition, has his arm raised in readiness to throw. Whether the boy at the left front of the sleigh is reacting in alarm to the prospect of being hit with a snowball, or is troubled by the boy dancing a jig in the snow near the oxen, is unclear, but his expression suggests that mayhem of some sort is about to erupt.[4] The sleigh driver, the only adult present, smiles with tolerant patience, clearly well used to the mischievous ways of his young charges.

Ranney's *The Sleigh Ride* celebrates the uncomplicated pleasures of American rural life, and does so without overt sentimentalizing. It was the type of picture that found ready acceptance among patrons in New York, many of whom no doubt cherished memories of similar events from their own childhood. As America began to evolve in the middle decades of the nineteenth century into a more urbanized and industrial society, such memories would increasingly become tinged with romantic nostalgia, and genre paintings—at least in some hands—would become more and more sentimental. *Franklin Kelly*

1. (New York, 1867), 432. On Ranney's importance as a painter of western subjects see Linda Ayres, "William Ranney," *American Frontier Life* [exh. cat., Amon Carter Museum] (Fort Worth, 1987), 79–107.
2. For example, *Boys Crabbing*, c. 1855, The White House, Washington.
3. One reviewer found *the countenances of the occupants of the sleigh, especially the old driver . . . harmoniously natural*; *The Herald* (New York), 21 April 1852; quoted in Francis S. Grubar, *William Ranney, Painter of the Early West* [exh. cat., Corcoran Gallery of Art] (Washington, 1962), 40.
4. Precisely what the boy near the oxen is doing and why the other appears alarmed remain unclear. Given the levels of topical content in some mid-nineteenth-century American genre paintings, it is possible their actions relate to meaning that has thus far eluded deciphering.

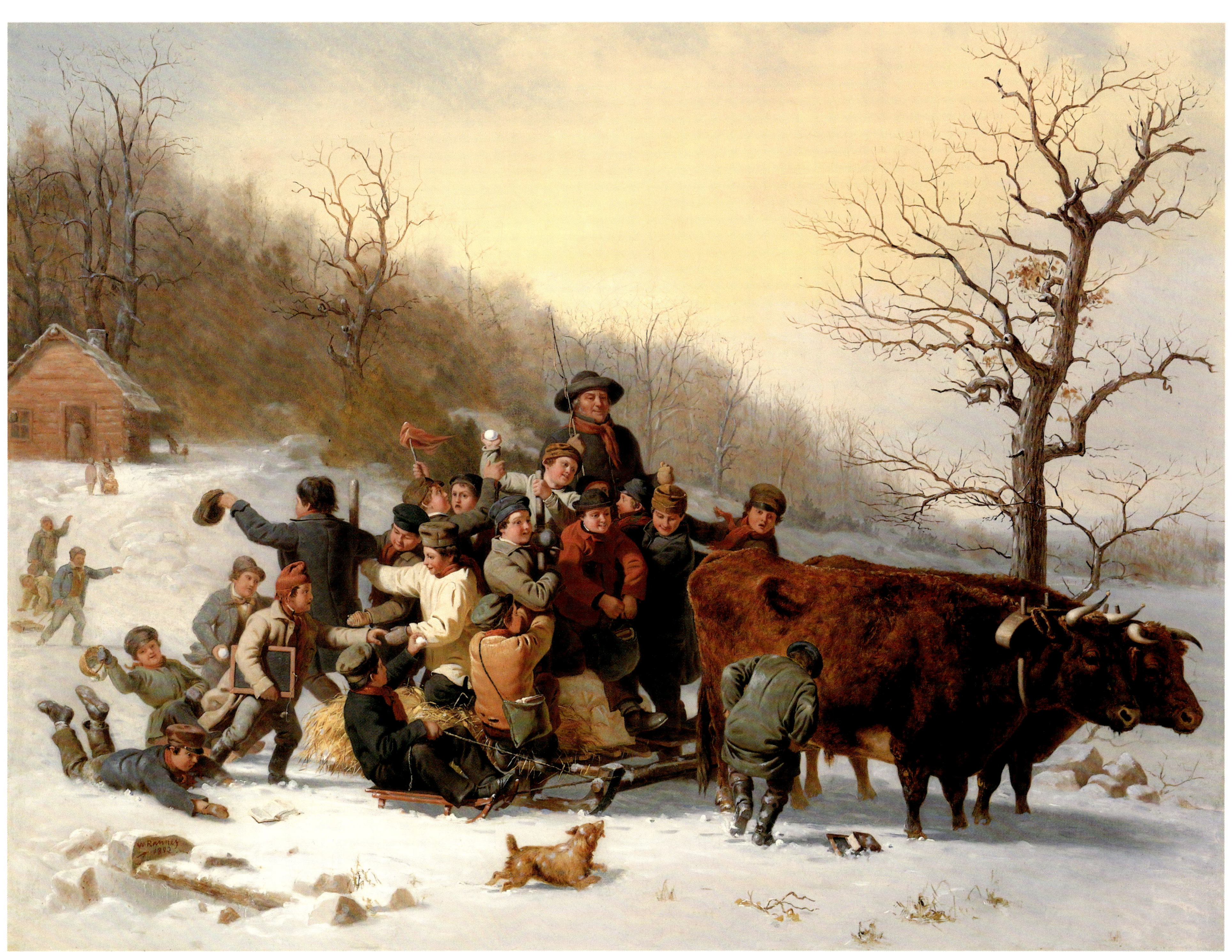
W Ranney

25

George Henry Durrie (1820–1863)
The Half-Way House 1861
oil on canvas, 36 x 53¾ (91.4 x 136.5)

One of a number of innyard paintings executed during the last few years of his career, *The Half-Way House* is a full-blown manifestation of Durrie's mature style.[1] Though he had painted the subject many times throughout the 1850s, the painting's enormous size (Durrie's works were generally quite small), complex composition, breadth of detail, and masterful handling of light and atmosphere suggest that Durrie was channeling all of his well-rehearsed effort into creating the work. These factors and Durrie's full inscription with signature, date, and locale (New Haven) confirm that this was the painting that Durrie exhibited at the National Academy of Design in 1862.[2]

Durrie utilized a complex composition typical of his later works, setting a variety of structures in the middle ground, which is visually approached by the sleigh's diagonal path. Within the scene, Durrie attempted to include the fullest possible range of subject matter and stylistic effects. A hazy view of overlapping distant hills provides the backdrop for the bright, carefully detailed innyard. The broad range of landscape effects is complemented by Durrie's inclusion of no less than six genre vignettes, each depicting some aspect of farm work or winter leisure. Despite Durrie's characteristic idealization of the scene, the facial features of the two men are unusually specific compared with other works in his oeuvre, and may be portraits.[3]

Durrie completed *The Half-Way House* at a time when his artistic energy and desire for recognition were at their peak. In addition to showing the work at the National Academy in 1862, Durrie exhibited a landscape at the Pennsylvania Academy of the Fine Arts, and in December held a major sale of his paintings at Snedicor and Company, New York. *Sarah Cash*

1. "Half-way house" was a common nickname for nineteenth-century inns and, especially considering Durrie's working methods, cannot be linked with a particular hotel. In fact, Durrie probably intentionally obscured the lettering on the sign in the paintings, which reads *H.*[I?] *F.R.B./HOTEL.*
2. Martha Hutson, *George Henry Durrie (1820–1920), American Winter Landscapist: Renowned Through Currier and Ives* (Santa Barbara, 1977), 109, remarks that the painting's exceptional size suggests a commission; this remark, however, does not agree with her subsequent statement that the work was the one exhibited at the National Academy of Design, since it is listed in the catalogue as for sale. National Academy of Design, *Catalogue of the Thirty-Seventh Annual Exhibition* (New York, 1862), no. 478.
3. The bearded figure is especially unusual for Durrie, and is possibly a self-portrait; a photograph of the artist and a self-portrait, both from c. 1860 (reproduced Hutson, *George Henry Durrie*, fig. 156 and fig. 151, respectively), show him with a beard. Durrie's diary entries, which record his love of sleighing (Hutson, *George Henry Durrie*, 49), support this suggestion.

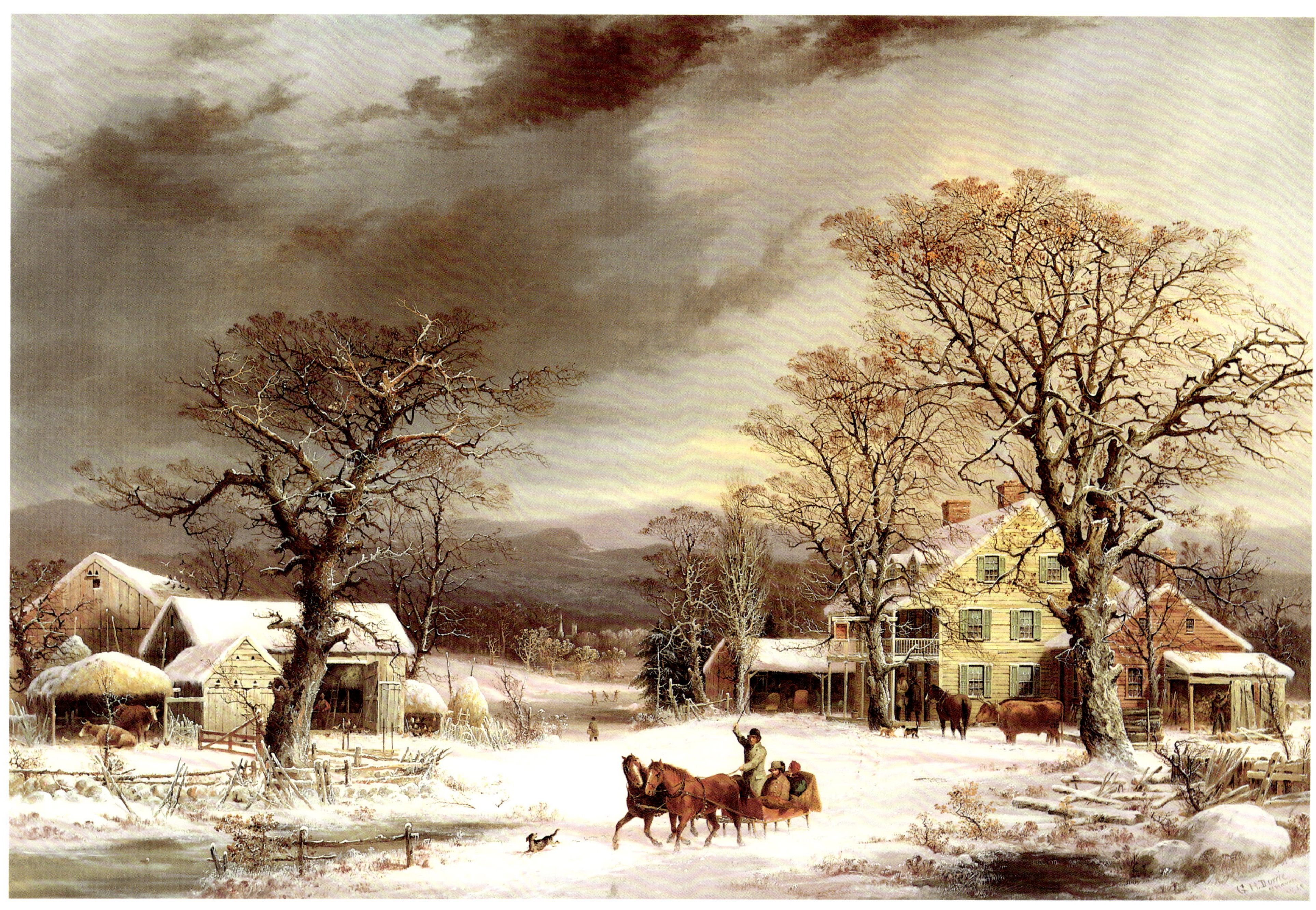

26

Francis William Edmonds (1806–1863)
The New Scholar 1845
oil on canvas, 26¾ x 34 (67.9 x 86.4)

The New Scholar, the first of three paintings on educational themes, comes from Francis W. Edmonds' most productive period, between 1842 and 1855. Under the auspices of the American Art-Union, the painting and an engraving of it were distributed in 1847 and 1850 respectively.[1] The composition of figures played against the geometric framework of an interior with a doorway to another room is derived from the Dutch tradition of genre painting. The disposition of light and shade, favorably noted in a review,[2] focuses attention on the figures. Edmonds' usual still-life elements are here clearly subordinated to the human drama.

The subject appears to have autobiographical significance for the painter. Edmonds' two children were then old enough to experience their first day at school. The switch held behind the teacher's back is perhaps a reflection upon Edmonds' own punishment for drawing a caricature of his schoolmaster when he was a boy.[3] Edmonds' empathy with this subject was perceived by the critic who wrote that the painting . . . *appeals not to the intellect but to the heart*.[4]

A preliminary oil sketch for *The New Scholar* establishes the setting and the placement of the figures but contains only a few of the still-life details. One of the two main changes in the figures from the study to the painting is the addition of the dog to the principal group.[5] Edmonds' wary dog may result from the example of David Wilkie's equally suspicious pet in *The Letter of Introduction*, which Edmonds could have known through the engraving of 1823.[6]

A deeper level of interpretation is consonant with Edmonds' belief in Jacksonian democracy. *The New Scholar* and the painting exhibited with it, *Facing the Enemy* (a temperance subject), were Edmonds' first works to show his awareness of current social issues. The preliminary study for the painting shows the two students in the next room roughhousing. By changing the boys' behavior to a model of studiousness, Edmonds undoubtedly meant to remind the viewer of the value of education as the means for advancement in a democratic society.[7]

Sarah Towne Hufford

1. For an explanation of the distributions of the American Art-Union, see cat. 32, note 1.
2. Review in the American Art Union Press Book as quoted in Maybelle Mann, *Francis William Edmonds, Mammon and Art* (New York, 1977), 104.
3. H. Nichols B. Clark, *Francis W. Edmonds, American Master in the Dutch Tradition* [exh. cat., Amon Carter Museum and participating museums] (Washington, 1988), 83–84.
4. Review in the American Art-Union Press Book as quoted in Mann 1977, 104.
5. Washington 1988, 85, fig. 54.
6. Clark has noted other probable borrowings from engravings of Wilkie's work. Washington 1988, 42, 76–77.
7. Washington 1988, 80, 85.

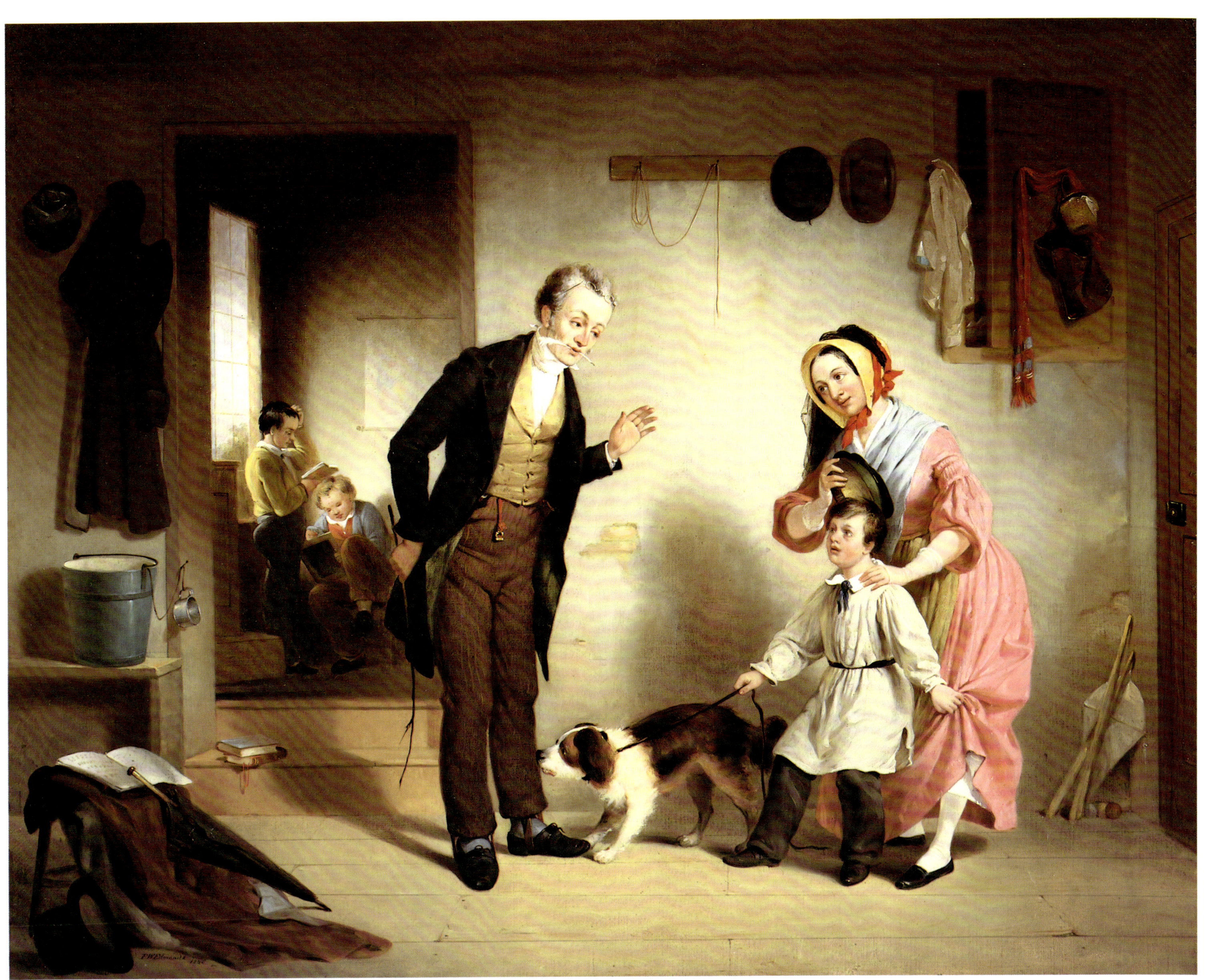

27

Enoch Wood Perry (1831–1915)
Mother and Child 1881
oil on canvas, 28⅝ x 36¾ (72.7 x 93.3)

In 1867, after a number of years of study and travel in Europe and of painting portraits in such different and disparate places as New Orleans, San Francisco, Hawaii, and Salt Lake City, Enoch Wood Perry settled in New York.[1] There he was part of a group of painters who, in the years immediately following the Civil War, devoted themselves to native subjects and the development of a native style—to the cause of painting what the critic Eugene Benson, who strongly supported it, called *home subjects*.[2] The group included such notable artists as Eastman Johnson, E. L. Henry, J. G. Brown, Seymour J. Guy, Thomas Waterman Wood, and Winslow Homer. Perry became one of its most important members: *Mr. Perry at the present time*, a critic wrote in 1875, *occupies a position very nearly at the head of our* genre *painters*.[3] He was also one of its most dedicated participants, exhibiting home subjects in almost every exhibition of the National Academy of Design from 1867 to the end of the century, and painting them long after others (such as Eastman Johnson and Winslow Homer) had forsaken the cause.

Mother and Child is an example of that dedication. In 1881, when it was painted, it was distinctly old-fashioned. It had been superseded by the more overtly modern subject matter and style of younger artists such as William Merritt Chase (see cat.51). But it was also deliberately historicizing; in every respect—costume, furniture, architecture—the painting deliberately re-created the past. This may have been fed by the historical revivalism of post-centennial America. But Perry's antiquarianism preceded the centennial itself by at least a decade. As early as 1866 one of his pictures was described as *an old-fashioned interior of a house with a woman spinning*, and in 1869 he made the first of several trips to Hurley, New York (one of them with Winslow Homer), to study *the quaint old Dutch interiors which abound in that neighborhood*;[4] for Perry brought to his paintings, as it was reported in 1873, *the most conscientious and thoughtful research*.[5]

To the antiquarianism of *Mother and Child*—which, despite his erudition, was more flavorful than factual—Perry added an art-historical reference. The light that streams through the window at the right and falls on the nursing mother and child is one of the painting's most truthful elements and a splendid bit of realist observation. But anyone familiar with the iconographic practice particularly of early Netherlandish painting, as Perry himself seems clearly to have been, must recognize it also as a piece of disguised symbolism. Light passing through a window was a symbol of the Virgin's purity and the miracle of her conception (as the piece of fruit apparently so casually placed on the table symbolizes the Fall and explains Christ's redemptory role). This mother and child in an ordinary domestic interior (as the group is usually situated in Netherlandish art) is thereby translated into the Holy Mother and Child.

Perry's iconographic sophistication may stem from the knowledge of European art that he acquired as a student. But it must also be seen against a background of revived interest in the nineteenth century in "primitive," "pre-Raphaelite" art,[6] in the study of Christian iconography, and in religious art (George de Forest Brush's and Abbott H. Thayer's transformations of their wives and children into Holy Families beginning in the early 1890s is an example similar to Perry's). *Nicolai Cikovsky, Jr.*

1. As a summer intern at the National Gallery, Patricia Burda collected an impressive amount of material on Perry from which I have borrowed liberally. With his usual generosity, Merl M. Moore, Jr. allowed me unrestricted access to his file on Perry. I am, of course, immensely grateful to them both.
2. "Fine Arts," *New York Evening Post*, 17 May 1869. Another critic said *pictures of domestic life* were *the most important part* of that year's National Academy of Design exhibition. ("Fine Arts. Forty-fifth Exhibition of the National Academy of Design," *The Nation* 8 [29 April 1869], 340). A few years earlier, James Jackson Jarves predicted that *the dawn of a respectable school of* genre *and home painting is nigh at hand. We say* home, *because there is no other word which includes so entirely, to the Anglo-Saxon ear, all those feelings, sentiments, and ideas which have their origin and growth under the family roof and in social training. Its motives are healthful, aims excellent, spirit patriotic, but as yet the flesh is weak to execute.* (*The Art-Idea* [Cambridge, Massachusetts, 1960 (first edition 1864)], 182–183).
3. "American Painters.—E. Wood Perry," *The Art Journal* [New York], n.s. 1 (1875), 216.
4. "The American Pictures. What Our Artists Are Doing," *New York Evening Post*, 29 December 1866; "Art Notes," *The Albion*, 10 July 1869, 398; "Art Notes," *New York Evening Post*, 8 July 1872.
5. "Art, Music, and Drama," *Appleton's Journal* 10, 16 August 1873, 219.
6. The most stridently vocal group of artists in New York when Perry began his career as a genre painter in the late 1860s were the American Pre-Raphaelites of the Association for the Advancement of Truth in Art.

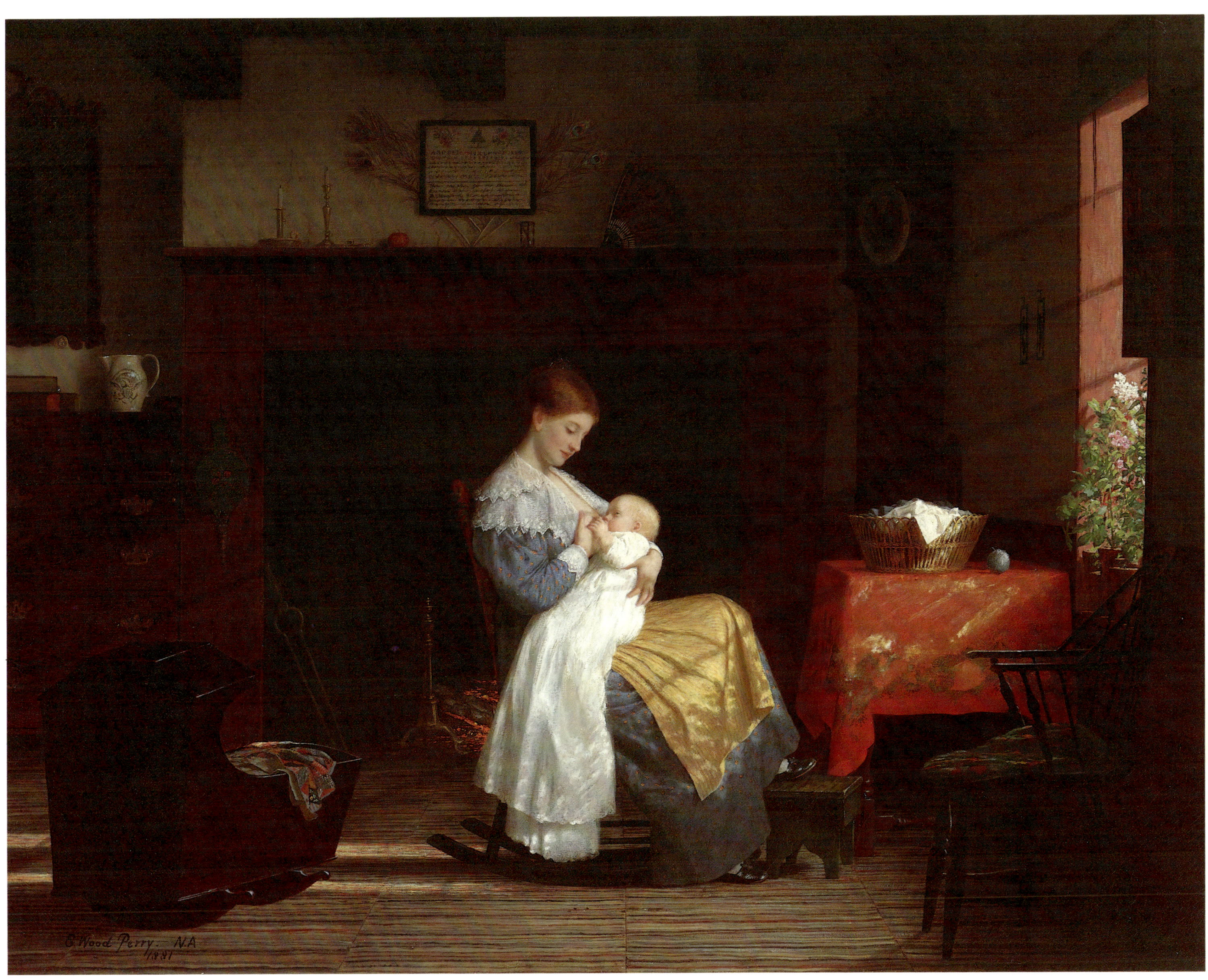
E. Wood Perry. N.A
1881

28

Edward Lamson Henry (1841–1919)
Parlor on Brooklyn Heights of Mr. and Mrs. John Bullard
oil on panel, 15⅜ x 17⅝ (39.1 x 44.8)

The *Parlor on Brooklyn Heights of Mr. and Mrs. John Bullard* belongs to the tradition of the conversation piece, an informal portrait on a small scale that had antecedents in the Netherlands and France but was developed more fully in England in the 1720s. The rise of the middle class created a demand for a new style of portraiture that was compatible with smaller-scale bourgeois homes.[1] Although conversation pieces were painted in America in the eighteenth century, the conditions that most favored their commission occurred during the last half of the nineteenth century.

John Bullard's leather and tanning business had made him a millionaire.[2] This painting was meant to memorialize the Bullards themselves, their wealth, and their taste as reflected in the richly appointed parlor. Decorated in the most current version of the Renaissance revival style, the room is filled with books and art. The sculpture and vases complement the classical detailing of the woodwork, bookcases, and mantel. That the Bullards were patrons of contemporary artists is indicated by the marble bust of *Medusa* by the American sculptress Harriet Hosmer.

E. L. Henry's interest in architecture and his meticulous style and attention to detail made him especially suited to execute this type of painting. Perhaps these qualities as much as the Bullards' preferences caused Henry to emphasize the room rather than the sitters. The composition, which appears to be one of two versions,[3] is similar to that in Henry's *The Library of Jonathan Thorne* of 1868. As with Henry's careful renditions of railroad stations, one value of this "interior portrait," in addition to its aesthetic merit, lies in the documentation it provides of nineteenth-century life. *Sarah Towne Hufford*

1. Sir Ellis Waterhouse, *Painting in Britain* (London and Baltimore, 1953), 140.
2. Edgar de N. Mayhew and Minor Myers, Jr., *A Documentary History of American Interiors from the Colonial Era to 1915* (New York, 1980), pl. 23.
3. The photograph of a painting of the same title from Henry's album reproduced in Elizabeth McCausland, *The Life and Work of Edward Lamson Henry, N.A., 1841–1919* (New York, 1970), 127, shows less of the left wall of the room, Mr. Bullard reading a book, and Mrs. Bullard looking toward the viewer.

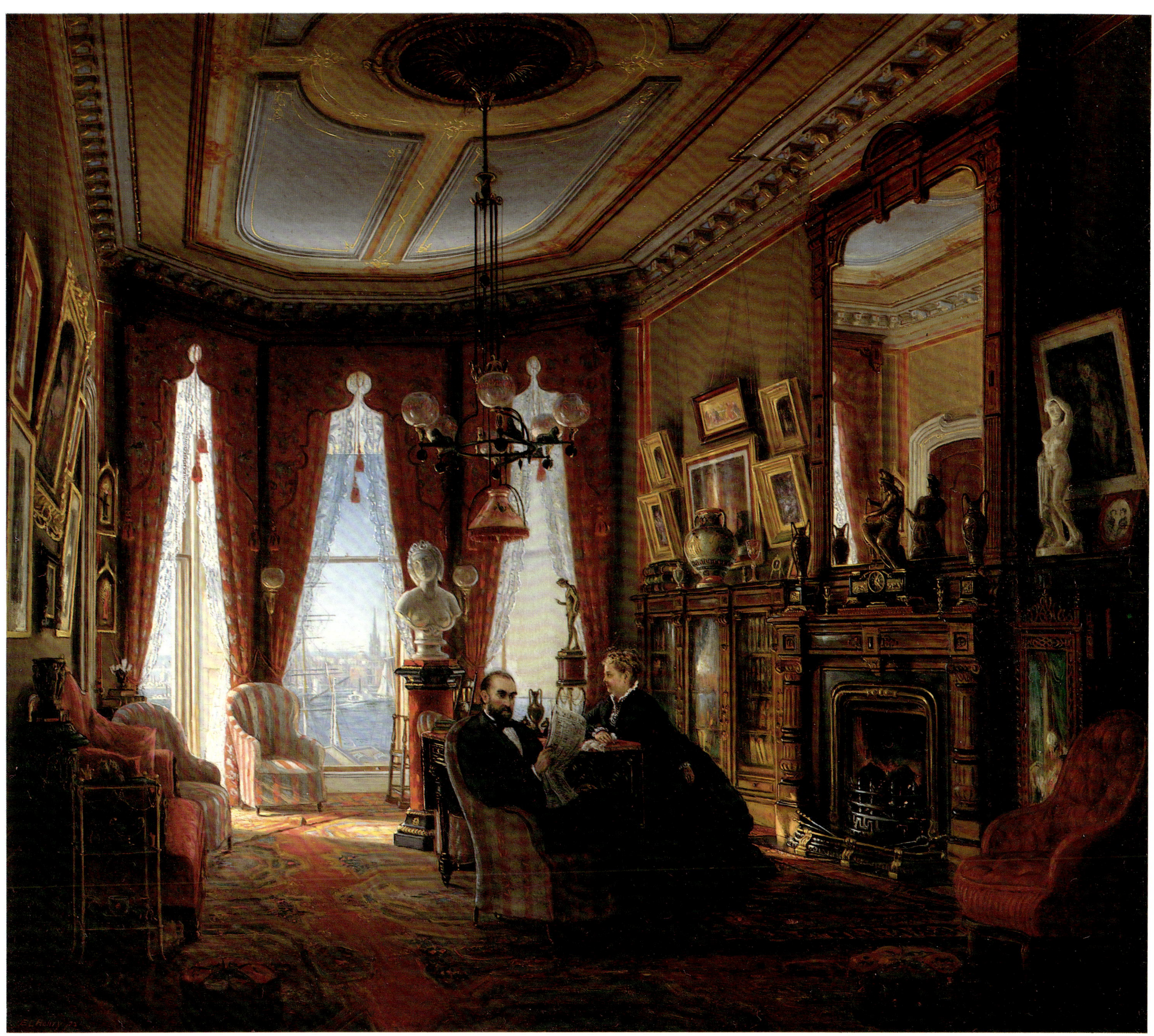

29

Arthur Fitzwilliam Tait (1819–1905)
The Life of a Hunter: A Tight Fix 1858
oil on canvas, 40 x 60 (101.6 x 152.4)

We have not seen a painting for some time which has pleased us so much, wrote a columnist in the *New York Herald* in the spring of 1858. Thus was this bear-hunting scene by Arthur Fitzwilliam Tait singled out for praise from the many canvases at the annual spring show of the National Academy of Design: *One of the most spirited pictures in the exhibition. The drawing is admirable and the tints strictly true to nature.*[1] The only professional art journal at the time, *The Crayon*, judged it to be *a large picture of great power; there can be no question as to the dramatic force with which this story is told.*[2]

As the first painting with the unlikely theme of a bear fight to grace the academy's walls, this auspicious beginning was quickly followed by a history of controversy, anecdote, and speculation.[3]

It began when an anonymous correspondent in another newspaper accused Tait of failing to acknowledge assistance on the canvas. The picture itself, he added, with its *awkward* composition, was *full of impossible attitudes and incongruous forms.*[4] Tait's published letter affirming that the picture was entirely his own handiwork was accompanied by a note from one of his patrons offering to pay $500 for any painting done within half a year on the same subject which, in the opinion of the president of the academy, was equal to Tait's bear fight in *originality, boldness, execution and truthfulness to nature.*[5] A notice in the *Daily News* criticized the scene for serious flaws in design and perspective: *This state of things is quite enough to put the painter "in a tight fix," and doubtless suggested the title of the picture.*[6] Two days later, *Harper's Weekly* published an amusing caricature of the canvas (fig. 1).

Although the locale of Tait's painting was the Chateaugay Woods in New York's northern Adirondacks, the work was bought for $500 by a Mr. J. Campbell, Esquire, whose business address was the Pacific Bank. The painting was lost from public sight until it was rediscovered in 1967 in California at the Elks Lodge in Redlands, quietly on view there for as long as anyone could remember. Campbell was a Californian who may have acquired the picture for its subject, for the bear was a local patriotic symbol. In the summer of 1846 a small group of Americans near San Francisco had proclaimed their independence from Mexico. They fashioned on the spot a primitive flag depicting a grizzly bear (much respected as a fighter) and, though it "did not excel in artistic merit," they hoisted it to the top of the flag pole in the Sonoma town plaza.[7] While that historic cloth ensign was lost in the earthquake of 1906, the official California flag still depicts the bear.

Back east, with the onset of the Civil War and an increased demand for inexpensive prints to entertain the American people, Tait resumed his occasional commissions for Currier & Ives and painted a second, quite different version of the bear fight. However, this canvas seems to be lost and the lithographic stone of 1861 accidentally broken, for no more than a dozen impressions of the published print survive (fig. 3). When a copy sold for $3,000 in 1928 its reputation was made, and the large folio scene has been breaking records ever since.

As one of the most valuable nineteenth-century American lithographs, *A Tight Fix* again attracted notoriety and critical scrutiny. A Mississippi Valley professor, studying the history of the region's backwoods lore and humor, argued in 1939 that Tait's composition was borrowed[8] from an illustration in a popular biography of Daniel Boone (fig. 2), echoing the charge of plagiarism that had been made almost a century earlier against the first painting. *The bear*, the critic had declared in 1858, *is copied from one that may be found in all the primmer* [sic] *books*,[9] a probable reference to the widely circulated Davy Crockett almanacs noted for their vivid woodcuts of the legendary hunter's exploits.

It is remarkable that these critics, decades apart, assumed that the artist's compositions were indebted to literary sources from the South. Tait had been hunting bears for sport and art for many years in the forests of northern New York. If his imagination needed more inspiration, the region boasted a rich repertory of bear stories. Three local tales he may well have heard firsthand serve here as a representative sample of Adirondack lore.

The first yarn concerns an encounter between Bruin and a wayfaring man near the steep banks of the Ausable River not far from Lake Champlain. As the bear stood on its hind legs to give the traveler a powerful hug, the man grasped each of the bear's ears and began to push, making it walk backward to the river's brink. Forcing it into the water, he held its head under until the beast drowned. "A piece of cool presence of mind," observed the narrator.[10]

Tait's works for Currier & Ives were advertised in the widely circulated sporting newspaper *The Spirit of the Times*, which published this brief report from a Mr. Baker of Saranac Lake about his neighbors, Cortez Moody and wife. Paddling along the shore, they spied a large bear crawling on a dead tree out into the water, as if to intercept their progress. It took seven rifle shots to finally subdue the animal, but not before the upset of their boat and a tussle in the shallow water. *With great exertion*, the account concluded, *the victors put their booty in the boat and returned in a terrible plight, muddied from top to toe, but in capital spirits for all that.*[11]

Finally, the most famous piece of Adirondack folk poetry, "Allen's Bear Fight Up in Keene," was on everbody's lips in Essex County at the time of Tait's two pictures. Allen, a country newspaper editor, was appointed to take the federal census, and visited each of the tiny and widely separated settlements. Trudging through the wilds toward Lake Placid, he met a bear with two cubs. Lacking a gun, he held her off with a large stick and, after a fearful struggle, succeeded in killing her with his knife. An unknown local poet immortalized the event by writing a long series of rhyming couplets, including this plea by Allen for discriminating divine intervention:[12]

Against the rock with giant strength
He held her out at his arm's length.
Oh God! he cried in deep despair,
If you don't help me, don't help the bear.

From the gently amusing to the grotesque, such yarns about bears were so universal they became the archetype of a distinctive species of our vernacular literature, the tall tale.[13] Such narratives characteristically strain our credulity by overdrawing the prowess of the hero, the size and ferocity of the beast, and the improbabilities of the circumstances.

The caricature published in *Harper's Weekly* after the original painting of *A Tight Fix* also assumed that Tait was telling an unlikely yarn. It is still amusing today because the caption mocks the braggadocio of the tall tale by the ingenious device of reversing the role of the raconteur.

A fresh look at Tait's two versions of *A Tight Fix* reveals that he chose not to paint a tall tale at all, but a quite different sort of story, and confirms the mistake of past critics in denigrating the pictures. The lithograph of 1861, where the sportsman is posed like a gladiator confronting his adversary, is a fluid and balanced composition with drama and machismo. It has no stylistic resemblance to the flat stiffness of the primitive Daniel Boone motif, but anticipates the realism of "hunting-camp" illustration that became popular later as covers of outdoorsmen's magazines and posters to advertise high-powered rifles.[14]

Turning finally to Tait's original canvas of *A Tight Fix*, we do not see today those defining characteristics of a nineteenth-century tall tale, a *comic lie or impossible exaggeration.*[15] Nor does the painting owe anything to the crude woodcuts[16] of the Davy Crockett almanacs tinged with mayhem. The distinguished art historian Joshua C. Taylor has suggested that those raw pictorials had some redeeming value for those *in search of a myth on which to base a distinctly American culture.*[17] This was not Tait's meaning or intention.

In this painting the hunter's tight fix is not simply that he has dropped his gun and is awkwardly immobilized on the slippery snow, or that he has only one hand free and is too close to the bear for his companion to risk a shot. The hunter's real predicament is his vulnerability for the few moments until he can find his feet. Only then can he exercise his option to fight or flee. The clumsy posture of the bear, be it noted, mirrors the same uncomfortable ambiguity.

Tait's focus on such a moment of unexpected helplessness is perhaps a parable, a reminder of those rare occasions when we have no immediate control of our destiny and are beyond the reach of helping hands. As a universal hazard of the human condition, it is a fitting theme for an artist.

Warder H. Cadbury

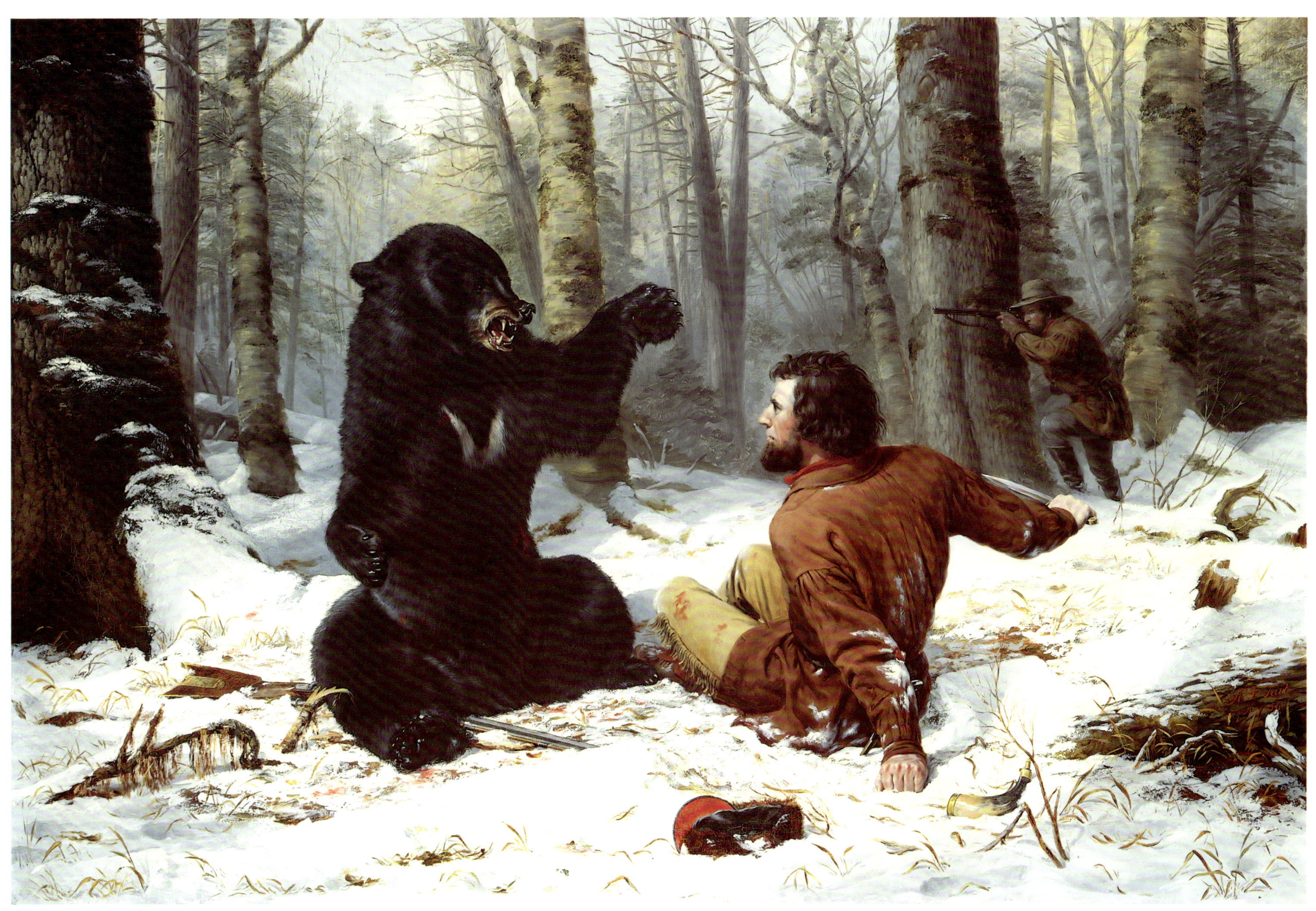

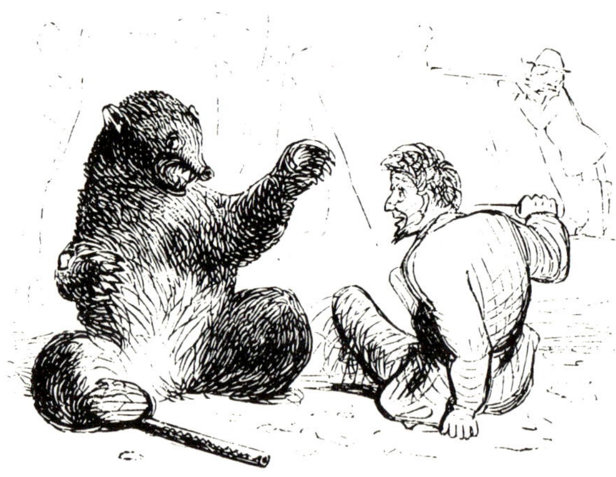

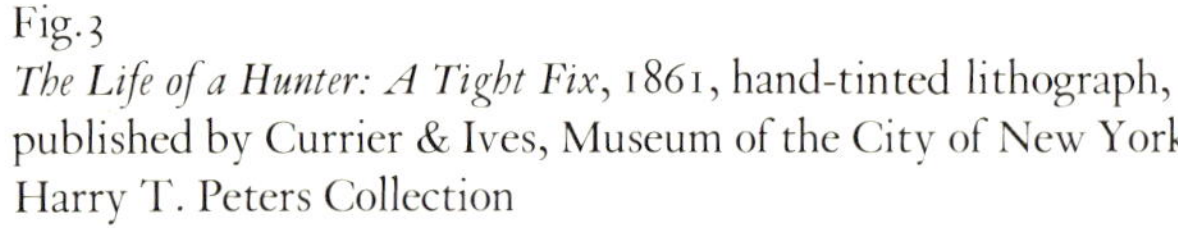
No. 182. An Old "Bar" narrating his Adventures to an intensely-interested Hunter.—Tait.

Fig. 1
Harper's Weekly (15 May 1858), 320

Fig. 2
From Timothy Flint, *The Life and Exploits of Col. Dan'l Boone, the First Settler of Kentucky* (Cincinnati, 1850), 70

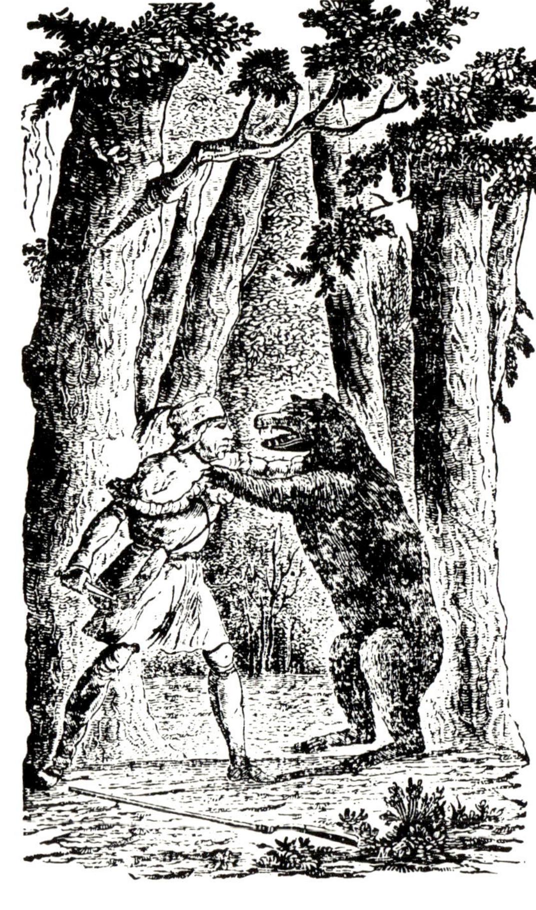

Fig. 3
The Life of a Hunter: A Tight Fix, 1861, hand-tinted lithograph, published by Currier & Ives, Museum of the City of New York Harry T. Peters Collection

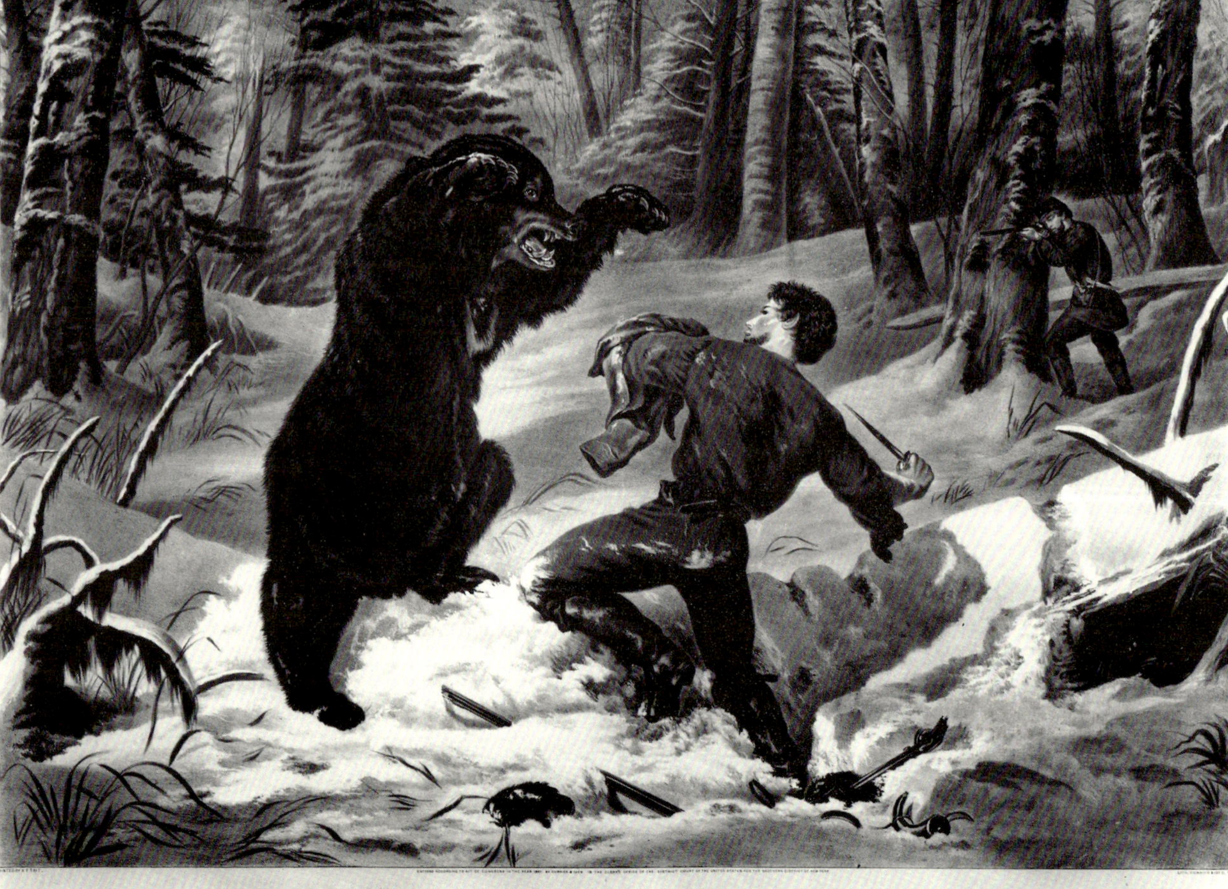

1. *New York Herald*, 23 April 1858, 3.
2. *The Crayon* 5 (1858), 177.
3. Alfred Jacob Miller, a member of the National Academy of Design, painted a bear hunting scene in 1837, but did not exhibit it in New York. He wrote: *To capture the grizzly bear is considered a signal honor, and a great coup. The relating of it is the* creme de la creme *of stories at the campfire, listened to with the most eager attention and admitting a vast amount of embellishment*. Quoted in Michael Bell, ed., *Braves and Buffalo, Plains Indian Life in 1837* (Toronto, 1973), pl. 96.
4. *New York Morning Express*, 4 May 1858.
5. *New York Morning Express*, 8 May 1858.
6. *New York Daily News*, 13 May 1858, 1.
7. Quoted in A. H. Greeley, "More Light on the Original Bear Flag of California," reprinted from *Yale University Library Gazette* 24 (April, 1953) by North American Vexillological Association (Winchester, Massachusetts, n.d.), n.p. See also John Adam Hussey, "New Light on the Original Bear Flag," *California Historical Society Quarterly* 31 (September 1952), 205–217.
8. Philip D. Jordan, "A Possible Source for 'A Tight Fix,'" *Antiques* 35 (January 1939), 28–29. See also his "Humor of the Backwoods, 1820–1840," *The Mississippi Valley Historical Review* 25 (1938), 25–38.
9. *New York Morning Express*, 4 May 1858.
10. Cited in Richard M. Dorson, "Just B'ars," *Appalachia* 24 (December 1942), 177.
11. "A Bear Adventure," *The Spirit of the Times* 23 (10 September 1853), 352.
12. The entire poem is published in many sources, but the definitive account is Edward P. Alexander, "The Man and the Legend," *High Spots, The Yearbook of the Adirondack Mountain Club* (January 1939), 38–44.
13. The name tall tale was coined in a famous bear story more than a century ago, Thomas Bangs Thorpe's "The Big Bear of Arkansas." See Paul Shepard and Barry Sanders, *The Sacred Paw, The Bear in Nature, Myth and Literature* (New York, 1985), 163.
14. See Richard Baldwin, "Hunting-Camp Gallery," *The American Sportsman* 2 (winter 1969).
15. Carolyn S. Brown, *The Tall Tale in American Folklore and Literature* (Knoxville, 1987), 11.
16. Richard B. Hauck, *Crockett, A Bio-Bibliography* (Westport, Connecticut, 1982), 79.
17. Joshua C. Taylor, *America as Art* (New York, 1976), 90.

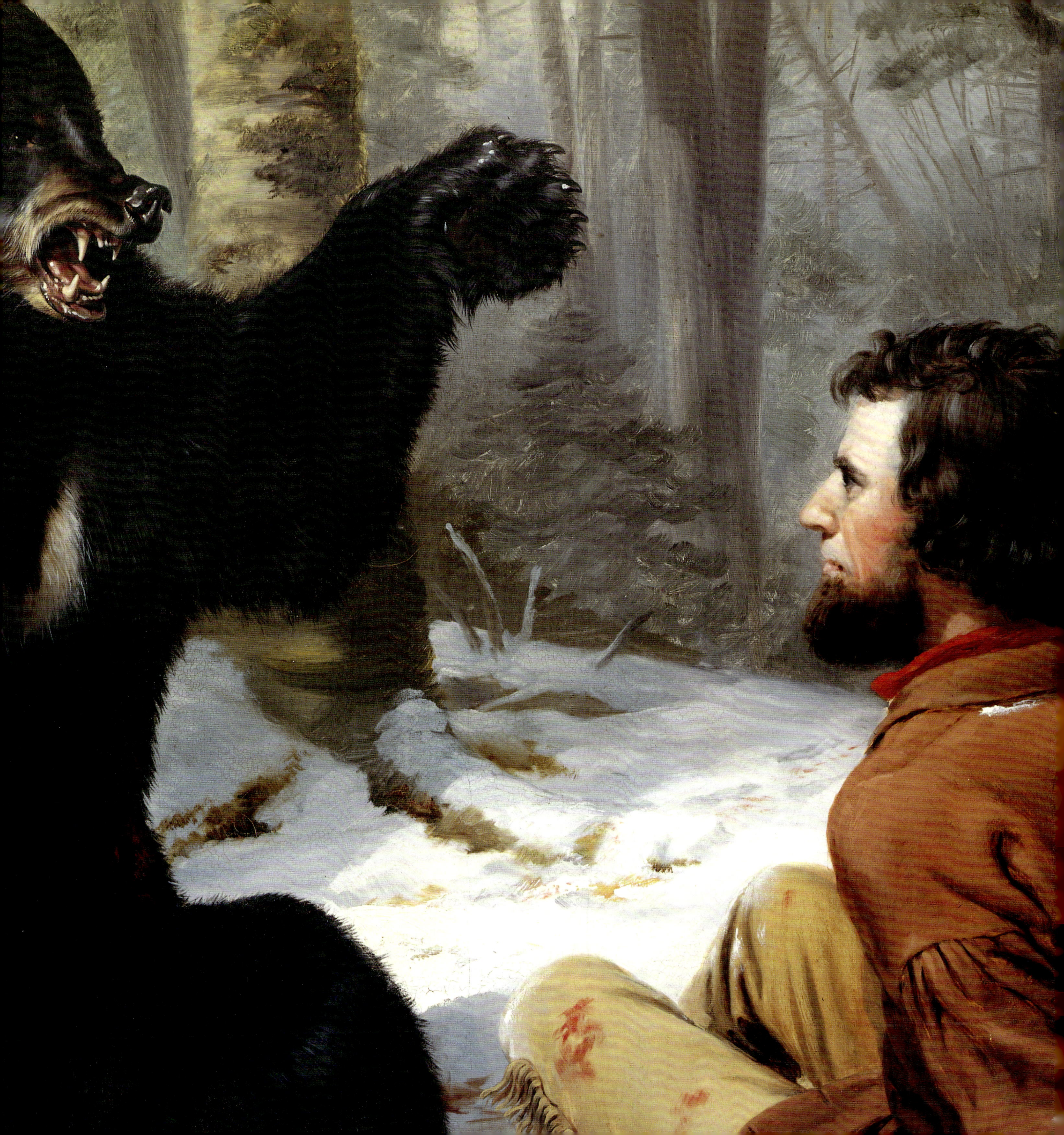

30

James Goodwyn Clonney (1812–1867)
The Trappers 1850
oil on canvas, 17⅜ x 14 (44.1 x 35.6)

The Trappers, exhibited at the American Art-Union in 1850, is a fine example of Clonney's rural genre scenes.[1] The composition of *The Trappers* might have been influenced by the figures in William Sidney Mount's *Catching Rabbits (Boys Trapping)*, 1839, and the landscape in *Trap Sprung (The Dead Fall)*, 1844.[2] Although *The Trappers* and *Catching Rabbits* each has a boy holding a rabbit while his companion resets the trap, Clonney has arranged these two figures in a completely different way. Clonney's more compact composition and the silhouetting of the figures against the sky emphasizes the captured prey. Adding a sense of triumph is the lively pose of the boy with the rabbit.[3] The gaze of the kneeling boy and the direction in which the rabbit is thrust implies an active relationship with something in the space outside the painting. The recipient of this attention is an invisible third person whose existence is confirmed by the shadow in the lower left.[4] These compositional devices coupled with the expressions on the boys' faces give *The Trappers* considerably more dramatic intensity than is found in Mount's picture.

This type of genre focused on the importance of hunting to the livelihood of farmers and frontiersmen. The subject of young boys portrayed as hunters alludes to the realities of rural life in which boys were expected to kill animals for food and fur or because they were pests.[5] The reference to the third person expands the narrative content of *The Trappers* by suggesting that this is a learning experience for the boys.[6] Clonney's clever use of the invisible character serves both the formal and iconographical interpretation of this painting. *Sarah Towne Hufford*

1. There are four drawings, nos. 1972.716–1972.719, at the Museum of Fine Arts, Boston, that relate to this painting.
2. Clonney could have known both of Mount's paintings through engravings.
3. Clonney was familiar with ancient sculpture, having won second prize at the National Academy of Design for a drawing after the antique. See Lucretia H. Giese, "James Goodwyn Clonney (1812–1867): American Genre Painter," *The American Art Journal* 11 (autumn 1979), 6. Rather than being identical to the flat-footed, three-quarter pose of Mount's boy, Clonney's pose with its greater lightness and hint of contrapposto was quite likely informed by knowledge of the Apollo Belvedere, an antique sculpture that was particularly admired in the eighteenth and nineteenth centuries.
4. Clonney's concept is similar to that of the invisible complement in the sculpture of Giovanni Lorenzo Bernini (1598–1680).
5. Patricia Hills, *The Painters' America, Rural and Urban Life, 1810–1910* (New York, 1974), 34.
6. The boys look as though they are deriving equal satisfaction from this experience even though they are of a different race and economic status. This is a departure from the more stereotypical depictions of blacks in the pre–Civil-War era.

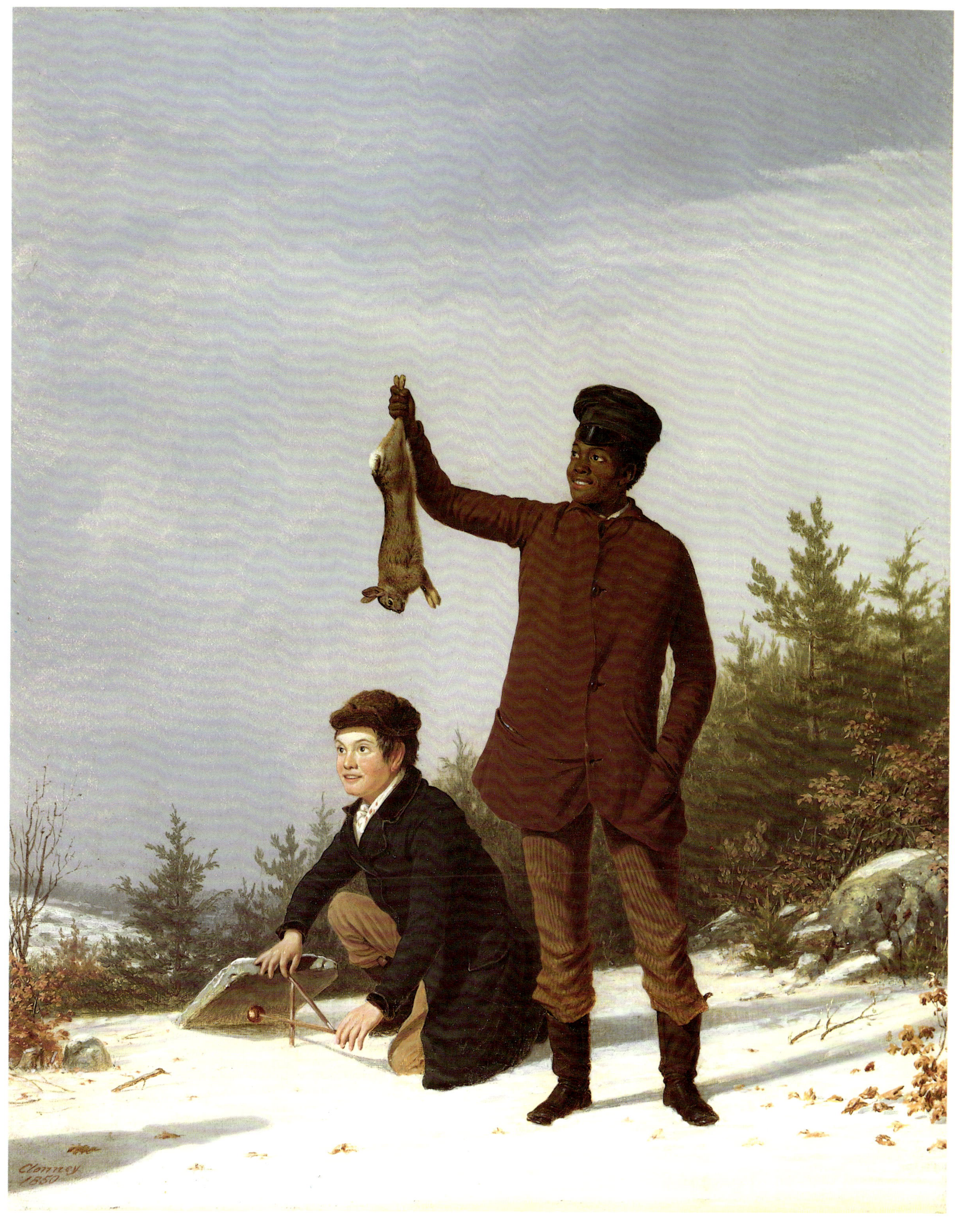
Clonney
1850

31

Martin Andreas Reissner (1798–1862)
The Forest Queen in Winter 1857
oil on canvas, 30⅛ x 40⅜ (76.5 x 102.6)

The identification of the specific locale depicted in *The Forest Queen in Winter* remains as elusive as information about Reissner himself. Family tradition passed down to a former owner of the painting holds that it depicts the artist and his family along the banks of the Ohio River in Covington, Kentucky, looking directly across to Cincinnati.[1] The same tradition maintains that the painting was executed in the front yard of the previous owner's great grandmother, supposedly a friend of Reissner's.

The correlation of the steamship *Forest Queen* with the side-wheeler by that name built in Cincinnati in 1851 supports the traditional identification of the scene.[2] Likewise, the railroad along the river's edge corresponds to the situation in Cincinnati of the Ohio and Mississippi Railroad, which opened in 1857.[3] However, the distant view does not resemble the part of Cincinnati seen from Covington, but rather is similar to the riverside scenery just west of the city. In fact, the painting almost exactly fits an 1857 railroad traveler's account of this area: *The Ohio River monopolized the attention of the traveller for nearly twenty miles, the railroad being built right upon its bank, and between it and a range of low hills to the north or west of the stream. This narrow strip of level land is exceedingly rich, covered with beautiful gardens, from which rise many neat and tasteful gardeners' cottages, presenting an agreeable picture of prosperous and contented industry. On the steep sides of the hills which rise backward from this garden strip, cling the vineyards to which we are indebted for the Catawba wines.*[4]

The carefully composed, meticulously detailed scene clearly betrays Reissner's background as a panorama painter. Like a theatrical backdrop, the scene is somewhat flattened, its space compressed to preclude any recession beyond the mountainside. Reissner drew on the conventions of panorama painting by presenting the viewer with a broad spectrum of minute detail throughout. Other elements, too, signal Reissner's dramatic flair: the strong contrast between the silhouetted figures and tree and the crisp, icy blue background; the threatening, curling black cloud at the right; even the distant mansion lawns, landscaped as if they were stage thrusts. Reissner's unique, almost magical style is not without humor, for in a device not uncommon among landscapists, he depicted himself in the foreground painting the scene, and, in a final touch, illusionistically signed and dated the painting in the snow. *Sarah Cash*

1. This information described the painting in the catalogue for Christie's New York sale WENDY-5400, 28 September 1983, lot 207.
2. This information also appeared in the Christie's catalogue (see n. 1) but was not part of the family tradition mentioned here. According to Frederick Way, Jr., comp., *Way's Packet Dictionary, 1848–1983* (Athens, Ohio, 1983), 169, the *Forest Queen* ran local trades from Cincinnati, probably to Lawrenceburg, Indiana. She measured 283 tons and disappeared from shipping lists in 1859.
3. That Reissner painted the scene in the same year suggests that he may have been commissioned to do so by someone involved with the opening of the railroad. The train's proximity to and implied imminent overtaking of the steamboat may be symbolic of the shift occurring in American transportation and trade.
4. William Prescott Smith, *The Book of the Great Railway Celebrations of 1857* (New York, 1858), 218. I am grateful to Alfred Kleine-Kreutzmann, curator of rare books and special collections, The Public Library of Cincinnati and Hamilton County, for this reference.

   Reissner seems to have embellished the "neat and tasteful gardeners' cottages" to suit his aesthetic purposes. Or, he may have painted a composite of the riverside area Smith described and the more elaborate residences that would have been found either along the Kentucky banks of the Ohio or elsewhere in Cincinnati; such a working method would not have been inconsistent with Reissner's background as a scene painter. The largest porticoed house in the painting, for example, is virtually identical in style to several mansions that dotted the side of Mount Adams, a part of Cincinnati directly across the Ohio from Newport, Kentucky (these may be seen in an 1848 daguerreotype of the city taken by Fontayne and Porter, collection The Public Library of Cincinnati and Hamilton County). Mount Adams, too, had a winery on its side and sloped steeply down to the Ohio, but was much more developed by this date than Reissner's landscape.

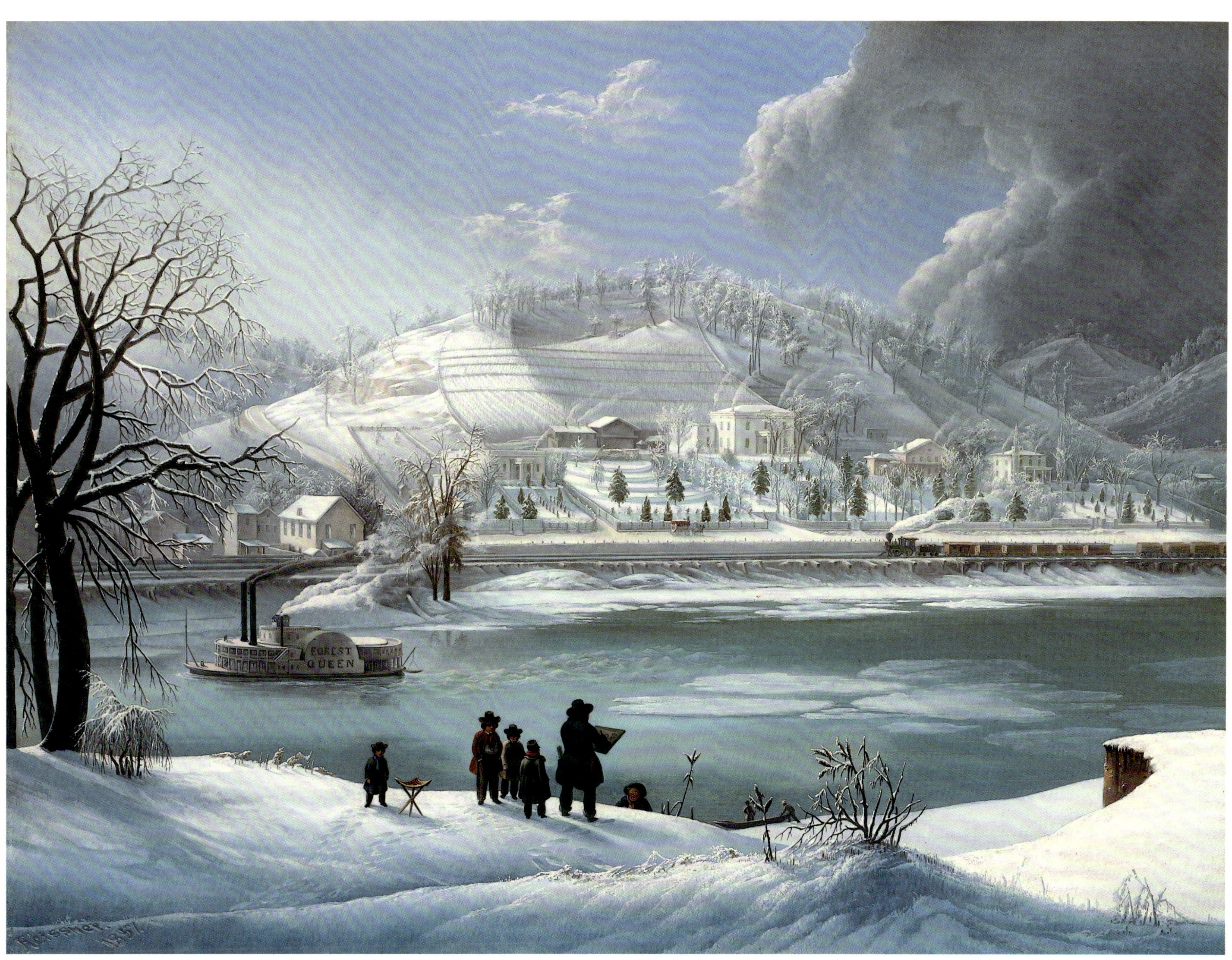
FOREST
QUEEN

32

Charles Deas (1818–1867)
Long Jakes 1844
oil on canvas, 30 x 24⅞ (76.2 x 63.2)

Four years before the enthusiastic reception of his painting *Long Jakes, "the Rocky Mountain Man"* at the American Art-Union of 1844, Charles Deas left New York to travel in the West. For more than a year, beginning in the spring of 1840, he traversed the Wisconsin Territory and painted scenes of Native American life he observed during visits to forts and journeys onto the frontier. By November of 1841 he had taken up residence in Saint Louis, where he would remain until 1848.

Saint Louis, a former Indian trading post and rendezvous for trappers, was a hub of life on the western frontier and one of the gateways to the west. George Ruxton, a British traveler and chronicler of the mountain man, noted that the city retained a *large . . . population still connected with the Indian and fur trade, who preserve all their characteristics unacted upon by the influence of advancing civilization.* Ruxton found *the most singular* [of Saint Louis'] *casual population* [to be] *the mountaineers, who, after several seasons spent in trapping, and with good store of dollars, arrive from the scene of their adventures, wild as savages, determined to enjoy themselves for a time, in all the gaiety and dissipation of the western city.*[1]

Such a mountaineer, whose colorful appearance in Saint Louis so impressed Ruxton, was the subject of Deas' first great success at the Art-Union in New York. *Long Jakes* was the first western picture Deas exhibited there and it caused what one critic called a *sensation among the audience* at the December distribution of pictures.[2]

Deas' red-shirted and bearded trapper, astride a dark brown stallion, turns in his saddle to direct his gaze at something the viewer cannot see, but which has attracted the trapper's attention and alarmed his horse. We know Long Jakes is dressed as Deas himself liked to dress, for we have a portrayal by Lieutenant J. Henry Carleton who noted the artist's exotic appearance in *a broad white hat—a loose dress, and sundry traps and truck hanging about his saddle, like a fur-hunter.*[3]

Carleton's description of Deas' attire and its correspondence with that of a fur trapper may lead us to approach the painting as a kind of self-portrait. Although Long Jakes and Deas do not share similar features (we know of Deas' appearance only from an 1840 *Self-Portrait* in pencil at the National Academy of Design), the image of the trapper as a wild man with a core of urbane chivalry might describe the artist, whose background of family prominence and classical education existed beneath his new persona as frontier resident.

The popularity of *Long Jakes* lay in this appealing vision of a western hero *from the outer verge of our civilization . . . wild and romantic,* yet with *traits of former gentleness and refinement in his countenance,* who *sits upon his horse as though he were fully conscious of his picturesque appearance.*[4] Deas, a man who could not gain admittance to the U.S. Military Academy, may have identified further with the trapper's escape from eastern conventions and the ensuing opportunity to prove his heroic fiber on the frontier. He must have been pleased at the narrative his painting inspired in Henry William Herbert's long essay written to accompany the published engraving of *Long Jakes* by W. G. Jackman. Herbert wrote that Long Jakes was a *man of energy, and iron will, and daring spirit, tameless, enthusiastic, ardent, adventurous, chivalric, free—a man made of the stuff which fills the mould of heroes.*[5]

To us, the reddened nose and battered hat from which a bite appears to have been taken may appear slightly humorous, but to Herbert and his readers *that bold frank sun-burned face, with its keen and pervading eye, farsighted as the soaring eagle's, and its expression of indomitable courage* and *the broad brimmed sombrero, well suited to guard the eyes alike from the overpowering splendor of the level sunbeams . . . and from the driving hail or sleet of winter*[6] were far from comic. The American public and critics embraced the potential of *Long Jakes* for narrative embellishment and as a political symbol of independence. They elevated Deas to a new position of prominence in New York and Saint Louis.

Hunters, natives of the continent, and a singular picture inspired by James Fenimore Cooper's novel, *The Prairie,* were Deas' subjects between 1845 and 1848 as he continued to live in Saint Louis and to exhibit there and back east. In two paintings, each titled *The Voyageurs* (c. 1845, Museum of Fine Arts, Boston, M. and M. Karolik Collection; and fig. 1), he depicted traders of French descent. These *voyageurs,* who often intermarried with Indians, usually procured pelts through trade with the Indians rather than by trapping the beaver. They traveled with their families along the Missouri in dugouts to transport the furs from trading posts in the wilderness to markets like Saint Louis and to carry merchandise back to the posts.

Long Jakes appears to be no *voyageur.* Although sometimes called *Jacques* in reviews of the Art-Union exhibition, Long Jakes memorializes an American rather than a French or Canadian trapper. First of all, he is shown alone without the company of a family. Secondly, he is presented as a hero, far from the characterization of the *voyageur,* whose pastimes, when not a family man, were defined by Charles Lanman as *generally of a rude and licentious character.*[7] Lastly, *Long Jakes* may be regarded as one of a pair of paintings, for its pendant, *The Death Struggle* (fig. 2), shows an episode in the same man's life that graphically portrays the consequence of trapping (or, in this case, probably poaching) rather than trading for pelts.

In *The Death Struggle,* our trapper, who has the same features and wears the same red shirt but who now rides a white rather than a dark brown horse, is engaged in deadly combat with an Indian. According to the *Broadway Journal, A trapper has been found trespassing upon the Indian hunting ground* and in the ensuing fight for the beaver, still in its trap, both Indian and mountain man are wounded; their horses legs entangled in vines and *maddened by the wounds which had been dealt out alike to man and beast, break from the control of their riders, and rush headlong towards a frightful precipice.*[8]

This horrific scene of bloodshed and almost certain death for men and animals alike contrasts sharply with the outwardly calm comportment of *Long Jakes.* We are aware, however, of some perceived danger, for the trapper has stopped his forward movement and turned his sunburned face to look behind him. Although as a hero he appears fearless, we sense concern in the intensity of his gaze; his horse's bulging eye and startled gait show fear at an unseen human or animal presence. Danger, whether fulfilled in *The Death Struggle* or threatening in *Long Jakes,* is characteristic of almost all of Deas' western subjects. The tensions of pursuit and combat may have their sources in the demons raging within the mind of the artist, for he was judged insane and committed to an asylum in the summer of 1848.

The image of *Long Jakes* retained its power in the American imagination. Not only engraved by Jackman and published in 1846, it also was lithographed by Leopold Grozelier about 1855 (fig. 3).[9] The popularity of this lithograph inspired a number of copies of *Long Jakes,* many by folk artists, such as William G. M. Samuel's *Man on Horseback* (Collection of Daughters of the Republic of Texas at the Alamo, San Antonio). At least seven copies are known, none by the artist's hand, and although Deas himself painted other versions of the subject, not one of these has come to light.[10]

Deas chose to paint a character from an earlier moment in American history. By 1844 the price of beaver pelts had declined, settlers had invaded the territories, and the brief heyday of the mountain man had passed.[11] But in the national imagination his apotheosis as the vigorous ideal of independent manhood was complete as embodied in Deas' *Long Jakes.* *Carol Clark*

1. George Frederick Ruxton, *Life in the Far West,* ed. Leroy R. Hafen (1849; reprint ed., Norman, Oklahoma, 1951), 52–53.
2. *Broadway Journal,* 4 January 1845, 13. Between 1839 and 1851 the Apollo Association and its successor (after 1844), the American Art-Union, distributed by lottery to members at the end of each year pictures the organization had purchased from exhibitions.
3. Lieutenant Carleton's journal of the 1844 expedition to the Pawnee was published anonymously in serial form in the *Spirit of the Times* (9 November 1844–12 April 1845) and then reprinted as Lieutenant J. Henry Carleton, *The Prairie Logbooks: Dragoon Campaigns to the Pawnee Villages in 1844, and to the Rocky Mountains in 1845,* ed. Louis Pelzer (Chicago, 1943), 28.
4. *Broadway Journal,* 4 January 1845, 13.
5. Henry William Herbert, "*Long Jakes,* The Prairie Man," *New York Illustrated Magazine* 2 (July 1846), 169. Dawn Glanz reinforces the heroism of our trapper by noting the similarity between the mounted Long Jakes and Jacques-Louis David's *Napoleon Crossing the Alps*; cf. Dawn Glanz, *How the West Was Drawn: American Art and the Settling of the Frontier* (Ann Arbor, Michigan, 1982), 45.
6. Herbert, *Long Jakes,* 1846, 171.

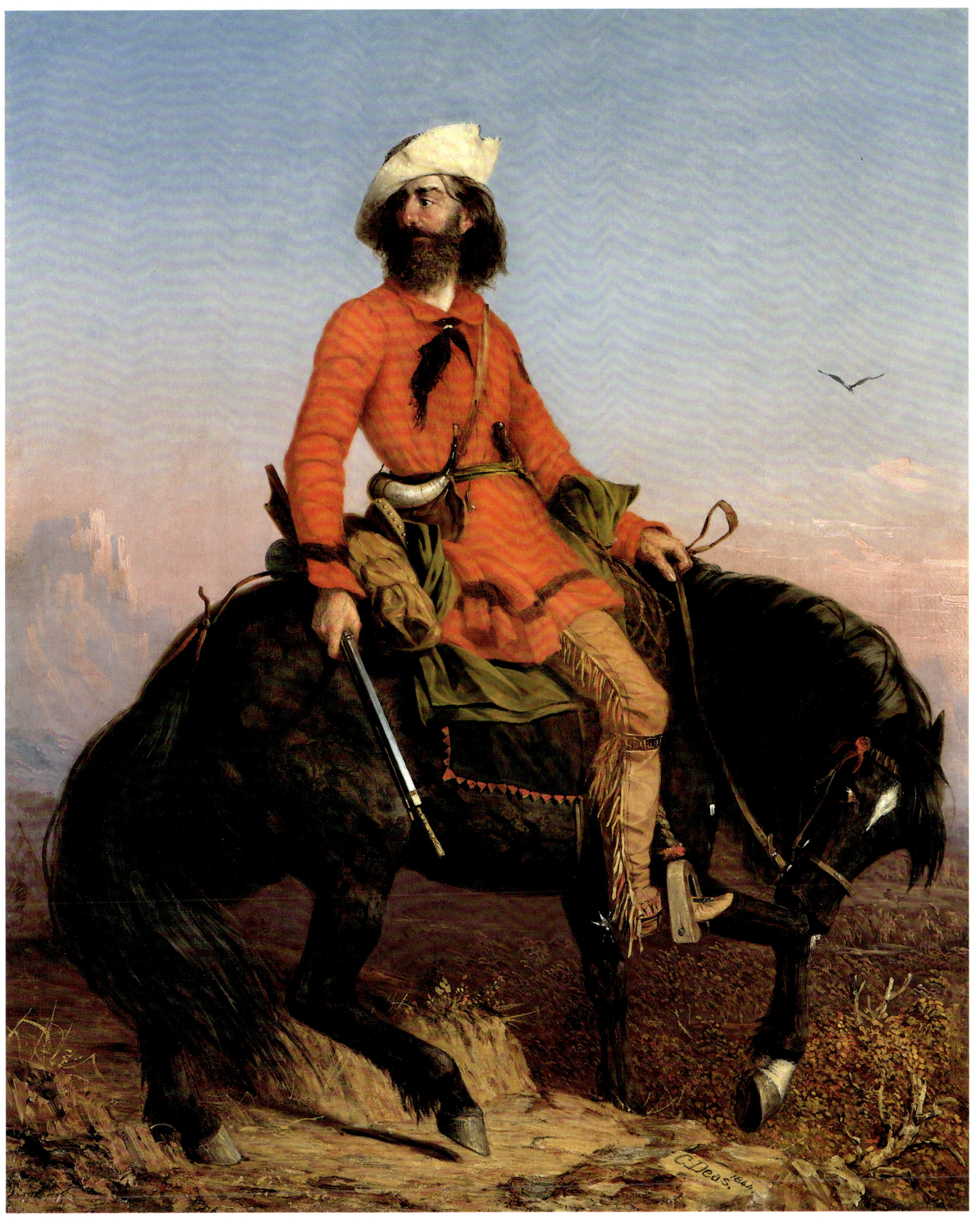
C. Deas. 1844.

7. Charles Lanman, *A Summer in the Wilderness* (New York, 1847), 146.
8. *Broadway Journal*, 13 September 1845, 154.
9. The lithograph was printed at J. H. Bufford, Boston, and published by M. Knoedler, New York.
10. On the Samuel painting, see Cecilia Steinfeldt, *Texas Folk Art: One Hundred Fifty Years of the Southwestern Tradition* (Austin, 1981), 24. The critic for the Saint Louis *Weekly Reveille* (8 February 1847), 1163,carefully described one version of *Long Jakes* that he calls *The Trapper*, which was on view in Saint Louis in 1847. Although many of its features are similar to the Manoogian picture, it is distinguished by a skull in the foreground. This feature, as well as the fact that *Long Jakes* was distributed at the Art-Union in December 1844 to G. F. Everson, confirms the existence of at least one other version. John F. McDermott, in "Charles Deas' Portrait of a Mountain Man: A Mystery in Western Art," *Gateway Heritage* 1 (spring 1981), 2–9, argues for the authenticity of four of these versions. I disagree fundamentally with his conclusions.
11. For a concise and informative essay on the mountain man, see William H. Goetzmann, "Lords at the Creation: The Mountain Men and the World," in *The Mountain Man* [exh. cat., Buffalo Bill Historical Center] (Cody, Wyoming, 1978), 9–31.

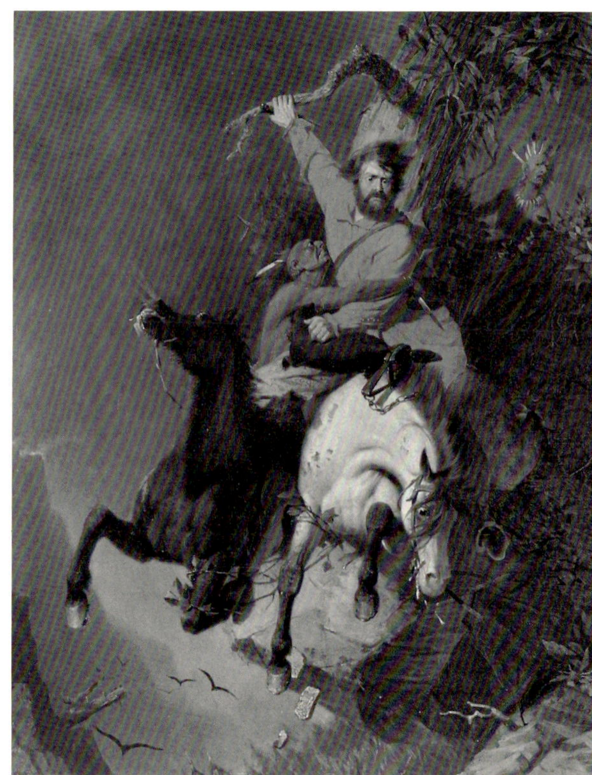

Fig. 2
Charles Deas, *The Death Struggle*, 1845, oil on canvas, 30 x 25 (76.2 x 63.5), The Shelburne Museum, Shelburne, Vermont

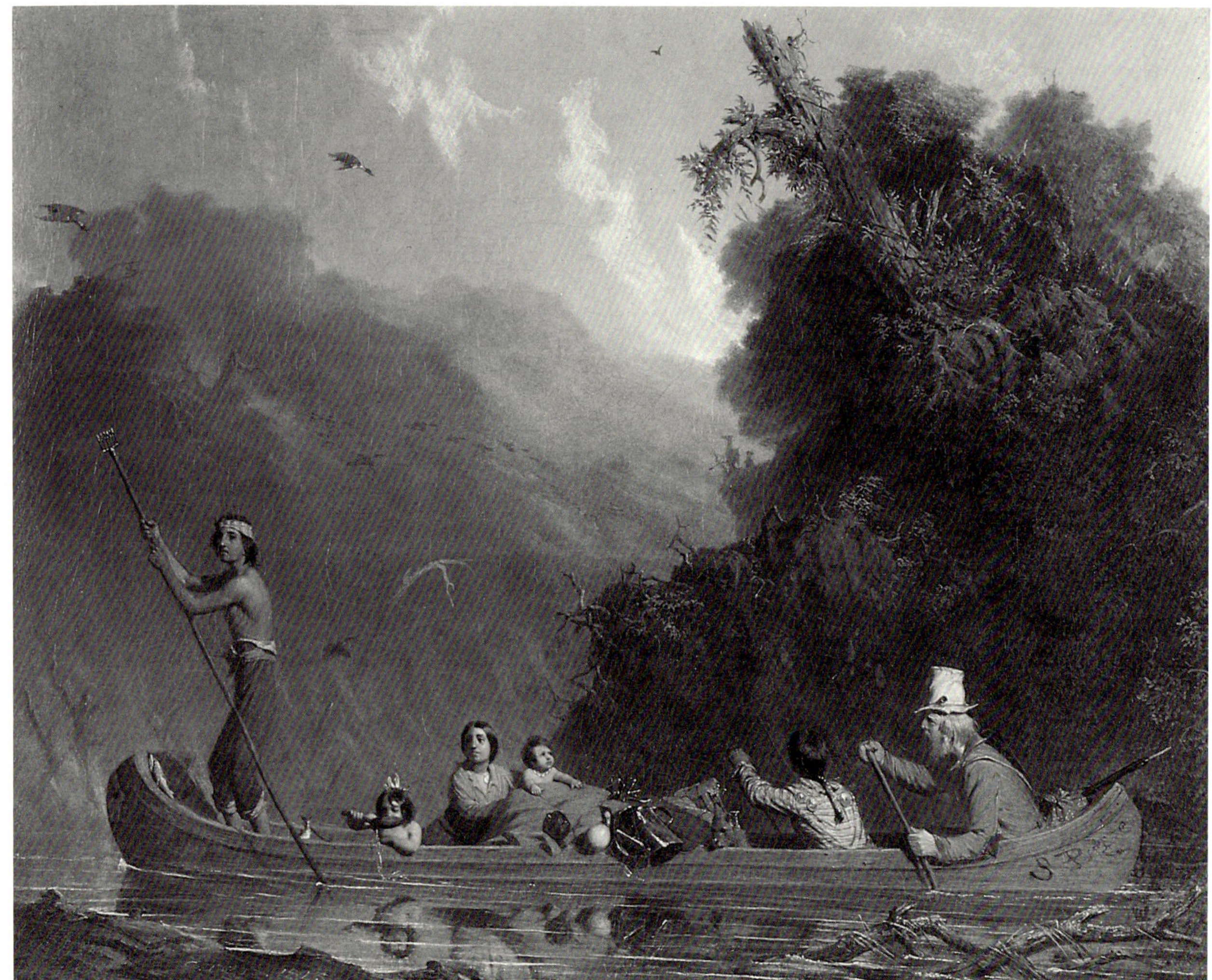

Fig. 1
Charles Deas, *The Voyageurs*, 1845, oil on canvas, 24 x 29½ (61.0 x 74.9), Rokeby Collection, on loan to The Metropolitan Museum of Art, New York

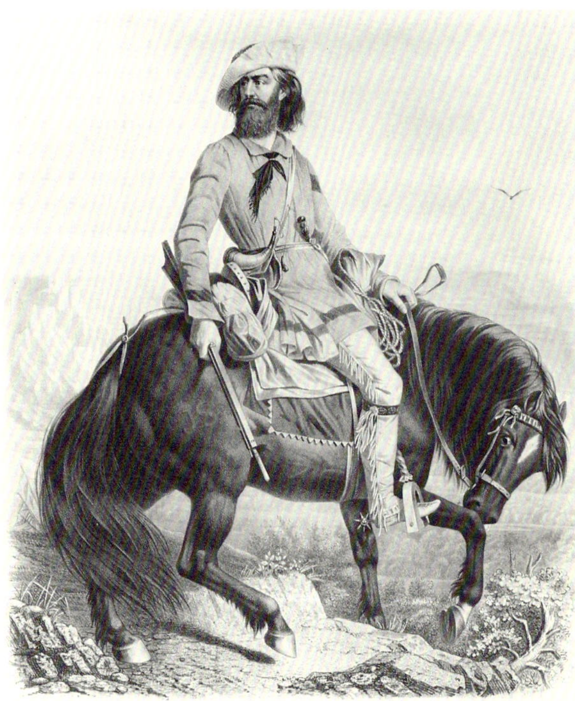

Fig. 3
Leopold Grozelier, after Charles Deas, *Western Life—The Trapper*, c. 1855, lithograph (proof), printed by J. H. Bufford, published by M. Knoedler, 5¾ x 4¾ (14.6 x 12.1), Amon Carter Museum, Fort Worth

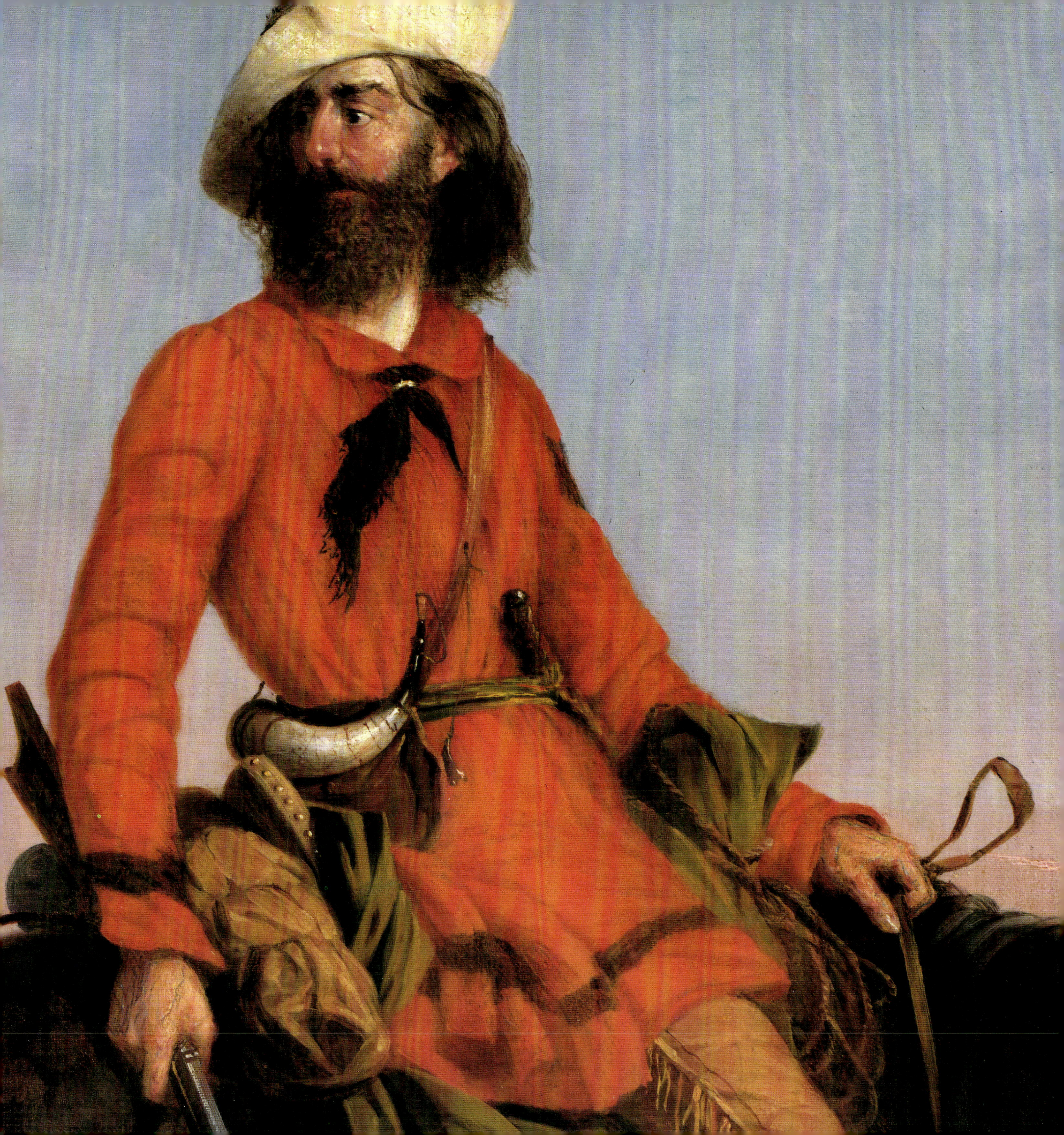

33

Albert Bierstadt (1830–1902)
Indians Traveling near Fort Laramie 1861
oil on canvas, 23 x 40⅛ (58.4 x 101.9)

Albert Bierstadt traveled west for the first time in the spring of 1859 with Frederick W. Lander's Honey Road Survey party. Following the Oregon Trail, the Lander party reached Fort Laramie early in June. En route they camped near Chimney Rock, the distinctive geologic landmark visible in the far distance of *Indians Traveling near Fort Laramie*. The diminutive size of this natural monument confirms the relatively early date of Bierstadt's painting, for in later western views by the artist the landscape itself emerges as the chief protagonist, dwarfing foreground figures. In this early work, however, the artist's interest is focused on a group of Plains Indians preparing for travel.

While on the trail with the Lander expedition, Bierstadt kept friends and family abreast of his progress through a series of letters that were published in the *New Bedford Daily Mercury*. Paraphrasing from one such letter, the *Mercury* reported that when a group of Indians unexpectedly visited the artist's camp, *Mr. Bierstadt obtained stereoscopic portraits of several of the party*, and *succeeded in sketching some fine studies including a picturesque groupe* [sic] *of Indians—a travelling party, the horses with the tent poles fastened to their sides, one end dragging upon the ground, and seated upon the poles, a squaw and papoose, with blankets and other camp articles.*[1]

Drawing upon such sketches and photographs, Bierstadt later composed *Indians Traveling near Fort Laramie* in his New York studio. Deftly arranging horses and figures to illustrate several stages in the moving process, he began the sequence at the far right where a single figure sorts the lodge poles, skins, storage bags, and other items from which a travois, the chief vehicle of Plains Indian transport, would be assembled. At the left, the process has been carried one step further. A range pony, already loaded with elaborately decorated storage bags, or parfleches, waits while two Indians prepare another set of poles for mounting. At the center, the process has been completed. Comfortably seated atop a fully assembled travois, a woman and two children wait for the journey to begin.

Unlike Bierstadt's later paintings of soaring western mountains, *Indians Traveling near Fort Laramie* celebrates the horizontal grandeur of the Great Plains. Beneath an enormous canopy of sky the land the artist described as *perfectly flat* stretches without limit.[2] *Nancy Anderson*

1. *New Bedford Daily Mercury*, 18 June 1859. No sketch directly related to this painting has come to light and only a few of the glass-plate stereographs taken on the Lander expedition survive. One of these, now in the collection of the Kansas State Historical Society, may be the source for one of the mounted figures in *Indians Traveling Near Fort Laramie*. See Gordon Hendricks, *Albert Bierstadt: Painter of the American West* (New York, 1974), fig. 44. A full-page illustration after *Indians Traveling near Fort Laramie* appeared in *Heart of the Continent* (New York, 1870), Fitz Hugh Ludlow's account of a western journey he and Bierstadt made together in 1863.
2. *New Bedford Daily Mercury*, 18 June 1859.

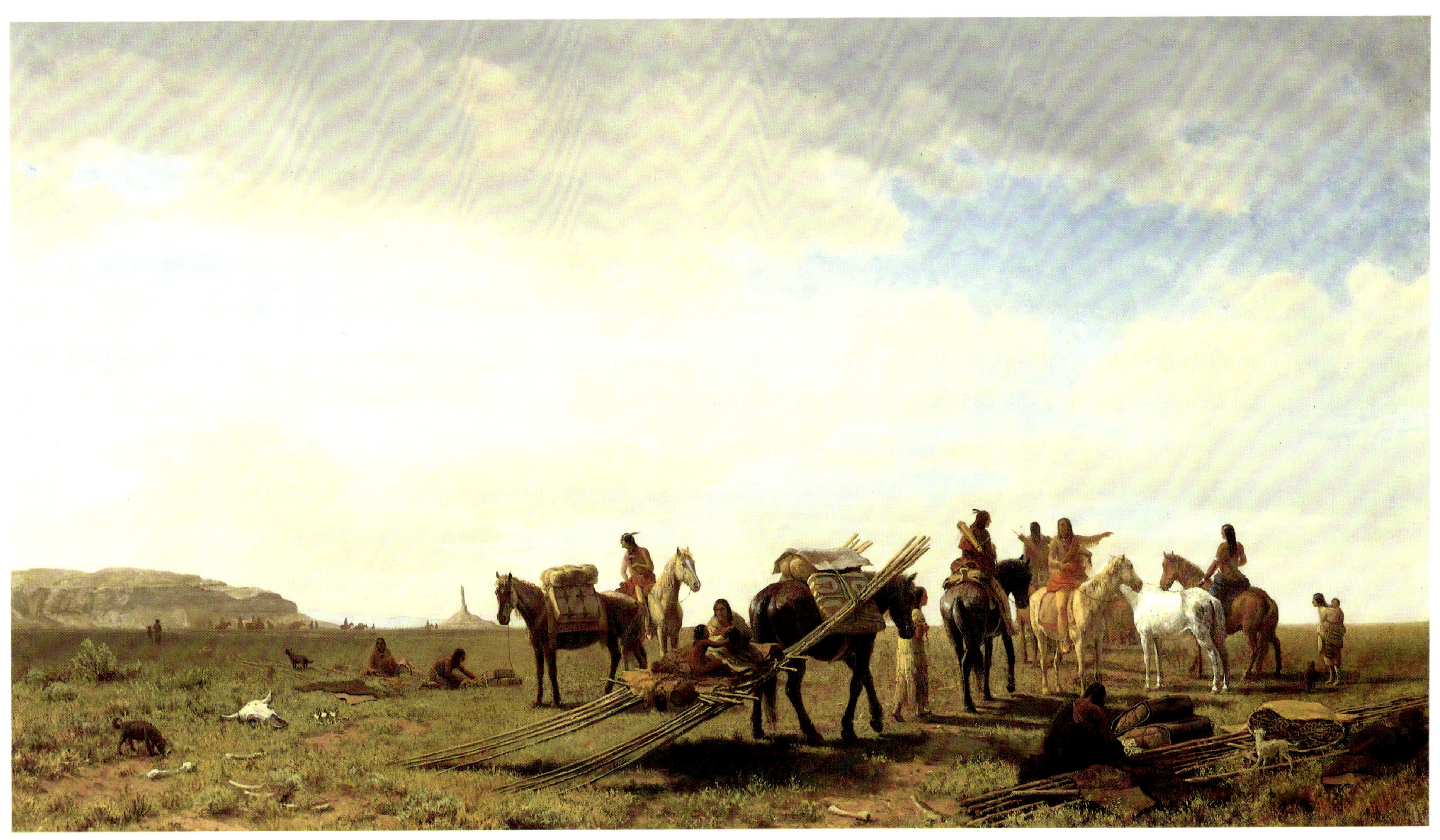

34

George de Forest Brush
Silence Broken 1888
oil on canvas, 26¾ x 18¼ (67.9 x 46.4)

George Deforest Brush spent six years studying at the Ecole des Beaux-Arts, Paris, and returned to the United States in 1884. By painting natives of the American continent as subjects he Americanized French academic painting, and conversely by replacing classical figures with Native Americans, Brush ennobled his subjects. He believed they *were superb and symmetrical men . . . their beardless faces reminding one always of the antique; their constant light exercises, frequent steam baths, and freedom from overwork develop the body in a manner equaled, I must believe, by the Greeks.*[1]

Silence Broken embodies such a character. The figure is treated not as a curiosity but as a noble hero. The influence of Jean-Léon Gérôme, Brush's teacher in Paris, is apparent here; the figure is strongly delineated with emphasis placed on his expression and his geometrically correct body. Additionally, Brush introduced an aural effect in a visual medium through the figure's attention to the sound of the goose in flight. Brush's earlier work in this series concentrated on a more exacting representation of the Native American; however, he eventually turned to a more idealized depiction, writing *I do not paint from the historian's or antiquaries' point of view; I do not come to represent them in any curious habits which could not be comprehended by us; . . . if I were required to resort to this in order to bring out the poetry I would drop the subject at once.*[2]

In later years Brush changed his style and subject matter, and looked toward Italian Renaissance paintings for inspiration. These works became extremely popular, and soon began to dominate his oeuvre, exhibitions, and sales. As one contemporary wrote in reference to Brush's change in style, *It would be difficult to find lovelier pictures than* Silence Broken *or* The Sculptor and the King. . . . *You never see reproductions of them. They rarely appear on the market, but when one does turn up, it is bought almost at once by a private collector.*[3] *James W. Tottis*

1. George de Forest Brush, "An Artist Among the Indians," *Century Magazine* 30 (May 1885), 55.
2. Brush 1885, 57.
3. Nancy Douglas Bowditch Papers, Archives of American Art, Smithsonian Institution, Washington. Roll 2830, notes by Berry Faulkner, frame 820.

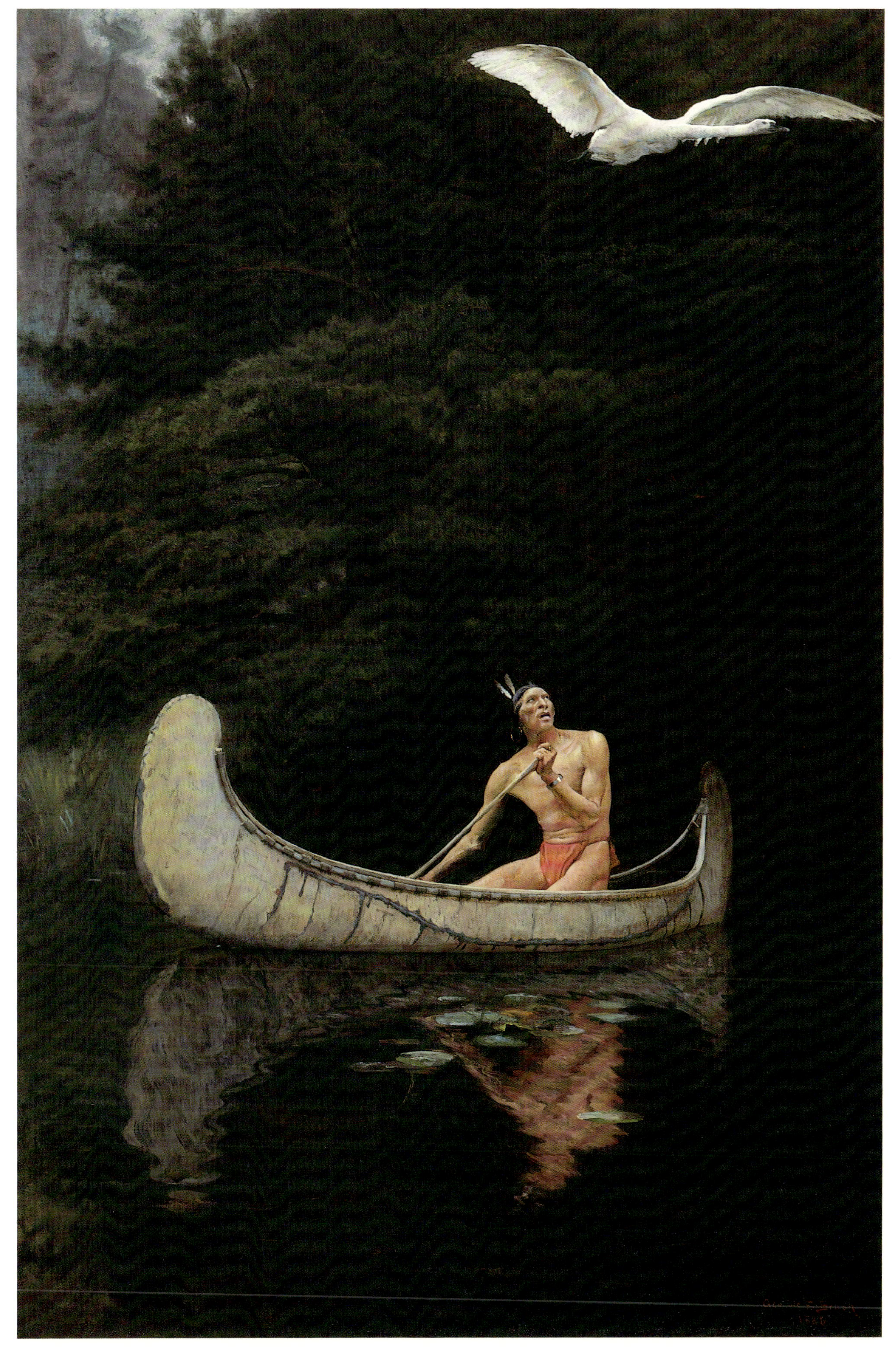

35

Henry F. Farny (1847–1916)
In the Foothills of the Rockies 1898
oil on canvas, 22 x 40¼ (55.9 x 102.2)

Henry Farney, with his younger contemporaries Frederic Remington and Charles Russell, was one of the chief portrayers of the American West in the last quarter of the nineteenth century. Farney specialized in paintings of Native American life. Although he knew it from first hand experience from several trips to the far western United States (in 1881, 1883, 1884, and 1894), his paintings are not simply direct witness accounts. They were concocted in Farny's Cincinnati studio from artifacts, photographs, and drawings that he collected on his western trips; a writer who reported Farny's return to Cincinnati from his 1881 trip said, *He brings back with him a great quantity of Indian loot*.[1] What is more, Farny, a well trained and highly sophisticated artist, recast his images of the West in particularly artful and knowing ways. *In the Foothills of the Rockies* is characteristic of Farny's mature art in its use both of conventions of pictorial organization derived from Japanese art, and a palette influenced by the coloration of impressionism.

As *In the Foothills of the Rockies* shows, the landscape settings of Farny's paintings are as convincing and compelling as their figures and artifacts. Though his landscapes were, like his figures, painted from memory in the studio, they depict the vegetation, light, and, above all, the space of the American West with extraordinary visual truth, aesthetic sensitivity, and expressive feeling.

When Farny painted it the West was spanned by railroads and occupied with settlers (the frontier was officially closed in 1890), and the native inhabitants were relentlessly confined to reservations to live a life very different from the one Farny portrayed with such apparent authenticity in *Foothills of the Rockies*. He knew that it was different. He went to Montana specifically to witness the completion of the Northern Pacific Railroad in 1883, and he saw Indians on reservations dependent on government rations for survival.[2] *It breaks my heart*, he admitted in 1910, *to see the prairies cut up with barbed wire, and to see the once noble Red Man debauching himself with fire water on reservations. The golden West isn't what it used to be*.[3] But he preserved its myth. *Nicolai Cikovsky, Jr.*

1. "Mr. Farny Among the Sioux," *Cincinnati Daily Gazette* (8 November 1881), quoted in *Henry Farny 1847–1916* [exh. cat., Archer M. Huntington Art Gallery, The University of Texas at Austin] (Austin, 1983), 22. Some of that "loot" can be seen in an undated photograph of Farny in his studio. See Denny Carter, *Henry Farny* (New York, 1978), 29.
2. See *Henry Farny* 1983, 22.
3. Quoted in Carter, *Farny* 1978, 28.

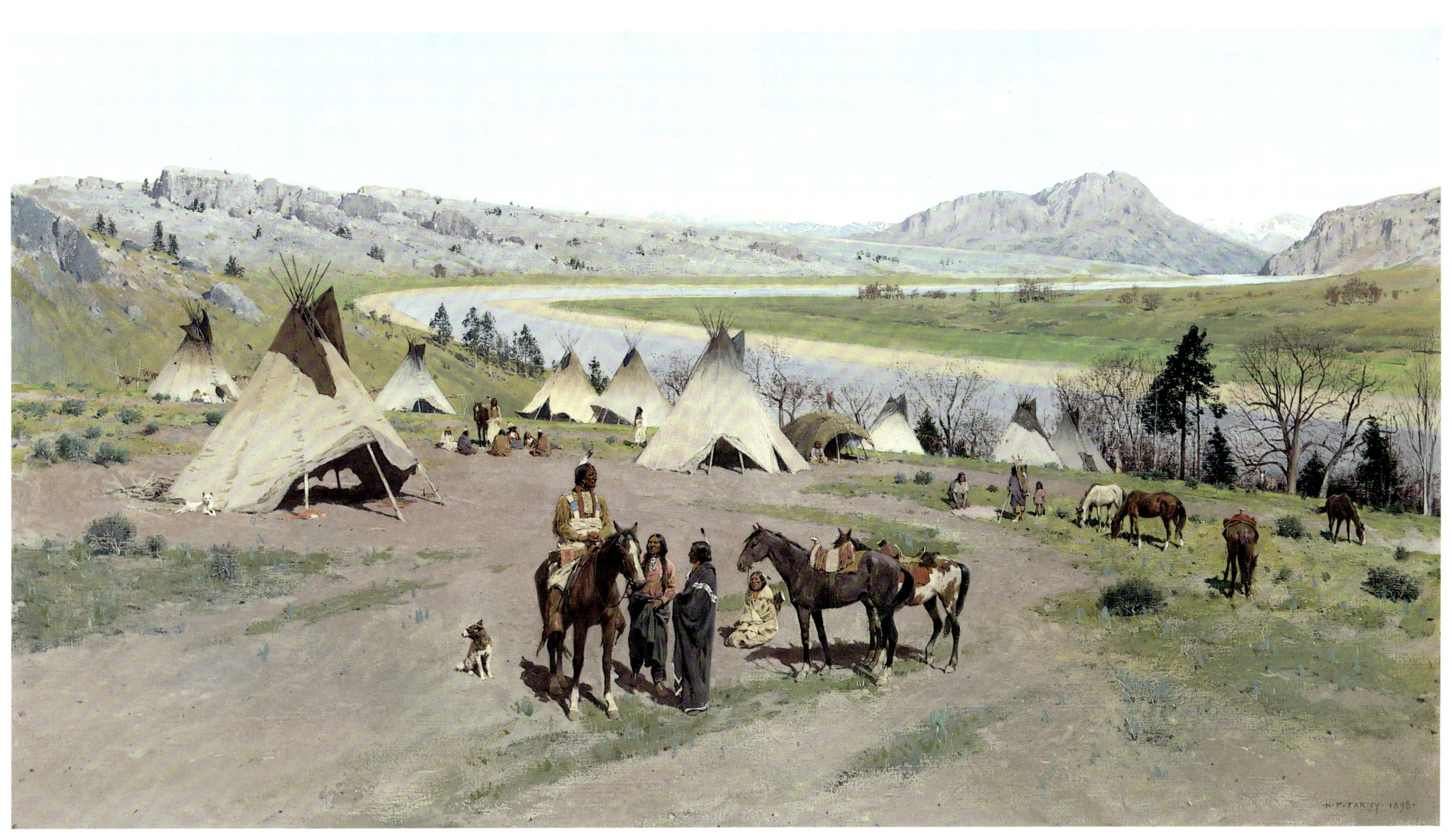
·H·F·FARNY·1898·

36

Johannes Adam Oertel (1823–1909)
Capturing Wild Horses 1855
oil on canvas, 40⅛ x 60¼ (101.9 x 153)

Capturing Wild Horses is one of a whole genre of paintings reflecting the fascination with the West and the way of life of Native Americans. Although Oertel had not been farther west than New Jersey by 1855, he would have been able to see popular prints, George Catlin's books, and paintings on western themes by Alfred Miller and William Ranney at the exhibitions of the National Academy of Design and the American Art-Union. Oertel's most likely sources for this subject were Catlin's *Wild Horses at Play*, *Lassoing Wild Horses*, and *Breaking Down the Wild Horse*, which were all published in one or more of his books.[1] The first and last subjects were also lithographed by Currier & Ives.[2] Paintings like Ranney's *Halt on the Prairie* and *The Retreat*, exhibited in 1850 and 1851 respectively, may have influenced the low vantage point, the close-up view, and the minimal landscape in Oertel's composition.

Despite the presence of the Indian with the lasso, the true subject is the horses themselves. Exuberant and robust, they are thoroughly romantic conceptions resembling those of Théodore Géricault and Rosa Bonheur rather than the ones in American artists' works. Like Géricault and Bonheur, Oertel must have spent considerable time observing horses to be able to portray them with such convincing anatomical detail. The spirited poses also seem to have been influenced at least as much by Bonheur's *The Horse Fair*, 1853, as by Catlin's depictions.[3] Oertel ultimately gained a considerable reputation for his animal paintings, which were compared favorably to those of Bonheur and Sir Edwin Landseer.[4] *Sarah Towne Hufford*

1. Catlin's paintings are illustrated in William H. Truettner, *The Natural Man Observed: A Study of Catlin's Indian Gallery* (Washington, 1979), 286–287.
2. Gale Research Co., compiler, *Currier and Ives, A Catalogue Raisonné* (Detroit, 1983), 749, 93, respectively. Although the lithographs are undated, it seems reasonable to assume that they were issued before 1855, since Catlin had exhibited and first published his paintings in New York in 1837.
3. Oertel would no doubt have been familiar with Géricault's lithographs of horses. Bonheur's *The Horse Fair* was a huge success at the Paris Salon of 1853. An etching of it was reproduced in *L'Artiste* 11 (1853).
4. J. F. Oertel, *A Vision Realized: The Life Story of Rev. J. A. Oertel, D.D., Artist, Priest, Missionary* (Milwaukee, 1917), 47–48, 228–229.

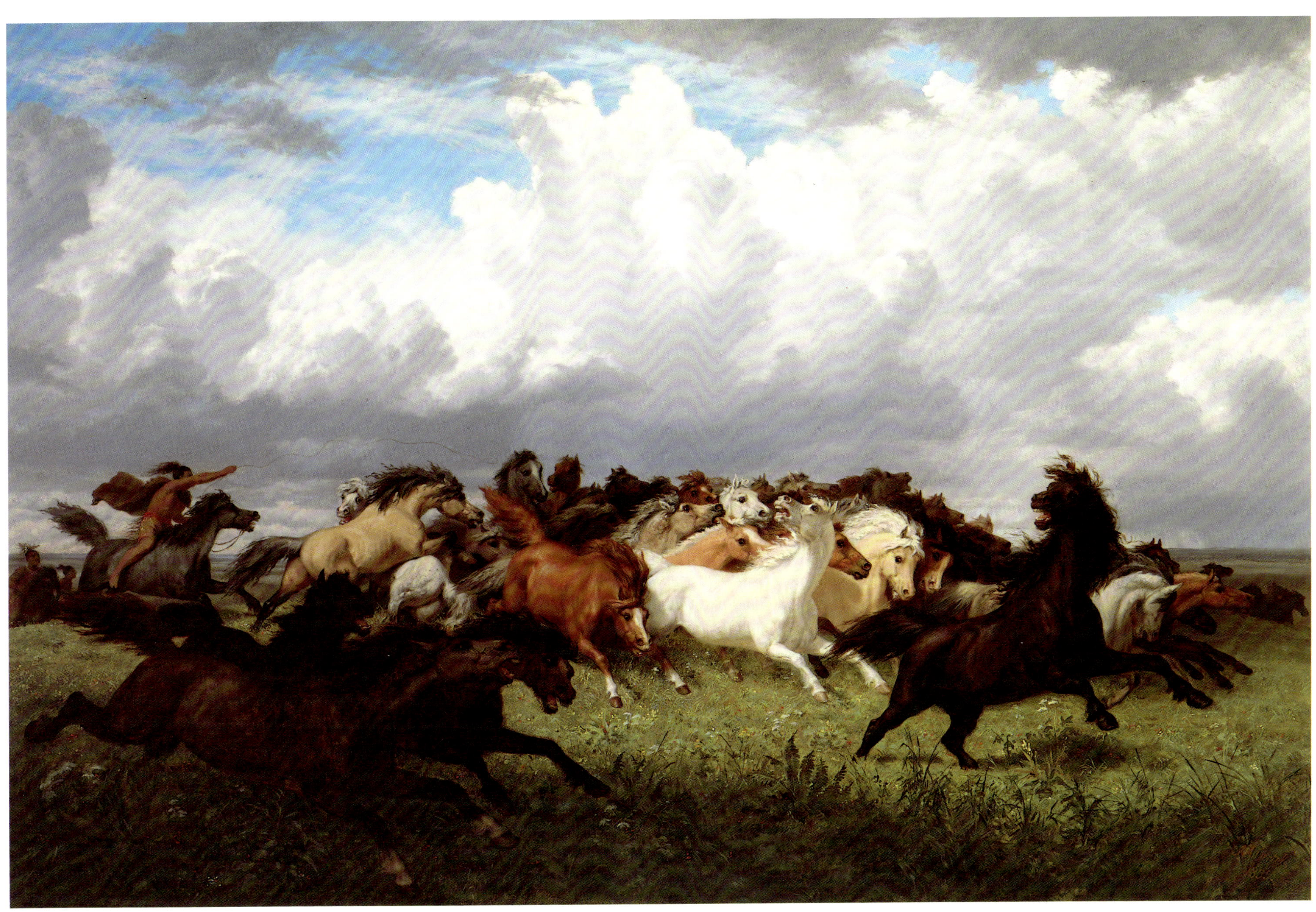

37

Raphaelle Peale (1774–1825)
Fruit in a Silver Basket 1814
oil on panel, 12½ x 19½ (31.8 x 49.5)

All the world's a stage,
And all the men and women merely players:
They have their exits and their entrances,
And one man in his time plays many parts,
His acts being seven ages.
(William Shakespeare, *As You Like It*, Act II, vii).

Still life has been viewed variously as the lowest and highest form of artistic expression. French academic theory in the seventeenth century put it at the bottom of a hierarchy of genres, trailing history painting, portraiture, and landscape.[1] By contrast, Wolfgang Born, author of the first survey of American still-life painting, compared it to chamber music.[2] For modern viewers, honed on abstraction and depreciating narrative, Born seems closer to the mark. Still life is like chamber music in its spareness, its emphasis on purity of form, its affirmation of reason over emotion. The scale is small, intimate. False notes are embarrassingly apparent; nothing is hidden beneath grandiose orchestration. Perfection seems near, yet so far. The appeal and power of still life, like chamber music, lies not only in its comprehensible scale, but in the fact that extraneous details are stripped away and what is left speaks to the responsive eye, simply and directly, of matters large and small. Of what do still lifes speak? Of relationships—connections, reflections, support, power, balance; of cause and effect; of things that have happened and will happen; of taste, touch, and smell; of man and nature; of markets and appetites and genetics and diet; of time, mortality, and regeneration. If we are to understand what a still life signifies, we must attend closely.

Raphaelle Peale's *Fruit in a Silver Basket*[3] depicts a small universe, perhaps two feet wide and shallower in depth, populated with things natural and man-made, seen and unseen, real and illusory. Three peppers, half a melon, and a silver basket containing golden apples and purple grapes sit on a shallow wooden ledge, possibly the top of a table.[4] An apple in the background peeks out from beneath the grapes. Presumably another piece of fruit behind the apple on the right keeps it from rolling back into the basket. A source of light, perhaps a window up and to the left, centered behind the front edge of the tabletop but in front of the produce, casts shadows and creates reflections. What the eye reads as the bottom of the center apple is actually the reflection of the tabletop in the curved side of the silver basket. The stem of the bunch of grapes behind the apple on the left and the far end of the basket handle are hidden from view.

There are special alliances and relationships within this small world. A golden band of three apples constitutes the strongest single visual element in the picture. In contrast to the coloristic consistency of the apples, three peppers introduce a note of change. The pepper on the left is dark green, its ripening neighbor lightens as it shades off from green to orange-red toward the stem, the one on the right is red with green stem and collar.

The silver basket engages in a formal dialogue with the melon. The basket resembles a boat with its stem pointing left while the stem end of the melon points right. The smooth, shiny shell of the silver vessel contrasts with the rough, yellow and dark-green mottled rind of the melon. Both are oval containers: the basket contains pieces of fruit; the melon is filled with its own flesh, white nearest the rim and light green around the seed-filled cavity. The trefoil punchwork around the rim of the basket, colored yellow by the apple behind it, echoes the melon's row of seeds.

The apples are regular in shape and color; the peppers are consistent in shape but changeable in color. The melon, grapes, and basket form a third triad of objects, similar in size but different in color, texture, and character. Parallel to the basket handle, the grapes tilt up to the right, pointing away from the melon and basket. It is as if these three elements have their backs to each other, affirming their individuality. Moreover the grapes blend into the dark background, truncating the pyramid of objects above which they seem to float. The composition becomes more insubstantial as it rises. In the lower register light projects the shadows of solid objects onto the wood surface. Above, there are reflections as well as shadows in the basket, trefoil voids instead of palpable seeds, and handles and tendrils that trace arcs in space as linear abstractions of the spherical solids below.

The scalloped outline of apples and melon strikes a motif of curves that pervades the image—the shapes of fruit and basket; looping tendrils, stems, and handle; the circles of collars and reflected highlights on the shiny peppers; round spots and blemishes on the apples; oval seeds, seed cavity, basket, and trefoils; the arrangement of objects curving forward from the green pepper on the left to the melon on the right, and then back through the fruit in the basket.

This is a silent world, but it is not static. Variety and change are introduced by contrasts, oppositions, and changing relationships that play throughout the picture. There is a basic contrast between that which is man-made and that which is natural. Wood has been planed to form a flat surface, and silver shaped into a geometrical version of natural form. Durable artifacts support and contain the perishable yield of nature. The table is flat, the objects it bears are round. The organic surfaces of wood and produce are warm to the touch, the silver appears cooler. The wood, silver, melon rind, and peppers are hard, or at least firm; the flesh of the melon, the grapes, and in varying degrees the apples are more yielding. The peppers, apples, and grapes are closed forms; the melon and basket are open. The fruit is sweet (and juicy); the red pepper is sweet too, in contrast to the green one.

Although the edge of the tabletop delineates a threshold and marks our exclusion from the pictured world, we are close to it. The openings at the left and right edges allow us visually, and almost physically, to embrace the scene as the basket holds the fruit. The peppers and melon frame a shallow proscenium, inviting the eye to enter through the opening center, our eye attracted by the bright reflection on the base of the basket, the brilliant red pepper, and the compositionally pivotal hinge located between melon, apple, and pepper where the diagonals of the receding melon and basket intersect.

The viewer is not the only human presence. The fruit and vegetables were picked and arranged on the table by an unseen hand; the melon was sliced. The artist has inscribed his name on the edge of the table on the right where the fruits and vegetables are most ripe and succulent, recording his act as well as his vision and his presence. The still life rests on a flat wooden surface; the artist has painted it on a flat wooden panel. The painting is the fruit of his effort, the produce of his hand. He marks the moment by inscribing the date. Time is sliced like the melon.

Although we witness a place and an instant of time memorialized for posterity, the image also speaks of past and future, of ripening and decay, of the slow, relentless rhythms of nature. Reading it temporally as well as spatially, we encounter a transformation that begins with the dark green pepper on the left and ripens to the red pepper. In the lower right a fully ripe melon, sliced open to reveal its sweet flesh, turns the composition back to the left and up to the adjacent mature golden apple. The next apple is marked with brown spots, the beginning of decay, while to the left, in the prow of the basket, a third apple rots, its skin broken open. The passage of time is recorded from unripeness through fruition to decay. But there is no tragedy. The melon, sliced open by a human act, reveals the promise of seeds, of regeneration. The rotting apple will open by itself in time, releasing the seeds that are hidden within. The movement through time, like the arrangement of the fruit and vegetables, is circular.

The line that leads from the melon to the rotting apple offers an alternative route. Instead of proceeding toward decay, the eye can turn up through the ascending grapes that fade into the background toward a more spiritual resolution, suggested by the halolike loop of the handle around the ripe apple. Here the promise is of eternal ripeness and sweetness rather than earthly decay and regeneration. Even the orbitlike path of the handle, reminiscent of an orrery, suggests the heavenly character of this region.[5]

The image evokes a sense of fullness. The table, basket, and melon are laden with content; the peppers, apples, and grapes are plump. The myriad circles also suggest fullness in the sense of completion, of return to beginnings. This is physical, but it is also temporal, the fullness of time. In its suggestions of the circular motion of time, Peale's *Fruit in a Silver Basket* is an abstract statement of a larger theme—

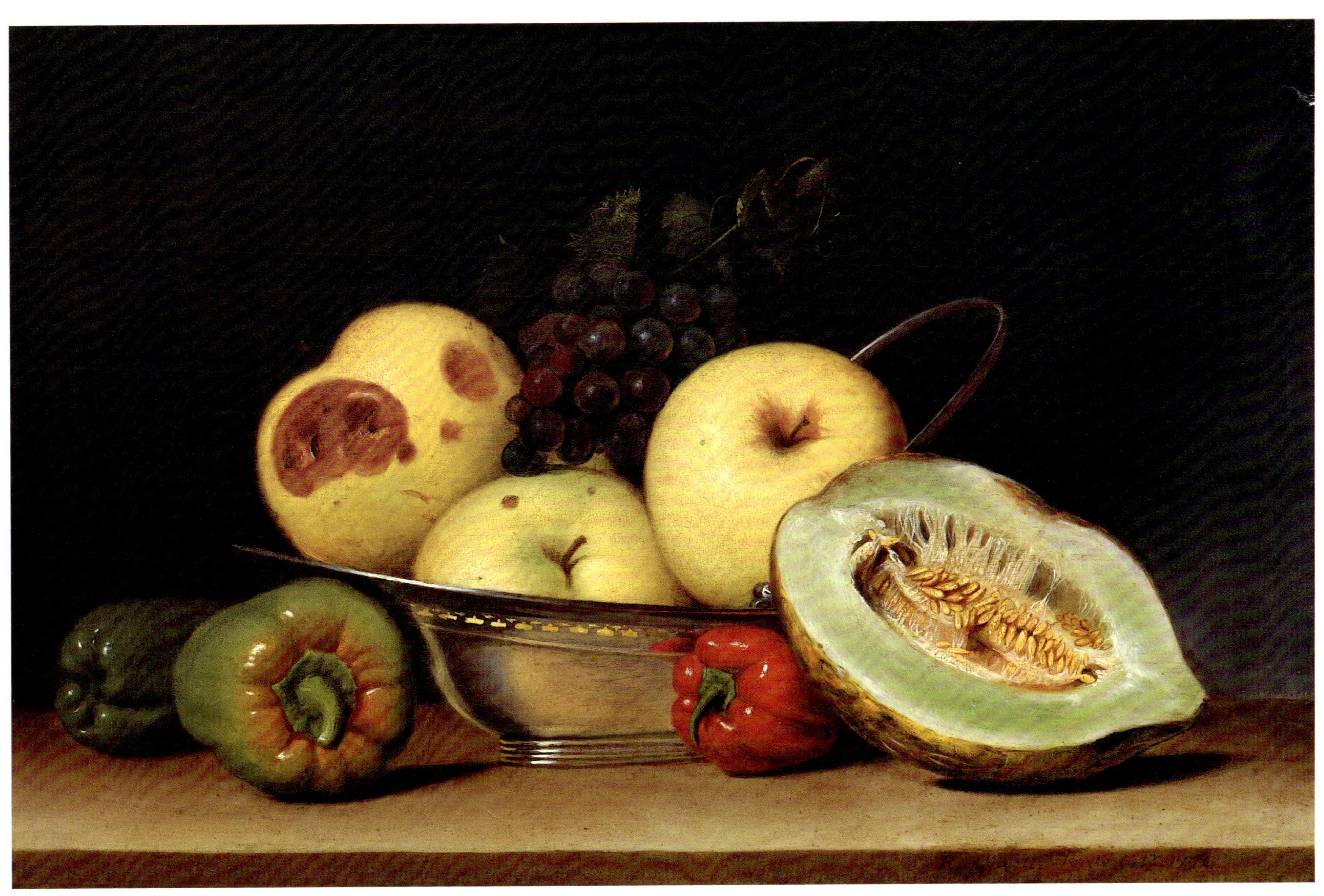

the cycle of life. With the grapes fading into the background, the other seven prominent pieces of fruit paraphrase and ennoble popular imagery of the seven stages of life, often shown as circular or as taking place on steps leading up to maturity and then down. But this *nature morte* is a more profound contemplation of the mystery of existence, of life and death, of physical and spiritual regeneration. Like chamber music, it carries simple means to complex ends. *Jules David Prown*

1. Rensselaer W. Lee, "*Ut Pictura Poesis*: The Humanistic Theory of Painting," *Art Bulletin* 22 (1940), 212–213.
2. Wolfgang Born, *Still Life Painting in America* (New York, 1947), 3.
3. This still life may very well be the one Peale offered to Charles Graff of Philadelphia in a letter dated 6 September 1816: *My old and inveterate enemy, the Gout, has commenced a most violent attack on me, two months previous, to its regular time—and most unfortunately on the day that I was to commence still life in the most beautiful productions of Fruit. . . . my left hand is in a most dreadful situation, & my Right Getting so bad as to be scarcely able to hold my Pen* [in] *this situation it is necessary to dispose of the Picture the fruit of which you so much admired, any alterations you may desire in the Picture on my recovery I will Exicute with a great deal of Pleasure, my fixt price was & would have been, but for this unfortunate attack, 40 dollars—therefore Sir if you feel disposed to Serve me I make a tender of this Picture to you for 30 Ds.* American Philosophical Society Library, quoted in Nicolai Cikovsky, Jr., *Raphaelle Peale Still Lifes* [exh. cat., National Gallery of Art] (Washington, 1988), 103–104.
4. It is difficult to resist the speculation that the produce depicted in this work was grown at Belfield, the farm outside Germantown that Peale's father, Charles Willson Peale, had acquired in 1810. Several months before this picture was completed, on 31 July 1814, the elder Peale had written from Belfield to his son Rembrandt that *My Garden is in good order* [?], *as indeed it ought to be for the expense of keeping a Gardiner that does no other work.* See Lillian B. Miller, ed., *Microfiche Edition of the Collected Papers of Charles Willson Peale and His Family* (Millwood, New York, 1980).
5. In 1803 Peale had published a new theory of the movement of astral bodies in space.

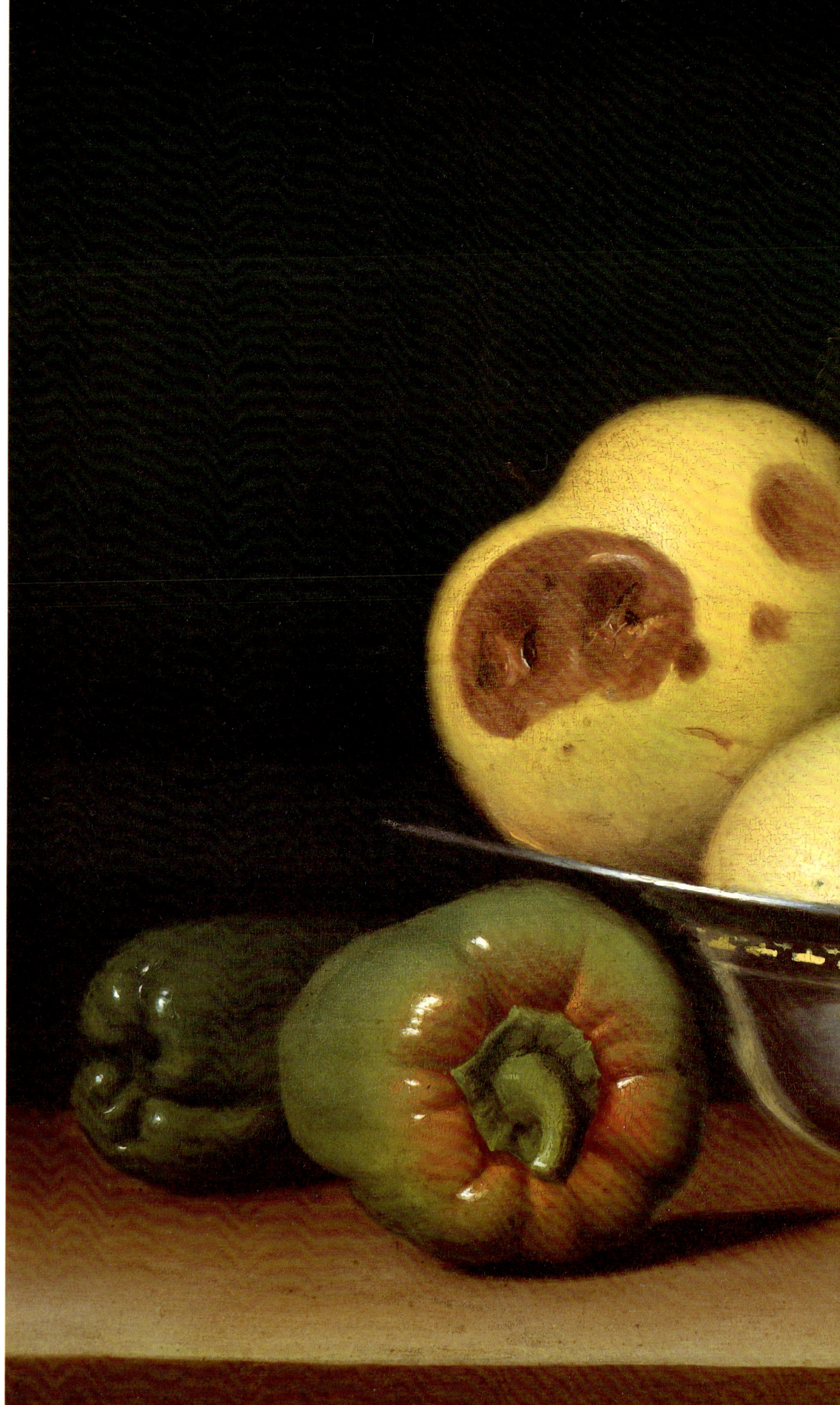

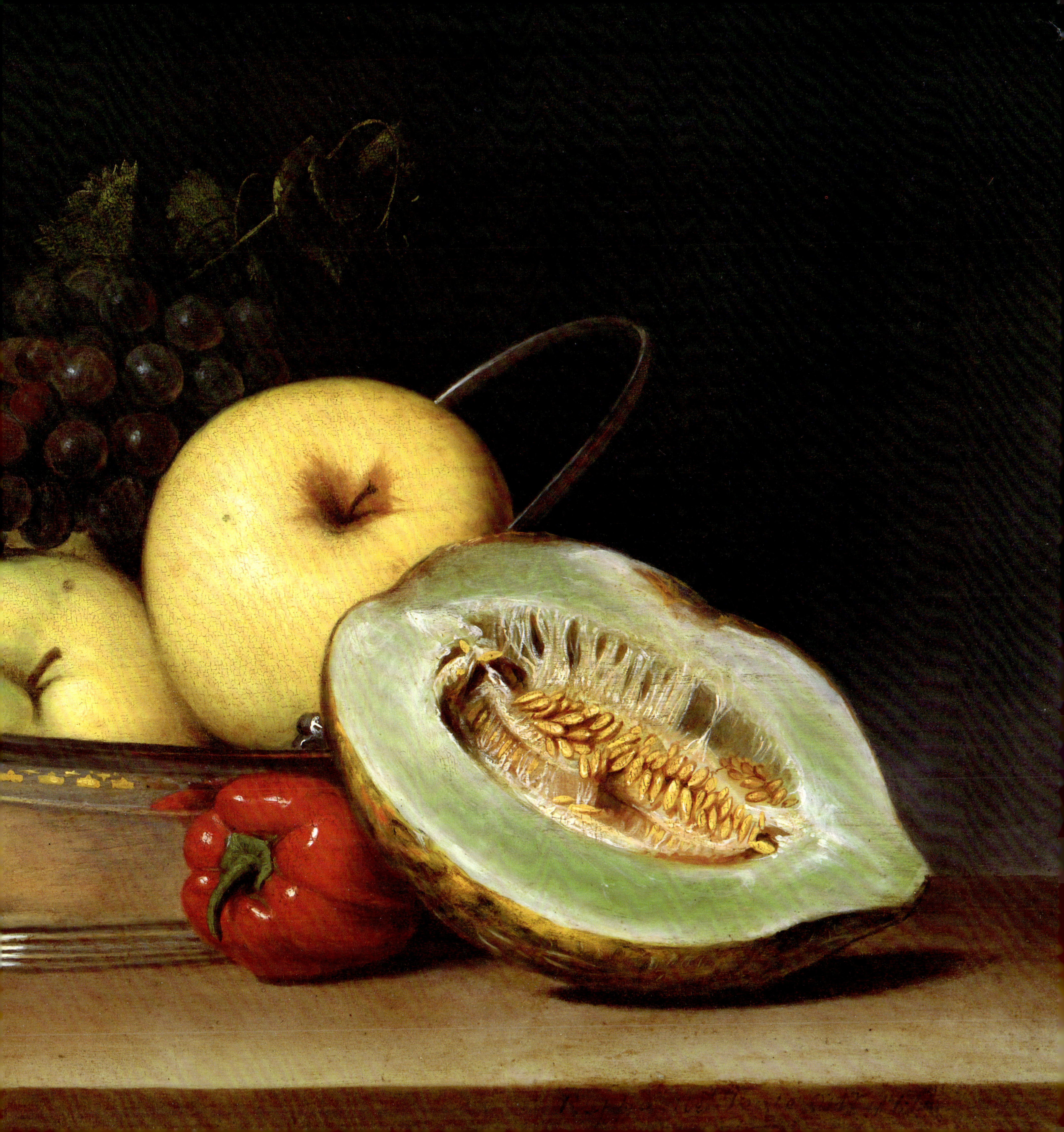

38

Robert Spear Dunning (1829–1905)
Apples 1869
oil on canvas, 19¾ x 25⅜ (50.2 x 64.5)

From his studio in Fall River, Massachusetts, Robert S. Dunning produced a plethora of still-life paintings that found their way into collections throughout the Northeast. His work typically consisted of an ornate piece of crystal or silver surrounded by a bounty of lush fruit. These seductive compositions frequently contained a honeycomb and a decorative fabric, all resting on a highly polished table.

In *Apples*,[1] however, Dunning departed from his opulent Victorian fruit pieces, and turned his composition into a moral commentary. The abundantly filled bag spills forth apples, sharing its bounty with the tattered straw hat; thus contrasting the believed relationship between bounty, plenty, and wealth to that of want, need, and poverty, and the joy of charity and giving. Dunning made a similar statement in his undated pendant *Still Life* (Samuel J. Doinsife Collection), where he added human elements to his composition to illustrate the act of giving or charity.[2]

Even though Dunning's work was not in the vanguard, his appeal was high. Bryant Chapin of the *Fall River Evening Herald* mentioned *Apples* in his review of the Dunning memorial show. *The old hat is amazingly natural both in color and texture and the tree trunk is worked out in infinite detail but keeps its place in complete subordination to the rest of the picture. Taken as a whole it is a unique concept and finely handled.* His review continued, *Poetic feeling and refinement are rare qualities in still life pictures but they exist in these pictures to a high degree.*[3] However, modern opinions began to find Dunning's work a bit staid for the twentieth-century eye, and with the exception of Fall River his work was to fall off into near obscurity. *James W. Tottis*

1. This work has been previously exhibited as *Autumn's Bounty*. The present title is based on historical descriptions of the work.
2. William H. Gerdts and Russell Burke, *American Still Life Painting* (New York, 1971), 174.
3. *Fall River Evening Herald*, 14 December 1911, 15.

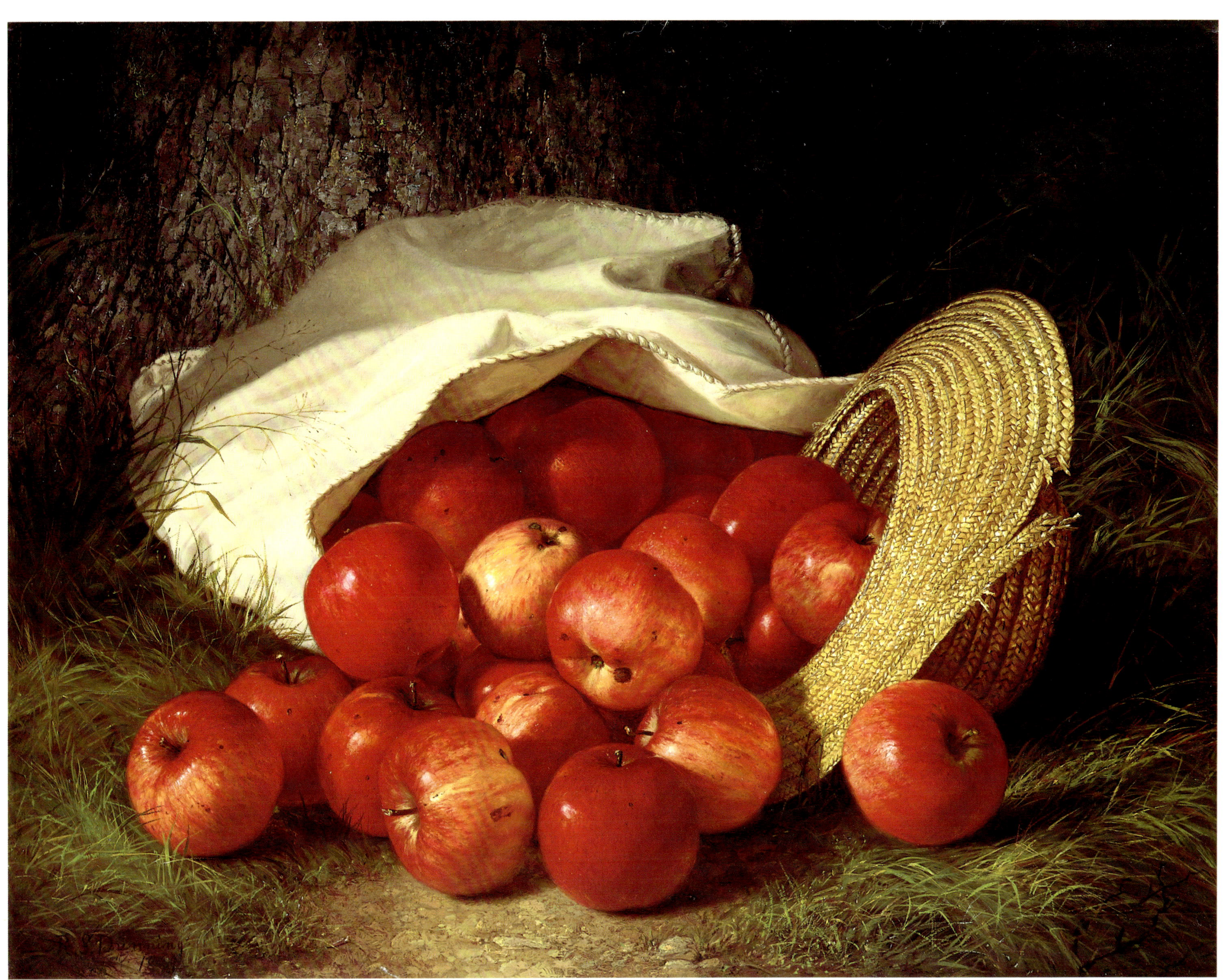

39

William Michael Harnett (1844–1892)
The Social Club 1879
oil on canvas, 13½ x 20¼ (34.3 x 51.4)

To a society obsessed with the idea of amassing collections of household objects that varied in interest and worth, William Harnett provided the perfect pictorial answer. He supplied the type of canvas that was well accepted in the male-dominated arenas, the office, club, and tavern. The compositions, especially those of his early years, consist of collectable objects, including beer steins, books, and pipes. *The Social Club* provides a key example of such a composition. Consisting of a collection of pipes with tobacco and a cigar box, Harnett arranged them as if they were a floral bouquet. He placed the four used pipes and four struck matches in a manner to suggest that a group of four persons had just left after "casually" placing their pipes on the marble shelf. For this post-party composition, Harnett created a surrealistic, dreamlike atmosphere where quiet solitude has replaced the joyous activity of a conversation group. Stylistically, it is representative of his early period, employing humble models (once Harnett moved to Europe his models became more elaborate). Painted in 1879, *The Social Club* was Harnett's sole representation that year at the Pennsylvania Academy in Philadelphia.[1]

Although the painting was sold, neither it nor Harnett received positive reviews. An anonymous critic considered his work to be not much more than a curiosity, and compared the trompe l'oeil composition to the work of a sign painter. The writer went further to say that great artists only use these devices as play and never as serious work.[2] This attitude was consistent with many contemporary critics, especially during the early years of Harnett's career. However, the same anonymous author dismissed Martin Johnson Heade's *Tropical Flowers* in much the same manner. Whatever varied opinions arose, Harnett's work sold well enough to send him to Europe in 1880. *James W. Tottis*

1. Kennedy Galleries, Inc., *The National Academy of Design Exhibition Record, 1861–1900*, vol. 1 (New York, 1973), 394.
2. Alfred Frankenstein, *After the Hunt: William Harnett and other America Still Life Painters 1870–1900* (Berkeley and Los Angeles, 1953), 50.

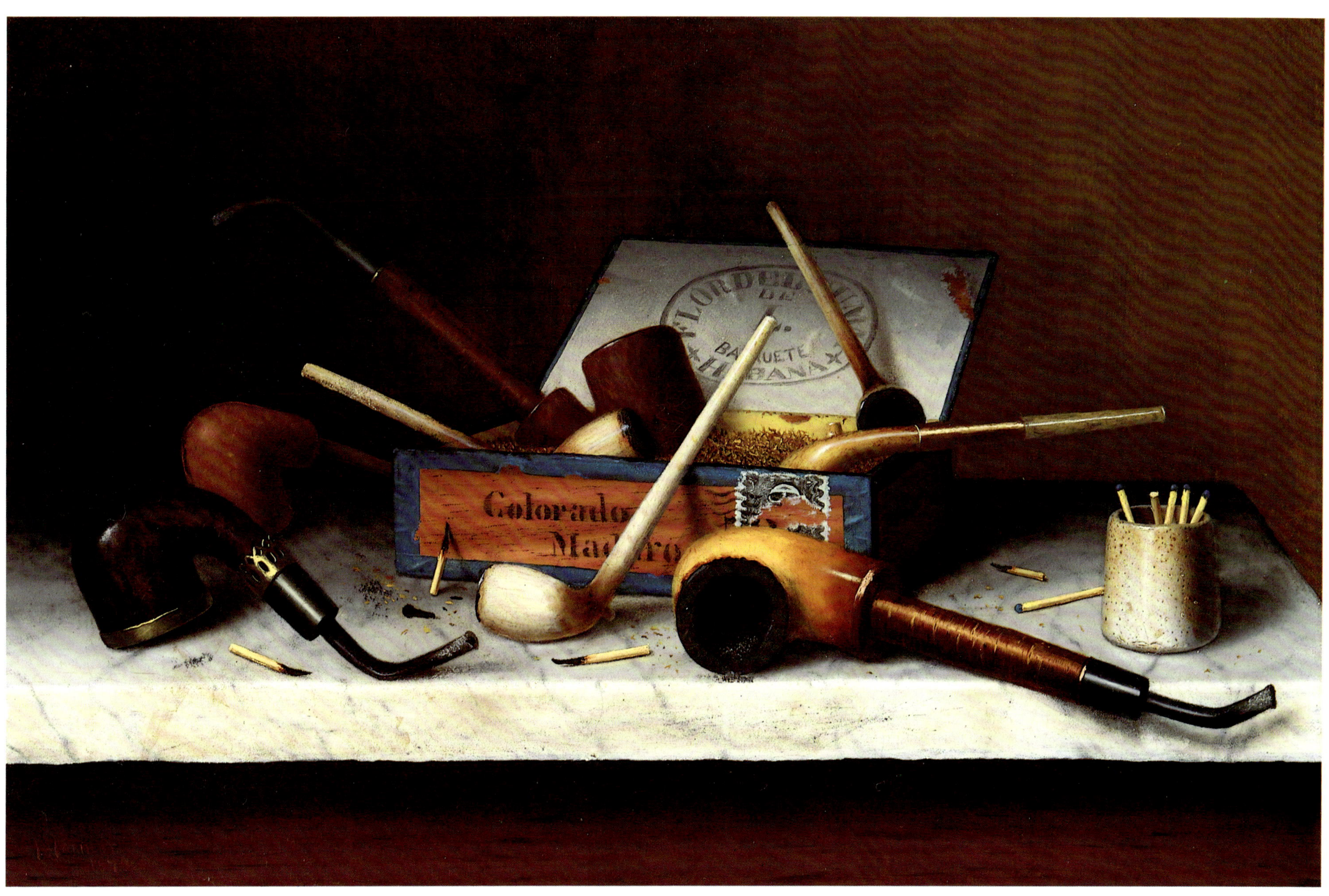
Colorado

40

William Michael Harnett (1844–1892)
Music 1886
oil on canvas, 46¼ x 38½ (117.5 x 97.8)

Harnett's work, as was his career, is often intertwined with mystery and intrigue. This work is a case in point. Previously titled *Still Life*, it is one of the larger canvases of his oeuvre. Painted in 1886[1] upon his return from Europe, it probably was based on a smaller work of 1885, *Still Life with Violin* (present whereabouts unknown). Exquisitely painted, Harnett seductively arranged some of his most treasured models—the porcelain jar, the old violin, one of his Turkish (Anatolian) rugs, and a Roman lamp—in a manner that allowed him to combine texture, tone, and substance on a life-size scale.

Harnett collected objects passionately for use as models. By the time of his death his studio was filled with scores of treasures, and in February 1893 these objects were sold at auction.[2] Lot 70, a Roman lamp from this sale, was described in the catalogue as appearing in his celebrated *Music*, as well as in works that were painted while he was in Europe.[3] Other objects used for this work, such as the Turkish rug, the violin, and the pitcher/jar, were also listed in the catalogue as appearing in *Music*. Contemporary accounts of *Music* tell us that it was commissioned by Theodore Stewart, who also purchased Harnett's 1885 version of *After the Hunt* (The Fine Arts Museums of San Francisco). An anonymous critic described it as a *clever painting called* Music—*a table on which rest some sheets of music, a violin, a lamp,* [and] *an old velum book. . . .*[4] Because Stewart died in 1887, *Music* had to be painted between Harnett's return to New York in 1886 and Stewart's death. This time frame and the descriptions make it clear that the dated Manoogian painting is *Music*. *Music* was a great success, therefore it is not surprising that Harnett painted a second smaller version, which was in his sister's collection (*Still Life*, 1887, Potamkin Collection).

Music is a superb example of Harnett's most lucrative period, in which he teases the senses and whets the appetite of his patron with the rich opulence of his antique models. Understandably, this canvas captured the admiration of the late-nineteenth-century public.

James W. Tottis

1. The Manoogian painting was previously dated as 1888. Close visual observation of this painting has shown that it was actually signed and dated 1886.
2. *Alfred Frankenstein Papers*, Archives of American Art, Smithsonian Institution, Washington, roll 1374, Blemly scrap book, Birch and Sons Catalogue.
3. *Frankenstein Papers*, Birch and Sons Catalogue. In the sales catalogue lot 69, another Roman lamp was pictured as lot 70. This is a known error because the description of lot 69 fits the lamp used in one of Harnett's last pictures, *Professor's Old Friends* (1891, William A. Farnsworth Library and Art Museum, Rockland, Maine).
4. *Alfred Frankenstein Papers*, Archives of American Art, Smithsonian Institution, Washington, roll 1374, Blemy scrap book, anonymous review, frame 328.

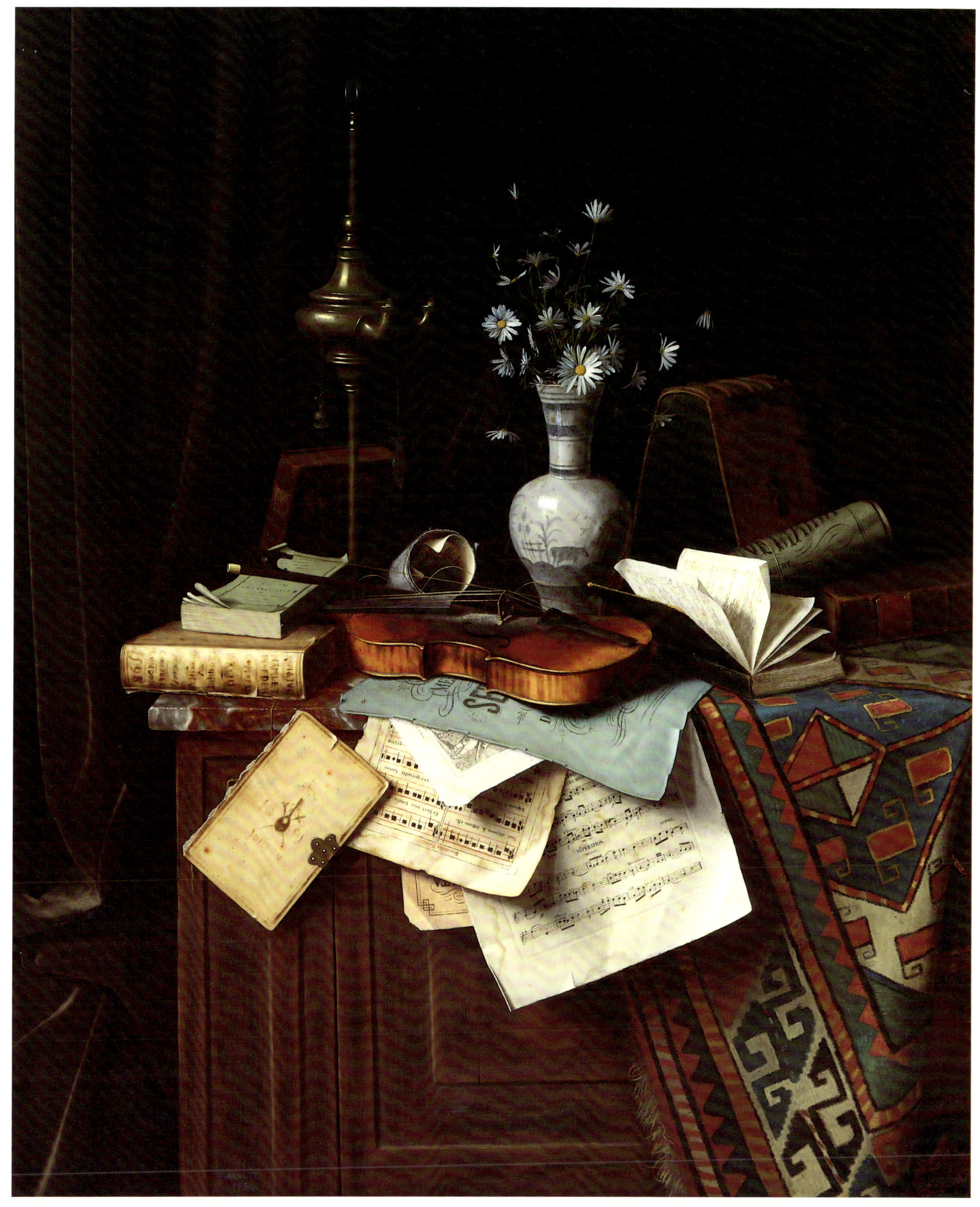

41

John Frederick Peto (1854–1907)
The Writer's Table: A Precarious Moment
probably 1890s
oil on canvas, 27⅛ x 22 (68.9 x 55.9)

As a Philadelphian trained at the Pennsylvania Academy, Peto was certainly familiar with that city's venerable and preeminent tradition of still-life painting, beginning with the works of the Peale family early in the nineteenth century and continuing to mid-century with the regularly exhibited examples of John F. Francis and Severin Roesen. Americans had variously looked to earlier European precedents in Dutch and Spanish seventeenth-century painting, and by the end of the nineteenth century there was also a revival of awareness of Chardin's still-life achievements. Aspects of this rich background find echoes in Peto's sensuous and sometimes stark tabletop compositions. Perhaps the most immediate conditioning influence on his style was the meticulous technique of his colleague William Michael Harnett's still-life arrangements of worldly objects and Victorian bric-a-brac. But after the early association in Philadelphia, Peto emerged from Harnett's shadow in mature work such as this, exploiting much more personally and forcefully rough textures of paint, strong combinations of color, and brightly lit forms set against often mysterious, impenetrable backgrounds. Here the variations of blues below and orange-reds above coexist as much in tension as in harmony. Peto has arranged his objects in a grouping that similarly seems caught between accident and contrivance. The eye is initially lulled into reading the solid and stable geometries of books, candlestick, inkwell, and mug, only to become aware of the awkwardly leaning positions of these forms, the bunched folds of the tablecloth, and the candle snuffer pushed to the unstable foreground edge. Books for Peto were embodiments of learning, here isolated before us to contemplate, even as their frayed condition insists on reminding us of time's sad passage. *John Wilmerding*

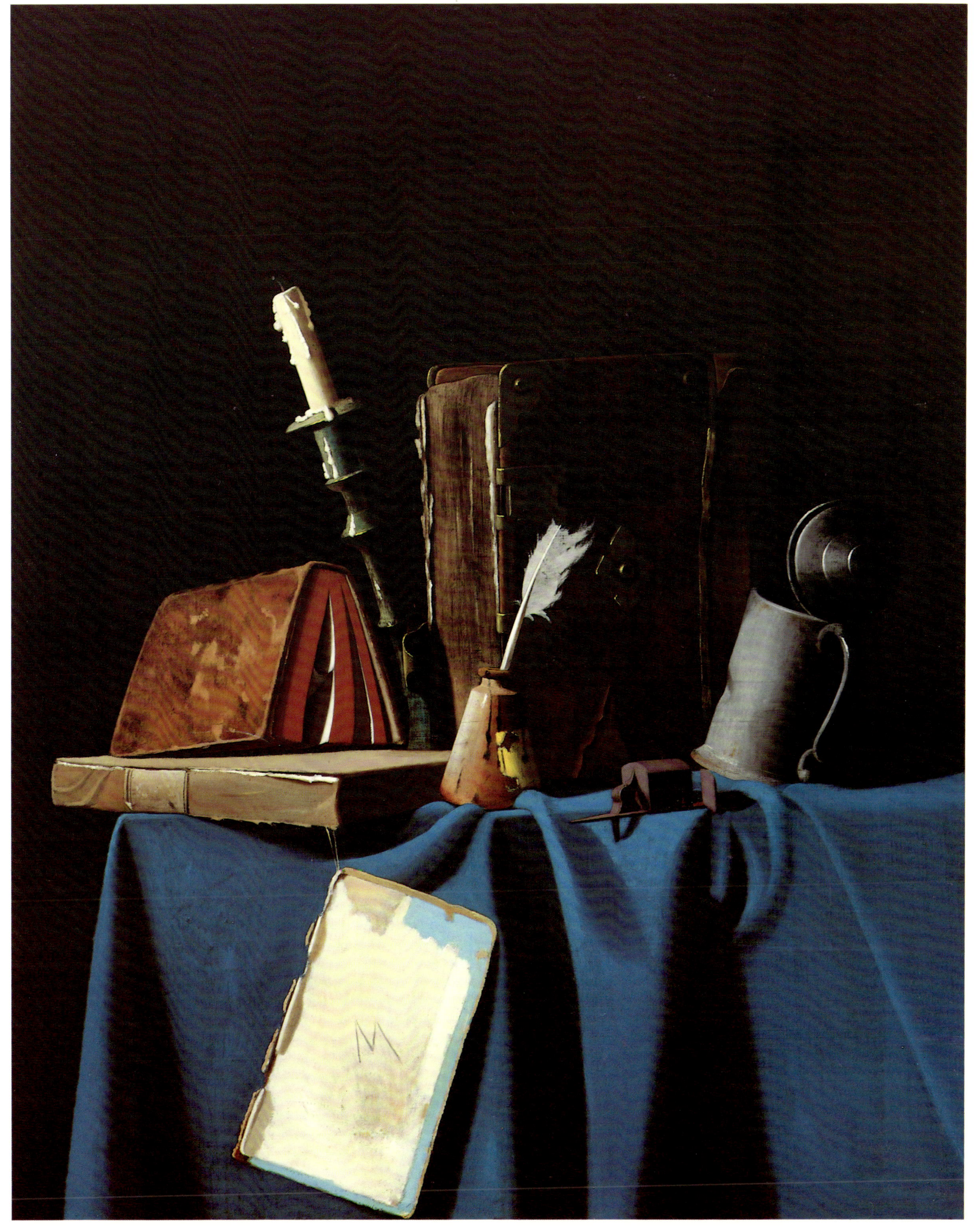
M

42

John Haberle (1856–1933)
The Changes of Time 1888
oil on canvas, 24⅜ x 20¼ (61.9 x 51.4)

Of the three major practitioners of trompe l'oeil still life in the United States during the last quarter of the nineteenth century—William Harnett, John Peto, and John Haberle—it is Haberle, according to Alfred Frankenstein, who was *the greatest American master of this tradition.*[1] The first paintings to bring Haberle attention concentrated for the most part on the subject of money; they depicted paper currency, sometimes combined with postage stamps, newspaper clippings, and photographs—other two-dimensional objects whose flatness made them effective subjects for "fool-the-eye" illusionism. Currency not only gave Haberle free rein to demonstrate his technical skills, but, since money was a widely popular artistic subject during the last quarter of the nineteenth century, it also allowed him to cater to a preexisting audience.[2]

Edward Nygren and Bruce Chambers recently have explored the theme of money in American painting, tracing its social, economic, and political relevance following the Civil War in the materialistic era known as the Gilded Age. They conclude that the Greenback party, the government policy on bimetallism, financial speculation and corruption, rapid industrialization, the emergence of the American millionaire and the subsequent growing chasm between the rich and the poor, the rise of counterfeiting, and appearance of the economic novel all fueled the nation's interest in money during the late nineteenth century and the artists' fascination with the subject.[3]

William Harnett's *Five Dollar Bill* (1877, Philadelphia Museum of Art) is the earliest known example of the currency genre. Its depiction of a single bill, seen against a plain dark background parallel to the picture plane, was at first imitated, then used by other artists as a springboard for more elaborate paintings. Counterfeiting, which had been a rampant problem following the Civil War, was still a significant concern to the national government in the 1880s, and Harnett stopped painting money in 1886 at the request of the Secret Service, which that year also seized one of his paintings. John Haberle, on the other hand, though the government's concern about money paintings was foolish and he seems to have enjoyed teasing the authorities. Haberle exhibited his *Imitation* (1887, Berry-Hill Galleries) in 1887 at the National Academy of Design in New York. The painting contained not just one bill but two, plus coins, stamps, and a tintype photograph of the artist. Harnett himself was reported to have said *that he had never seen such reproduction anywhere.* And the bills were so accurate that they elicited a warning from the Secret Service that probably only encouraged the artist.[4] In any case, he created a number of similar paintings and exhibited them widely (*Reproduction*, c. 1887, private collection; *U.S.A.*, c. 1889, Collection of Jo Ann and Julian Ganz, Jr.; *Can You Break a Five?*, c. 1888, Amon Carter Museum, Fort Worth; *One Dollar Bill*, 1890, Berry-Hill Galleries, New York; and *Twenty Dollar Bill*, 1890, Museum of Fine Arts, Springfield, Massachusetts).

Just a year after the exhibition of *Imitation*, Haberle produced a currency painting of intricate complexity, a work that concerns money, illusion, history, and the theme of *vanitas*. *The Changes of Time*, exhibited at the 1889 exhibition of the Pennsylvania Academy of the Fine Arts, is the culminating statement of John Haberle's series of currency paintings. In its complex composition and illusionistic detail, it is arguably his masterwork.[5]

On a dark blue-gray weathered cabinet door Haberle placed a disorderly pile of postage stamps, coins, and paper currency. The oldest pieces, two Connecticut Colonial shilling notes, are in the upper part of the composition, while more recent bills—fifty-dollar and one-dollar bills from the Confederacy, twenty-five and fifty cent fractional notes, and a one-dollar greenback—occupy the middle and lower parts of the door. Haberle, in an ironic bow to the Secret Service, revealed on the reverse side of the greenback the government's warning against counterfeiting.[6] The most prominent bill in the group is the newest, a five-dollar bill, the denomination first painted by Harnett. But, unlike Harnett's five, Haberle's is a crisp silver certificate with a portrait of U. S. Grant from a series of 1886, the year Harnett was warned to stop painting currency.[7] The white bill contrasts with the others, which are yellowed and worn with use, and it forms the focus of a strong diagonal line, anchored at opposite ends by a photograph of a young woman at upper left and a blue envelope at lower right, addressed to Haberle in New Haven. The envelope dates the painting (there is an *88* near the stamp that is the counterpart to the partially obscured *88* at the upper left of the door) and reinforces the identity of the artist, whose tintype portrait sits on top of the envelope.[8] The letter within demonstrates Haberle's remarkable skills; the paper is so thin that we can see the writing on the reverse.

A less obvious diagonal line, creating an "X" with the other, runs between a clump of stamps at lower left and a magnifying glass at upper right that appears to hang from a nail by a frayed cord. Like the pair of spectacles Haberle depicted in *Can You Break a Five?*, the lens of the glass is cracked and partly covers a torn newspaper clipping with words of praise about Haberle's first money painting: *entirely with a brush and with the naked* [ey]*e*/*"Imitation" No. 362, by J. Haberle . . . a*/[r]*emarkable piece of imitation of natura*[l] *ob-*/ [j]*ects and a most deceptive* trompe l'oil [sic]. The lens of the magnifying glass aptly replaces most of the word *eye*. The minute detail and invisible brushwork that allow us to read this tiny message distinguish Haberle's work from that of Harnett and Peto.[9]

What does the door on which these objects rest conceal? We glimpse a piece of paper jutting out, enticing us to look inside. But even if we could open the satyr's-head lock with the key dangling from its mouth, we would be unable to see inside, since the door is nailed shut above the lock and at bottom right. Haberle tweaks the viewer's inquisitive nature.

The cabinet door is framed by a border that resembles oak-colored wood with "carved" medallions containing portraits of the presidents (some of which are echoed on the bills and stamps). The inner edge of the border includes their dates of office, correct except for the three most recent.[10] Washington is at top center, encircled with laurel leaves. John Adams is to the right, Jefferson to the left. Then the presidents alternate from left to right sides until Hayes, where they begin to follow the left side of the border. The last president depicted is Benjamin Harrison, a Republican elected by a narrow margin in the year the painting was executed, but not inaugurated until 1889. This tells us that the painting, which is dated 1888, was created in either November or December. A U.S. Navy button, having slipped from its place above, obscures the end of Harrison's term, which would have been unknown to Haberle at this time, while four vacant medallions at the right side of the lower border remain to be filled by the presidents who will lead the country into the twentieth century. Between each medallion are fasces, bundles of rods which were common in political imagery of the nineteenth century and became symbols, in the 1850s and early 1860s, of union.[11]

Group portraits of the presidents go back to at least the time of James Madison. Usually done at the time of inauguration and featuring the current president in the center, they sometimes also enframed historical scenes or other patriotic images. By late in the nineteenth century, presidential portraits served as border decoration not only in prints, but also in other political memorabilia such as broadsides, sheet music, and even handkerchiefs. Haberle's "frame," then, might at first glance be dismissed as merely traditional decoration. However, the fact that, in Haberle's painting, the presidents surround money in various forms (even postage stamps were used as money during the Civil War) gives the painting a different connotation. It is money that has the place of honor and veneration, surrounded by our national leaders, past and present. Money is at the center of politics.[12]

The painting's title, *The Changes of Time*, appears at the bottom center of the painting, tacked over the medallion in the form of a coin (surrounded by laurel leaves like the Washington portrait directly above it). As with other Haberle paintings, the title carries multiple layers of meaning. The formal succession of presidents symbolizes the orderly changes and passage of time, from the beginning of our country to the present. The various types of currency also imply change, though in not such an orderly fashion, and recall our nation's trials and triumphs. Colonial shillings remind us of the Revolutionary War, the bill depicting Washington likewise calls to mind the founding of our nation, the Confederate bills portraying Jefferson Davis and Stonewall Jackson signify the Civil

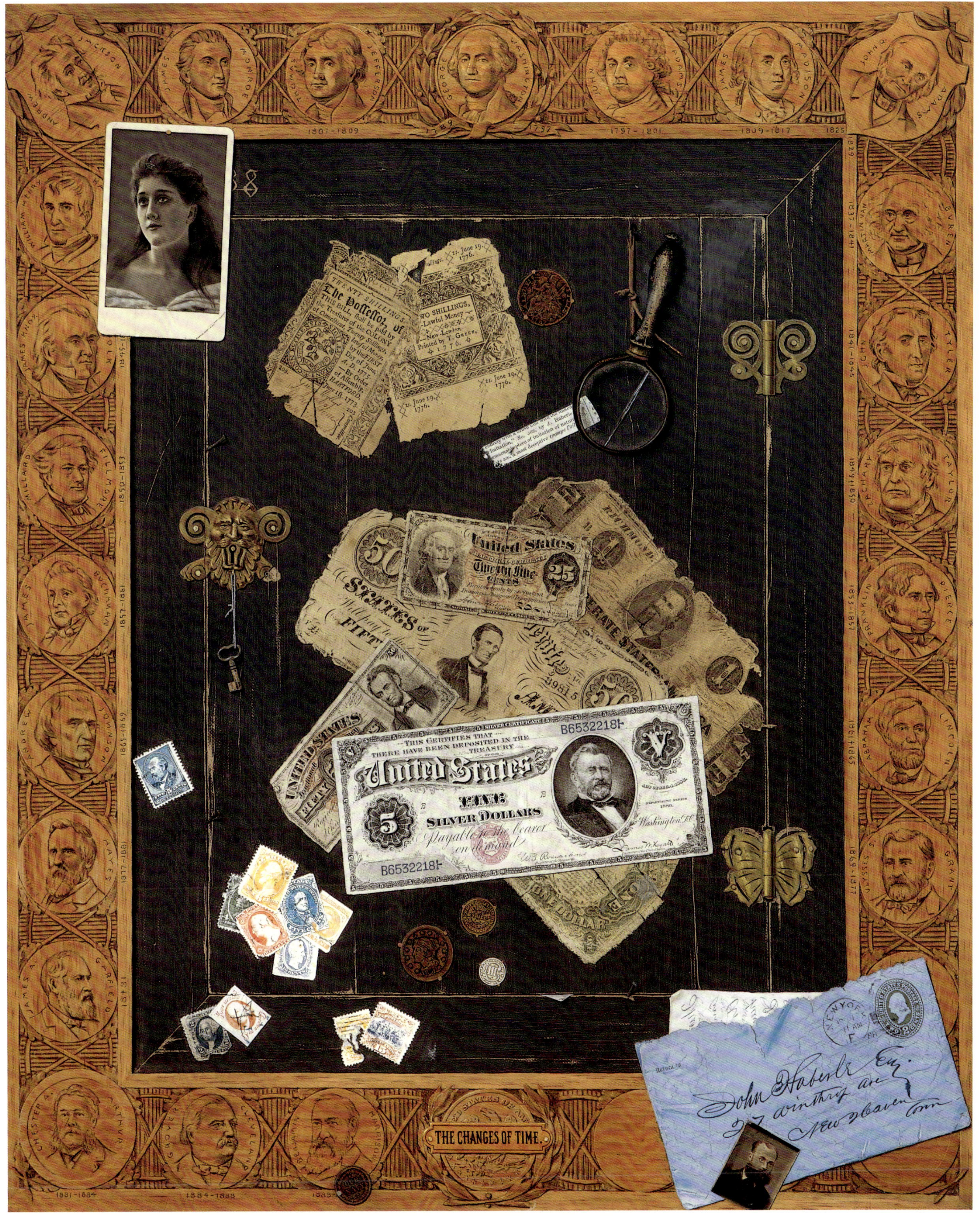

THE CHANGES OF TIME.
United States
FIVE
SILVER DOLLARS
B6532218
TWO SHILLINGS,
Lawful Money
United States
Twenty five
CENTS

War, and the fifty-dollar bill with Lincoln the assassination of that president. The most recent bill features U. S. Grant, whose term was known for its corruption.

For the pun-loving Haberle the coins and fractional notes are another kind of change, the smaller money you get in exchange for a larger bill.[13]

The concept of the passage of time is reinforced by the wear and tear exhibited by the objects in the painting, particularly the older currency, newspaper clipping, cabinet door, postage stamps, and magnifying glass. The transience and vanity of material possessions, especially money, is called forth by these worn and tattered objects, symbols of *vanitas*. The seemingly disorderly arrangement of the currency emphasizes its relative worthlessness, and it seems inevitable that the crisp five-dollar silver certificate will eventually become as decrepit as the other notes. The beauty of the young woman in the photograph, too, will gradually fade.

Finally, this tour-de-force of illusionism is a brash advertisement for Haberle himself. His name, address, and photographic portrait, placed over the four empty medallions, indicate he may have immodestly seen himself as an important presence in the nation's—or at least the art world's—future. And the newspaper clipping, praising Haberle's achievements (actually a combination of two earlier reviews), has been selectively edited to omit the critic's reference to his trompe l'oeil painting as *without being in any sense a work of art*.[14]

In *The Changes of Time* Haberle invites the viewer to contemplate such sober issues as the passage of time, vanity of earthly possessions, and the country's preoccupation with money while, with an irreverent wit and hearty bravado, he entices us to laugh at his tricks and marvel at his technical accomplishments. *Linda Ayres*

1. Alfred Frankenstein, *After the Hunt: William Harnett and Other American Still Life Painters* (Berkeley and Los Angeles, 1953, rev. ed. 1969), 115. It was reported in 1898 that Haberle's *imitative work, now that Harnett is dead, is held as the best in the country*. Jane Marlin, "John Haberle: A Remarkable Contemporaneous Painter in Detail," *Illustrated American* 24 (30 December 1898), 516.
2. William M. Harnett (1848–1892), John F. Peto (1854–1907), Jefferson David Chalfant (1856–1931), Otis Kaye (1885–1975), Nicholas A. Brooks (active 1890–1904), Victor Dubreuil (active 1880–1910), and Haberle ranked among those artists for whom money served as subject matter.
3. Edward J. Nygren, "The Almighty Dollar: Money as a Theme in American Painting," *Winterthur Portfolio* 23 (summer/autumn 1988), 129–150, and Bruce W. Chambers, *Old Money: American Trompe L'Oeil Images of Currency* [exh. cat., Berry-Hill Galleries, Inc.] (New York, 1988). Nygren noted on page 129 that money was repeatedly referred to in the popular press and cartoons of the day. I thank both authors for sharing information with me.
4. Letter, Thomas B. Clarke to W. M. R. French, 12 July 1888, in Gertrude Grace Sill, *John Haberle: Master of Illusion* (Springfield, Massachusetts, 1985), 9. Alfred Frankenstein, "Haberle: or the Illusion of the Real," *Magazine of Art* 41 (October 1948), 224, reported that a newspaper clipping found in Haberle's house stated that the *artist painted bank bills so accurately that the Secret Service men compelled him to desist*.

   As Bruce Chambers points out, the title *Imitation* might refer not only to Haberle's accurate imitation of currency—which extended to authentic serial numbers and signatures on the bills—but also to his imitation of the work of the more established artist Harnett. Chambers, *Old Money*, 24. It was reported that the illusionism in *Imitation* was so persuasive that in *strict violation of the rules of the Academy, glass was finally put over the picture to keep the fingers from picking at the canvas*. Marlin, *Haberle*, 516. *U.S.A.* also caused problems for Haberle when it was exhibited at the Art Institute of Chicago in 1889. A local critic accused Haberle of pasting real bills to the canvas. Haberle traveled to Chicago to prove otherwise, and a retraction was printed in the Chicago *Inter-Ocean* on 7 July 1889. See Frankenstein, *After the Hunt*, 117.
5. Frankenstein, *After the Hunt*, 118, reported that Haberle asked the relatively high price of $2,200 for the painting at the time of the exhibition. *The Changes of Times* was purchased by Marvin Preston, who collected Haberles and hung them in Churchill's, the Detroit saloon he managed.
6. Haberle also used this conceit in *Can You Break a Five?*, which reveals even more of the warning.
7. Chambers, *Old Money*, 27–31, 35, 36, discussed the silver certificate and its significance in light of the late-nineteenth-century debate in America between the monometallists and the bimetallists. He also noted that Haberle omitted important types of money, including state and national banknotes. He believes that the "sound money" party, whose philosophy he feels Haberle shared, would have considered the money depicted as worthless.
8. The tintype is also seen in *Reproduction* and *Imitation*. Sill, *Haberle*, 21–22, discussed items that Haberle recycled in various paintings.
9. Frankenstein, *After the Hunt*, 116, believes that Haberle's meticulous style can be attributed to the scientific illustrations he created for Othniel Charles Marsh at Yale. Although Haberle was not credited with any of the illustrations, it appears likely that he created some of the drawings of fossils and was working with Marsh as early as 1876. See Zelda Edelson and Barbara L. Narenda, "John Haberle, A Great American Artist and His Links to the Peabody Museum," *Discovery* 20 (1987), 24–30.

   The clipping actually combines quotes from two separate reviews. The first part of the clipping is also seen in *U.S.A.* and *Can You Break a Five?*. The second part comes from the New York *Evening Post* which included the misspelling of trompe l'oeil. Sill, *Haberle*, 42.

   Chambers, *Old Money*, 35, theorizes that the magnifying glass in place of the "eye" might refer to the artist's deteriorating eyesight.
10. The dates for Monroe, Jackson, and W. H. Harrison and the end date of Polk's tenure are covered by the photograph of the young woman. Haberle was usually meticulous in the information presented—even to the point of placing a cross between the dates of those presidents who died in office—but he inexplicably erred in the dates for Arthur (1881–1885), Cleveland (1885–1889), and B. Harrison whose term of office began in 1889. I thank Bruce Chambers for pointing out the crosses.
11. I am grateful to Bruce Chambers for identifying the Navy button, previously thought to be a coin. The significance of the button in unknown; Benjamin Harrison had served as a brigadier general.

    Fasces were borne before Roman magistrates as an emblem of official power and symbols of the Roman republic. Fasces were used in Lincoln's campaign and also as symbols of the nativists, the group of second- and third-generation Americans who were anti-immigrant and anti-Catholic. I thank Bernard Reilly at the Library of Congress for the information on fasces in political imagery.
12. Nygren, "Dollar," 139, fig. 10, illustrated an earlier version of the genre, Nathaniel Currier's *The Presidents of the United States*, 1844, Library of Congress.

    Haberle's painting may have served as inspiration for a large print produced in 1889 in celebration of the hundredth anniversary of George Washington's inauguration. *The Presidents of the United States* (Beckerman Brothers Art Publishers, Chicago) features similar presidential portraits in medallions, with simulated wood planking behind them. I thank Bernard Reilly for calling this print to my attention.
13. This was pointed out by Sill, *Haberle*, 42.
14. See note 9.

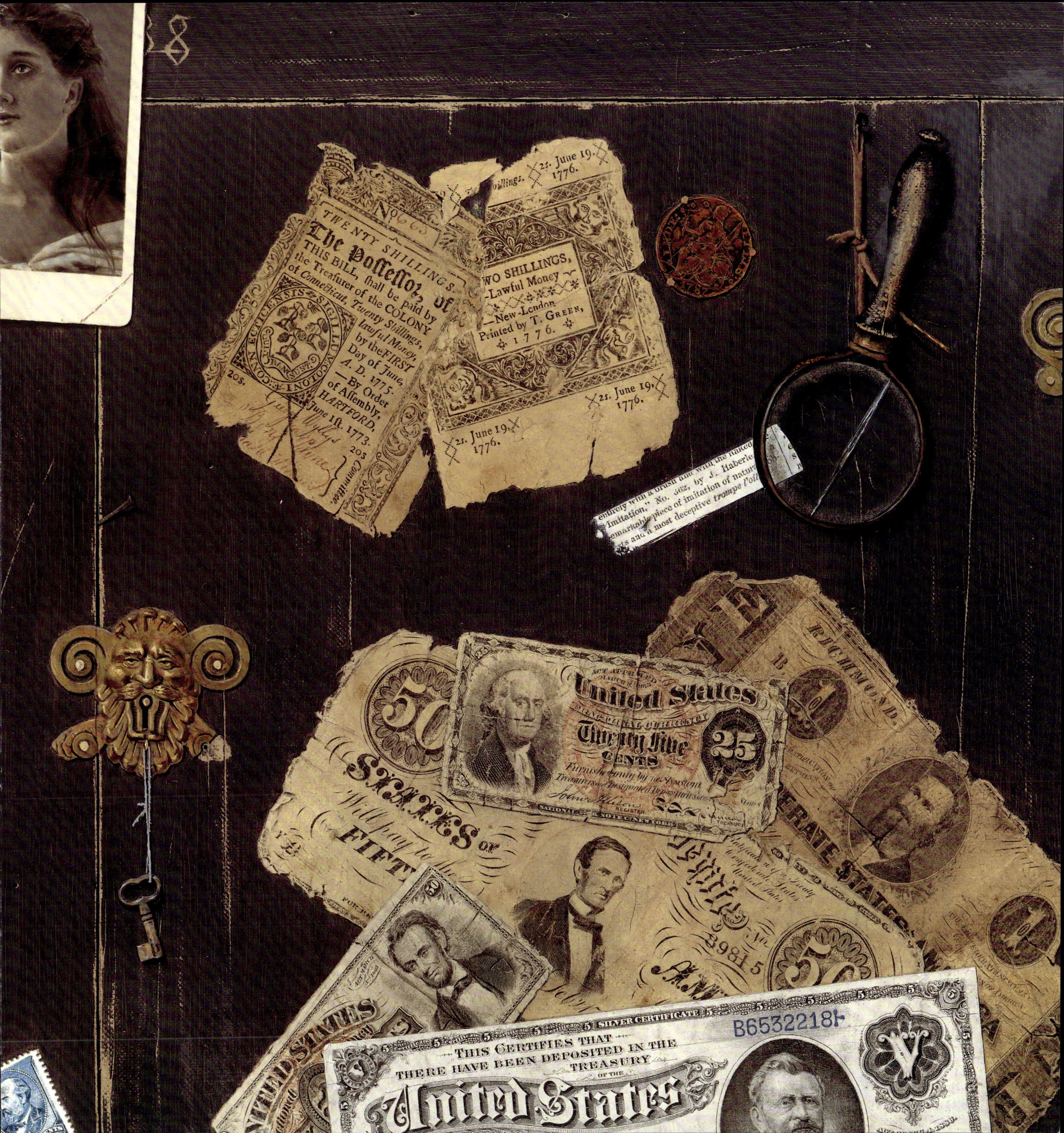

43

John Frederick Peto (1854–1907)
Old Time Letter Rack 1894
oil on canvas, 30 x 25⅛ (76.2 x 63.8)

In his fully mature style Peto evolved two distinct types of still-life painting: tabletop compositions and arrangements of hanging objects on illusionistic wall boards or doors. Whereas the former concentrated on the three-dimensional textures and masses of forms tightly set on the receding platforms of a table or shelf, this second category exploited the even more demanding illusionism of objects placed against an upright flat plane at one with the canvas itself. As with many of Peto's subjects, there were well-known precedents for this format in seventeenth-century Dutch and eighteenth-century English art as well as in examples occasionally executed by his friend Harnett and other contemporary colleagues such as John Haberle. But far more than they, Peto became intensely preoccupied by the so-called office board and letter rack designs, both as forms of personal history and as challenging exercises in visual playfulness. These works incorporated not only the commonplace bric-a-brac of his daily life and household, but also subtler references to the more private pressures of his inner thoughts and artistic concerns. The cropped upside-down photograph, for example, at the center left here is almost certainly a portrait bust photograph of Lincoln that Peto often used at this time, thought to have been an image of untimely loss associated with the recent death of Peto's father. The general wear and tear of things more broadly evokes the poignant sense of change in fin-de-siècle America, while the striking abstraction of design and color signals Peto's unconscious predictions of modernism.

This particular rack picture began the second of two series Peto undertook, the first in the late 1880s much lighter in palette and crisper in execution. After a period devoted to other themes, he took up the format again in the late nineties and early 1900s with a greater feeling of gravity and psychological resonance. This painting is also notable for its history of having long borne a false Harnett signature, symptomatic of the confusion in artistic personalities that has haunted our appreciation of Peto until recent years. *John Wilmerding*

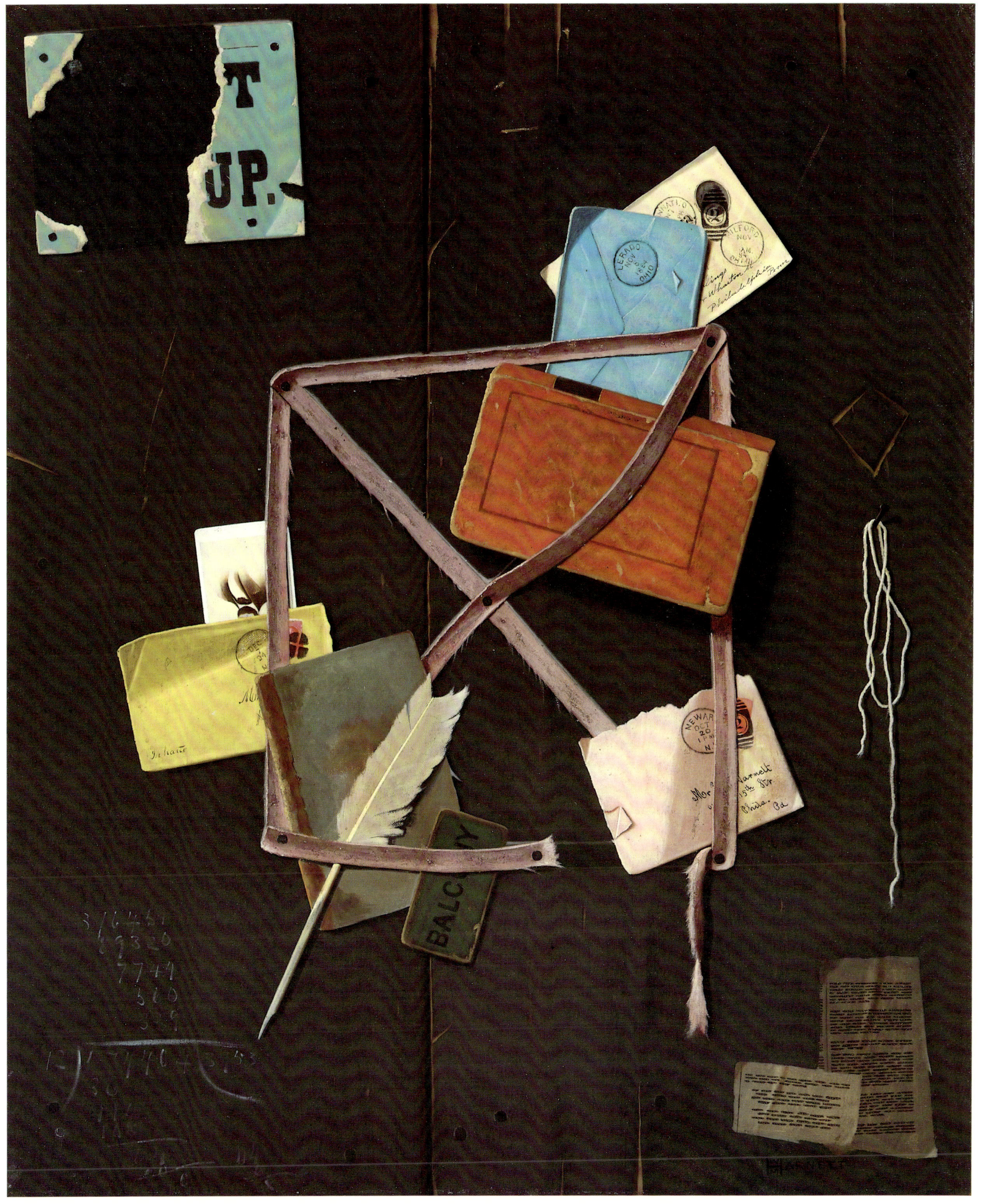

44

Martin Johnson Heade (1819–1904)
The Gems of Brazil c. 1863–1864
sixteen oil paintings on canvas, each 12¼ x 10 (31.1 x 25.4), mounted on four panels

upper left: Ruby-Topaz (Chrysolampis mosquitus)
upper right: Brazilian Ruby (Clytolaema rubricauda)
lower left: Black-throated Mango (Anthracothorax nigricollis)
lower right: Amethyst Woodstar (Calliphlox amethystina)

The Gems of Brazil was the most complex and ambitious project of Martin Johnson Heade's entire career. Although he apparently finished the twenty individual works that composed the series, he was never able to complete the project he intended, the publication of a lavish book illustrated with chromolithographs of the paintings.[1] *The Gems* thus might be seen as a metaphor of sorts for Heade's artistic career. They were works of great originality and beauty and were conceived with considerable intellectual effort and creative energy. Yet the artist failed to achieve with them all that he envisioned and hoped for, whether through poor timing, misjudging his audience, or simply because of bad luck. *The Gems* might have made Heade famous in America in the 1860s, when successful painters were among the most admired, and most richly compensated, citizens of the land. But they did not; few of his contemporaries probably even knew of their existence, and fewer still ever saw them. Over the course of his career Heade would find fame and recognition always elusive, even though he created works of often startling beauty and imagination, and even though he was a master of several genres. He was known to New York artists and art critics and to a few patrons, but remained just enough out of the mainstream to be regarded as eccentric. Despite moments of exceptional creativity and achievement, as in *The Gems of Brazil*, Heade never enjoyed the success that he must have felt was due him.

The origins of Heade's fascination with hummingbirds are unknown, but he admitted that he had been since *early boyhood . . . almost a monomaniac* on the subject.[2] Nor is it clear just when and how he arrived at the idea of writing and illustrating a book describing Brazilian hummingbirds. It has been suggested that the idea came from his friend the Reverend James C. Fletcher (1823–1901), a diplomat, writer, and naturalist.[3] In a lengthy book Fletcher coauthored, entitled *Brazil and the Brazilians*, he took special note of hummingbirds, one of which he described as a *little winged gem*.[4] Moreover, Fletcher was acquainted with the young emperor of Brazil, Dom Pedro II (1825–1891), who had a strong interest in natural history and the arts and who may well have been involved in the initial conception of *The Gems of Brazil*.[5] Whatever the case, Heade was in Brazil by late 1863 and would remain there for about a year.

If the *Gems of Brazil* project was the major impetus for Heade's first South American trip it was not the only one, because while there he also painted several landscapes. One of these, *Sunset—View of Rio de Janeiro, from São Domingos* (fig. 1), was exhibited in 1864 at the Academy of Fine Arts in Rio.[6] Heade was just beginning to find his way as a landscape painter in the early 1860s, yet *Sunset—View of Rio* is painted with considerable authority and sophistication. Although it may have owed something to the South American works of Heade's friend Frederic Church, the painting suggests that Heade was fully capable of making his own powerful statement about the lush beauty of the tropical landscape. The ability to capture the special character of the Brazilian scene was of importance to Heade, for in *The Gems of Brazil* landscape would play a key role in establishing a realistic setting for the hummingbirds. In this way, Heade's *Gems of Brazil* were

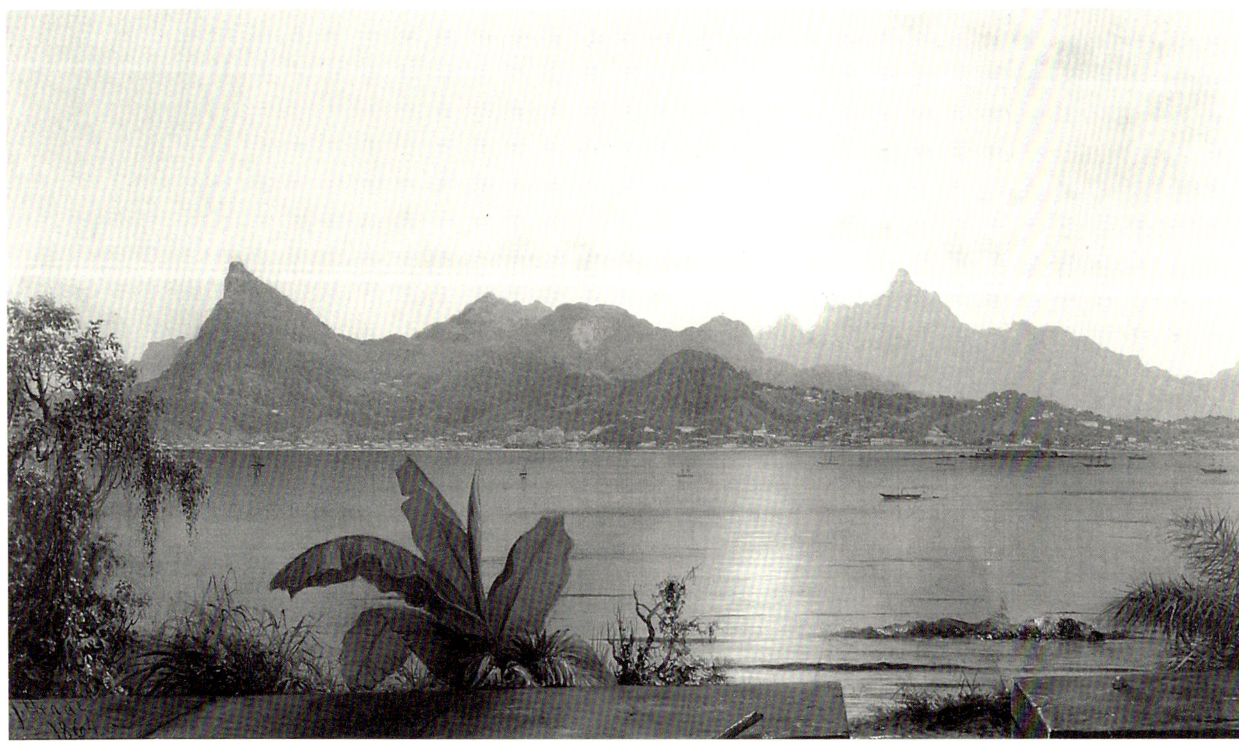

Fig. 1
Martin Johnson Heade, *Sunset—View of Rio de Janeiro, from São Domingos*, 1864, 20⅛ x 35 (51.1 x 88.9), The Pennsylvania Academy of the Fine Arts, Philadelphia, Henry C. Gibson Fund

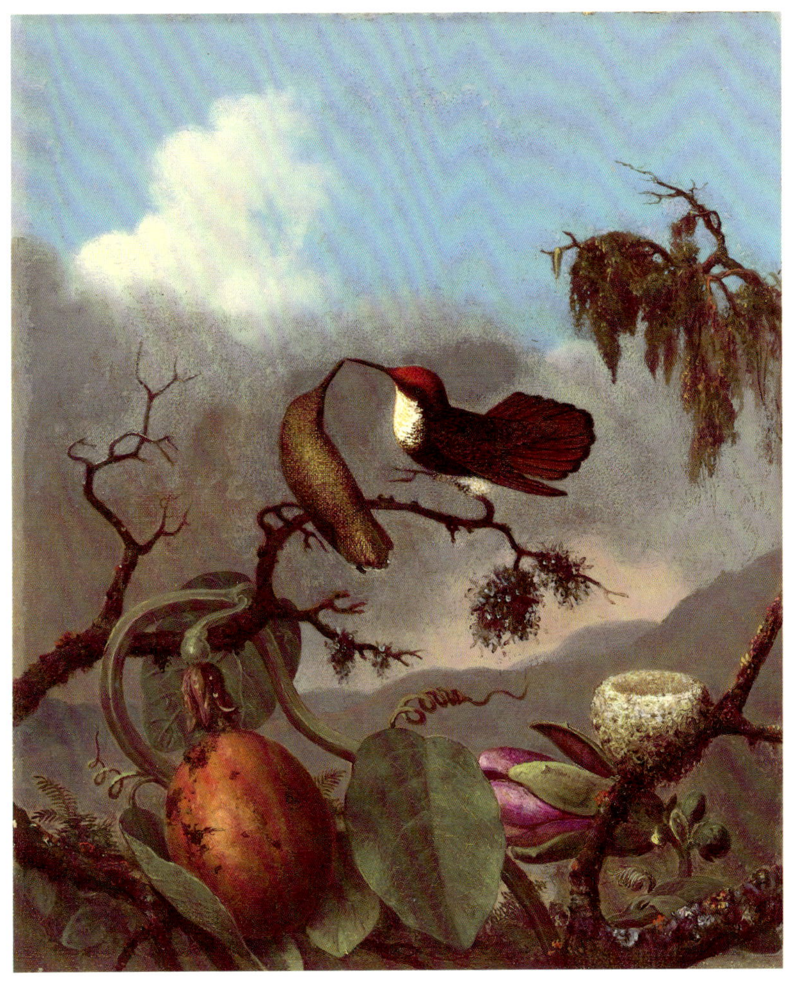

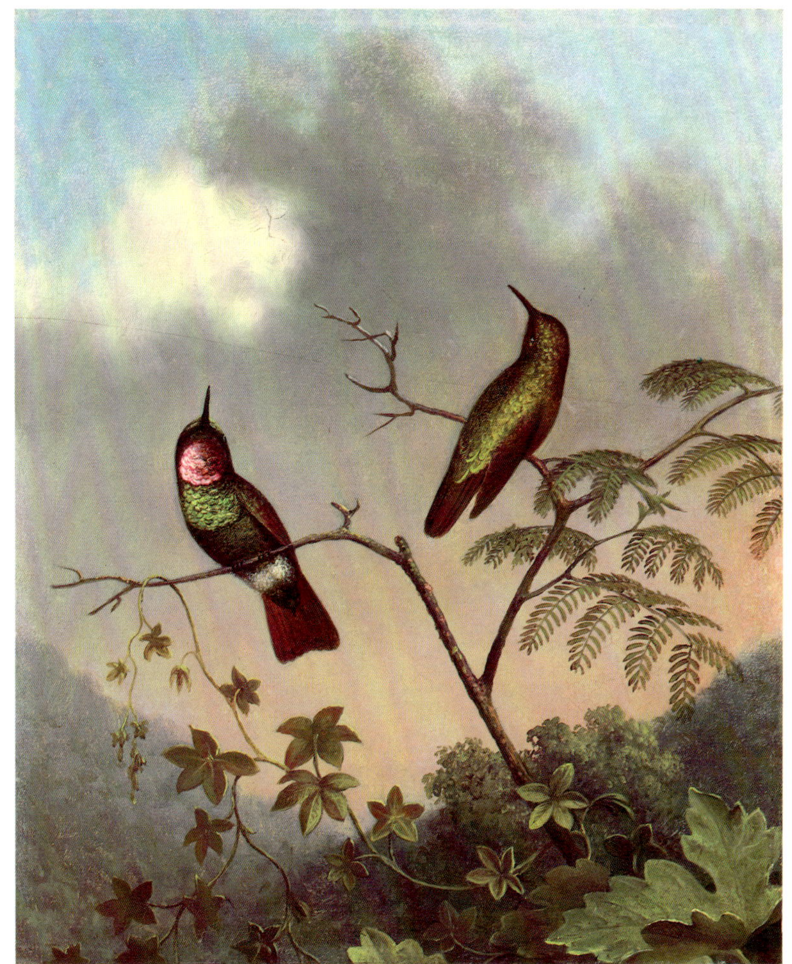

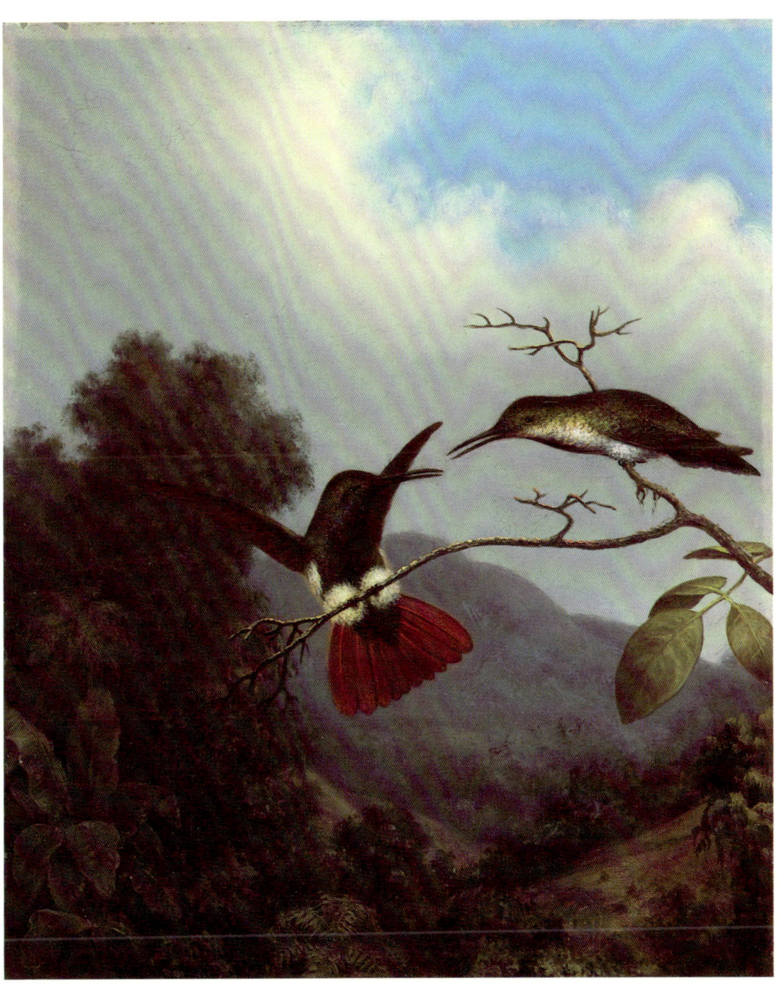

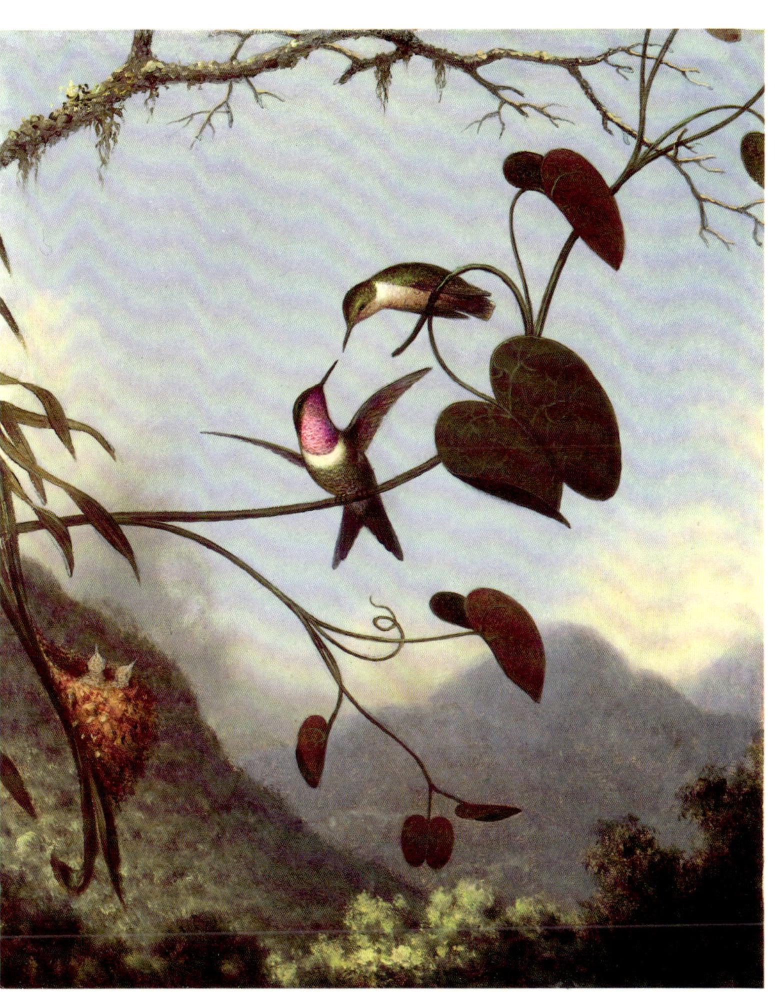

unlike any of the well-known hummingbird illustrations that had preceded them.

Among the numerous earlier depictions of hummingbirds that might have been an influence on Heade, two are of particular relevance.[7] John James Audubon included illustrations of the four species of hummingbird known to inhabit North America in his famous book *The Birds of America* (1827–1838). Although Audubon followed the general conventions of ornithological illustration, the drama and complexity of design of his images, which set them apart from all others, may well have inspired Heade.[8] Of even greater importance for Heade, however, was the Englishman John Gould's five-volume *Monograph of the Trochildae* (1849–1861), which was well known throughout England and America and which included some 360 lithographic illustrations. Gould was almost single-handedly responsible for a tremendous rise of interest in hummingbirds, especially among the English. In 1851 Gould displayed more than 1,500 hummingbird specimens, many shown posed with wax flowers, at the London Zoological Garden.[9] Over 75,000 people attended, including Queen Victoria, Prince Albert, and Charles Dickens. Queen Victoria thought it *impossible to imagine anything so lovely as these little Humming Birds*, and Dickens was of the opinion that *the most vivid colours of the painter's palette cannot duplicate their ever-varying tints.*[10] Gould's success with popularizing hummingbirds, both in England and America, helped pave the way for Heade's endeavor, because the artist certainly intended for his own book to appeal to the same audiences. But one has to wonder why Heade was not, in fact, discouraged by Gould's example, because he clearly could not hope to equal the Englishman's *Monograph of the Trochildae*, let alone surpass its excellence as a scientific text. Heade must have felt that he could do something that Gould had not done, and it is only by recognizing just what that was that we can fully appreciate his achievement in *The Gems of Brazil* and understand the reasons for the ultimate failure of the project.

Heade knew that in one very important respect he had an advantage over Gould when it came to depicting Brazilian hummingbirds, for the Englishman had *never set his foot on South American soil, the habitat of this large family of birds.*[11] Thus, no matter how scientifically accurate Gould's illustrations were, and no matter how many specimens he might possess, he could not claim to have seen a living Brazilian hummingbird, as could Heade.[12] Heade realized that by combining extant scientific knowledge about hummingbirds with his own observations and the reports of others intimately familiar with the birds he could bring to his own book considerable authority. This is evident from the draft of his introduction: *Without assuming for this monograph the importance of a scientific character, it has been the object of the author, by consulting the works of various Trochilidists, as* [well as] *by gleaning all the information possible relating to the birds in their native country to make it as reliable in the little ground it covers in this extended branch of Natural History as any work yet published on the subject.*[13] But Heade also sensed that there was something lacking in all other illustrated texts on hummingbirds, for none was able to evoke the mysterious beauty of living birds and the way they harmonized so perfectly with their natural setting. He wrote: *For one who is in the least degree attuned to poetic feeling, they have a singularly fascinating power which the subtlest mind is unable to explain, but which all who have studied them must acknowledge to have felt.*[14]

Heade would endeavor in *The Gems of Brazil* to capture this fascinating power on canvas, using the skill and creative imagination that he, an artist, possessed but more purely scientific illustrators did not. He clearly felt that hummingbirds were capable of evoking deeper associations than just scientific curiosity, for he quoted Audubon in his introduction to *The Gems of Brazil: Where is the person, I ask, who on observing this glittering fragment of the rainbow would not pause, admire, and turn his mind with reverence toward the Almighty Creator, the wonders of whose hand we at every step discover, and of whose sublime and beautiful conceptions we everywhere observe the manifestations in his admirable system of creation?*[15] To evoke such associations Heade would have to make his paintings do more than just illustrate the literal appearance of the hummingbirds; they would also have to capture the less tangible truths of God's *system of creation.* To understand this one miraculous aspect of the world was to take a step toward understanding the greater system; as the German naturalist Alexander von Humboldt wrote in *Cosmos*, his famous book, *Nature, in every region of the earth is indeed a reflex of the whole.*[16]

The Gems of Brazil convincingly suggest the natural settings in which the tiny birds actually lived, because Heade paid careful attention to depicting the vines, flowers, and trees that made up their principal habitat. He also arranged his compositions so that one looks through a foreground screen of foliage toward distant jungle, hills, and sky, making it clear that these habitats are part of a much greater whole.[17] As such, his view of the hummingbird was distinctly different from that of Audubon or Gould, who even though they showed the birds with flowers, divorced them from any further context. It has recently been suggested that the theories of Charles Darwin, which proposed an organic and dynamic relationship between animals and their surroundings, may have played a role in the formation of Heade's view of the hummingbird.[18] This idea gains further credence when one realizes that *The Gems* as a series must have been intended to outline the very life cycle of hummingbirds. One sees simply birds together in some of the pictures (as if in courtship), birds around empty nests in some, birds around (or, in one case, sitting on) nests with eggs, and birds around nests with young in others. Heade realized that one hummingbird will rarely tolerate the presence of another, but also knew that they were often seen together during mating season, especially around the nest.[19] He had corrected what must have seemed to him a grave fault in other depictions of hummingbirds, which showed several

upper left: Frilled Coquette (Lophornis magnifica)
upper right: Tufted Coquette (Lophornis ornata)
lower left: Black-breasted Plovercrest (Stephanoxis lalandi)
lower right: Fork-tailed Woodnymph (Thalurania furcata)

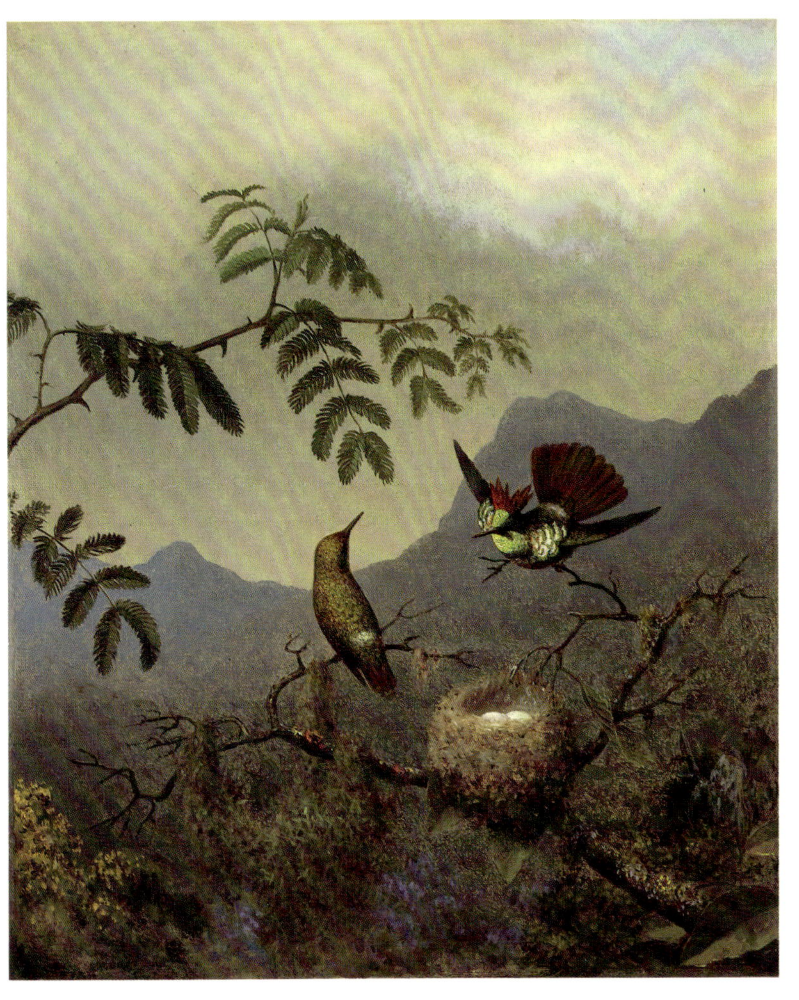
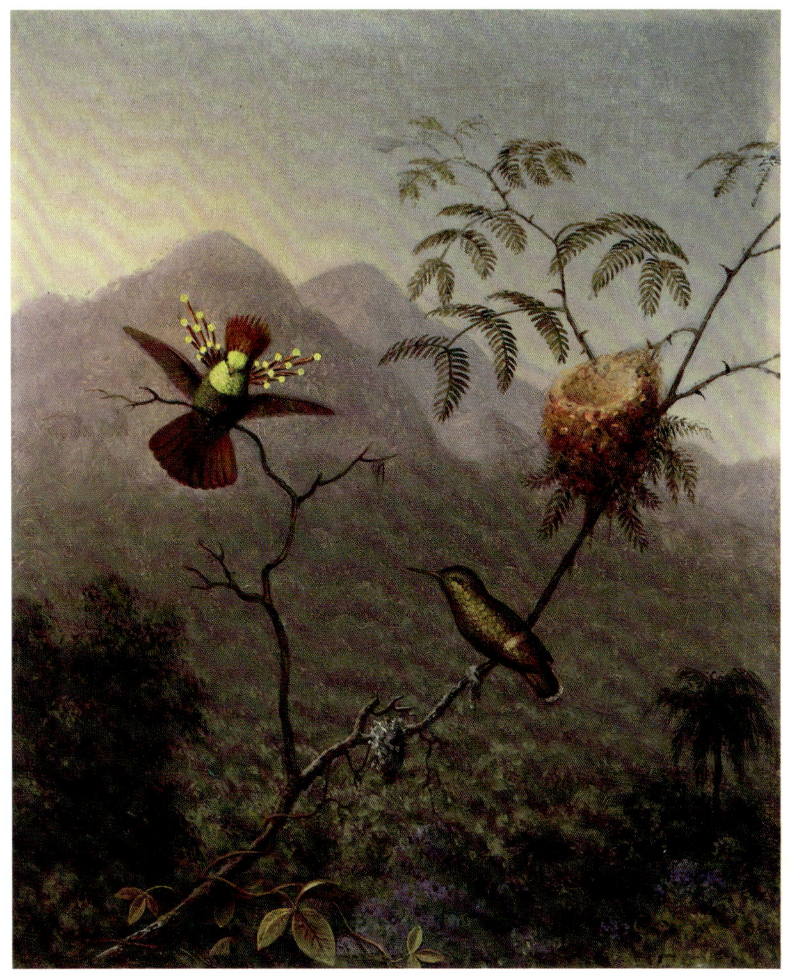
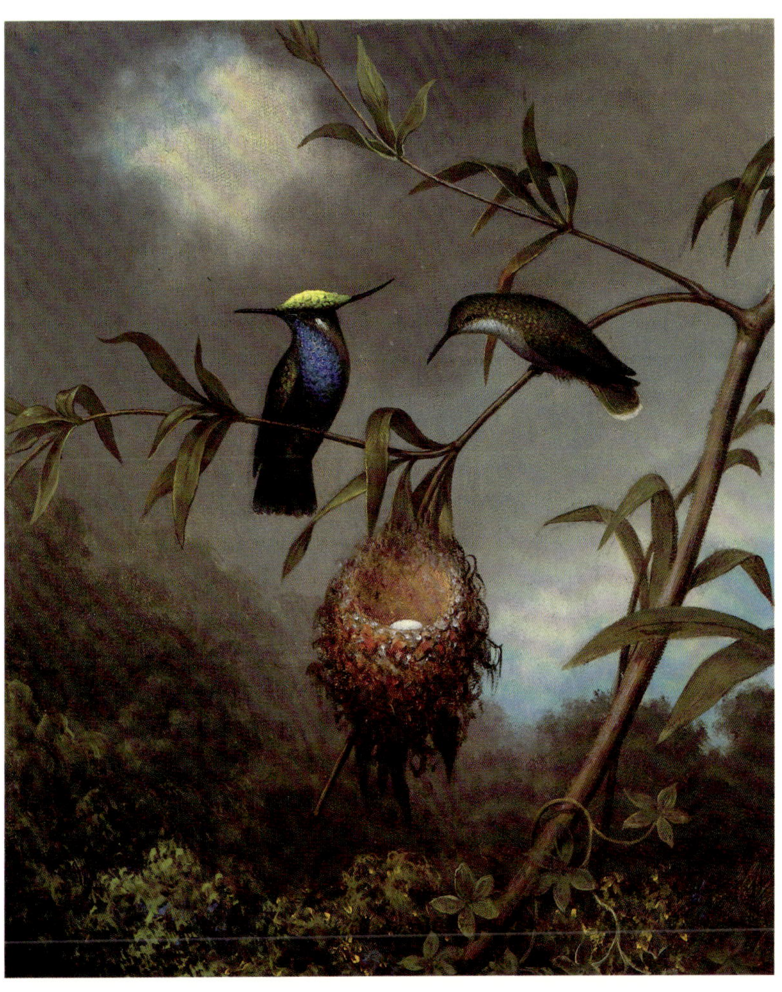
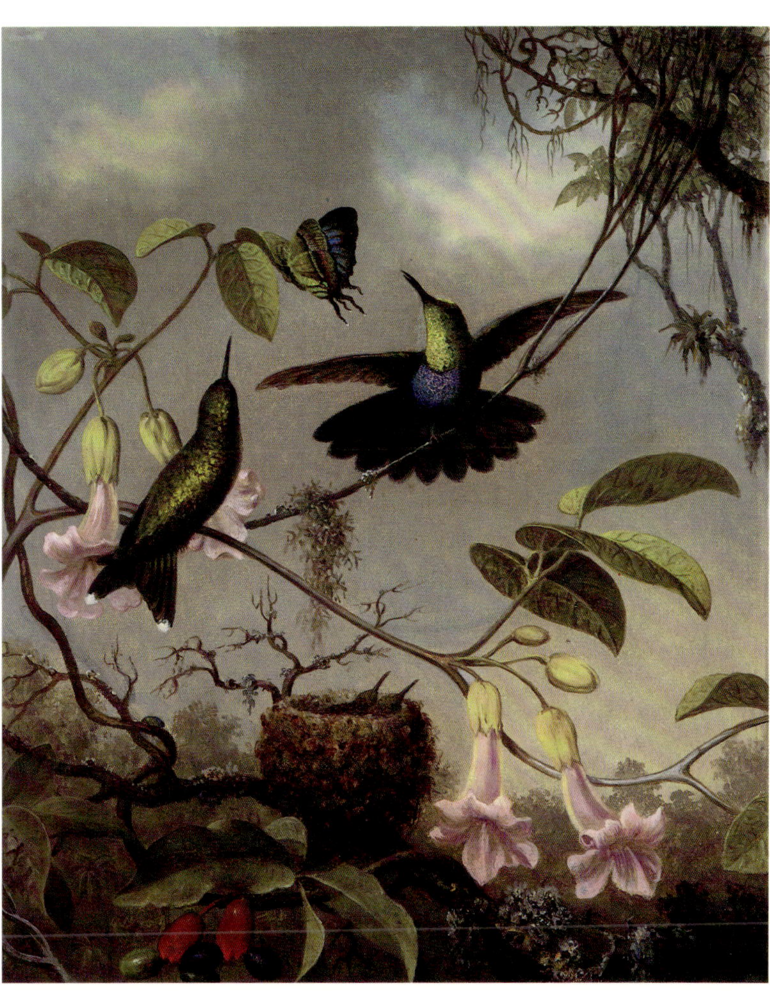

birds together in one setting without justification.

Heade's *The Gems of Brazil* thus pioneered a new, more naturalistically accurate portrayal of the hummingbird that provided a picture of the birds as they actually lived. This must have been one reason why he (and perhaps Fletcher) felt they might succeed, but there was also a further reason. Heade invested considerable attention in capturing the elusive iridescent colors of the various species of hummingbird (which not only Dickens, but many others, felt were beyond the reach of any painter), and it was his hope that it would be possible to duplicate them through chromolithography. When he exhibited twelve of the finished paintings in Rio de Janeiro in 1864, the catalogue noted that the full series of twenty *would be chromolithographed and published in London,* where Heade would travel after leaving Brazil. The title page of the planned book announced that the work would be done by *the best artists of Europe from the original pictures.*[20] However, as Theodore Stebbins has discussed, this phase of the project was unsuccessful.[21] Surviving prints reveal that there were severe problems with reproducing the colors and tones of Heade's originals, and particular difficulties with the landscape backgrounds. In short, many of the very qualities that would have made Heade's images of hummingbirds superior to all others were lost in the translation from one medium to another. Although he experimented with retouching the prints in an effort to salvage them, the project was soon abandoned. The original paintings were purchased by the Englishman Sir Morton Peto in London and Heade returned to New York late in 1865, his grand project unrealized.[22]

Heade, of course, did not abandon his interest in hummingbirds after the failure of *The Gems of Brazil.* He apparently brought back from South America a *fine collection of tropical birds,* and these, together with the sketches and paintings he retained, provided him with inspiration for the rest of his career.[23] By 1871 he had created his first paintings combining South American hummingbirds with orchids in tropical landscapes (fig. 2). Although in these lushly romantic images Heade abandoned the scientific approach he had tried to follow in *The Gems of Brazil,* he achieved a new level of evocativeness and beauty (fig. 3). The frequency and energy with which Heade created such paintings for the next thirty years suggests that they may have served as an outlet for his frustrations over the failure of *The Gems of Brazil.* If so, that ambitious project paid a rich dividend indeed, because Heade's best orchid and hummingbird paintings are surely among the most original and beautiful works in all of nineteenth-century American painting. *Franklin Kelly*

upper left: Hooded Visorbearer (Augastes lumachellus)
upper right: Crimson Topaz (Topasa pella)
lower left: Stripe-breasted Starthroat (Heliomaster squamosus)
lower right: Snowcap (Microchera albocoronata)

Fig. 2
Martin Johnson Heade, *Cattleya Orchid and Three Brazilian Hummingbirds,* 1871, 13¾ x 18 (34.8 x 45.6), National Gallery of Art, Washington

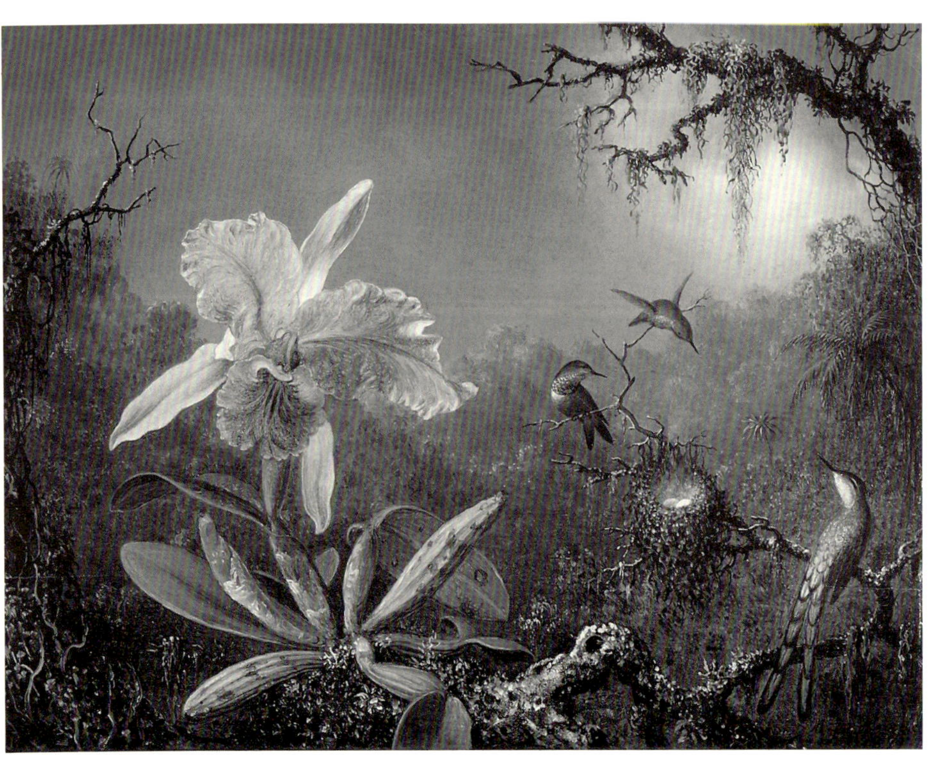

Fig. 3
Martin Johnson Heade, *Cattleya Orchid, Two Hummingbirds, and a Beetle,* 14¼ x 22¼ (36.2 x 56.5), Manoogian Collection

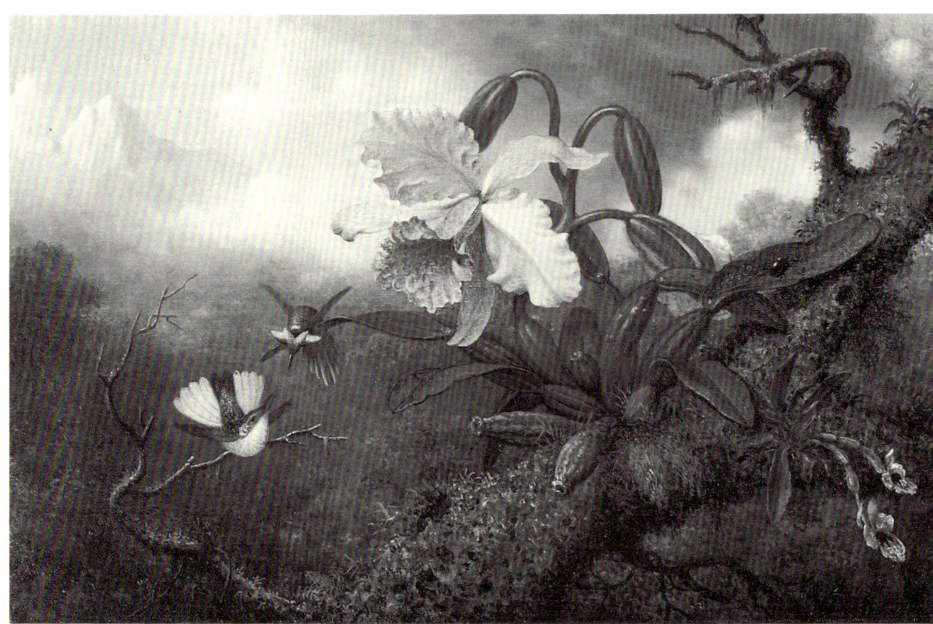

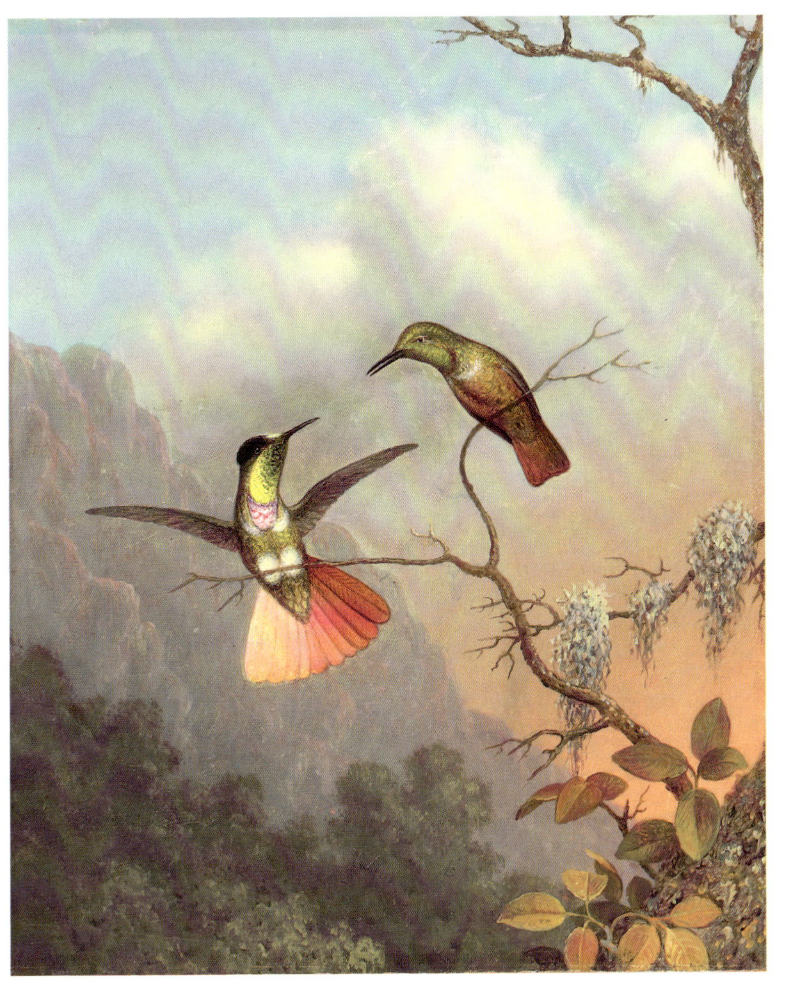
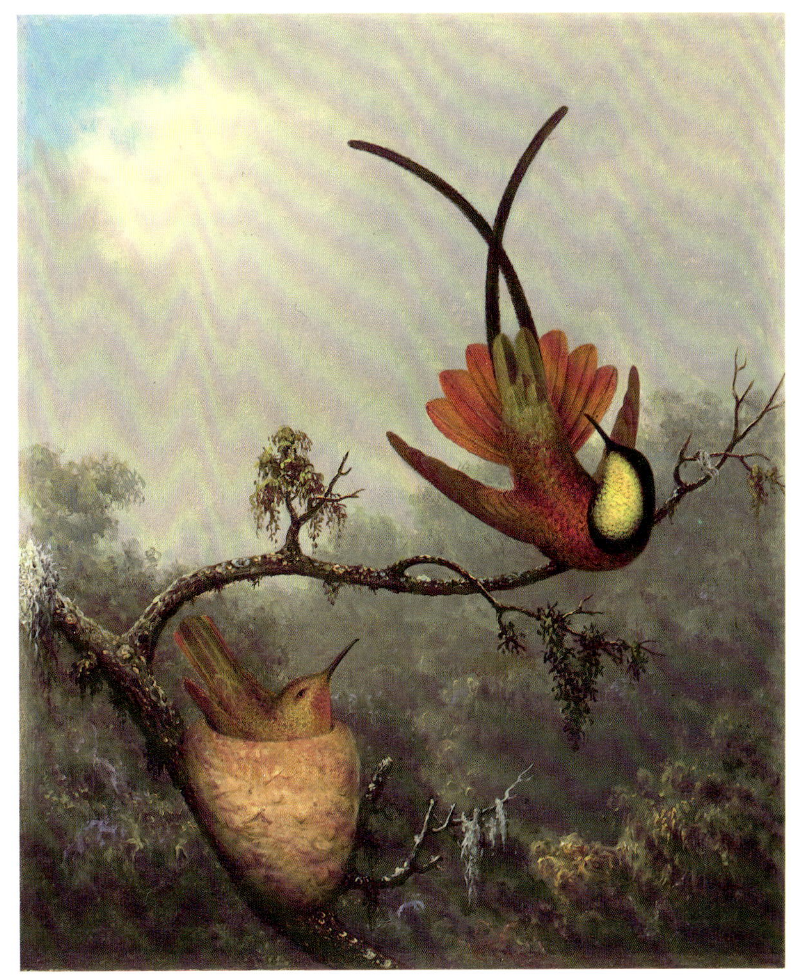
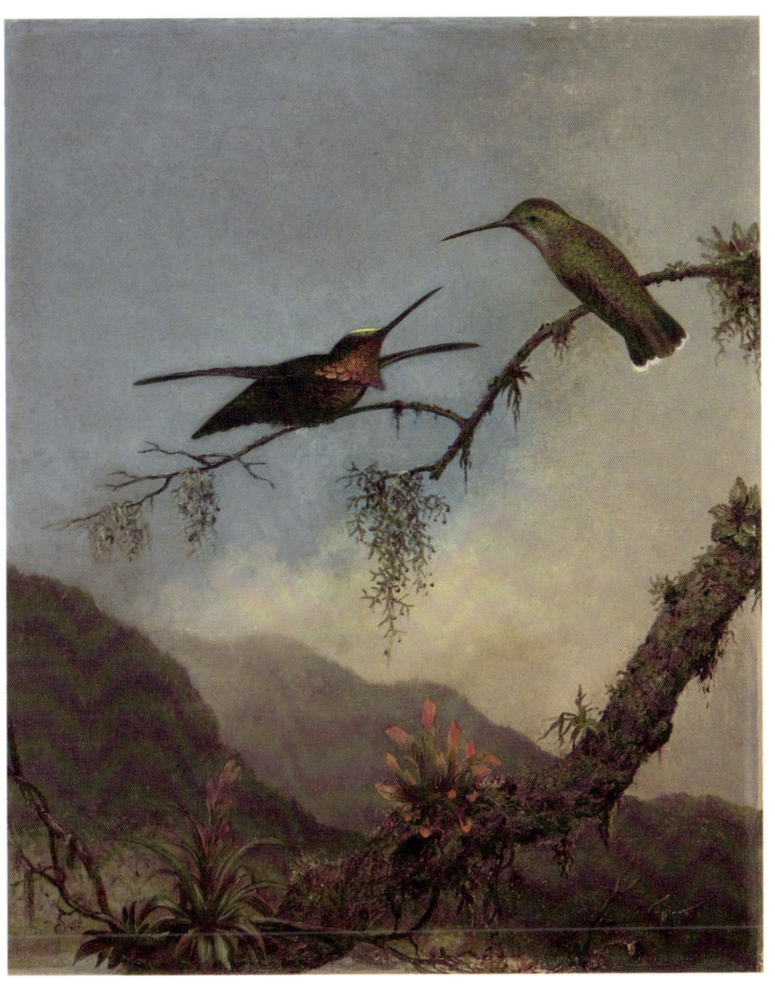
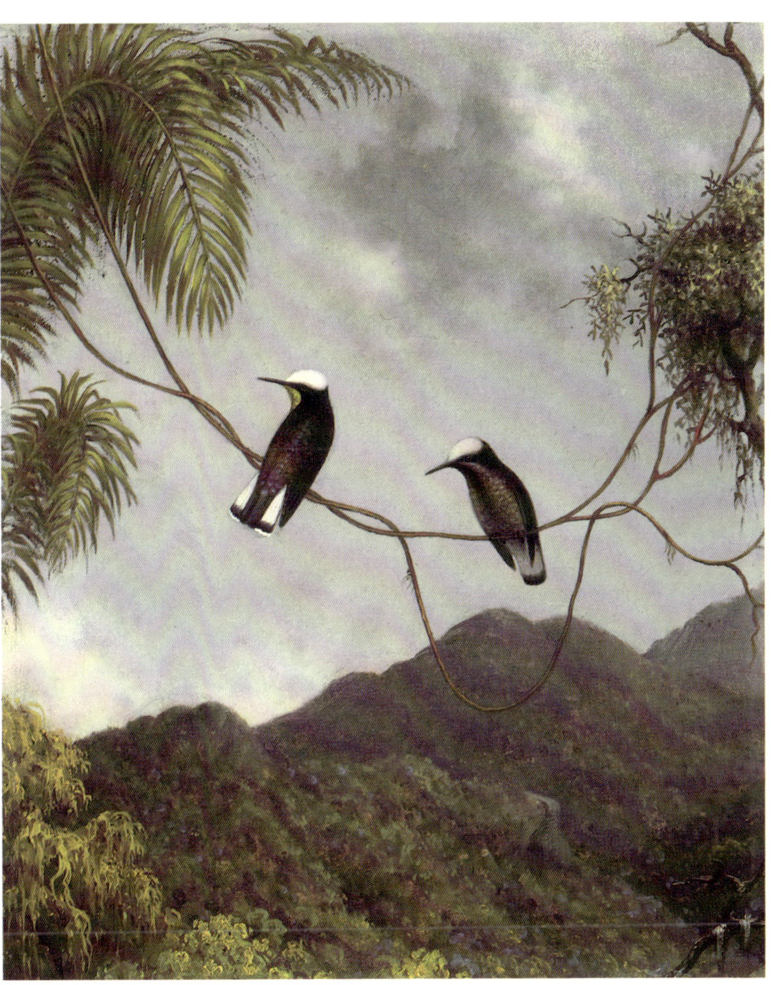

1. These sixteen paintings came to light in 1981 in a private collection in London, where they had been for at least fifty years. Unfortunately, there is no evidence available concerning prior ownership. The paintings were framed in the same manner, in groups of four, and though the actual frames have been changed, the order and placement of the pictures remains the same. If Heade did indeed complete twenty *Gems*, then four (perhaps also framed together) must have been separated from the original group at some point. Theodore E. Stebbins, Jr., in *The Life and Works of Martin Johnson Heade* (New Haven and London, 1975), 131, 226–227 believed he could identify two of the *Gems* (numbers 73 and 81 in his catalogue raisonné), which would leave two yet to be accounted for. However, the fact that one of the sixteen paintings discussed here depicts not hummingbirds, but a butterfly, raises an additional problem. Was the butterfly part of the original series of twenty? If so, there is no mention of it in any of the known contemporary references to the project. Henry Tuckerman (*Book of the Artists* [New York, 1867], 542), did, however, note that Heade had brought back from South America *a fine collection of tropical birds and butterflies*, suggesting that Heade developed an interest in butterflies at the time he was working on *The Gems of Brazil*. Perhaps Heade included the butterfly in the series as yet another example of nature's magnificent coloring. For the present, the answers to such questions and a definitive discussion of *The Gems of Brazil* must await publication of Stebbins' forthcoming revised edition of his Heade catalogue raisonné.
2. Heade, "Taming Hummingbirds," *Forest and Stream*, 14 April 1892, 348; quoted in Stebbins, *Heade*, 129.
3. Stebbins, *Heade*, 47, 85, 127–128.
4. Coauthor D. P. Kidder (Philadelphia and New York, 1857), 484.
5. Stebbins, *Heade*, 127.
6. *Exposição das Belles Artes de 1864* [exh. cat., Academy of Fine Arts] (Rio de Janeiro, 1864), no. 75, 11. I am grateful to Murilo Lellis, librarian, Museu Nacional de Belas Artes, Rio de Janeiro, for providing me with a xerox copy of the catalogue.
7. Stebbins, *Heade*, 127–129.
8. For a brief discussion, see Carlotta J. Owens, *John James Audubon: The Birds of America* [exh. cat., National Gallery of Art] (Washington, 1984).
9. Gordon C. Sauer, *John Gould the Bird Man: A Chronology and Bibliography* (Lawrence, Kansas, 1982), 128–130, 221, 277; Maureen Lambourne, *John Gould—Bird Man* (London, 1987), 80.
10. Lambourne, *Gould*, 85; Sauer, *Gould*, 198–199.
11. Heade, "Taming Hummingbirds"; quoted in Stebbins, *Heade*, 129.
12. Gould confirmed that he did not see a live hummingbird until 1857, when he was shown a rubythroat while on a visit to Philadelphia (Stebbins, *Heade*, 129–130). Even though thousands of hummingbirds (and other exotic species) were shipped as specimens into England during the Victorian period for study, none apparently were cultivated in aviaries. Gould himself later tried to cultivate hummingbirds, but they always died (information from Dr. Richard Zusi, curator of vertebrate zoology, Museum of Natural History, Smithsonian Institution, Washington; I am also grateful to Dr. Zusi for his help in identifying the various species of hummingbirds depicted in Heade's *The Gems of Brazil*).
13. "Introduction," from *The Gems of Brazil*, handwritten draft, Archives of American Art, Smithsonian Institution, Washington.
14. "Introduction," *The Gems of Brazil*. Heade also noted in the introduction that not all of the birds he had chosen to depict were strictly Brazilian species, because some were found in other countries.
15. "Introduction," *The Gems of Brazil*.
16. *Cosmos: A Sketch of a Physical Description of the Universe*, trans. Edward Sabine (London, 1848), 2:86.
17. In some cases the landscape backgrounds seem to continue from one picture across to the next, although it is unclear whether or not this was intentional.
18. Ella M. Foshay, "Charles Darwin and the Development of American Flower Imagery," *Winterthur Portfolio* 15 (winter 1980), 229–314.
19. Stebbins, *Heade*, 132.
20. Robert G. McIntyre, *Martin Johnson Heade, 1819–1904* (New York, 1948), plate XXIV.
21. Stebbins, *Heade*, 134–137.
22. Clara Erskine Clement and Laurence Hutton, *Artists of the Nineteenth Century and Their Works* (Boston, 1880), 340.
23. See Tuckerman, *Book of the Artists*, note 1, above.

upper left: Black-eared Fairy (Heliothryx aurita)
upper right: White-vented Violetear (Colibri serrirostris)
lower left: Ruby-throated Hummingbird (Archilochus colubris)
lower right: Blue Morpho Butterfly

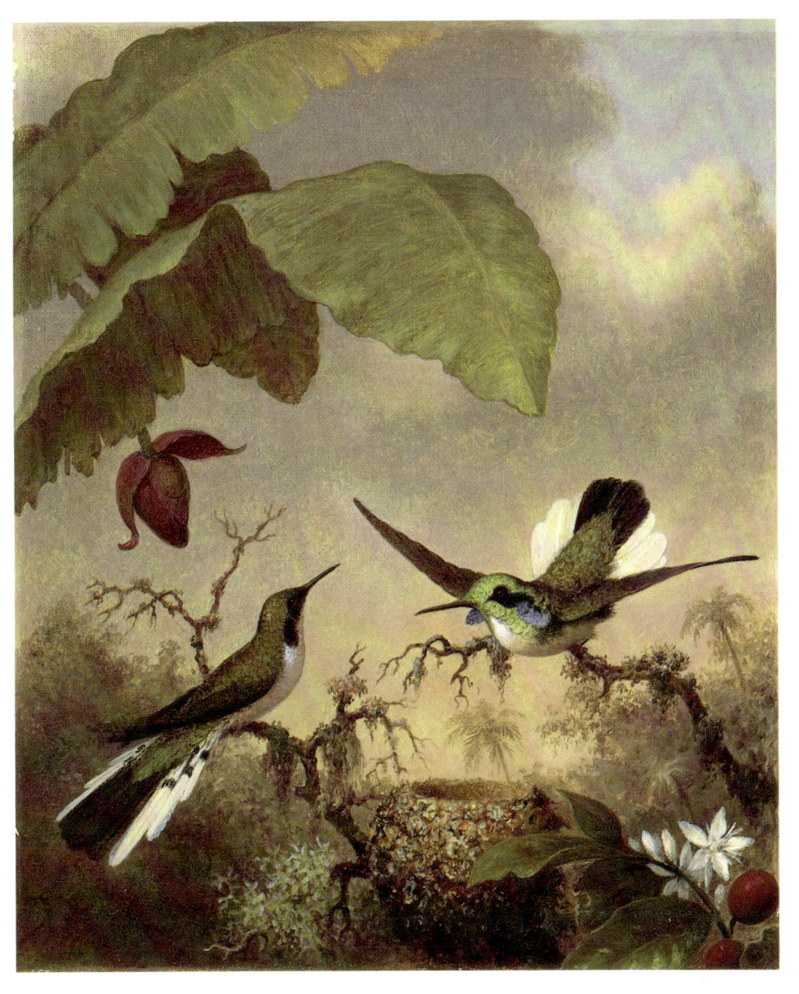
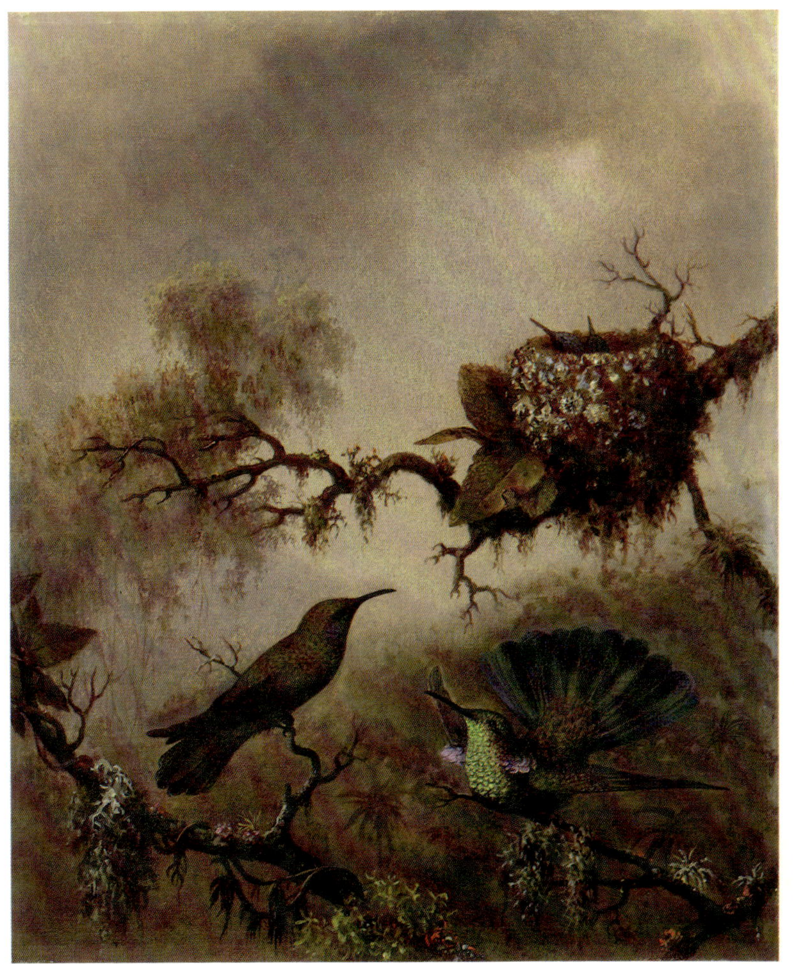
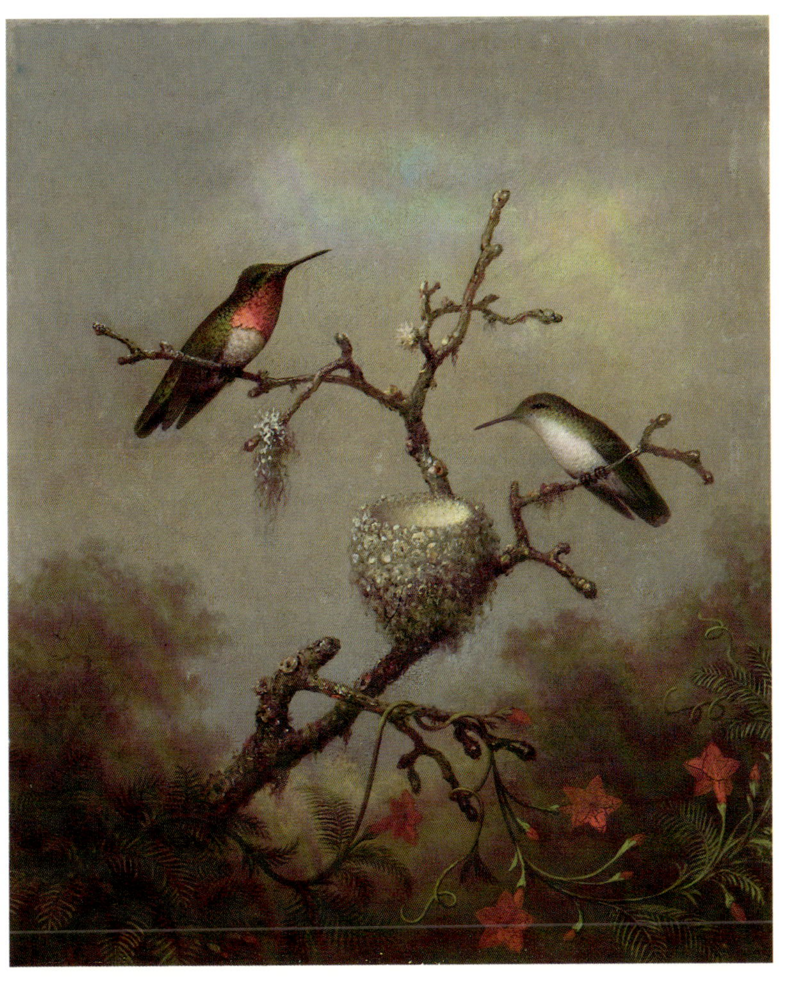
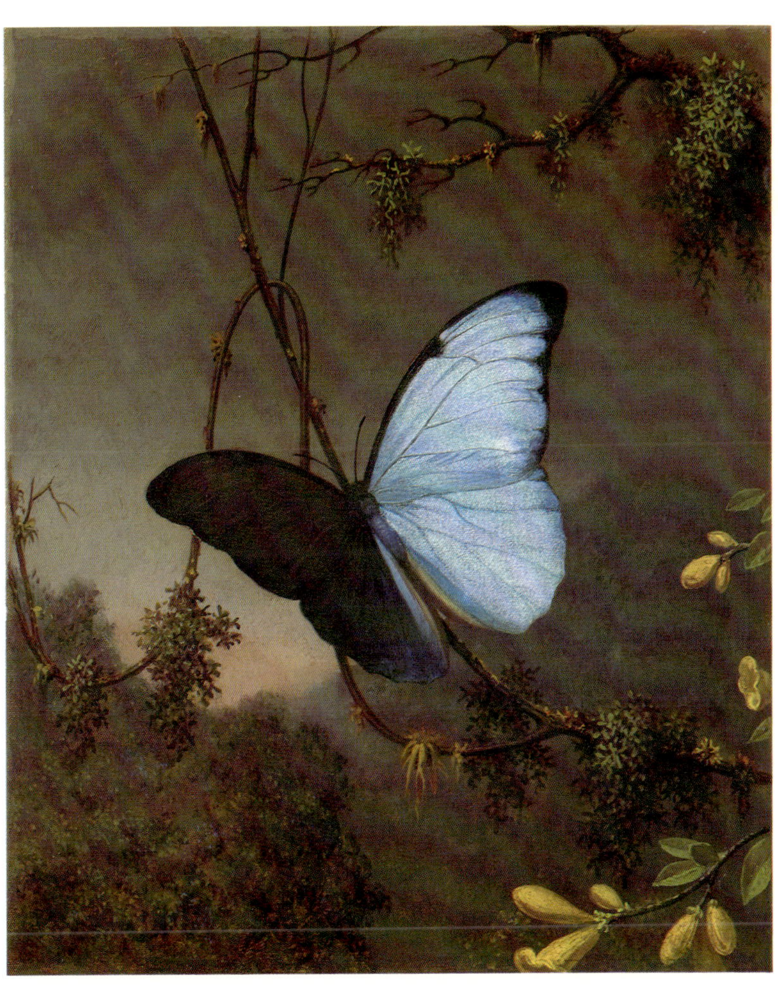

45

Martin Johnson Heade (1819–1904)
Magnolias on a Blue Velvet Cloth c. 1885–1895
oil on canvas, 15⅛ x 24¼ (38.4 x 61.6)

Martin Johnson Heade was the only major American artist of the nineteenth century to make important contributions both in landscape and still-life painting.[1] Virtually all of his still lifes were floral pieces, starting with elegantly simple pictures of flowers in vases in the early 1860s (such as *A Vase of Corn Lilies and Heliotrope*, 1863, Saint Louis Art Museum) and culminating in the 1880s and 1890s in a glorious series of roses, magnolias, and other flowers spread out on velvet cloths. Although Heade continued to paint landscapes until the end of his life, the flower pictures—and, most especially, the magnolia paintings—are considered the strongest of his late works.[2] Only one of the dozen or so known pictures of giant magnolias is dated (*Magnolia Grandiflora*, 1888, collection of Jo Ann and Julian Ganz, Jr., Los Angeles), but most were doubtless executed around the same time.

After a lifetime of restless travel, uneasy personal relationships, and only modest critical and popular success as an artist in the northeast, Heade finally married and settled permanently in Saint Augustine, Florida, in 1883. There he found his first and only important patron, Henry Morrison Flagler, who purchased his works on a regular basis through the 1880s and 1890s. At the age of sixty-four Heade had at last found personal and professional stability, and the renewed energy and interest in painting evident in the magnolia pictures may well have been inspired by his new circumstances.[3] The paintings in the series vary in size, in the number of flowers depicted, and in the color of the velvet, but the most successful examples generally show two or three blossoms against a blue background. Heade was obviously intrigued by the play of the shapes of leaves, petals, and folds of cloth, and infused the paintings with a sinuous rhythm of lines formed by the curving edges of flowers and leaves. But he was apparently also fascinated by contrasts of color, texture, and tone, because the brilliantly lit yet softly glowing petals stand out sharply from the dark green leaves, which shine with almost metallic brilliance.

Heade's magnolia paintings are among the most original still lifes of the nineteenth century, having no obvious precedents in either American or European art.[4] It is not clear whether the artist intended for them to carry specific meaning, even though his orchid and hummingbird pictures are often undeniably charged with sexual connotations. Nevertheless, the sensuous tones, curving contours, and beautiful opulence of the magnolia paintings are deeply suggestive, bringing to mind, as John I. H. Baur once observed, *odalisques on a couch*.[5]

Franklin Kelly

1. Theodore E. Stebbins, Jr., *The Life and Works of Martin Johnson Heade* (New Haven and London, 1975), 111.
2. Stebbins, *Heade*, 166.
3. *A New World: Masterpieces of American Painting, 1760–1910* [exh. cat., Museum of Fine Arts] (Boston, 1983), 282.
4. Stebbins, *Heade*, 166.
5. *Commemorative Exhibition: Paintings by Martin J. Heade and F. H. Lane from the Karolik Collection in the Museum of Fine Arts, Boston* (New York, 1954); quoted in Stebbins, *Heade*, 176.

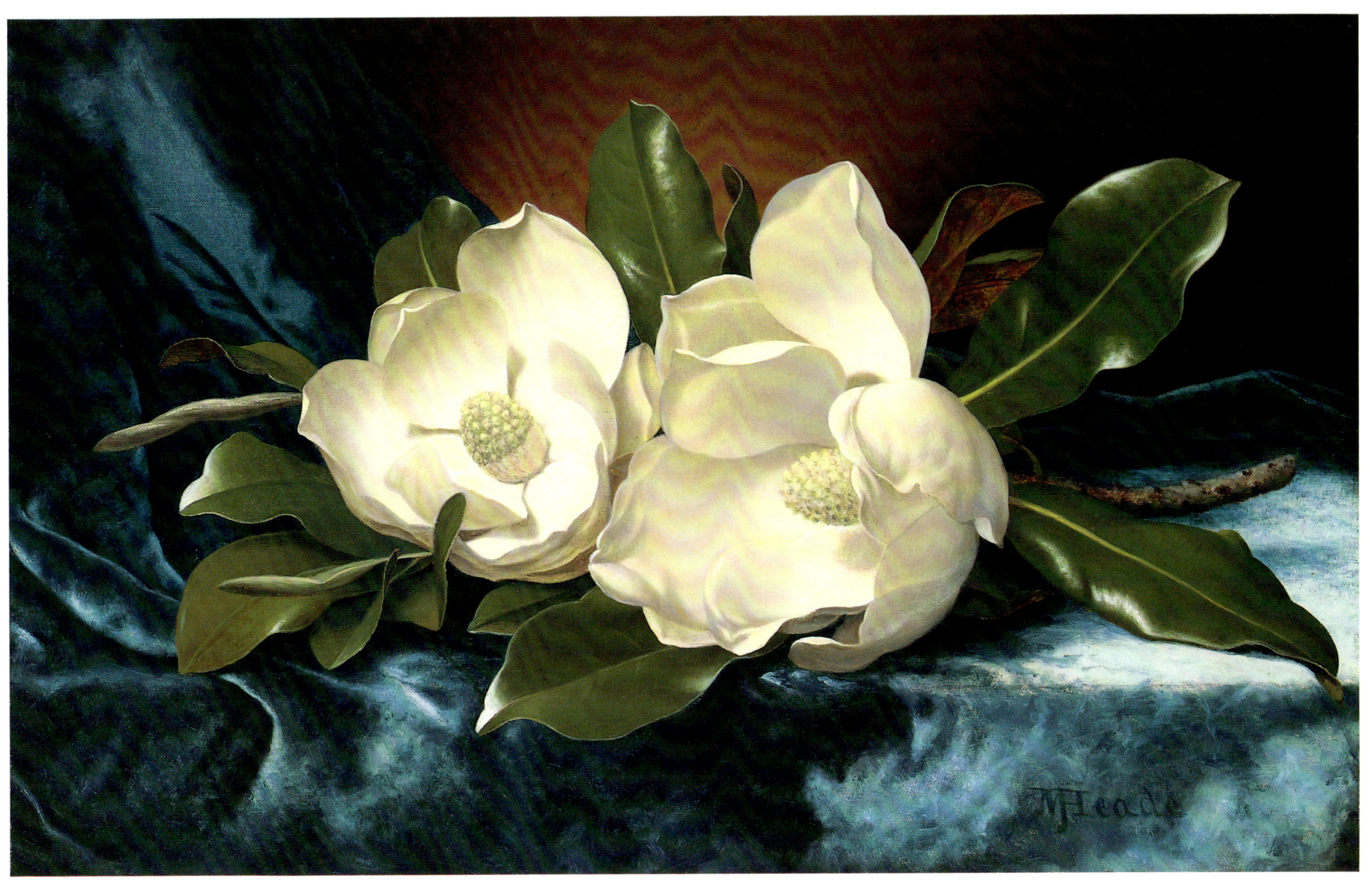
MJHeade

46

Thomas Eakins (1844–1916)
The Art Student (Portrait of an Artist) c. 1890
oil on canvas, 42 x 32 (106.7 x 81.3)

Virtually all of Thomas Eakins' paintings were, in some form or other, portraits. But during the years around 1890, at the time he painted *The Art Student*,[1] the function and the form of Eakins' portraiture underwent a profound change. Before that time his portraits usually depicted their subjects in context, in some characteristic activity or environment, while afterward—in paintings that Eakins' chief modern biographer, Lloyd Goodrich, called "head portraits"[2]—his attention focused on the subject itself, with little or no activity or setting (figs. 1, 2). The division is not hard and fast, of course. But for roughly the first twenty years of his professional life Eakins mostly painted the first kind of portrait, and for the last twenty (beginning about 1890), mostly the second.

In 1886, Eakins suffered *the severest blow of his professional career*,[3] his dismissal, with an aroma of scandal, as director of the school of the Pennsylvania Academy of the Fine Arts. This, more than any other single event, separates Eakins' early from his late work—the thematically varied and often ambitious paintings preceding it, which included such transcendent achievements as *The Gross Clinic* of 1875, from works following which, on the whole, were narrower in subject matter, simpler in composition, and smaller in size. Given the traumatic nature of his departure from the academy, it is possible to attribute this change to disillusionment and retrenchment, to an erosion of confidence and loss of creative energy resulting in paintings that were, Lloyd Goodrich believed, formulaic and routine.[4]

It is possible, however, to regard the later "head portraits" in a different and more favorable light. For perhaps they were not symptoms of decline but, on the contrary, composed a project—the major artistic undertaking in the last twenty years of his life—that Eakins pursued with an intense clarity of purpose and certainty of procedure that makes the thematic variety and sporadic ambition of his earlier art seem by comparison groping and uncertain.

Although Goodrich found the late "head portraits" disappointing, he nevertheless put his finger precisely, if unwittingly, on what they were about. *The head portraits of these later years*, he wrote, *have an element of repetitiveness, of formula: similar poses of head and shoulders, similar lights and shadows, similar blank backgrounds, and the same size canvases. . . . There was no loss of skill or strength, only a strict limitation in scope. . . . His continuing desire to paint these head portraits, his constantly asking people to pose, had reached the dimension of an obsession. He no longer had to work for a living; he was free to paint anything he wanted to. . . . One asks: why not more works calling on his mastery of the whole human body—not just the head? It is sad to see such powers expended on such limited material.*[5]

Goodrich also indicated statistically how the nature of Eakins' enterprise shifted beginning in the 1890s. The format of his "head portraits" was 24 x 20 inches. He painted only about ten such portraits in the 1870s, and twelve in the 1880s; but he painted forty in the 1890s and eighty-five in 1900–1910 (thirty-seven in 1903–1904 alone).[6]

The explanation of the change that these statistics graphically records lies in the answer to Goodrich's somewhat plaintive question, why, when he was free to

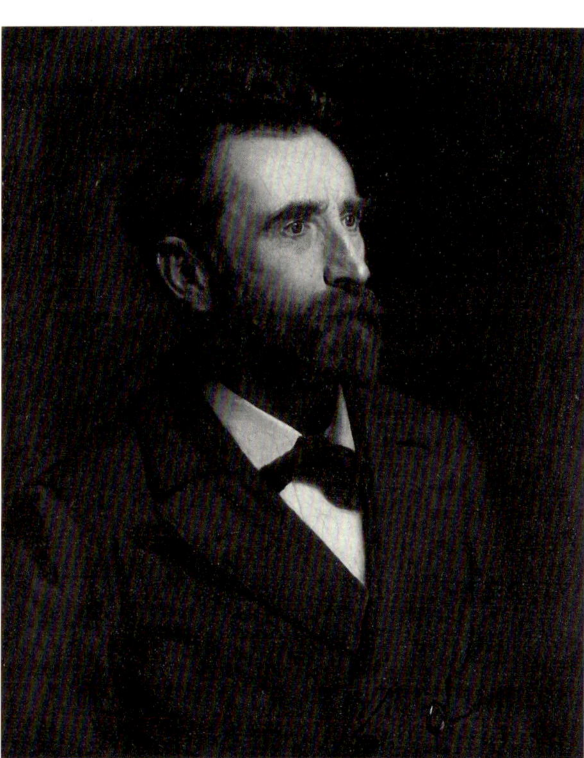

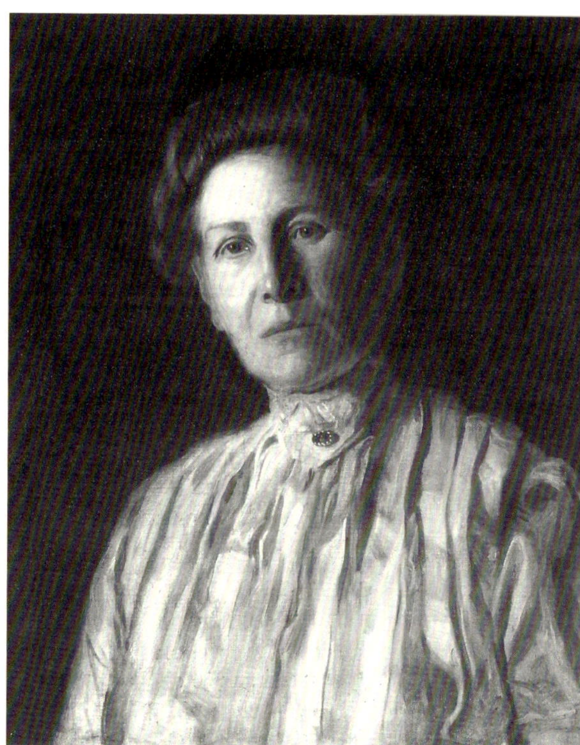

Fig. 1
Thomas Eakins, *Louis Husson*, canvas 24 x 20 (0.610 x 0.509), National Gallery of Art, Washington, Gift of Katharine Husson Horstick

Fig. 2
Thomas Eakins, *Mrs. Louis Husson*, canvas, 24 x 20 (0.611 x 0.509), National Gallery of Art, Washington, Gift of Katharine Husson Horstick

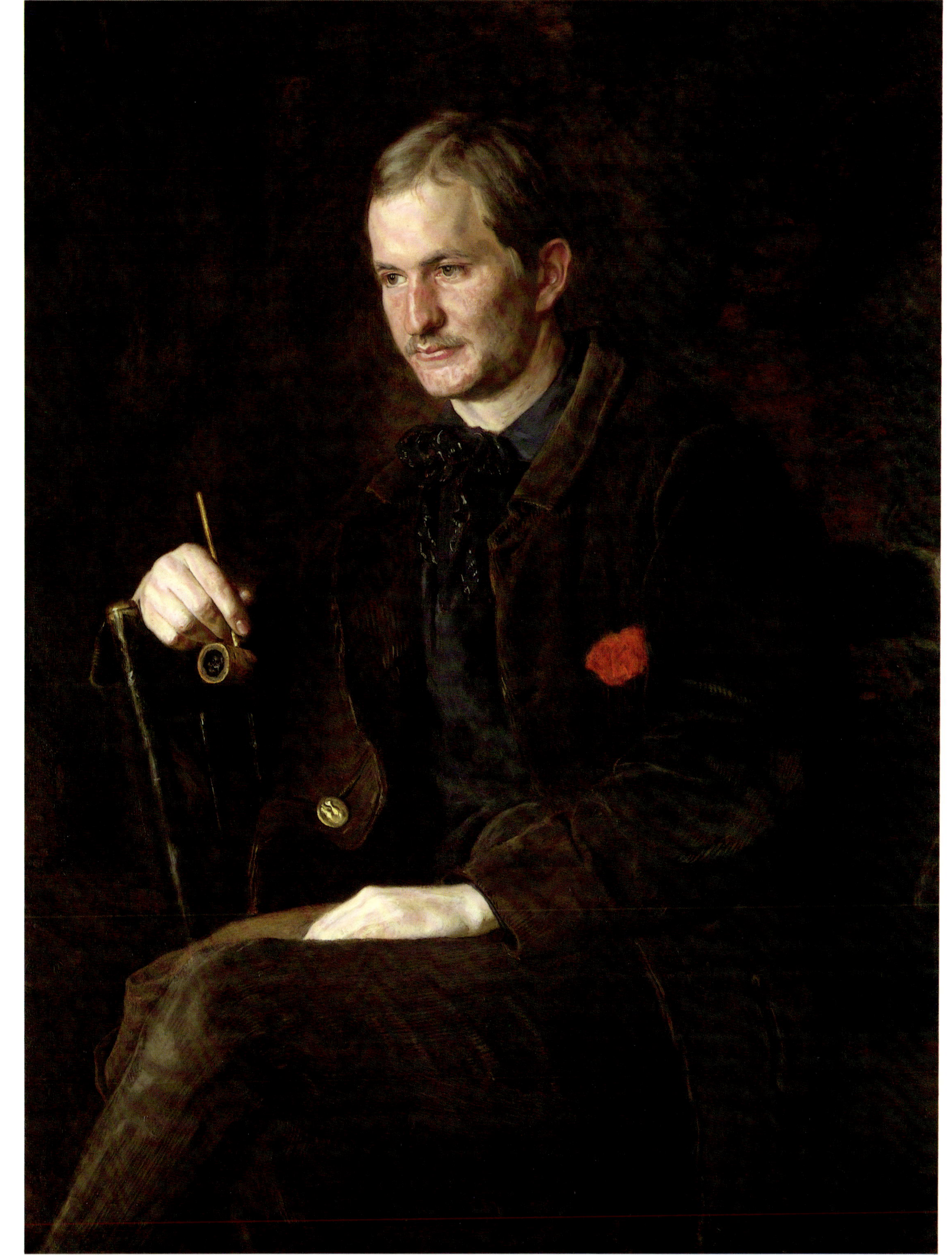

paint whatever he wanted to, Eakins did not paint more works that called upon his mastery of the human figure rather than portrait heads? Eakins' mastery of the human figure derived from two years of intensive academic study in France in the late 1860s. Although he pursued his study of the figure with an almost scientific rigor that seemed to go beyond the immediate needs of art, he surely knew that the human figure—especially in traditions that Eakins' academic training sanctioned and was dedicated above all to preserving—was the noblest subject that any artist of serious purpose could paint, and one more than any other inextricably associated with high art. The central pursuit, or problem, of Eakins' early art was to accomodate what his training had taught him, and principally the knowledge it gave him of the human figure, to the circumstances of late nineteenth-century life in his native city of Philadelphia. If, as it has been elegantly argued, the subject underlying all of Eakins' art was the *heroism of modern life*,[7] its depiction always depended upon, and was at times the pretext for displaying, Eakins' academically implanted knowledge of the figure and the essentially conventional belief in its artistic importance that went along with it. When in the 1890s, therefore, Eakins called less and less upon his knowledge of the figure, what he really called less and less upon, cared less and less about, and ultimately largely rejected, was not the figure itself but all the modes and methods of conventional art that had been traditionally invested in it.

What Eakins rejected it for, as Goodrich put it, was "just heads," works of *no . . . interest as compositions, as more complex works of art*. But it was not only this limitation of subject and diminishment of art and artistry that distressed Goodrich. Other limitations of Eakins' late portraits also saddened him: *similar poses of head and shoulders, similar lights and shadows, similar blank backgrounds, and the same size canvases*, and the singlemindedness with which Eakins pursued his project, the *continuing desire to paint these head portraits* which *reached the dimensions of an obsession*.[8]

What Eakins had in mind in the obsessional enterprise of his late portraits first becomes clear in his portrait of James Wright and other works like it painted in the years about 1890. James Wright was one of Eakins' students at the Art Students League in Philadelphia (an organization established by loyal students after Eakins' dismissal from the Pennsylvania Academy in 1886). Like most of his portraits, early and late, it depicted someone Eakins knew, and like most of them it was initiated by Eakins, not by the sitter. This relationship of artist to sitter was a special, indeed an almost singular, condition of most of Eakins' portraiture—and especially of his late portraits, for which he was *constantly asking people to pose*.[9] Because of the closeness of this relationship, and because his sitters, like Wright, are often reflective or introspective, Eakins' portraits appear to be psychologically probing. Yet beginning in the later 1880s Eakins seems to have understood the purpose of his portraits rather differently. For the title of this painting, *The Art Student* (or *Portrait of an Artist*),[10] refers not to an individual, despite Eakins' closeness to the person it depicted, but to the professional type he exemplified; its stress, in other words, is more taxonomic and typological than psychological. This was not an isolated case. Eakins used precisely the same form of title in other paintings made about 1890. When he exhibited portraits of William D. Marks (1886, Washington University, Saint Louis), Letitia Wilson Jordan (1888, Brooklyn Museum), Walt Whitman (1887–1888, The Pennsylvania Academy of the Fine Arts), and Samuel Murray (1889, John R. and Eleanor R. Mitchell Foundation, Mount Vernon, Illinois) at the Pennsylvania Academy in 1891 they were called respectively *Portrait of an Engineer*, *Portrait of a Lady*, *Portrait of a Poet*, and *Portrait of a Student*. The portrait of James Wright, entitled *Portrait of an Artist*, was part of this group. Other examples of this practice are the portraits of George Reynolds that Eakins called *The Veteran* (c. 1886, Yale University Art Gallery), and of Franklin Schenck called *The Bohemian* (c. 1890, Philadelphia Museum of Art).[11]

Ranging from the *Portrait of an Engineer*, in which Marks is depicted in his professional environment, through the three-quarter-length portraits of Letitia Jordan and James Wright, to the simpler and smaller "head portraits" of Whitman, Murray, Reynolds, and Schenck, these portraits have little in common apart from their titles. As this suggests, Eakins assigned typological titles to existing paintings as if to appropriate them for a project for which they were not originally made. And this, in turn, suggests that the project was still new to him and in its first stages. Only the portraits of Letitia Jordan and James Wright, their subjects both dressed, almost uniformed, she as a Lady and he—with corduroy coat, flowing tie, pocket handkerchief, and pipe—as an Artist, seem to have been painted with some typological function in view.

At the end of his life Eakins was asked his opinion on the present and future of American art. In the most memorable part of his answer he said, *American art students and painters* should *study their own country and portray its life and types*.[12] This was not hollow rhetoric. For what Eakins prescribed for American students and painters at the end of his life was the very same program—portraying the life and types of his own country—that had given shape and guidance to his own artistic undertaking during the preceding decades, the program that had been first proposed by the typological, or typologically titled, portraits of the late 1880s, such as the portrait of James Wright as *The Artist*.

That program was systematically enacted, however, only in the "head portraits" that Eakins began making in steadily increasing numbers in the 1890s. System itself was one of that program's essential elements; it was exactly what Goodrich found most troubling about the late paintings: similar poses, similar lighting, similar backgrounds, steadily increasing similarity of size, and the replacement of conventional artistic refinements and complexities by systematically ordered patterns of representation. And it was their system—or, more exactly, their classificatory systematics—that tells most clearly what these paintings endeavor to do.

Eakins' scientific interests, the studies of anatomy, perspective, and motion to which he applied himself with scientific rigor and mathematical precision, have been routinely noticed.[13] But what was perhaps his largest and most absorbing scientific project, the "head portraits" that he painted obsessively in the last twenty years of his life, has not. They were begun in earnest at just the time that the new and uniquely nineteenth-century social sciences, anthropology and sociology, were being consolidated as scientifically responsible and professionally respectable disciplines. Like them—indeed, with them as his models—Eakins undertook in his late paintings the description, regulated in pose, lighting, and size with the orderliness and objectivity of a scientific methodology, of American culture and society, the "life and types" of his own country. And he did so more particularly by using one of the favorite tools of the social sciences, typology, the classification of human beings according to physical and mental attributes, as well as by couching his pictorial language in scientific form. Dispensing with conventions of artistic portraiture and its subtleties of pose, expression, and setting, Eakins conformed his work instead to evidentially more accurate modes of typological portraiture, of which in his time the clearest if most extreme form was developed for the physiognomic description and identification of criminals, such as, for example, Thomas Byrnes' *Professional Criminals of America* (1886) or Alphonse Bertillon's *Identification anthropométrique* (1893)[14] (figs. 3, 4). Eakins used a similar method of systematically classifying human bodily types photographically in the "naked series" he made in the early 1880s[15] at approximately the same time that he worked with Eadweard Muybridge in photographically documenting human and animal motion.[16]

Eakins' most direct artistic heirs were not his actual students, like James Wright, but fellow Philadelphians of a younger generation, the realist painters of the Ashcan school: Robert Henri, George Luks, John Sloan, and William Glackens. More wholeheartedly than any other artists who worked under Eakins' example and spiritual influence, they individually and corporately carried out his charge to *American art students and painters* to *study their own country and portray its life and types*. They did so by painting "records" and "documents" of contemporary life, as their mentor Henri—interestingly, in language imported from the methodology of the social sciences—described them.[17] But they did so more particularly by means of typological portraiture, to the degree, in fact, that portraits of social and racial types composed the largest part of the work of Henri and Luks—paintings with titles like Henri's *Himself* and *Herself*, *The Laundress*, *Indian Girl*, and *El Segoviano*, or Luks' *The Little Milliner*, *The Old Dutchess*, *The Little Madonna*.[18] It would be preposterous, of course, to claim that such paintings as these

Fig.3
From Alphonse Bertillon, *Signaletic Instructions*, pl. 31 (Chicago, 1896)

Fig.4
From Thomas Byrnes, *Professional Criminals of America*, new and revised ed. (New York, 1895)

THE FOREHEAD

1 Inclination 2 Height 3 Width

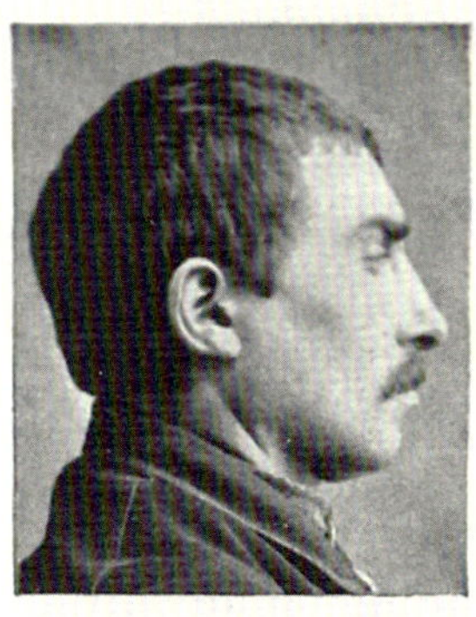

1. Forehead with inclination receding.

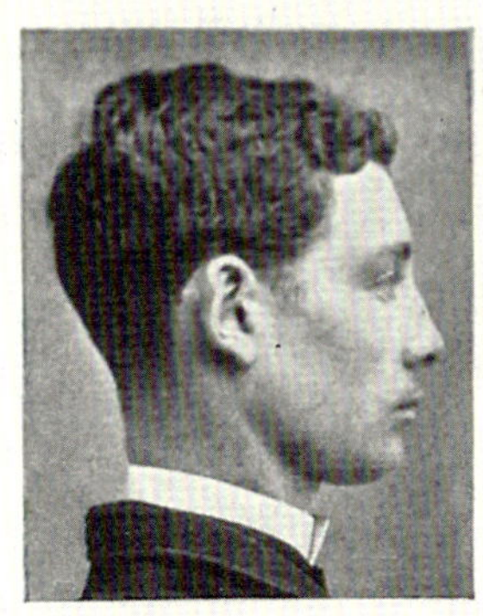

2. Forehead with inclination intermediate.

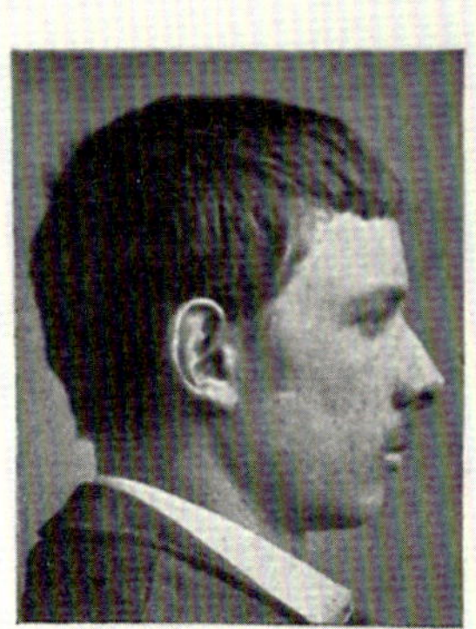

3. Forehead with inclination vertical.

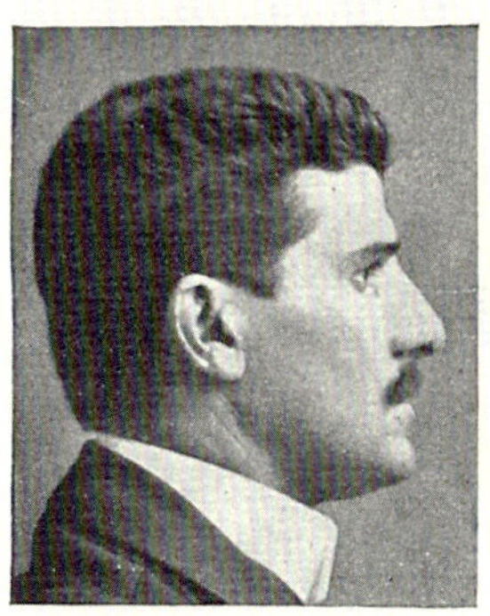

4. Forehead of little height.

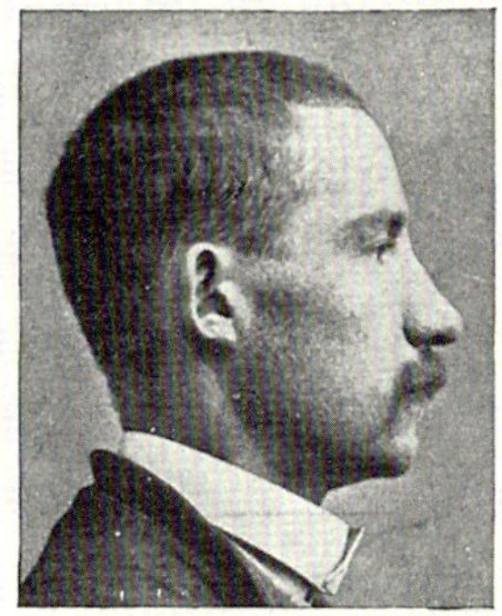

5. Forehead of medium height.

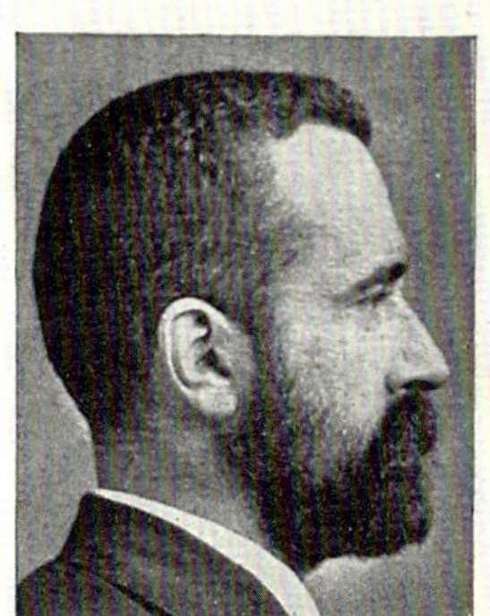

6. Forehead of great height.

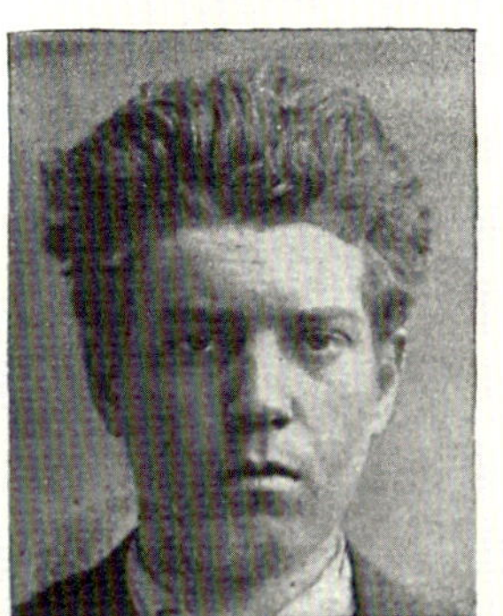

7. Forehead of little width.

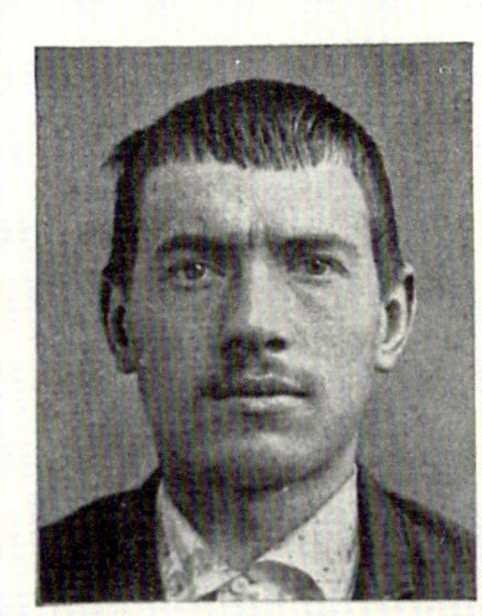

8. Forehead of medium width.

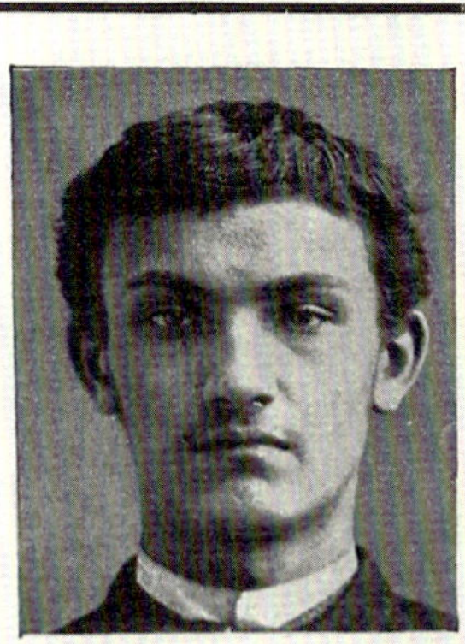

9. Forehead of great width.

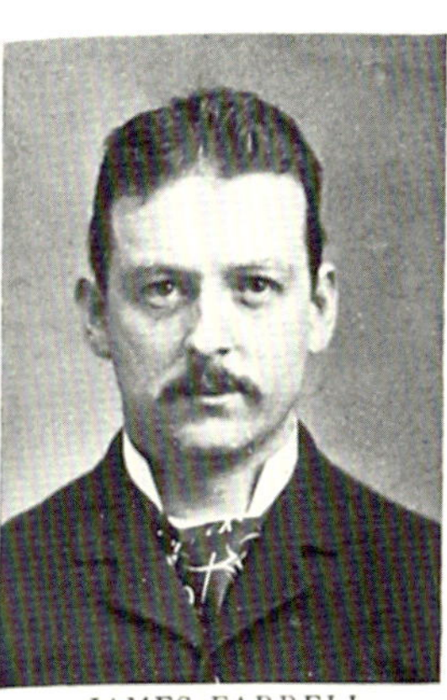

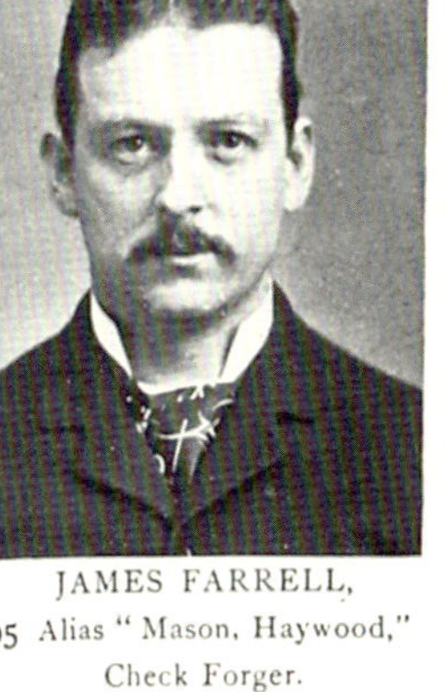

295 JAMES FARRELL, Alias "Mason, Haywood," Check Forger.

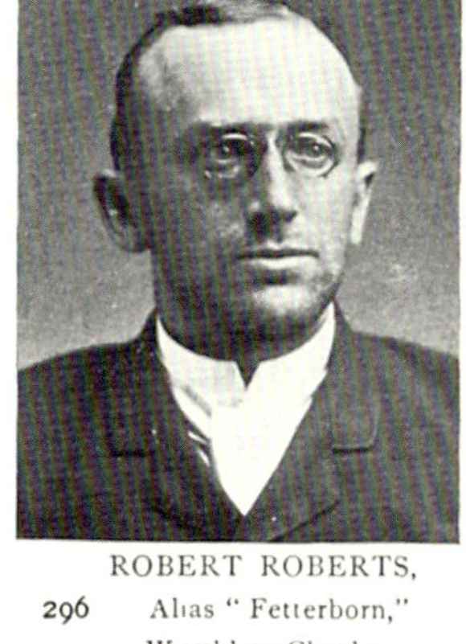

296 ROBERT ROBERTS, Alias "Fetterborn," Worthless Checks.

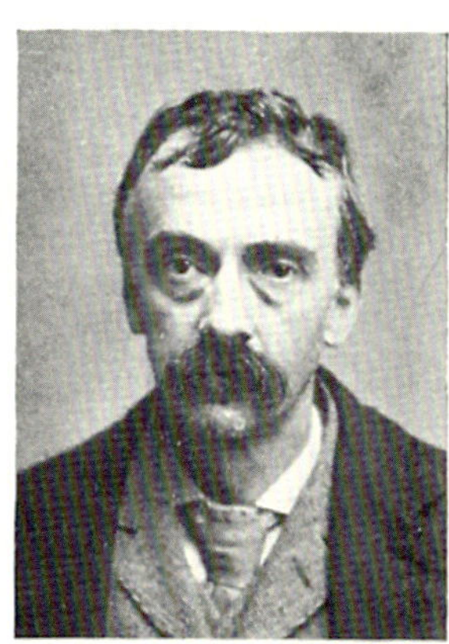

297 GEO. LINGARD, Forger.

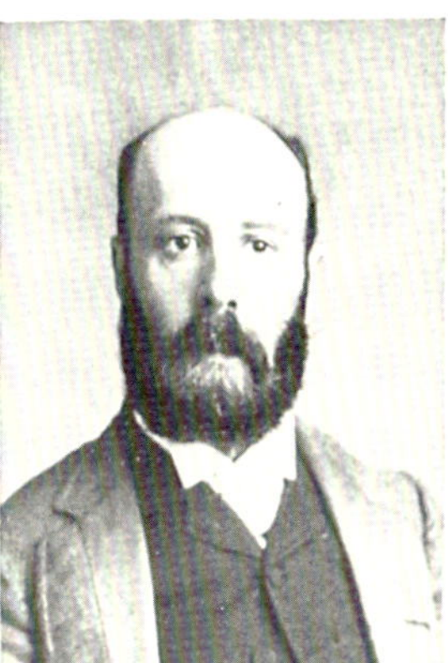

298 CHAS. H. LITTLE, Alias "Howard," Bogus Checks.

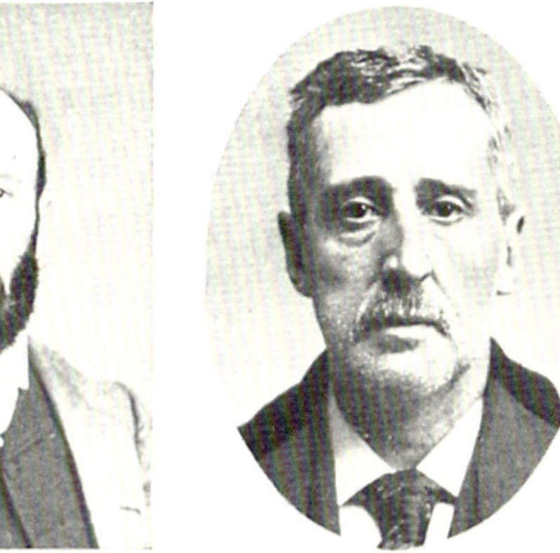

299 JOHN S. BRUSH, Alias "Jansen," Forger.

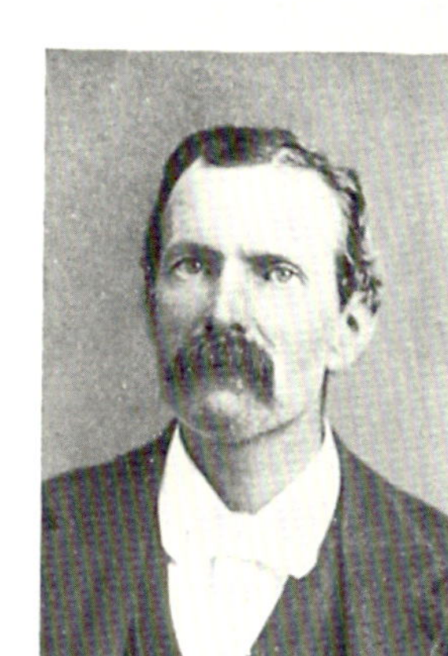

300 GEO. D. ARMSTRONG, Forger.

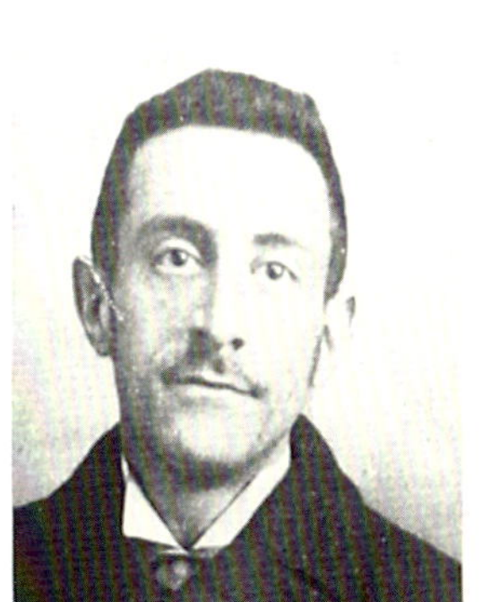

301 HUGO ADLER, Alias "Louis Allen," Forger.

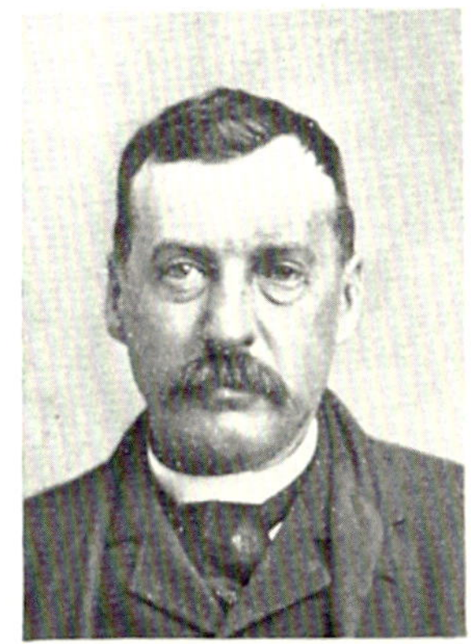

302 GEO. LOCKWOOD, Forger.

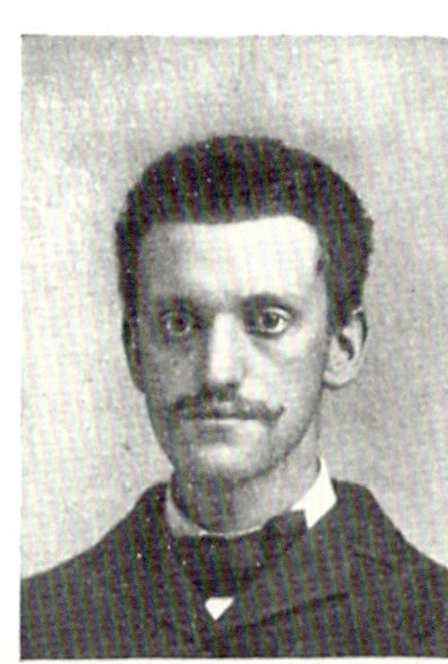

303 JOSEPH MEYERS, Alias "Mangus," Worthless Checks.

followed wholely and solely from Eakins' example; they descended from a multitude of sources and represented a practice widespread by the turn of the century. But for Henri, at least, Eakins' late portraits seem to have been compelling models. In them, with almost compulsive urgency, Eakins painted his friends more often than at any other time in his life. In the Eakins loan exhibition at the Metropolitan Museum of Art in 1917, these were the paintings to which Henri called special attention: *Being a great portrait painter*, Henri wrote his students, *he was, as usual, commissioned to paint only a very few. But he had friends and he painted his friends. Look at these portraits as well.*[19]

Nicolai Cikovsky, Jr.

1. See note 10 below for a discussion of the painting's title.
2. Lloyd Goodrich, *Thomas Eakins* (Washington, 1982) 2:220.
3. Goodrich, *Eakins* 1982, 1:295.
4. *Eakins* 1982, 2:215. For another description of this change see Evan H. Turner, "Thomas Eakins: The Earles' Gallery Exhibition of 1896," *Arts Magazine* 53 (May 1979), 100–107.
5. *Eakins* 1982, 2:215, 220.
6. *Eakins* 1982, 2:215.
7. Elizabeth Johns, *Thomas Eakins: The Heroism of Modern Life* (Princeton, 1983).
8. *Eakins* 1982, 2:215.
9. Goodrich, *Eakins* 1982, 2:220.
10. When the painting was first exhibited in the 1891 Pennsylvania Academy of the Fine Arts annual exhibition, its title, as given in the catalogue, was "*Portrait of an artist*. Property of James M. Wright." *Portrait of a Student*, exhibited in the same exhibition, depicted another of Eakins' pupils, Samuel Murray. In 1933, the portrait of James Wright was listed in Lloyd Goodrich's catalogue of Eakins' works (no. 258), without explanation, as *The Art Student*. It was owned by Wright and in the possession of a nephew. A painting entitled *The Art Student* was exhibited in the Eakins memorial exhibition held at the Pennsylvania Academy of the Fine Arts in 1917. It was owned by Mrs. Eakins, however, and therefore does not seem to have been the same painting.
11. Kate Kernan Rubin, "Thomas Eakins, *The Veteran*," *Yale University Art Gallery Bulletin* 39 (winter 1984), 20–24, very perceptively noted that Eakins' portraits, such as *The Veteran*, were "part of a project to document and record the observable human types of his day. . . ."
12. Quoted in Goodrich, *Eakins* 1982, 2:269.
13. See Lloyd Goodrich, *Thomas Eakins: His Life and Work* (New York, 1933), 40–43.
14. An English edition of Bertillon, titled *Signaletic Instructions, Including the Theory and Practice of Anthropometrical Identification*, was published in 1896. See Allan Sekula, "The Body and the Archive," *October* 39 (1987), 3–64. Kate Kernan Rubin related Eakins' project to the nineteenth-century "science" of phrenology. ("Thomas Eakins, *The Veteran*," 24). Eakins' slightly younger contemporary, Henry Farny, began to paint bust portraits of American Indians in the early 1880s; those hanging in his studio in 1894 prompted a Cincinnati newspaper to say that it *resembles a rogue's gallery composed of the prize murderers of the world.* Quoted in *Henry Farny 1847–1916* [exh. cat., Archer M. Huntington Art Gallery, The University of Texas at Austin] (Austin, 1983), 34.
15. See Ellwood C. Parry III, "Thomas Eakins's 'Naked Series' Reconsidered: Another Look at the Standing Nude Photographs Made for the Use of Eakins's Students," *American Art Journal* 20, no. 2 (1988), 53–77.
16. Rubin, "Thomas Eakins, *The Veteran*," 24.
17. *The Art Spirit* (Philadelphia and New York, 1939), 220–223, speaking of his colleagues Sloan and Glackens. Painting, he said also, "is the giving of evidence. It is the study of our lives, our environment." *The Art Spirit*, 113.
18. Before a visit to California in 1914 Henri wrote one of his former students there, "Of course, I shall want to paint interesting people. I'm told you have them all the way [from] up to date class to the half breed and gipsy." (Quoted in Martin E. Peterson, "Henri's California Visit," *Fine Arts Source Material Newsletter* 1 (February 1971), 29. In 1915 Henri wrote, "The people I like to paint are 'my people,' . . . the people through whom the dignity of life is manifest, that is, who are in some way expressing themselves naturally along the lines nature intended for them . . . . My love of mankind is individual, not national, and always I find the race expressed in the individual." (Quoted in *The Art Spirit*, 141–142).
19. *The Art Spirit*, 86–87.

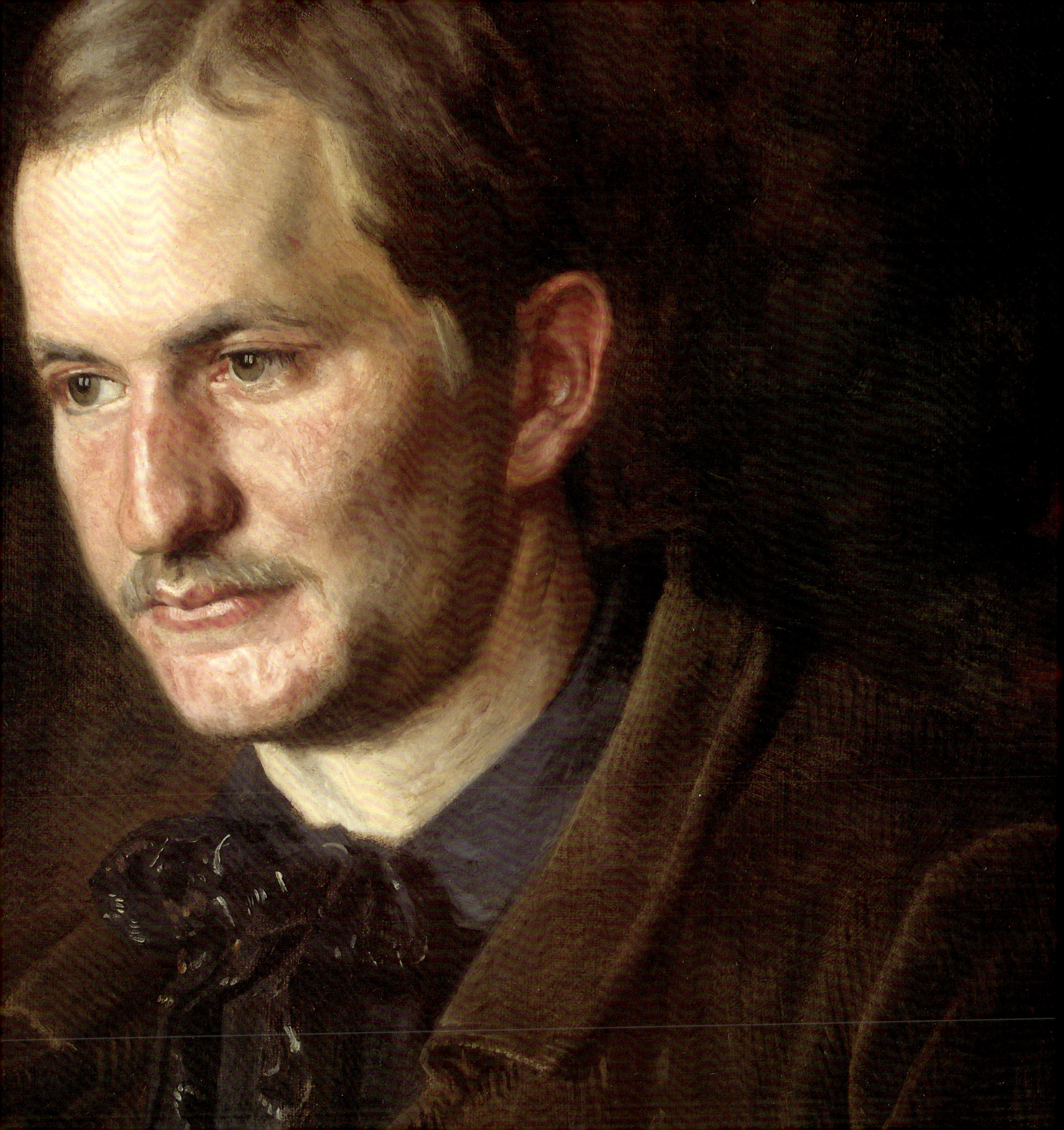

47

John Singer Sargent (1856–1925)
John Alfred Parsons Millet 1892
oil on canvas, 36¼ x 24⅛ (92.1 x 61.3)

John Alfred Parsons Millet was born in Broadway, Worcestershire, in 1888. Son of the painter Frank Millet (cat. 53), the boy had John Singer Sargent and the English landscape artist Alfred Parsons (1847–1920) as godfathers, and counted Henry James as a correspondent from the age of six onward. After schooling in England, Millet attended Harvard and the Harvard Medical School. He turned to psychiatry as a profession in the early 1920s and, along with his private Manhattan practice, worked at various times on the faculties of Buffalo, Cornell, and Columbia universities. He died in 1976.[1]

Sargent's earliest extant depictions of his godson are two pencil drawings done on 20 September 1888 (Hirschl & Adler Galleries, New York; and Fitzwilliam Museum, University of Cambridge). A witness later recounted: *In the days of my youth I was often* [at] *one of those delightful parties at the Frank Millet's* [sic] *house in Broadway—where Sargent, Abbey, Henry James, the Tademas and others foregathered. On the occasion of this drawing* [Fitzwilliam] *I had been wandering about the lovely old garden, carrying the Millet's baby, Jack. . . . Suddenly Sargent appeared, stopped, gazed at us, seized my sketchbook lying by me on the seat and proceeded to make this exquisite drawing—I am represented by the thumb to the left! He did various other sketches of us two and also of myself alone, which were snatched by my friends.*[2]

The same feeling of spontaneity pervades the portrait of the young boy now in the Manoogian collection. Alert and serious, the child studies the viewer. Three richly textured hangings—a maroon brocade, a crimson oriental silk, and a brown fur—lend a bold, abstract quality to the lower half of the canvas. Young Millet leans on these draped stuffs as if they were tribute from the European, oriental, and primitive worlds, the heritage of his cultured and adventurous father and godfather. The boy's cool, proprietary gesture belies the innocence implicit in his long, uncut, curling hair.

Throughout his career Sargent included children in some of his most ambitious portraits and genre works.[3] These portrayals generally earned him high praise for his accuracy, his sympathy, and for the respect he showed his subjects.[4] In spring 1891, Frank Millet had praised in print one of Sargent's most celebrated portraits of a child (*Beatrice Goelet*, 1890, private collection). He noted that Sargent captured the character, the distinguished aspects, and the evanescent expression of his sitters, concluding, *I have had three members of my family painted by him, and I should rather have a portrait of myself done by him than by anyone else of whom I know.*[5] This fourth family picture, dedicated to Frank Millet's wife, stayed in the Millet family until 1980.

Marc Simpson

1. Biographical material taken from Leon Edel, "John Alfred Parsons Millet," *The Century Association Yearbook, 1977* (New York, 1977), 226–228.
2. Nettie Huxley, quoted by Marvin Sadik, *American Faces* [exh. cat., National Portrait Gallery] (Washington, 1980), 101.
3. See, for example, *The Daughters of Edward D. Boit* (1882, Museum of Fine Arts, Boston), *Carnation, Lily, Lily, Rose* (1885–1886, Tate Gallery, London), and *Mrs. Carl Meyer and Her Children* (1896, private collection).
4. See the critical response to *Beatrice Goelet* as discussed in Trevor J. Fairbrother, *John Singer Sargent and America* (New York, 1986), 170–173.
5. "What the Artists think of Sargent's 'Beatrice,'" *Harper's Weekly* 35 (9 May 1891), 346–347. Quoted in Fairbrother, *Sargent*, 173.

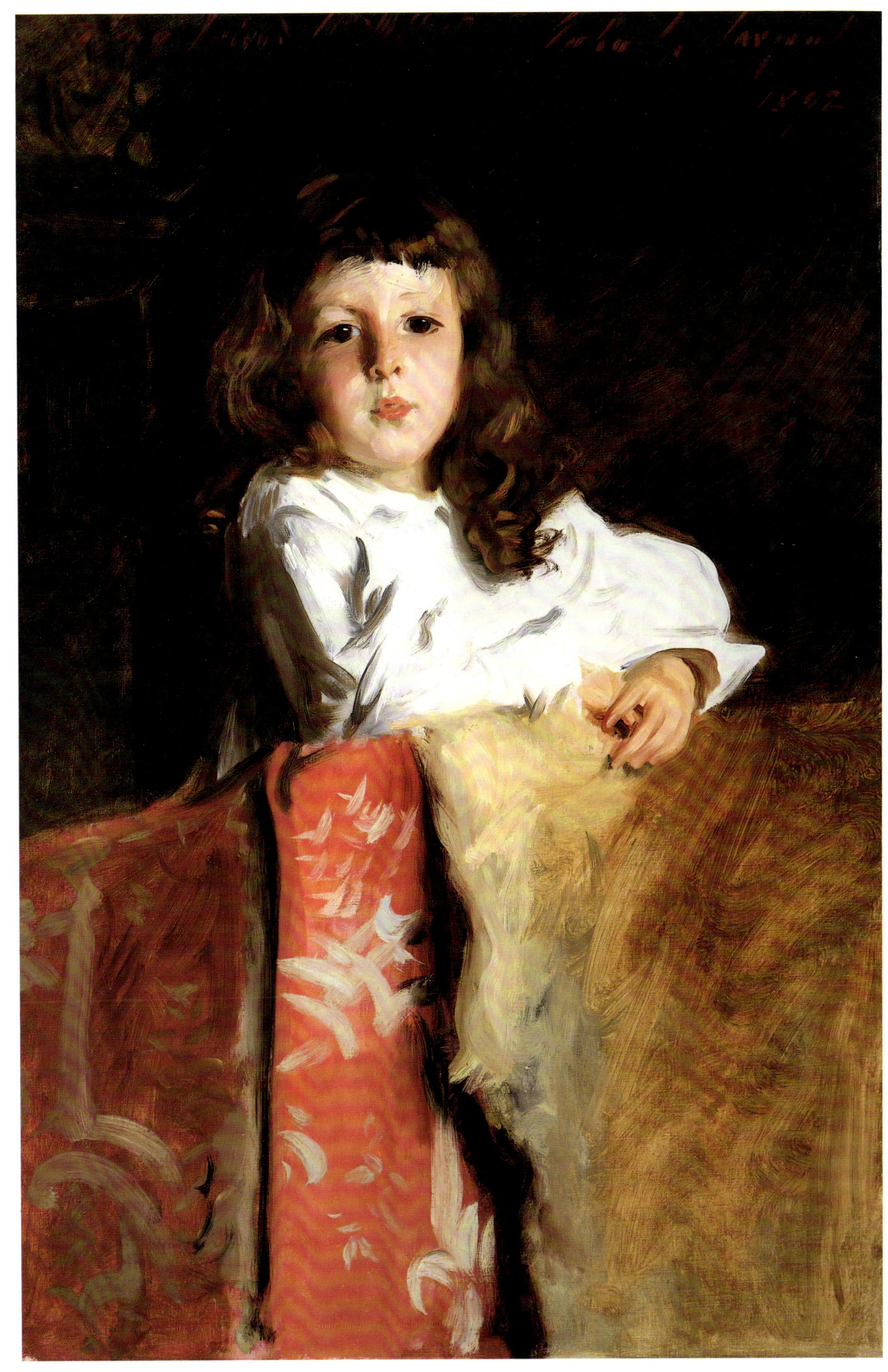

48

John Singer Sargent (1856–1925)
Miss Helen Dunham 1892
oil on canvas, 50⅜ x 43½ (128 x 110.5)

American critics of the early twentieth century looked on Sargent as the greatest living portrait painter, an artist who captured in his canvases not only the look of a specific individual but the character of the time. And repeatedly they characterized that time as *restless, vivid, spontaneous*, summarizing its spirit as *the nervous tension of the age*.[1] Sargent's *Miss Helen Dunham* epitomizes the energy and movement of this modern tenseness. The sideward glance, the taut neck, the position of her clasped hands (so dashingly and summarily painted) all signal the model's darting attention. Even the shimmer of her clothes, with light dancing off the cascade of rustling fabrics, betokens the present inability of Miss Dunham to sink back into the sheltering curves of the armchair and rest.

The vitality that Sargent portrays seems entirely appropriate. Helen Dunham, later Mrs. Theodore Holmes-Spicer, was a friend of Sargent's from at least 1890, when he invited her to the famous evening during which the fiery Spanish dancer Carmencita performed for Isabella Stewart Gardner.[2] Friendly with such bohemian blue bloods on both sides of the Atlantic as Mrs. Gardner and Vernon Lee, it was apparently Helen Dunham who brought together Sargent and the great Italian actress Eleanora Duse in 1893.[3] She was also responsible for introducing Sargent to her friend Gertrude, Lady Agnew, whose resulting portrait (1892/1893, National Galleries of Scotland) brought Sargent great popular success and prompted his election as an associate of the Royal Academy.[4]

The commission for Miss Dunham's portrait (and those of her sisters) came from her father, James H. Dunham of New York, at a time when Sargent was concentrating almost exclusively on his mural projects. The artist wrote on 7 March 1892: *This winter has been a capital one for me down here* [he was staying with Mr. and Mrs. Edwin Austin Abbey at Fairford, Gloucestershire]. *We make a very good household and there is nothing outside to take one from one's work which has been the Library exclusively. It is getting on very slowly as it need must—and requires more brain work than is good for a would be impressionist.*[5] Thus his portraits of the year, done in his London studio, are primarily of or for friends, such as this work or *John Alfred Parsons Millet* (cat. 47). Yet aside from the pose, Sargent did not treat the portrait of Helen Dunham informally, its scale and finish marking it a serious and fully conceived painting. Moreover, the artist himself clearly valued his accomplishment, for over the next five years he showed *Miss Helen Dunham* at major exhibitions in London, Chicago, and New York.[6]

Marc Simpson

1. See, for example, the comments of Charles Caffin, Christian Brinton, Royal Cortissoz, and John Van Dyke brought together in the catalogue *John Singer Sargent* [exh. cat., Grand Central Art Galleries] (New York, 1924), 9–12.
2. The event, held at William Merritt Chase's Tenth Street studio, was the subject of numerous anecdotes in memoirs and the biographies of many people who attended. Both Sargent and Chase painted full-length portraits of Carmencita. For a brief account, see Stanley Olson, *John Singer Sargent* (New York, 1980), 161–163.
3. See Richard Ormond, *John Singer Sargent: Paintings, Drawings, Watercolors* (New York, 1970), 247–248.
4. The portraits of Miss Dunham and Lady Agnew could almost be considered polar opposites. Using the same props and effects and comparable gowns, the one is all restless energy while the other becomes the epitome of elegant languor. Sargent used contrasting color schemes to heighten the emotional effect of each portrait, a rich and intense red for Helen Dunham, and cool blues and violets for Lady Agnew.
5. Sargent to Mrs. Charles Fairchild. Transcription in collection of the Boston Athenaeum, box 1, folder 14.
6. London, New English Art Club, 1892; Chicago, World's Columbian Exposition, 1893; New York, National Academy of Design, *Loan Exhibition of Portraits*, 1895; New York, Society of American Artists, 1897.

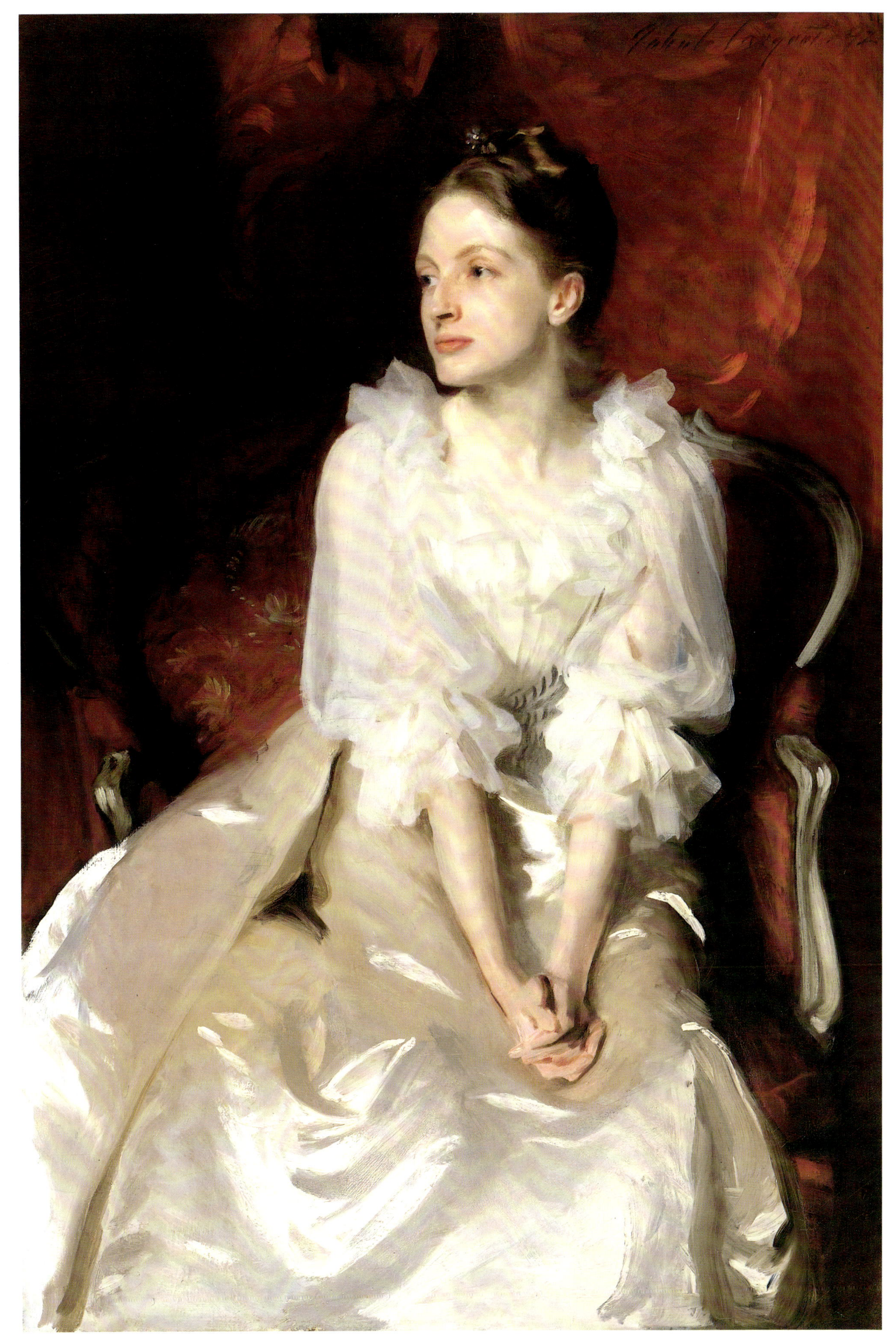

49

John George Brown (1831–1913)
Sunshine 1879
oil on canvas, 14⅛ x 20⅛ (35.9 x 51.1)

Less well known than his paintings of shoeshine boys and other urban street urchins, J. G. Brown's *Sunshine* was executed in the earlier part of his career, when many of his works reveal his interest in observing and translating the effects of natural light into oil on canvas.[1] In *Sunshine* Brown has captured the bright but hazy atmosphere of the seashore.

In the 1860s and 1870s, Brown's outdoor scenes rivaled those of Eastman Johnson and Winslow Homer. Similarities in the work of these three artists imply that they influenced each other. All had studios in New York; Brown and Homer worked in the Tenth Street Studio Building from 1872 through 1881. Brown began painting pensive young middle-class women alone outdoors by the mid-1860s several years before Homer was to do so.[2] The resemblance of the girl and her costume in *Sunshine* to those in a Homer drawing and a related painting of 1878 suggest a particular instance in which Brown may have been familiar with Homer's work or they may have used the same model.[3]

Since the 1840s, landscape paintings of the Hudson River School and literature had inspired Americans *to go forth, under open sky, and listen to nature's teachings*.[4] These romantic concepts of nature may have influenced Brown's decision to paint introspective young women in woodland settings. The population growth in the cities after the Civil War also encouraged people to plan outdoor excursions like picnics, camping, and ocean bathing. By placing his contemplative young lady within the context of an outing at the beach, Brown acknowledged both the romantic and the prosaic aspects of American life in that era. *Sarah Towne Hufford*

1. *Sunshine* must be the same painting as *A Sunny Day*, which Brown exhibited in 1879 at the National Academy of Design. A review in the *New York Times*, 20 April 1879, 10, describes *A Sunny Day* as . . . *a full-length minature portrait of a young girl lying on a sandy hillock on the beach*. Martha Hoppin has graciously provided this information from her monograph on John George Brown, which is to be published by Cambridge University Press about 1990.
2. Linda Ayres, "The American Figure: Genre Paintings and Sculpture," in *An American Perspective: Nineteenth-Century Art from the Collection of Jo Ann and Julian Ganz, Jr.* [exh. cat., National Gallery of Art] (Washington, 1981), 54.
3. The drawing by Homer is illustrated in *Winslow Homer, 1836–1910, A Selection from the Cooper-Hewitt Collection, Smithsonian Institution.* [exh. cat., Cooper-Hewitt Museum] (Washington, 1972), cat. 40. The related painting is *Peach Blossoms* in the Art Institute of Chicago.
4. *American Narrative Painting* [exh. cat., Los Angeles County Museum of Art] (Los Angeles, 1974), 140. The quotation is from William Cullen Bryant's poem "Thanatopsis."

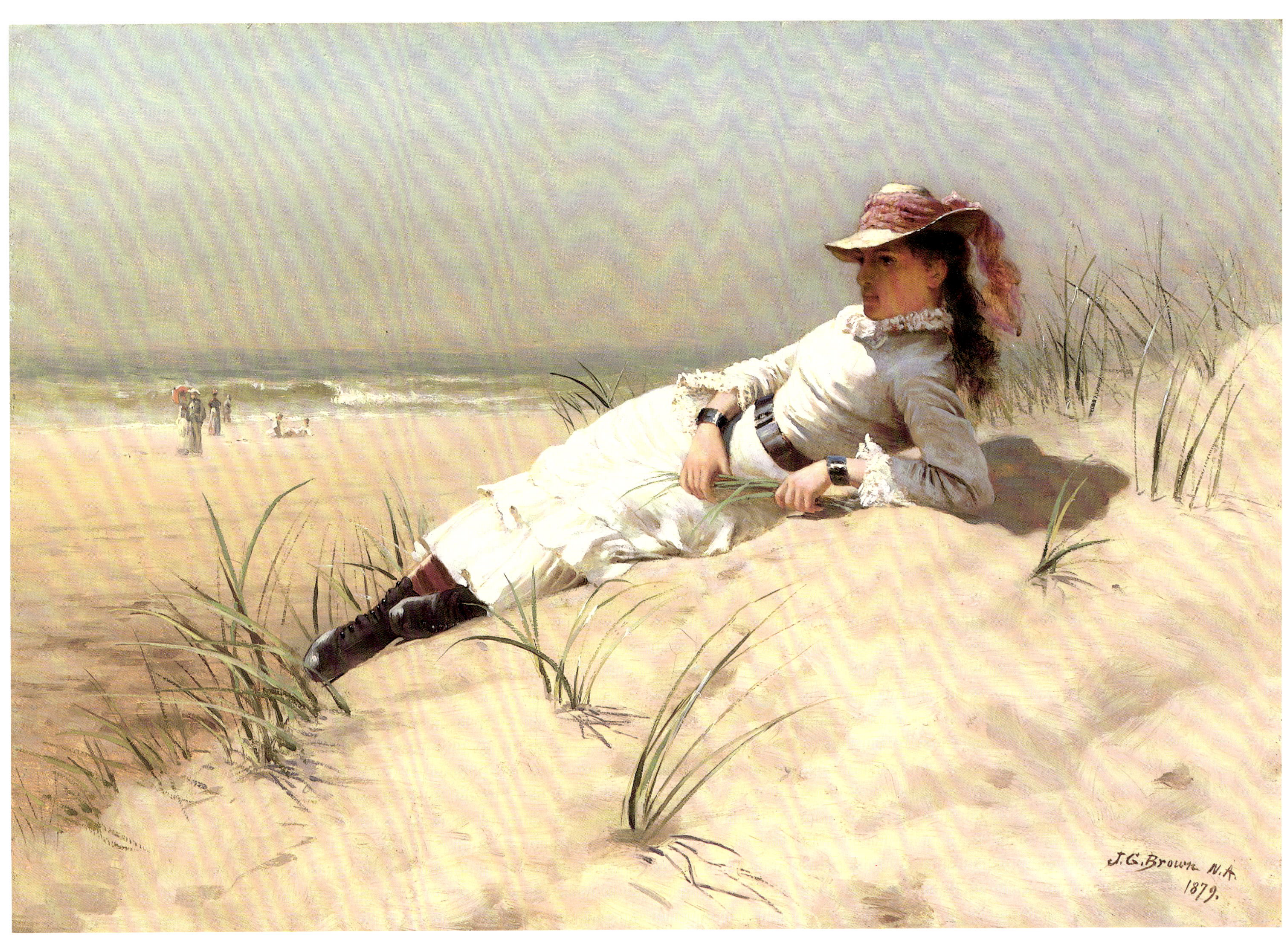
J.G. Brown N.A.
1879.

50

Charles Sprague Pearce (1851–1914)
Reading by the Shore
oil on canvas, 11⅞ x 18⅛ (30.2 x 46)

Reading by the Shore is an unusual painting in Charles Sprague Pearce's oeuvre in a number of respects. Compared to the larger-scale works with narrative content that Pearce regularly submitted to the Paris Salon for three decades after 1876, this work is more private in scale and sentiment. Its palette is high in value and its brushstrokes looser than his salon submissions, which critics noted were within a range of subtle, gray tonalities.[1] Most of Pearce's outdoor paintings tend to have an even distribution of lighting, but here the face of the subject is in shadow, and the focus instead is the brilliant, variegated color of the umbrella, which draws the viewer almost like a stained glass window. In common with Pearce's outdoor paintings is the high horizon line, which the critics indentified as a hallmark of his compositional technique.[2]

From 1885 Pearce resided about twenty miles from Paris in Auvers-sur-Oise, painting in a glass-enclosed outdoor studio. The large majority of his paintings over the next three decades, sentimental interpretations of rural life in northern France, were produced here. No other paintings of the seaside with figures by Pearce are known, although a finished oil sketch of a similar shoreline exists (private collection, Philadelphia). It is probable that Pearce, like large numbers of his contemporary American expatriates, visited the rocky coast of Brittany and Normandy with his wife, and there painted this intimate portrait of her reading.[3]

Pearce painted several portraits of his wife in the late 1880s, including the full-length *La Dame de la Directoire* (Elvejham Museum of Art, Madison, Wisconsin), c. 1888, and a three-quarter-length *Portrait of Madame P.* (unlocated), c. 1889, which was shown at the Exposition Universelle in Paris that year. Based on the age of the subject, and a similarity in certain passages of the handling of paint corresponding to the Elvehjam work, *Reading by the Shore* was evidently also painted in the late 1880s.

D. Dodge Thompson

1. George William Sheldon, *Recent Ideals of American Art* (New York and London, 1890), 10.
2. "Book of American Figure-Painters," *The Art Amateur* 16, no. 2 (January 1887), 47.
3. David Sellin, *Americans in Normandy and Brittany, 1860–1910* [exh. cat., Phoenix Art Museum] (Phoenix, 1982).

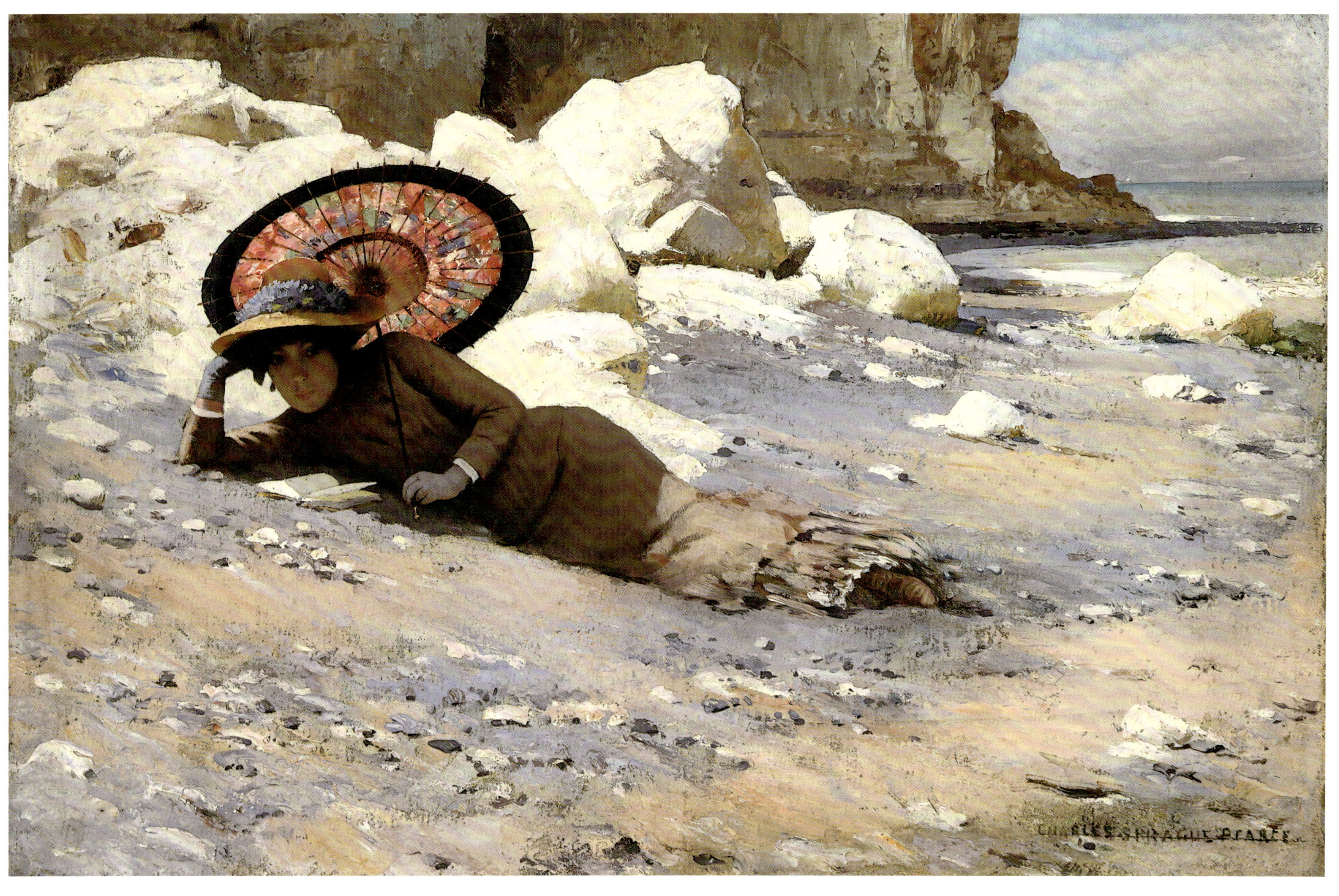

51

William Merritt Chase (1849–1916)
The Nursery 1890
oil on panel, 14⅜ x 16 (36.5 x 40.6)

By 1890, when he painted *The Nursery*, William Merritt Chase was at the height of his powers as an artist. With boundless self-confidence he had assimilated bits and pieces from the styles of many different artists and combined them with consummate skill to develop what is now recognized as his mature style. The bright, sun-filled expression, which he achieved in paintings done in the 1890s such as *The Nursery*, is considered to be Chase's ultimate statement in art.

In 1878 Chase completed his studies at the Royal Academy in Munich and returned to America, quickly establishing a reputation as a gentleman artist and spokesman for progressive art. His opulent studio in the Tenth Street Studio Building served as a meeting place for artists as well as a gracious setting in which Chase could entertain his wealthy patrons. Among the many paintings hanging on its walls were his own copies of Old Masters and portraits and figure paintings done in the dark tones and bravura brushwork favored by the Munich school. Landscape painting was not given priority; in fact, only one large landscape by Chase can be assigned to this period.

Chase first experimented with plein-air painting on a trip to Italy in 1877, accompanied by two other Munich-trained Americans, John H. Twachtman and Frank Duveneck. In Venice, Chase worked at capturing the bright light of the city reflected off the walls of houses and the waters of canals. These paintings were small, experimental, and of a personal nature; his major works from the period continued to be large figurative compositions.

After his return to New York in 1878, Chase became an active member of the emerging young art community. He joined the social/art group known as the Tile Club, whose summer excursions in the countryside reinforced his interest in plein-air painting. Also, during the early to mid-1880s, Chase made return visits to Europe, particularly to the Netherlands, where, under the influence of the painters of the Hague school, he began to devote even more time to outdoor painting. This shifting emphasis, combined with Chase's growing interest in the medium of pastel, resulted in a major change in his palette and subject matter, from dark, tonal portraits and figure pieces to bright, sun-filled landscapes painted outdoors.

During these summer trips abroad Chase met many of the leading figures of the art world, including the relatively academic Belgian painter Alfred Stevens and the French impressionist Edouard Manet. He also had the chance to see the works of other impressionists, including the pastels of Giuseppe de Nittis, an Italian artist working in Paris. The work of each of these artists had a profound effect on Chase's artistic development. Stevens encouraged Chase to lighten his palette and focus on contemporary subject matter; this advice was underscored by Chase's study of the work of the impressionists. Compositional devices were undoubtedly adopted from the impressionists, such as cropping the image to create both a candid effect and a sense of immediacy. Furthermore, the use of dramatic diagonals drawing the viewer into the composition, which Chase utilized most effectively, was a speciality of De Nittis. All of these influences can be detected in varying degrees in Chase's plein-air genre scenes of the 1880s, but they are cleverly combined into a style all his own.

In 1886 Chase married Alice Gerson and began spending his summer months at home, recording his own domestic milieu and translating what he had learned abroad into an American idiom. At first, Chase and his wife lived in his studio on Tenth Street, but when their first child was born they moved their home to the suburbs of Brooklyn. There Chase delighted in spending the summer painting Prospect Park as well as other parks in the area. From 1886 until 1889, these parks served as the perfect setting for Chase's genteel genre paintings. Then, after a park attendant reprimanded Chase for a minor violation, he moved on to Central Park, which became the new setting for his outdoor paintings.

By 1890, when Chase began painting his major series of Central Park scenes, he had clearly mastered the art of plein-air painting. Initially he chose to paint well-known sections of the park, such as the Central Park Terrace and the Boat Basin. He was also attracted to other picturesque settings such as the small pond where children sailed their miniature yachts. These scenes were immediately singled out and praised for their natural beauty and for their straightforwardness. One critic observed: *The art of Mr. Chase is objective and external, and he has trained himself to be a kind of human camera through whose lenses we see reflected . . . a new definition of beauty in things we have heretofore called dull and uninteresting.*[1] While Central Park was certainly not dull or uninteresting, most New Yorkers took its carefully planned landscape for granted. In one writer's assessment: *The practical man wonders how much a piece of road in Central Park costs. The ward politician looks at the Park, and dreams of filching money from the taxpayers by the time-worn methods.* However, the same writer went on to note: *The artist sees the beauty of the Park, watches the play of sunlight on lake, tree-top, and meadow, and picks out for its unexpected charm some corner neglected by the public.*[2] William Merritt Chase led the way on this artistic mission, with what his fellow artist Kenyon Cox described as *a wandering eye . . . finding out beauty in common objects and in unexpected places.*[3] Chase's painting *The Nursery* is a perfect example of how the inquisitive artist could discover beauty in even the remotest sections of Central Park. It also displays Chase's consummate skill as a plein-air painter, as well as his natural ability for capturing the characteristic look and spirit of Americans at leisure.

It was the foresight of Frederick Law Olmsted and Calvert Vaux, whose design "Greensward" was selected for the plan of Central Park in 1853, that provided varied spaces for the activities of New York's growing population. In this plan, specific areas of the park were designated for physical activity, while others were reserved for relaxation and contemplation. The area in which Chase painted *The Nursery* was originally designed to be an arboretum. The land, approximately forty acres located between Harlem Lake in the northernmost region of the park and Central Park's Upper Reservoir, was intended to feature every native American tree and shrub that the terrain and climate would support. When the arboretum plan proved to be impractical, a portion of the area was utilized as a temporary nursery.[4]

In Chase's painting *The Nursery*, the artist has taken what might otherwise have been viewed as a mundane subject and transformed it into a charming and candid view of a brief moment in the day of a young woman. The setting is Central Park's nursery, where seedlings were started early in the season in cold frames covered by glass. The young plants were then transplanted to flower beds and decorative urns throughout the park. The month is June, when all of the trees are in full leaf, and most of the seedlings have already been removed, as indicated by the cold frames in the foreground which have been taken over by weeds. Only a few of the frames in the far background remain filled with bright red and yellow flowers.

It is not known just what drew Chase's attention to the upper regions of Central Park to paint *The Nursery*. This area was described as *little frequented* except by those who lived in the area. But what he found, a *peculiar mixture of straight lines with crooked, of orderly ranks of seedlings with frames abandoned to the wildest growth*, he transformed into one of the boldest, most direct, and loveliest paintings of his entire career.[5] The composition is a daring combination of strong diagonals that draw the viewer swiftly into the composition. Then, through the use of increasingly brilliant shades of white, the eye is directed to the pivotal figure of the woman in the foreground. The eye stops, momentarily, to consider the woman's pensive expression and the tone of her skin, which reflects the red brick wall of the shed, then continues down to her tan gloves to an explosion of color in the bouquet of flowers she holds. The overall color is high-keyed, the light brilliantly manipulated as the artist keeps the right side of the composition somewhat subdued, yet without any distracting shadows—as if a cloud were overhead. In contrast, the composition is enlivened by the bright sunshine in the background and the strong morning light reflected off of the red building and the women's dresses.

In explaining this painting, a contemporary writer contended that *the lady in front to the left has obtained a dispensation from the rule not to pick the flowers* in the park.[6] This was a reasonable assumption on the part of the writer since the ordinances regulating behavior in the park were both strict and explicit: *All persons are forbidden: To cut, break, or in any way injure or deface the trees, shrubs, plants, turf*

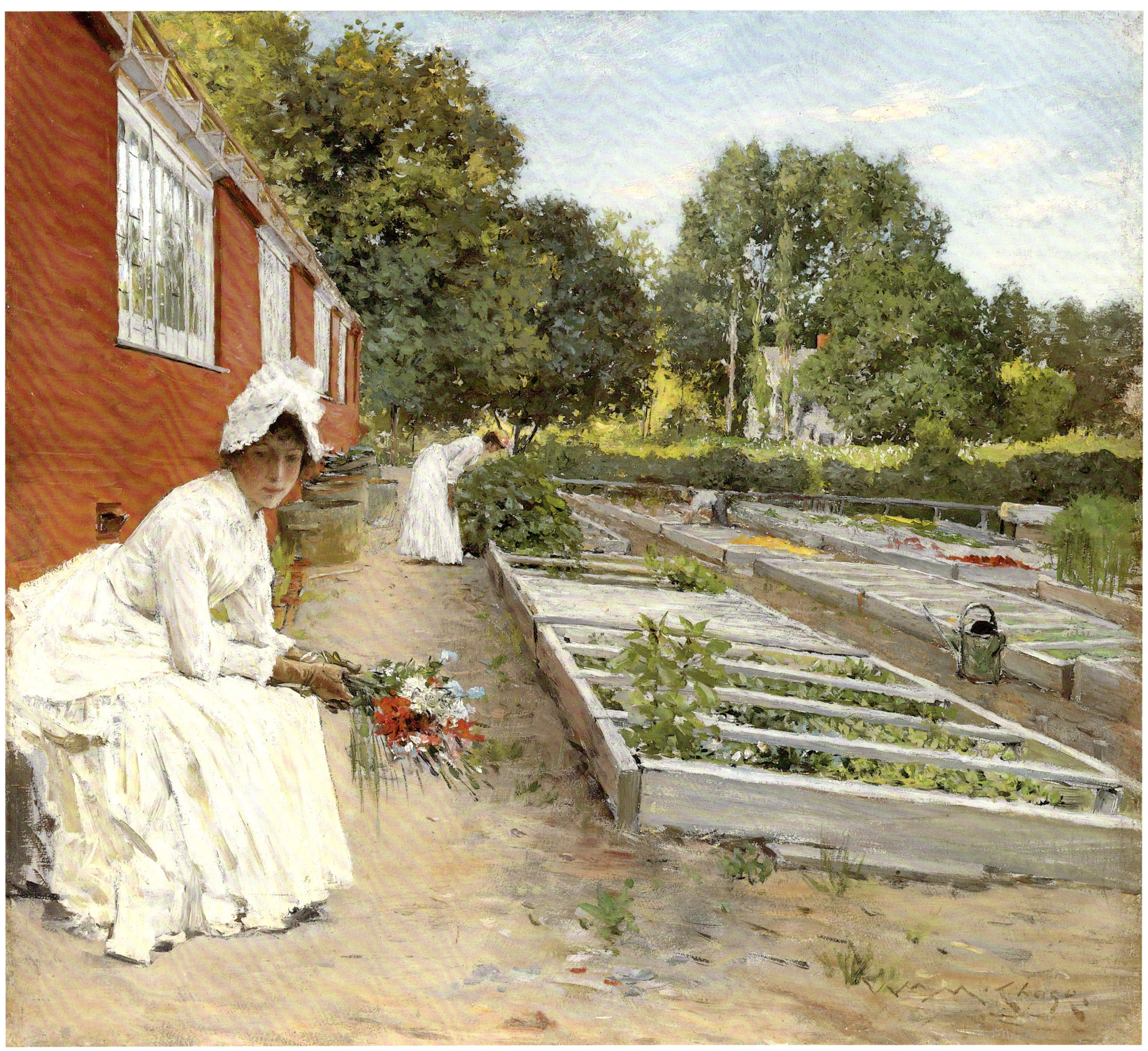

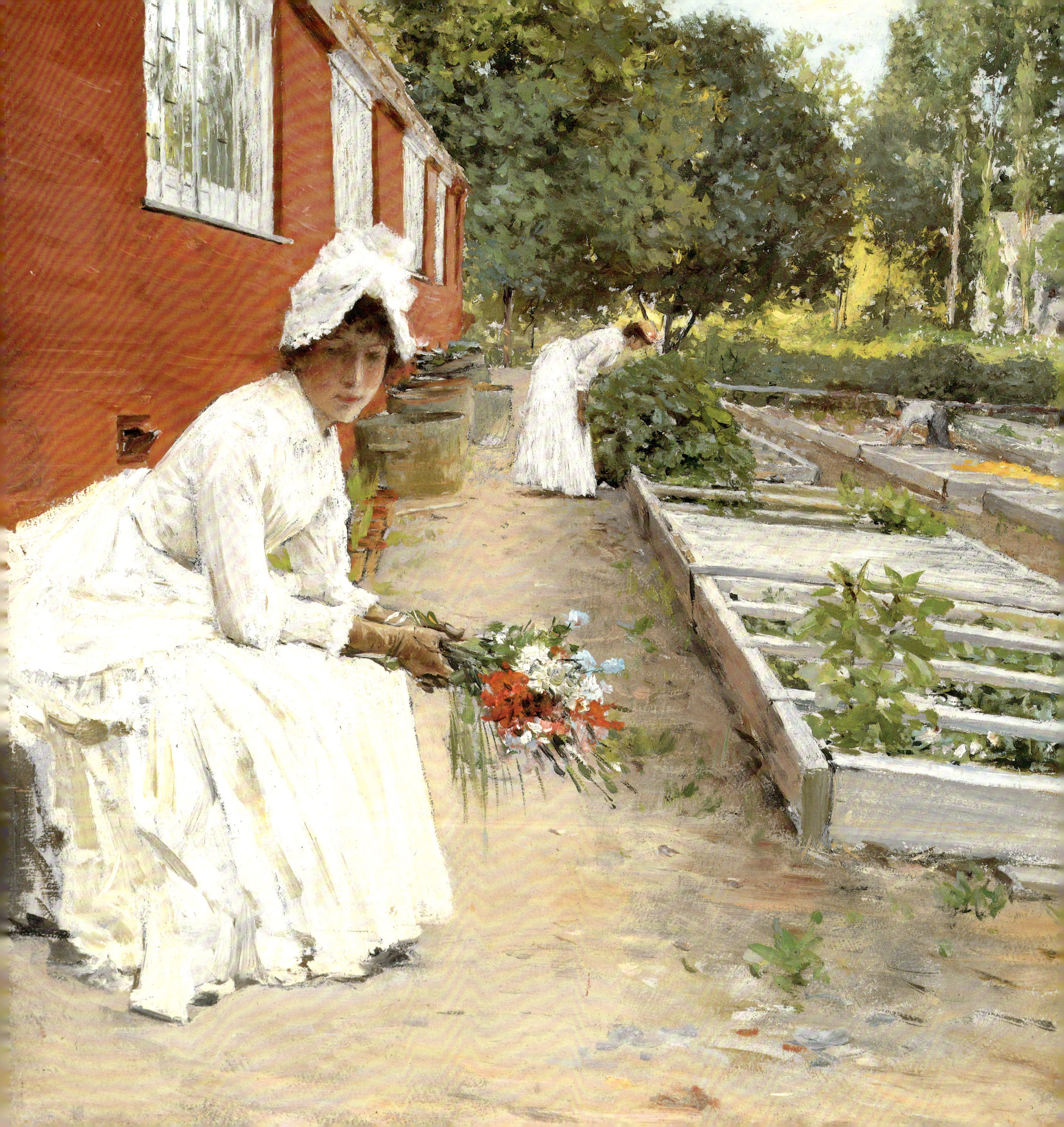

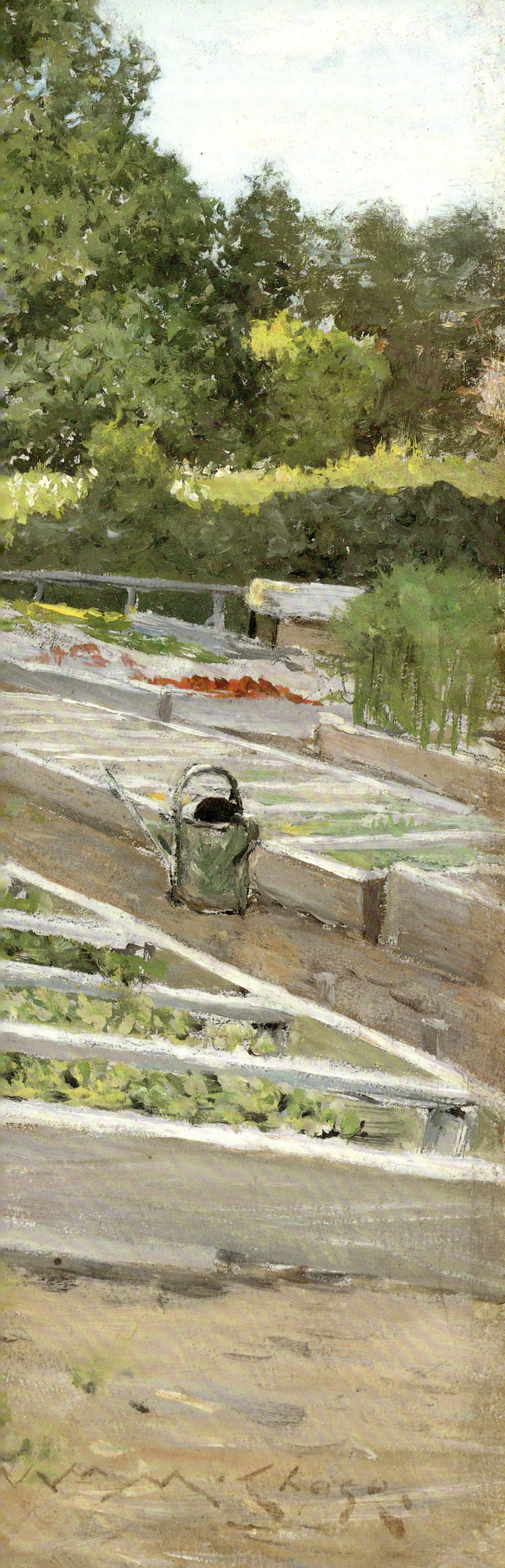

or any of the buildings, fences or other constructions upon the park. Another ordinance forbade bringing into the park *any newly plucked branch, plant or flower.*[7]

Chase did not intend his painting to carry a message or tell a tale, however, for he generally disdained such narrative art. Instead, *The Nursery* is a simple, straightforward scene, most likely unpremeditated. Chase described his approach to plein-air painting: *When I start to paint out of doors, I put myself in as light marching order as possible . . . I carry a comfortable stool that can be closed up in a small space and I never use an umbrella. I want all the light I can get. When I have found the spot I like, I set up my easel and paint the picture on the spot. I think that is the only way rightly to interpret nature.*[8] In this way Chase often took a prosaic subject and created an impressive, sparkling artistic statement. This is exactly what he accomplished in his painting *The Nursery*.

Ronald G. Pisano

1. Perriton Maxwell, "William Merritt Chase—Artist, Wit and Philosopher," *The Saturday Evening Post* (November 4, 1899), 347.
2. Charles De Kay, "Mr. Chase and Central Park," *Harper's Weekly* 35, no. 1793 (2 May 1891), 327.
3. Kenyon Cox, "William M. Chase, Painter," *Harper's New Monthly Magazine* 78 (March 1889), 556.
4. Henry Hope Reed and Sophia Duckworth, *Central Park: A History and a Guide* (New York, 1972), 133. This area was in use by 1873, as shown on a map reproduced in Elizabeth Barlow, *Frederick Law Olmsted's New York* (New York, 1972), 90–92.
5. De Kay, "Mr. Chase," 328.
6. De Kay, "Mr. Chase," 328.
7. T. Addison Richards, *Guide to Central Park* (New York, 1869), 99–100.
8. A. R. Ives, "Suburban Sketching Grounds: Talk with Mr. William M. Chase, Mr. Edward Moran, Mr. Leonard Ochtman," *Art Amateur* 25, no. 4 (September 1891), 80.

52

Robert Reid (1862–1929)
Reverie 1890
oil on panel, 11⅞ x 20⅛ (30.2 x 51.1)

Reverie is one of the few works by Reid known today that was executed between his return to New York in 1889 and the beginning of his involvement in mural work in 1892–1893. For the relatively minor role played by its figure, and the dominance of its sun-dappled landscape setting, *Reverie* has been viewed both as a brief aberration in a career devoted to mural work,[1] and as a precursor of Reid's later impressionist paintings.[2]

What exposure to or knowledge of impressionism Reid might have had in France is unknown. Certainly there is no indication of impressionist tendencies in the religious and sentimental narrative works that he produced for the Paris Salon.[3] Yet within two years of Reid's settling in New York, critics were describing his exhibited work as impressionist,[4] leading one to believe that Reid quickly absorbed a new aesthetic from his circle of artist friends in America. Among those who could have influenced Reid in this regard are his colleagues from the Boston Museum School, Edmund Tarbell (1862–1938) and Frank Benson (1862–1951), who had both returned from Europe and were teaching there by 1889; or New York artists with whom he would later be associated as a member of The Ten such as J. Alden Weir (1841–1926). Certainly the mood of *Reverie*, the quiet remove at which Reid described the figure and her reflective activity, demonstrate an attitude for which the Boston school as well as certain members of The Ten are well known, one embodied by the beautiful cultivated woman described in a setting and with a technique as refined as the subject herself.

In time, both the extent of Reid's academic training and his experience with mural design would temper the impressionist tendencies revealed in *Reverie*. The small, broken strokes of color, the soft, naturalistic palette, the forms defined by patches rather than contour, would all soon give way to broad strokes, distinct outlines, and tonal effects centered around a dominant hue.

Christian Brinton, writing in 1911, called attention to a *blitheness* in Reid's art, stating that *His world is devoid of any spiritual, philosophical, or philanthropic pretensions. It exists for itself alone, and persistently sings of youth, sunlight, flowers, and supple rhythmic forms and contours.*[5] Although Brinton was thinking of Reid's mature paintings, he described an inclination already evident in *Reverie*, a taste for simple, beautifully painted pictures concerned with color, light, and decorative effects. *Sally Mills*

1. H. Barbara Weinberg, "Robert Reid: Academic 'Impressionist,'" *Archives of American Art Journal* 15 (January 1975), 11.
2. William H. Gerdts, *American Impressionism* (New York, 1984), 182.
3. See Weinberg, "Robert Reid," figs. 3, 5, 6.
4. See, for example, the writer for the *Studio* who lamented in 1891 that Reid had been *bitten by the Impressionist tarantula* (quoted in Gerdts, *American Impressionism*, 182); or a review of the 1892 Society of American Artists show that grouped Reid's *A Letter* among *other Impressionistic paintings* and praised *the superior brilliancy* of its color (*The Critic* 20 [14 May 1892], 281).
5. Christian Brinton, "Robert Reid: Decorative Impressionist," *Arts and Decoration* 2 (November 1911), 34.

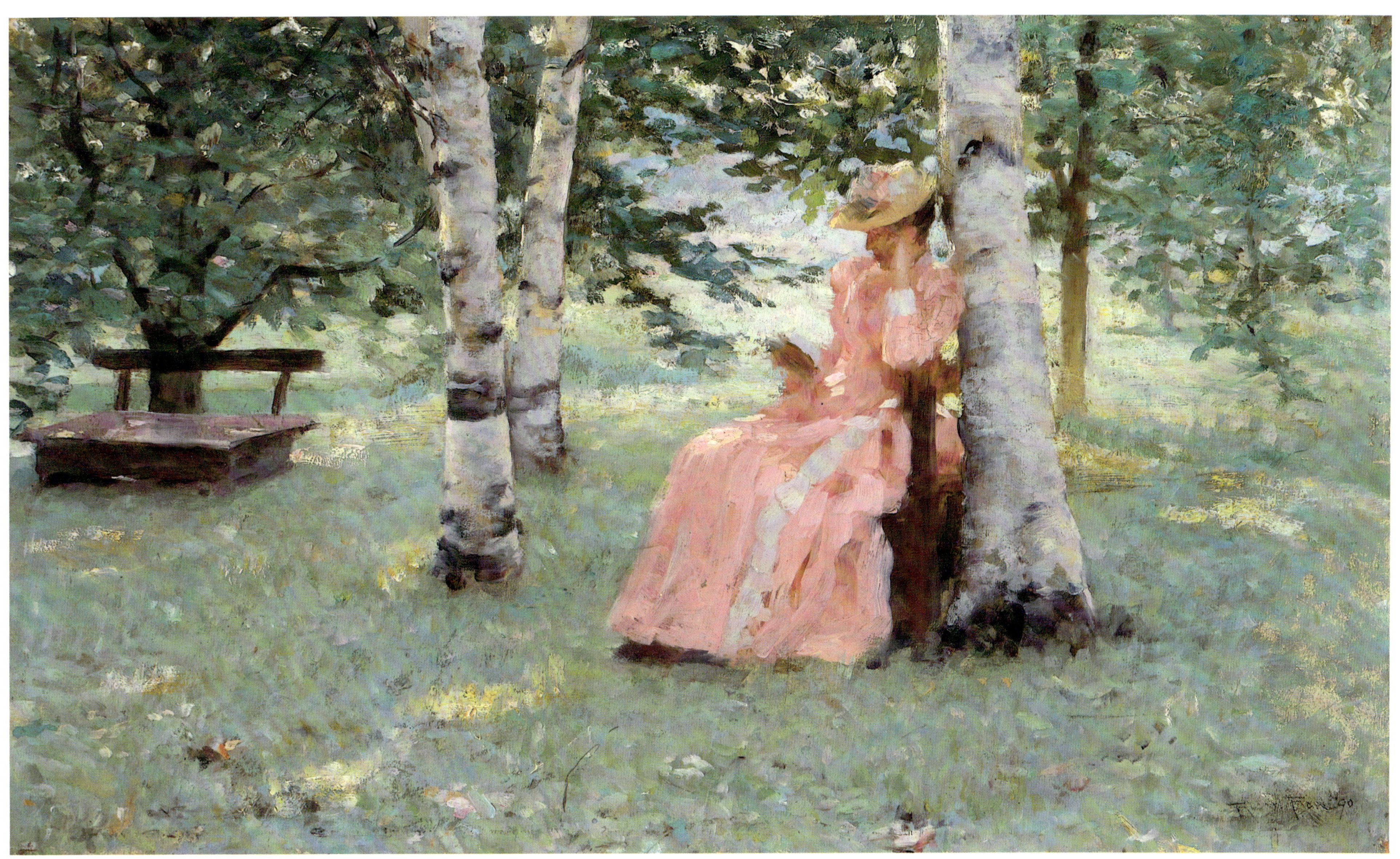

53

Francis Davis Millet (1846–1912)
The Window Seat 1883
20⅛ x 30¼ (51.1 x 76.8)

The Window Seat, in spite of its potentially sentimental subject, is a painting about light—interior and exterior light, light falling through glass and light filtered through muslin, light modeling form and light reflected off form. The figure in *The Window Seat*, a handsome young woman[1] dressed in a muslin dress and fichu of the early nineteenth century, sits off-center in the composition, her eyes intent on her fancywork. Through the windows behind her streams a cool light that dances off the polished surfaces of the interior—the table with its propped-open book and floral still life, the spindle chair on which the woman rests her feet—and glows within the varying layers of white curtains. The whole scene creates a mood of quiet domesticity that, together with the work's smooth technique, suggests the artist's admiration of seventeenth-century Dutch genre painting.

The Window Seat is one of Millet's earliest English subject pictures. The painting probably re-creates a scene that he first saw in summer 1883 while staying with a group of artists and writers connected with the Harper's publishing firm, among them Edwin Austin Abbey, at the White Lion Inn in the Oxfordshire village of Bidford-on-Avon.[2] It would be in the next summer that, with Abbey, he would discover the Worcestershire village of Broadway and establish his home as the center of a thriving Anglo-American art colony.

Millet first exhibited *The Window Seat* in London in December 1883 at the inaugural exhibition of the Institute of Painters in Oil Colours. The close-toned study of whites was reproduced in the catalogue, via a pen drawing of the figure by Abbey.[3] The painting's accurate representation of a light-filled interior moved one critic to note that it *evinces a fine sense of the harmonies of white, and light and shade, and solid and semi-lucid forms*, and another to call it *one of the most original works in the exhibition.*[4] The writer for *The Magazine of Art* wrote of it simply: *Of all the varied treatments of the single figure, that of Mr. F. D. Millet in "The Window Seat" is the most remarkable. . . . The lighting is most dexterously managed, and the cleverness of the picture is almost obsessive . . . the sense of luminous, ubiquitous daylight is powerfully rendered.*[5]

Millet clearly valued the painting. He exhibited it at the National Academy of Design annual in New York in 1885 and again as one of his eight paintings at the World's Columbian Exposition in Chicago in 1893. A writer upon the latter exhibition summarized the work as *one of the best illustrations of his effective and scholarly style. It is a simple story simply told.*[6] *Marc Simpson*

1. Reputedly Millet's wife, Lily. Francis Davis Millet Papers, Archives of American Art, Smithsonian Institution, roll 1096, frame 191.
2. See E. V. Lucas, *Edwin Austin Abbey*, 2 vols. (London, 1921), 1:130–131.
3. *Institute of Painters in Oil Colours* (London, 1883), ill. no. 90.
4. "Institute of Painters in Oil Colours" *Athenaeum* 2930 (22 December 1883), 822; and "The Institute of Painters in Oil Colours, London," *The Art Journal* (1884), 94.
5. "The Institute," *The Magazine of Art* (1884), 163.
6. Hubert Howe Bancroft, *The Book of the Fair*, 2 vols. (Chicago, 1893), 2:683, reproduced 682.

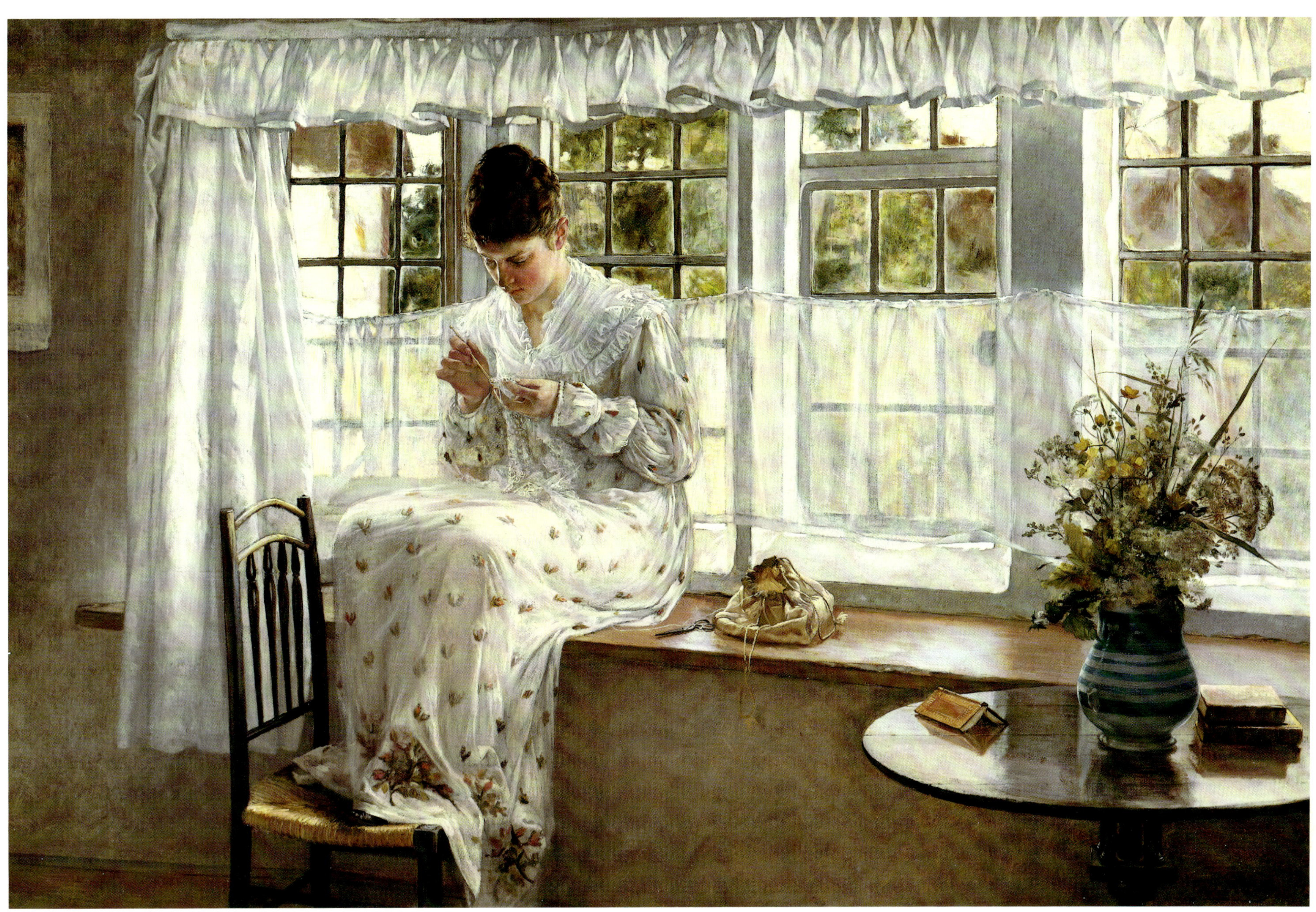

54

Mary Cassatt (1844–1926)
Susan Seated Outdoors Wearing a Purple Hat c. 1881
oil on canvas, 29⅛ x 36¾ (74 x 93.4)

Little is known about Susan, who was apparently a cousin of Cassatt's companion-housekeeper Mathilde Vallet. Susan posed for at least nine canvases painted by Cassatt between 1881 and 1883,[1] the last and finest being *Susan on a Balcony Holding a Dog* (1883, The Corcoran Gallery of Art, Washington), which received high praise when it was shown at the eighth impressionist exhibition in 1886.[2] Her brief but concentrated appearance in Cassatt's art at this time suggests that she was assuming a role previously held by Cassatt's sister Lydia. Lydia had been the model for many of Cassatt's most successful works of the late seventies and early eighties, but she suffered from Bright's disease and had grown steadily weaker in the year preceding her death in 1882. Susan replaced Lydia as Cassatt's steady model, her plain, unglamorous features serving to typify the artist's idea of a modern woman.

The composition of *Susan Seated Outdoors Wearing a Purple Hat* relates closely to Cassatt's painting of *Lydia Crocheting in the Garden at Marly* (1880, The Metropolitan Museum of Art, New York); they are among the few works by Cassatt that are set outdoors.[3] Both feature a seated woman, whose figure commands the foreground plane, while the line of a path recedes behind her at a sharp angle. The later work is sketchier and simpler; Susan is posed against a richly brushed but indistinct and nearly impenetrable wall of green. She wears a dark dress that draws attention to her gloved hands, her young face, and her distinctive purple hat. No narrative element explains her presence in this garden; Susan seems "all dressed up with no place to go."

Although set in a landscape, *Susan Seated Outdoors Wearing a Purple Hat* does not reveal the traditional impressionist concern for light. Like Degas, Cassatt preferred interior settings to outdoor light and maintained an emphasis on the figure, never allowing its contours to dissolve into the background. The dark colors and slashing strokes of this work reflect as well her admiration for Manet and the Spanish masters such as Velázquez. The very simplicity of her composition and description call attention to Cassatt's design, especially to the manner in which she has nearly eliminated a middle ground. Cassatt's interest in pattern and arrangement, concerns that would announce themselves later in the decade as "decorative," suggest ambitions quite apart from the impressionist motive of capturing a particular place and specific moment through the depiction of color and light.[4]

Sally Mills

1. Adelyn Dohme Breeskin, *Mary Cassatt: A Catalogue Raisonné of the Oils, Pastels, Watercolors, and Drawings* (Washington, 1970), nos. 105–112, 125.
2. See Charles S. Moffett and others, *The New Painting: Impressionism 1874–1886* [exh. cat., The Fine Arts Museums of San Francisco] (San Francisco, 1986), cat. 137.
3. William Gerdts related that around 1880, Monet advised Cassatt to pose her models out of doors. See *American Impressionism* [exh. cat., The Henry Art Gallery, University of Washington] (Seattle, 1980), 47.
4. See Fronia E. Wissman, "Realists among the Impressionists," in San Francisco 1986, 348–350.

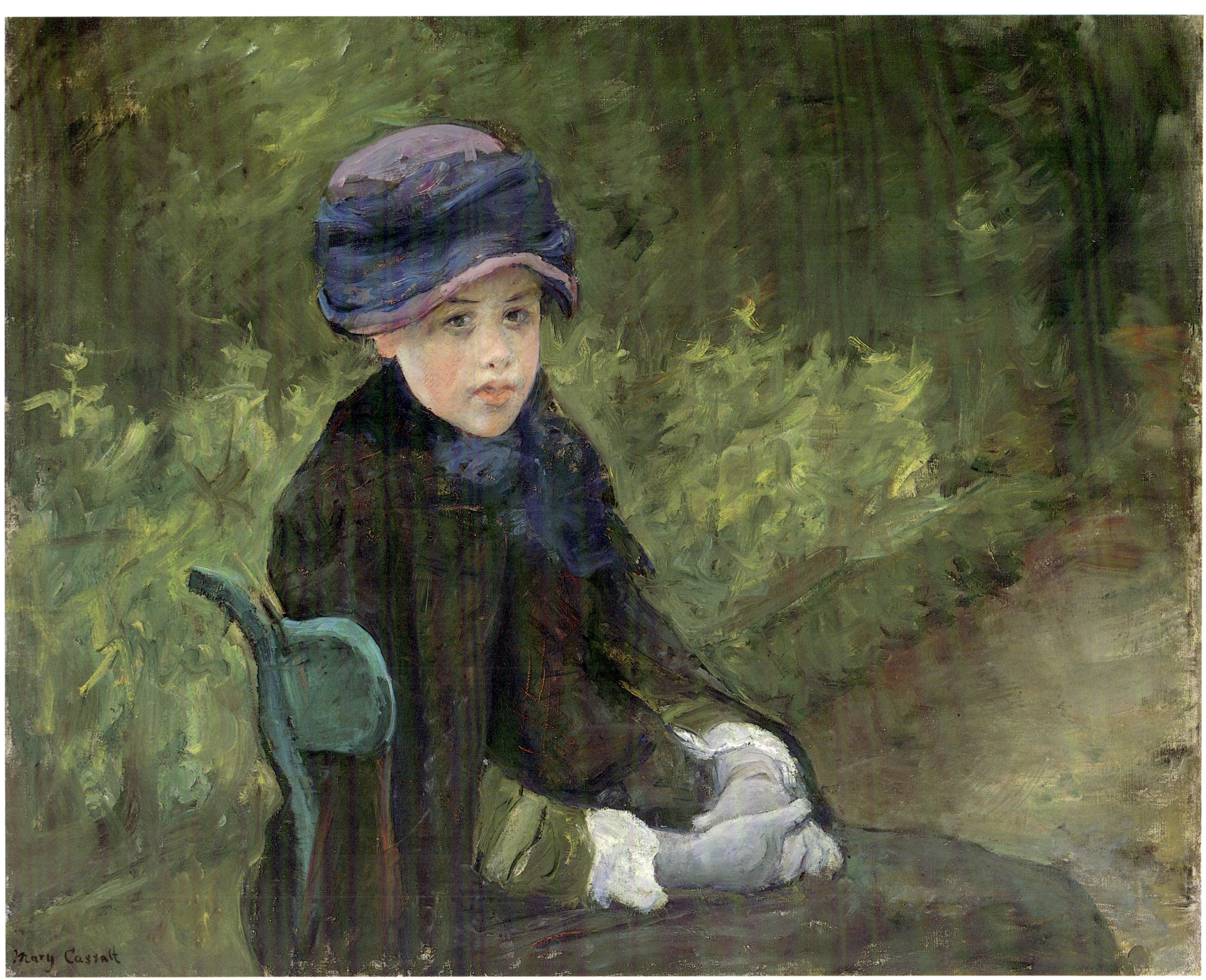
Mary Cassatt

55

Childe Hassam (1859–1935)
A Paris Nocturne 1890
oil on canvas, 27¼ x 20¼ (69.2 x 51.4)

In 1886 Hassam and his new wife left Boston for Paris. Unlike the majority of their fellow American artists who lived as students in that city, they settled comfortably into a large apartment and studio. Hassam made illustrations and sold other work through dealers in the United States while enrolled at the Académie Julian, where he studied traditional methods of drawing and painting. At the same time he was not oblivious to the impressionist movement; the brighter palette and emphasis on the quality of light in such works reinforced Hassam's own inclinations toward plein-air painting.

Hassam early showed an interest in depicting the more attractive aspects of city life under varying conditions. By the time he arrived in Paris he had already created the masterful *Rainy Day, Boston* (1885, Toledo Museum of Art, Ohio) and *Boston Common at Twilight* (1885–1886, Museum of Fine Arts, Boston). His first major Parisian street scene, *Une Averse, Rue Bonaparte* (1887, private collection, Wichita) received much critical acclaim when exhibited at the Salon that year. With its somewhat loose handling, it was a bridge between the straightforward Boston cityscapes and his truly impressionist work such as *Le Jour de Grand Prix* (1887, New Britain Museum of American Art, Connecticut), which won the gold medal in the Salon of 1888. In this sun-filled depiction of one of Paris' most festive occasions, Hassam first used the short, broken brushstrokes that would characterize most of his painting thereafter.

A Paris Nocturne is one of the more broadly handled of Hassam's works. The very sketchy quality of the foreground and the anonymous yet prominently placed wasp-waisted woman in the center of the composition lend the work something of the quality of an illustration. The location of the busy scene of Parisians clothed in evening garb was said, in a 1928 catalogue, to be the Champs Elysees,[1] but such generalized and ubiquitous elements as the flower stall and advertising kiosk do not make it possible to pinpoint the avenue shown.[2]

Hassam's great talent for capturing the beauties of the night are amply demonstrated in this composition. A zigzag of light formed by the street lamps, the illuminated kiosk with its fiery orange window, and the bright, cool, reflecting pavement form a dramatic contrast to the dark figure of the fashionably dressed woman. *Deborah Chotner*

1. Catalogue of the American Art Association sale, 1928, number 55, consigned by Mr. Lyman G. Bloomingdale of New York. I am grateful to Kathleen Burnside for providing this information.
2. *Les Grands Boulevards* [exh. cat., Musée Carnavalet] (Paris, 1985) is an excellent source of illustrations and information on this topic. Regarding the kind of advertising column depicted in *A Paris Nocturne*, it explains *ce type de kiosques hexagonaux ou octogonaux était réservé à l'affichage. Le soir, ils étaient éclairés de l'intérieur. Les affiches étaient disposées derrière des vitres.* 208, no. 431.

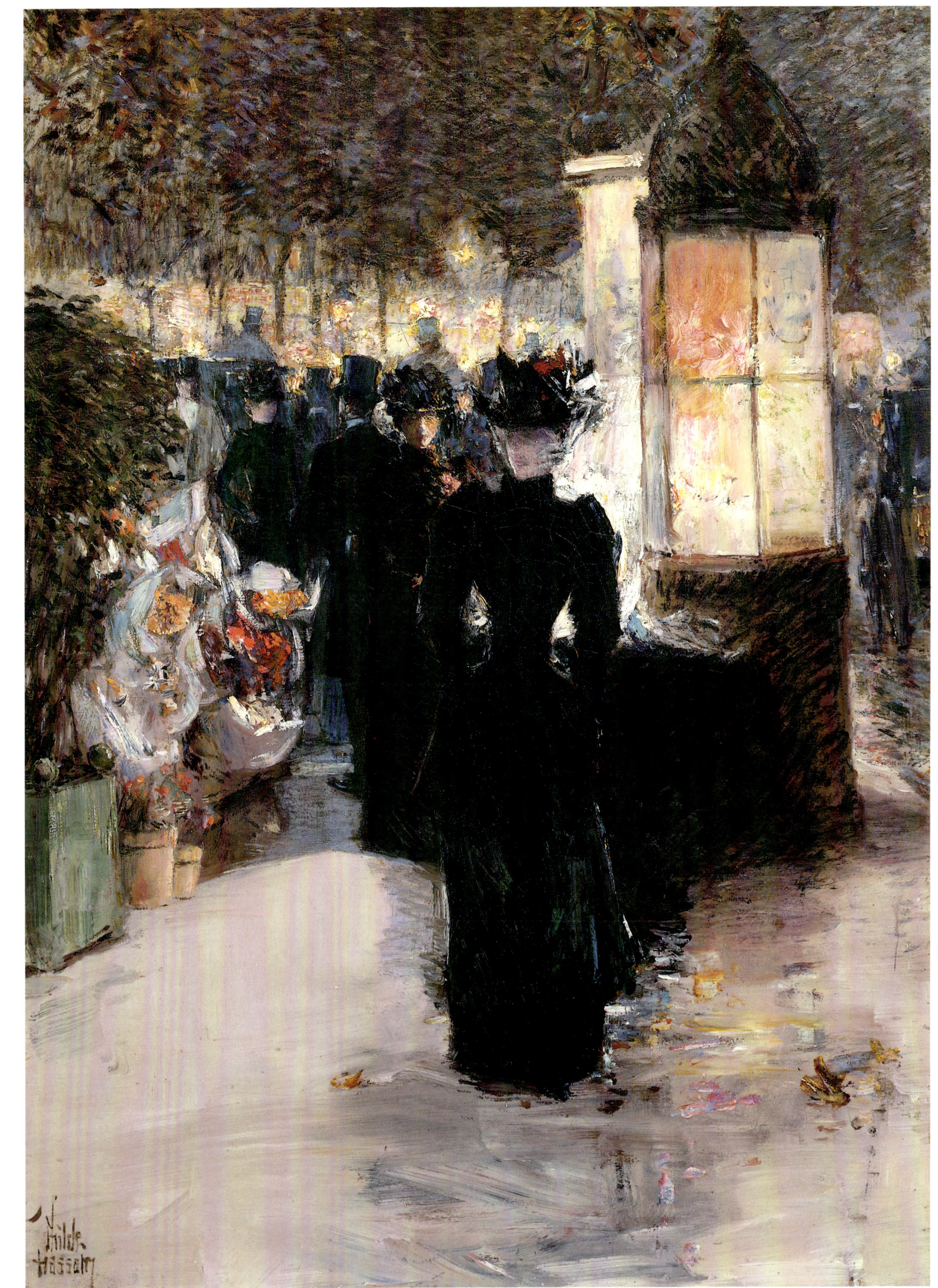
Childe
Hassam

56

Julius L. Stewart (1855–1919)
Summer 1880
oil on canvas, 33½ x 58¾ (85.1 x 149.2)

The Manoogian collection contains two of Julius Stewart's principal French landscapes, *Summer* and *On the Banks of the Seine at Bougival*, 1885 (not in exhibition).[1] Both paintings depict the landscape of the Ile de France, construct the composition around an oblique horizon line, and incorporate recognizable portraits in an anecdotal manner. Both works also portray intimates of the artist: Stewart family members in *Summer*, and the coterie of his patron James Gordon Bennett in *Bougival*. However, in *Summer* Stewart was primarily concerned with capturing the evanescent light and color of the French countryside on a summer day, with his family as staffage, while the emphasis of the later *Bougival* landscape shifted to the genre portraits of personalities of the Bennett clique.

Summer, of all Stewart's works, has the greatest emphasis on landscape; the figures are quite incidental. Stewart was highly attuned to changing fashions in the world of painting in Paris, and the picture demonstrates an early, if only momentary, recognition of plein-air impressionism. The man in the background is certainly the artist's father, the connoisseur and collector William Hood Stewart, presumably accompanied by the artist's mother. This identification is circumstantially corroborated by the fact that the painting was the only work by the son in the W. H. Stewart estate sale of 1898.[2] The likeness of the elder Stewart can be compared with the similarly ancedotal portrait of him in Fortuny's *The Antiquaries* (Boston, Museum of Fine Arts), one of the best-known contemporary works in his collection.

Summer was painted by Stewart in 1880. However, the artist was in Spain and North Africa, including Egypt, for part of 1880 and 1881 and did not submit any paintings to the Salon in those years. His regard for the picture is shown by his willingness to submit it to the Salon of 1882 two years after its completion, where it was accepted and exhibited with a full-length portrait of his sister, Ellen Stewart, probably included here as one of the foreground figures.[3] *D. Dodge Thompson*

1. For an illustration of *Bougival*, see D. Dodge Thompson, "Julius L. Stewart, a Parisian from Philadelphia," *Antiques* 130, no. 5 (November 1986), 1050–1051.
2. Thomas E. Kirby, *Catalogue of the Modern Masterpieces Gathered by the Late Connoisseur William H. Stewart*, American Art Association (New York, 1898).
3. *Catalogue illustré du Salon* (Paris, 1882), LX, nos. 2493 and 2494.

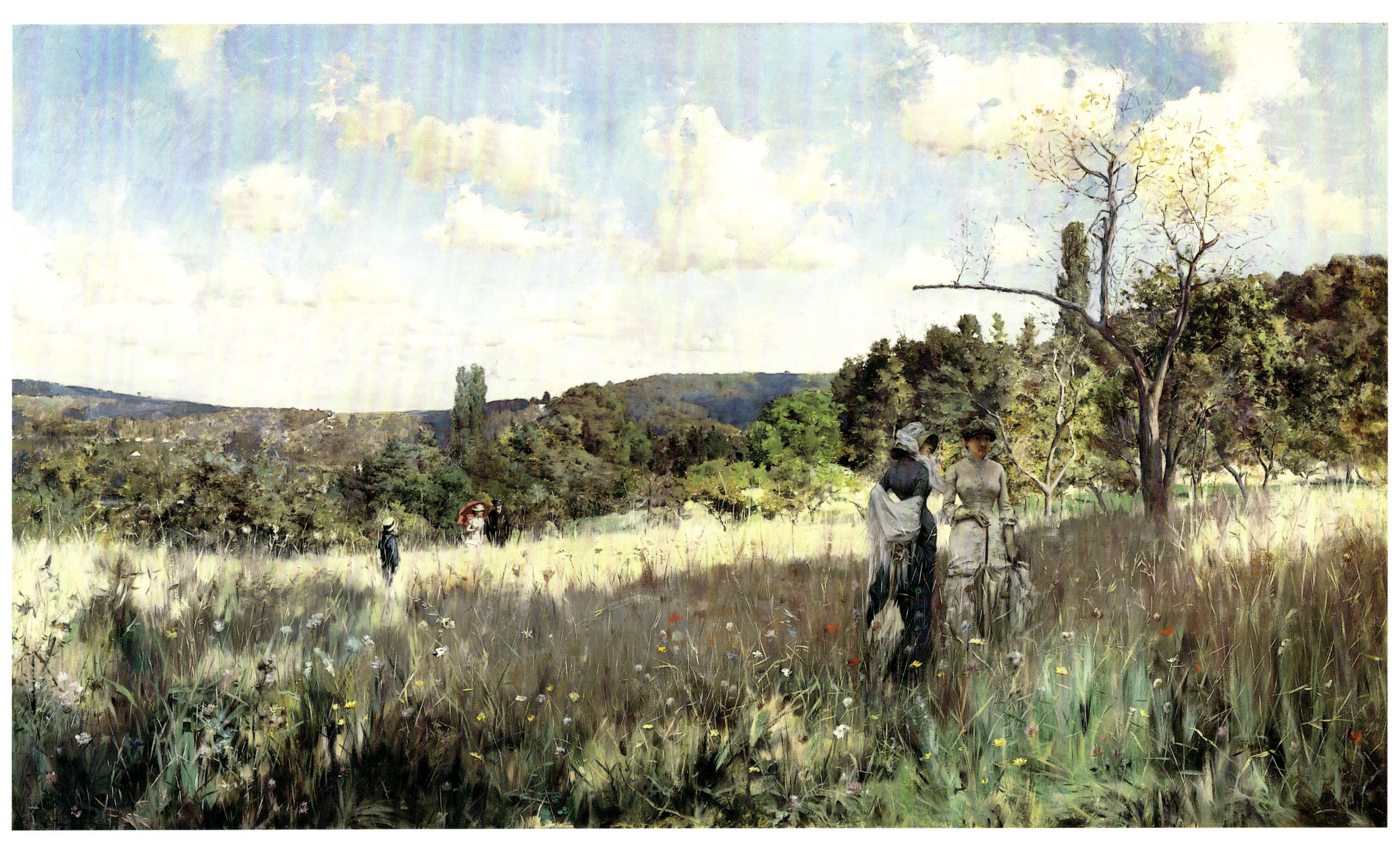

57

Theodore Robinson (1852–1896)
World's Columbian Exposition 1894
oil on canvas, 25 x 30 (63.5 x 76.2)

Artists are not always the best judges of their own work. For Theodore Robinson, *World's Columbian Exposition* was a difficult and problematic painting, one that he ultimately found wholly unsatisfactory. For most recent art historians, on the other hand, it is one of his most successful and accomplished late works, a monument in the history of American art.

The World's Columbian Exposition, Chicago's great "White City" set on the shore of Lake Michigan, was officially open to the public from May through October 1893. Vast exhibition halls filled with machinery, agricultural produce, ethnographic materials, and fine arts from around the world collectively celebrated the accomplishments of civilization. Robinson visited the exposition in March, before the official opening. His trip was probably prompted by the fact that he had three paintings included in the fine arts exhibition at the exposition—*The Layette* (The Corcoran Gallery, Washington), *Winter Landscape* (Daniel J. Terra Collection, Chicago), and *Roman Fountain* (ex coll. Charles Barney).

Robinson did not linger in Chicago; by the beginning of April he was once again in New York. Nor did the scenery in Chicago inspire him to record any visions of the fair. It was not until the next year, on 12 March 1894, that Robinson began work on the first of his two paintings of the Columbian Exposition. He recorded the event in his diary: *Began a World's Fair thing for Millet, a panoramic view of a part of the grounds and lake—no end of detail, windows, domes, minarets, etc. a fearful grind but will try to make it as amusing as possible—an autumn coloration to make it as gay as may be. The things are to be used for the book and then exhibited together I believe. Almost every one has a finger in the pie. Poor* [John] *Twachtman groans over his—has done one and will do another.*[1]

Millet was Francis Davis Millet (see cat. 53), who served as director of decoration for the fair, supervising all the decorative and mechanical painting, sculpture, and ornament of the exposition halls and grounds.[2] In the year after the end of the fair Millet and the architect Daniel Burnham attempted to assemble the definitive history of the enterprise in a deluxe, illustrated publication. This is the project for which Robinson, Twachtman, and many others were enlisted.[3] Robinson finished his autumn scene in less than two weeks, on 23 March recording in his diary: *Took my World's Fair thing to Millet who liked it and gave me another to do. Mine looked very poor to me.* [J. Alden] *Weir had a water-color very artistic—a lot of figures crossing a bridge—architecture, etc.*[4] Robinson's autumn-colored painting, *North Lagoon, World's Columbian Exposition* (fig. 1), is now in the collection of the Chicago Historical Society.

On 31 March Robinson officially received the second commission from Millet for the publishing venture, *a big World's Fair canvas, for colored plate* [the numbers 25 x 30 were added later to the diary manuscript]. This is the exhibited painting. The artist worked a long time on this second commission. After nearly a month had gone by, on 25 April, Robinson noted in his diary that the day was *Very warm and summery—I work at a World's fair thing with difficulty for Millet.* Four days later his dissatisfaction with the project is clear: *A lovely day—staid in my stinking studio and worked on my horrible "World's Fair."* Although Robinson's unhappiness with the work was strong, on 14 May he welcomed the prospect of income: *Worked a little on my World's Fair illustration and took it to Millet who was not in. Met* [Robert] *Blum who urged me to ask a good price—said the edition de luxe was subscribed for in advance $300,000.* But the artist was not to realize his high hopes. On 31 May he wrote in his diary that he had a *disagreeable visit to Millet—who gave me only 150. for my world's fair thing—which in truth looked beastly—so I left with a bad taste in my mouth.* That was apparently the close of Robinson's involvement with images of the World's Columbian Exposition, with one painting looking *very poor* and the other *beastly*. The very next day he reflected that *I am afraid I lose sight of my ideal in N. Y. and get to thinking too much of money success. I must get back to a singleness of aim and conviction I had a year or so ago.*[5]

The artist's evident dissatisfaction with *World's Columbian Exposition* (and its companion painting) is difficult to comprehend, for today it stands as one of his most glowing and vibrant works. One possible explanation lies in Robinson's model and ideal, Claude Monet. What Robinson valued above all else in the Frenchman's art was its vitality. He wrote that *it is, of course, the spiritual side of the artist's work that is really worth dwelling on. M. Claude Monet's art is vital, robust, healthy. Like Corot's, but in more exuberant fashion, it shows the joy of living. It does not lack thought, and many of his pictures are painted with difficulty; but there is never that mysterious something which often gets into a picture and communicates itself to the spectator, a sense of fatigue, or abatement of interest in the motive. There is always a delightful sense of movement, vibration, and life.*[6] For Robinson, then, the spirit that the painter brought to and infused into the painting was a principal component of its quality. And while to the contemporary viewer Robinson's painting of the lagoon is instinct with life and vibrancy, especially in the vivacious brushwork of water, sky, and foliage, the artist was well aware of his "abatement of interest" in the subject, and so apparently saw the work as lifeless. It is perhaps this unreal expectation of a continuing, heightened emotional interest on the artist's part, and his own reasonable departures from that state, that prompted Robinson's often-voiced discontents with much of his work throughout his final years.[7]

One of the more obvious reasons for Robinson's weariness with the subject was that the painting, rather than growing from his own observations, was instead a close copy after a photograph taken by Charles Dudley Arnold, the head of the bureau for photography for the exposition (fig. 2).[8] Robinson had long used photographs as an aid and economy in his figure paintings,[9] but never before the world's fair paintings had he followed someone else's photograph to literally form a landscape composition. This perhaps explains his use of the word "illustration" in describing his work.

Arnold's photograph was taken from the Illinois Building, looking up the East Lagoon past one arm of the Romanesque Fisheries Building, the high-domed U.S. Government Building, and the immense Manufactures and Liberal Arts Building, with the sweep of water leading to the obelisk at the far right. Robinson clearly relied upon the photograph, which had earlier been published in Hubert Bancroft's *The Book of the Fair* (1893), respecting even the chance position of the pedestrians on the walkways. Only in the left foreground did he make a major alteration, omitting the Merchant Tailors pavilion and simplifying the configuration of tents at the far left, thus opening up the composition to an immediate projection into the middle ground and easing the movement from left to right across the canvas. Robinson also increased the viewpoint's sense of height and distance by adding to the upper and lower edges of the scene. And even though with those exceptions he followed the photograph faithfully, yet still for most viewers he managed to dissolve that monochromatic armature during the creative process.[10]

The world's fair paintings stand out from Robinson's oeuvre on another count, in addition to the nonautograph photographic source. Rarely in his work does the artist focus so closely on architecture, especially highly developed, complex buildings such as those shown in *World's Columbian Exposition*. One factor (in addition to ever-pressing finances) that may have allowed him to accept the commission, so different from the rural views he most frequently chose, was again his admiration of Claude Monet. On seeing examples from Monet's Rouen Cathedral series in May 1892, Robinson wrote: *I saw Monet Monday and a dozen or so canvases he did at Rouen last winter. They are the Cathedral, mostly the facade, filling up all the canvas, and they are simply colossal. Never, I believe has architecture been painted so before, the most astonishing impression of the thing, a feeling of size, grandeur and decay, an avoidance of the banal side of the subject. . . . Isn't it curious, a man taking such material and making such magnificent use of it.*[11] Because the commission was from Millet, who most likely selected the panoramic photograph to be copied, Robinson could not emulate these works of Monet and their radical composition. Nor probably would he have wanted to. As he confided later to his diary: *They* [the *Cathedrals*] *are bewildering at first . . . the painting is so novel that it shocks even the faithful. And I . . . like best the Monets of an earlier date, when he is always thinner, gets there with more ease . . . but one gets to like and appreciate the later, wrought-out, elaborate visions.*[12] Among the Monets of an earlier date with which Robinson would have been familiar are views of architecture that share certain characteristics with *World's Columbian Exposition*, such

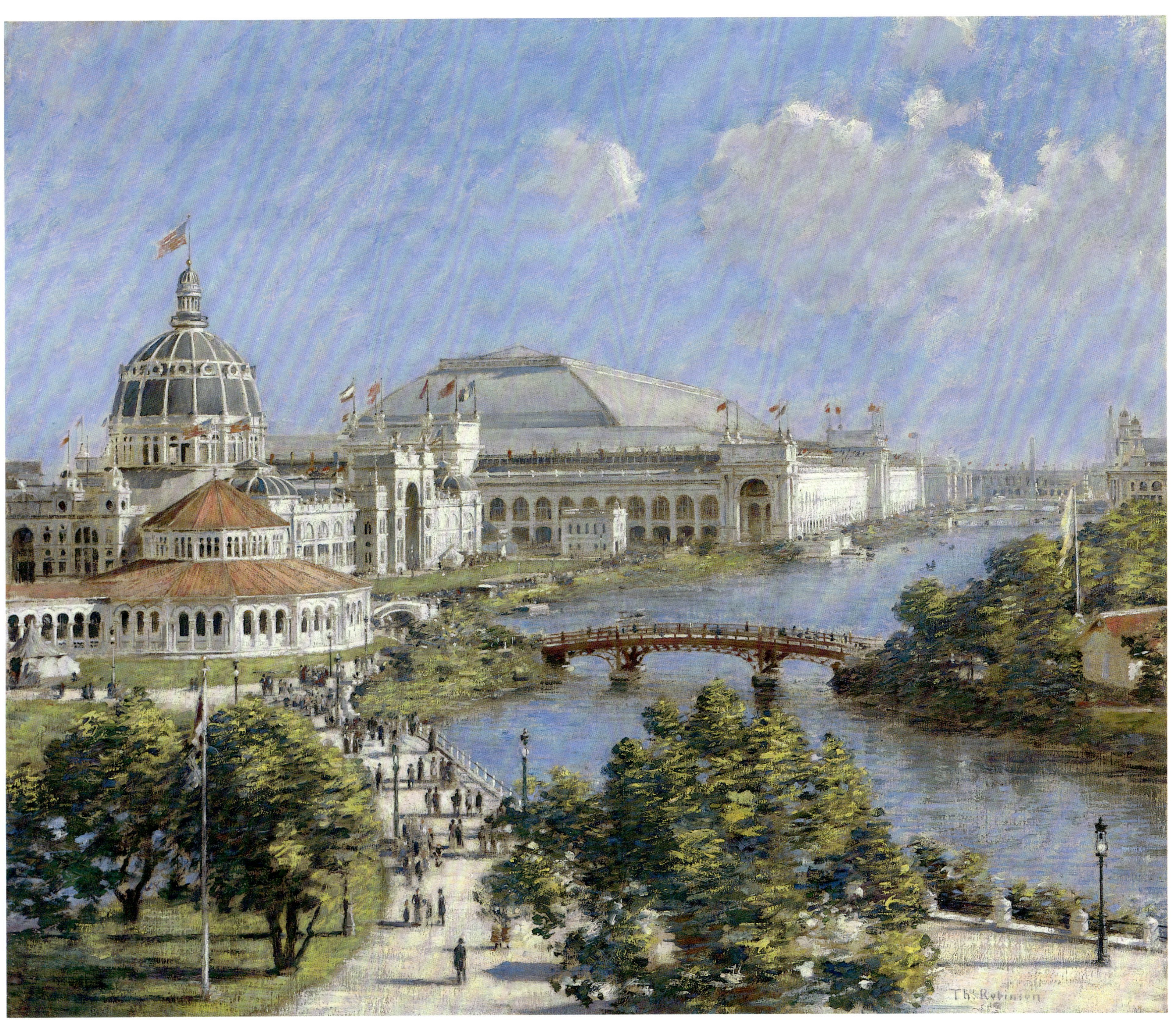
Th. Robinson

as the scene Monet painted from the Louvre in 1867, *Saint-Germain-l'Auxerrois* (Staatliche Museen Preussischer Kulturbesitz, Nationalgalerie, Berlin).[13] Although there are significant variations between the two works, they have in common a heightened viewpoint, a concentration on the details of elaborate architecture that stands in strong contrast to their summary handlings of foliage and pedestrians, a limited number of contrasting hues, and the reliance on sharp shadow patterns to animate the foreground. Further, Robinson was clearly thinking of Monet while at work on *World's Columbian Exposition.* His diary entry for 25 April begins with recording a visit from the writer and art critic Hamlin Garland, a major proponent of impressionist painting in America. Robinson records: *He* [Garland] *tells a story of Monet new to me. A young man shows him a landscape done much in his manner—too much in fact. Monet asks—"And do you really see Nature like that?" "Certainly, sir." "Impossible my dear friend, that is the way* I *see it.*"[14] Robinson's next full sentence goes on to relate his working *on a World's fair thing with difficulty for Millet.*

If Robinson was himself dissatisfied with *World's Columbian Exposition* because it bore too strong a superficial resemblance to Monet's works without carrying the American artist's own emotional response to the subject, it is nonetheless among the most ambitious and resolved of his late works. The painting's strong colors arrest attention while effectively conveying the sense of late afternoon light falling hard and crisp on crowds and buildings. Robinson's loosened brushwork on water, sky, and foliage animates the scene, lending a sparkle and vivacity to the whole that testifies to the artist's power of imagination, and convinces us (if not himself) that in this work, as he wrote of Monet's canvases, *Clouds are moving across the sky, leaves are twinkling, the grass is growing.*[15]

Marc Simpson

1. Theodore Robinson, Diaries. 1892–1896, 12 March 1894, manuscript in Frick Art Reference Library, New York.
2. After the opening of the fair Millet also assumed responsibility for music, fireworks, festival staging, and associated entertainments within the White City.
3. Millet wrote at about this time in a report to his alumni association: *At the close of the Exposition I returned to New York, and since that time have been occupied, in association with Mr. D. H. Burnham, director of works of the Exposition, in writing, illustrating, and publishing a book the purpose of which is best described on the title-page, "The Book of the Builders, being the Chronicle of the Origin and Plan of the World's Fair: of the Architecture of the Buildings and Landscape; of the Work of Construction; of the Decorations and Embellishments, and of the Operation."* ("Francis Davis Millet Papers," Archives of American Art, Smithsonian Institution, Washington, roll 1097, frames 1374–1375).

   Unfortunately, Millet and Burnham were only able to publish their work serially in the first six issues of *The Columbian Serial* (1894). They apparently could not bring the projected deluxe volume to completion. Robinson's designs are not included in these published portions.
4. Robinson, Diaries, 23 March 1894.
5. Both of the world's fair paintings were untraced when John I. H. Baur assembled his pioneering monograph on the artist in 1946, although Baur extrapolated from Robinson's diary entries to characterize the project as *some real potboiling.* Baur, *Theodore Robinson, 1852–1896* [exh. cat., Brooklyn Museum] (Brooklyn, New York, 1946), 38.
6. Theodore Robinson, "Claude Monet," *The Century Magazine* (September 1892). Quoted in Charles F. Stuckey, *Monet: A Retrospective* (New York, 1985), 136.
7. See Robinson, Diaries, 14 November 1894; quoted by Baur in Brooklyn 1946, 12, 27–28, 33, 42.
8. First noted in print by Carol Troyen in her catalogue entry on this painting in *A New World: Masterpieces of American Paintings 1760–1910* [exh. cat., Museum of Fine Arts] (Boston, 1983), 319.
9. See John I. H. Baur, "Photographic Studies by an Impressionist," *Gazette des Beaux-Arts*, ser. 6, 30 (October–December 1946), 319–330.
10. As Kirk Varnedoe wrote of Delacroix in "The Artifice of Candor: Impressionism and Photography Reconsidered," *Art in America* 68 (January 1980), 66–78.
11. Letter to J. Alden Weir, quoted in Sona Johnston, *Theodore Robinson, 1852–1896* [exh. cat., The Baltimore Museum of Art] (Baltimore, 1973), xxii.
12. Robinson, Diaries, 4 March 1896, quoted in Brooklyn 1946, 27.
13. *Saint-Germain-L'Auxerrois* was included in the exhibition *Monet-Rodin* at the Galerie Georges Petit in June 1889, when Robinson had just returned to France from a visit to New York.
14. Robinson, Diaries, 25 April 1894.
15. Robinson, "Claude Monet," 136.

Fig. 1
Theodore Robinson, *North Lagoon, World's Columbian Exposition*, 1894, oil on canvas, 16¼ x 25⅛ (41.3 x 63.8). Chicago Historical Society

Fig. 2
Charles Dudley Arnold, *Looking Up the East Lagoon*, 1893, photograph. From Hubert Howe Bancroft, *The Book of the Fair*, 2 vols. (Chicago, 1893), 1:392 [Photo by Joseph McDonald]

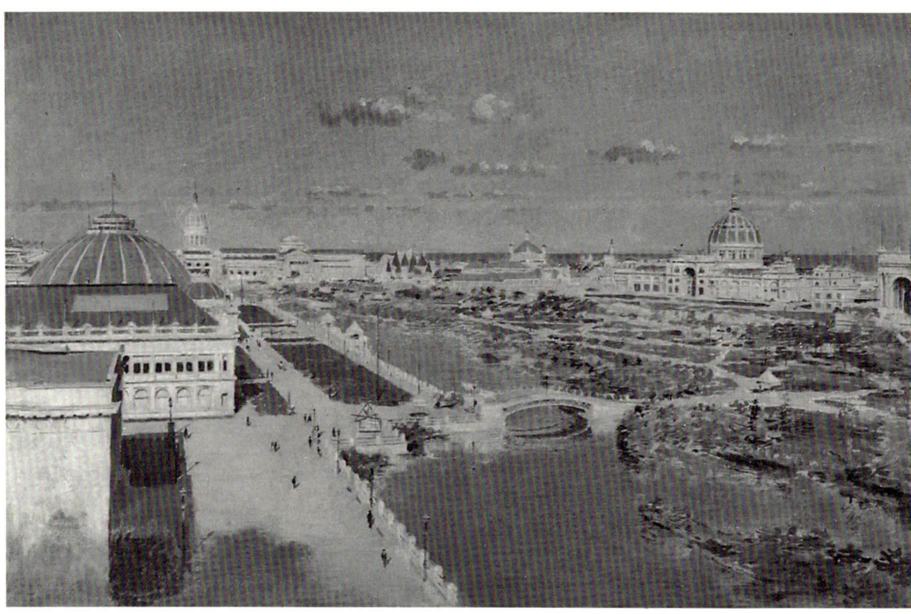

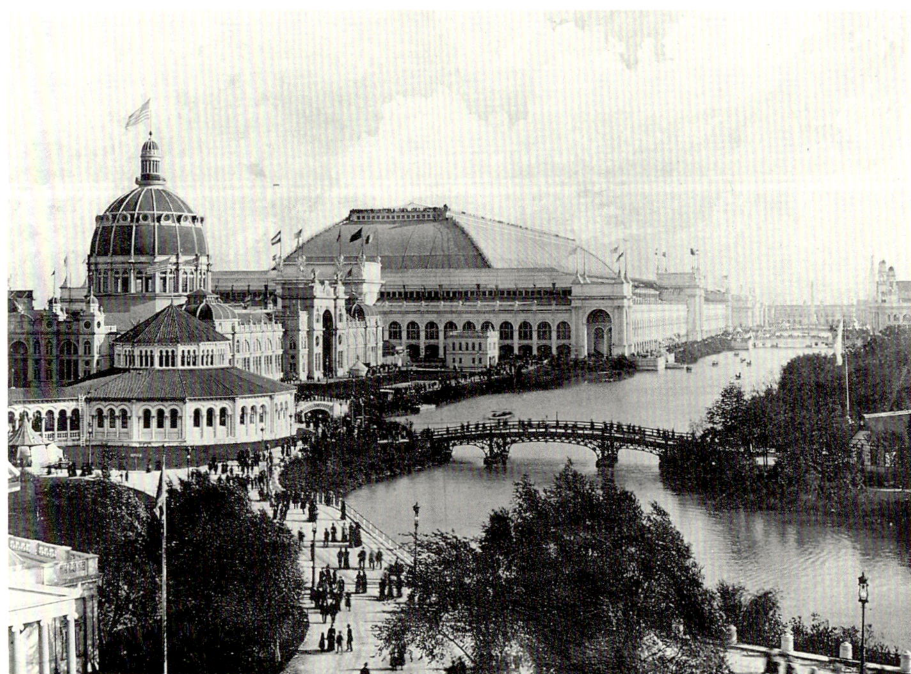

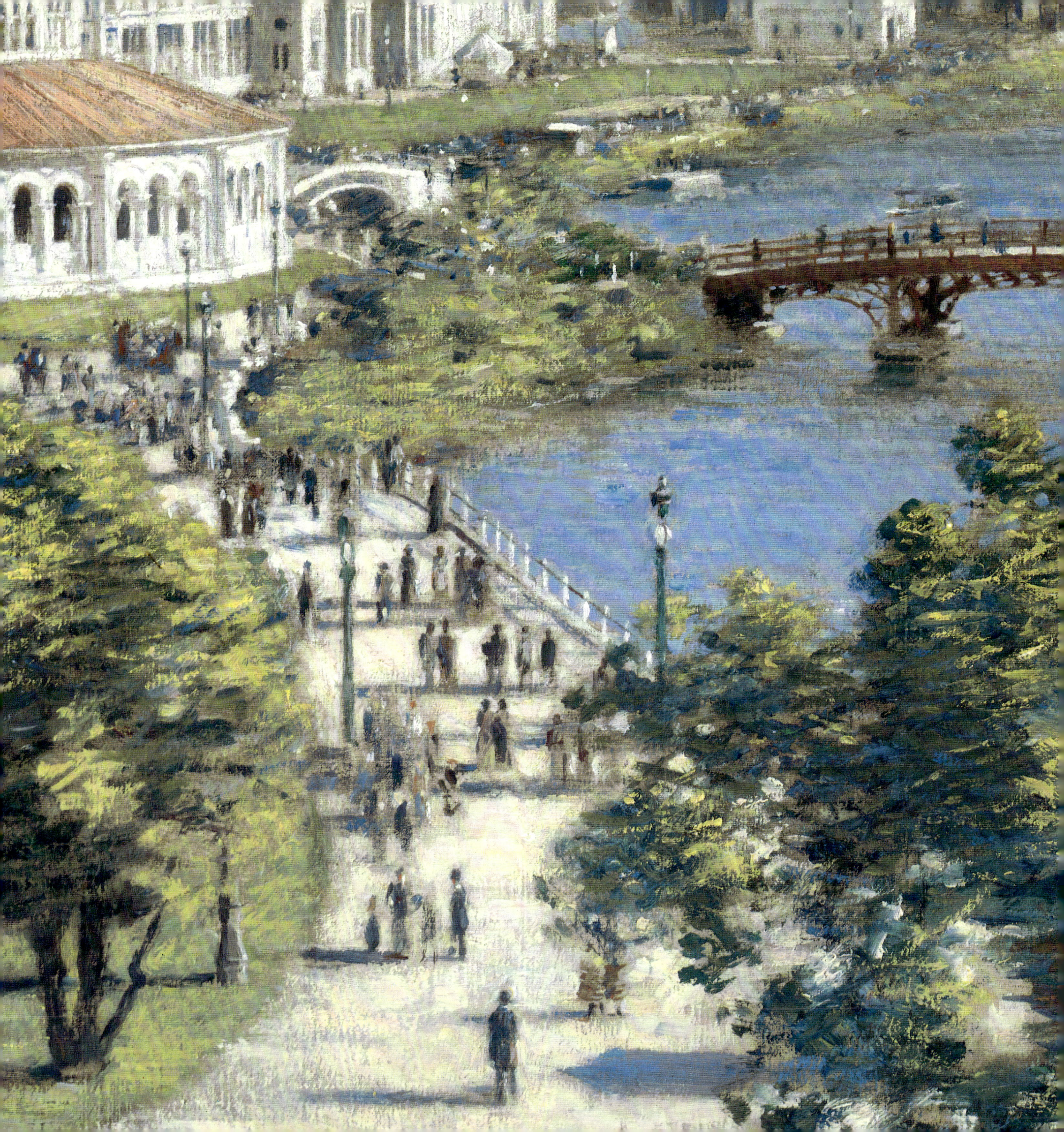

58

Theodore Robinson (1852–1896)
Low Tide 1894
oil on canvas, 16 x 22¼ (40.6 x 56.5)

Low Tide, painted at Cos Cob, Connecticut, in the summer of 1894, is one of the most serene and accomplished paintings of Robinson's career, a lyric evocation of coastal light and air. Two of the artist's closest friends, John Twachtman (see cat. 68) and J. Alden Weir (1852–1919), had established a summer school in Cos Cob in the early 1890s.[1] Under their influence Robinson traveled to the village on 1 June 1894, the day after submitting the just-completed *World's Columbian Exposition* (cat. 57) to his patron. He recorded in his diary, *To Coscob. pretty things around the boat-yard & mill—nice old houses. We will go there for a few weeks.*[2] Within days Robinson settled at Holley House, a local boarding house. The site pleased him immensely. On 7 June he recorded, *Walked around by the R.R. bridge to Mianus and back. Some fine things—little white boats near the Sound.* Two weeks later he rejoiced, *Am getting well and strong and work with interest—especially from the R.R. Bridge, late afternoon, the club house and little yachts at anchor, low-tide, patches of sea grass. It is particularly brilliant at about 5 p.m.*[3] This diary entry probably records the artist's work on *Low Tide* and the closely related *Low Tide—Riverside Yacht Club* (1894, Mr. and Mrs. Raymond J. Horowitz).

The Cos Cob paintings are first and foremost Robinson's eloquent responses to the specific beauties of the Connecticut shore, closely observed, with the canvases painted outdoors.[4] But they also reflect other art with which Robinson was familiar. There are similarities in compositional strategy to the works of William Merritt Chase (see cat. 51) from the late 1880s, for example, with their open foregrounds, high horizon lines, and bands of foliage and architecture running across the upper portions of the canvases. Further, although Robinson's manner of laying on paint is far more serene, there are strong thematic and emotional parallels in the Cos Cob works to the Argenteuil paintings of 1874 by Claude Monet. In their economy and elegance, the Cos Cob paintings are also a response to Robinson's enthusiasm for Japanese prints. As he noted the previous February: *My Japanese print points in a direction I must try & take: an aim for refinement and a kind of precision. . . . And the Japanese work ought to open one's eyes to certain things in nature, before almost invisible . . . and their extraordinary combination of the convention and the reality.*[5]

Robinson had to leave Cos Cob in July to assume his teaching responsibilities in New Jersey. He returned to the village for ten days at the end of the summer and even considered buying property in the area.[6] But the idyll in Cos Cob was over. The next summer he was in Vermont, and by the summer of 1896 he was dead.

The Cos Cob paintings, *Low Tide* among them, have played an important role in the appreciation of Robinson's art since his one-man exhibition at the Macbeth Gallery in 1895. As one critic later noted: *Out of little he made much. He painted light, air and colour. The purest lyric talent we have thus far produced, he sang a song steeped in outdoor brightness and objective tranquillity.*[7] *Marc Simpson*

1. Twachtman started the school perhaps as early as 1890. Weir also taught with him at least in 1892 and 1893. *Connecticut and American Impressionism* [exh. cat., The William Benton Museum of Art] (Storrs, Connecticut, 1980), 89.
2. Theodore Robinson, Diaries: 1892–1896. Manuscript in the Frick Art Reference Library, New York.
3. Robinson, Diaries, 19 June 1894, quoted in John I. H. Baur, *Theodore Robinson, 1852–1896* [exh. cat., Brooklyn Museum] (Brooklyn, New York, 1946), 68.
4. Robinson began a sketchbook in Cos Cob (private collection) that is filled with quick drawings of local scenery, sometimes accompanied by notations of time and atmospheric condition. The sketchbook is partially illustrated in Sona Johnston, *Theodore Robinson, 1852–1896* [exh. cat., Baltimore Museum of Art] (Baltimore, 1973), 72–73.
5. Robinson, Diaries, 17 February 1894. Quoted in Brooklyn 1946, 40. See also the entry for 10 December 1893, *we discussed Japanese art and other—Tw.*[Twachtman] *& W.*[Weir] *are rabid just now on the J.*"
6. Storrs 1980, 91.
7. Christian Brinton writing in 1915, quoted in Brooklyn 1946, 52.

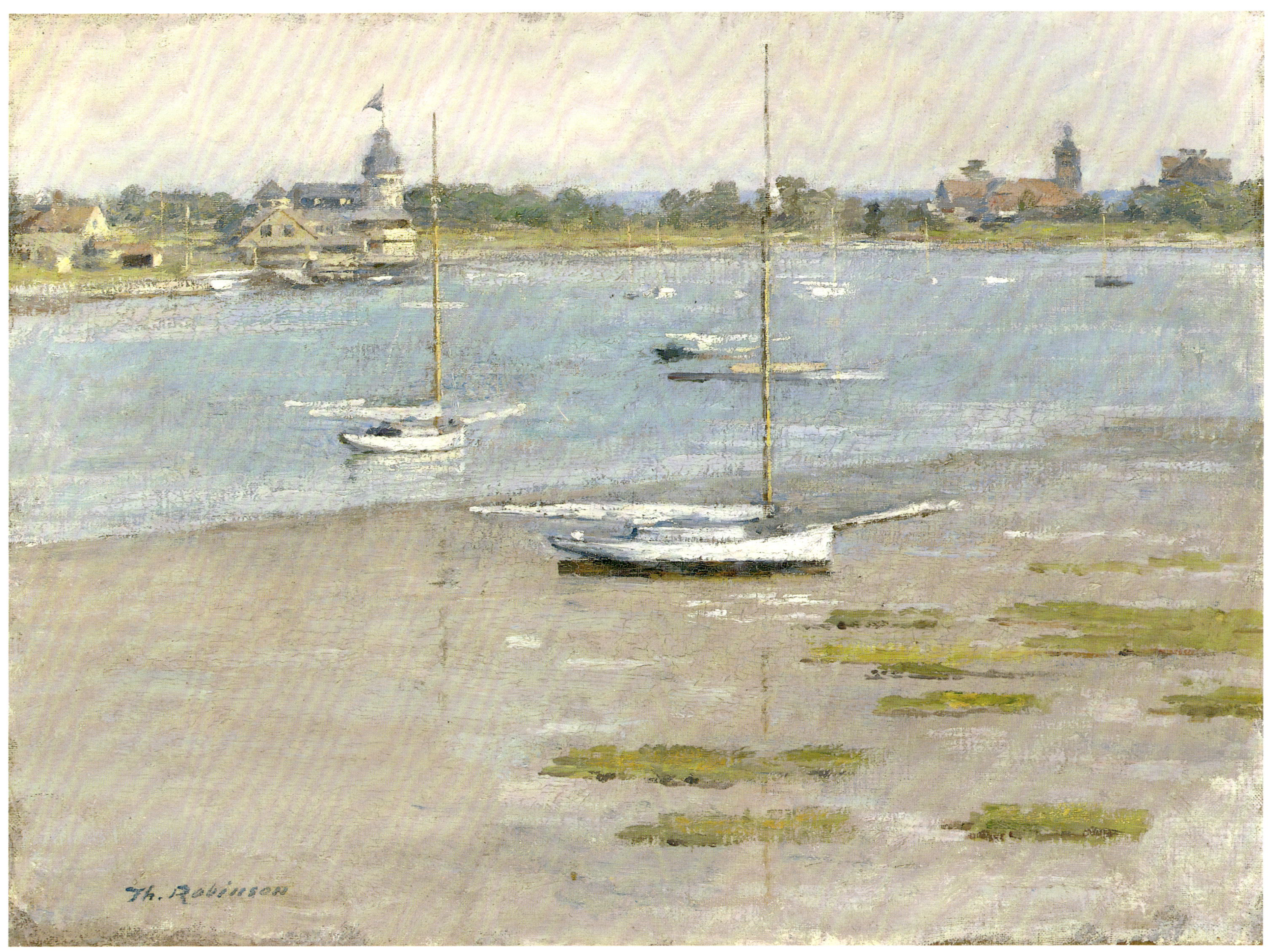
Th. Robinson

59

Thomas Worthington Whittredge (1820–1910)
Off Seconnet, Rhode Island c. 1898
oil on canvas, 14½ x 22¾ (36.8 x 57.8)

Among the major Hudson River School painters, Whittredge made the most varied choices in his subjects for paintings. As he wrote in his autobiography, *I have tried anything and everything which has struck me as interesting until I am hardly known as the painter of any particular class of landscape. Coast scenes, brook scenes, scenes on the plains, interiors of old New England houses; moonlight, firelight, and every picturesque feature that presented itself I have tried in some way to depict.*[1] Whittredge was equally adaptable in adjusting to changing styles of painting during the last third of the nineteenth century, and managed to keep working successfully when many of his Hudson River School colleagues had fallen out of fashion. Thus, even though he did not create a sustained body of work in one style or investigate one subject, as did his contemporaries Church, Kensett, Gifford, and Cropsey, his career was highlighted by periods of surprisingly fresh inspiration and achievement.

Soon after Whittredge had returned to America from abroad in 1859, he began making regular summer visits to Newport, Rhode Island. As he noted, *This part of the New England littoral, the paradise of summer dwellers, had great charm for me. . . . In short, it was the land of my forefathers.*[2] Whittredge's father had been born in Newport and was a sea captain early in life. The artist must have inherited from him a particular love of the Rhode Island seaside, because he returned to it often for inspiration and also built a summer home there. Beginning in the 1870s Whittredge painted numerous landscapes of Rhode Island scenery. The earliest examples of importance, such as *A Home by the Sea* (1872, Addison Gallery of Art, Phillips Academy, Andover, Massachusetts) successfully blended Hudson River School compositions with brushwork and coloring inspired by French Barbizon painting. In the 1880s Whittredge lightened his palette in response to the developments of impressionism, and began creating light-filled, open compositions such as *Second Beach, Newport* (c. 1881, Walker Art Center, Minneapolis). His last important paintings, in the 1890s, were executed in the Newport area and across Sakonnet Bay in the vicinity of Sakonnet.

Off Seconnet, Rhode Island[3] is freely and masterfully painted, fully worthy of comparison with the finest works of such younger artists as William Merritt Chase, Theodore Robinson, and Childe Hassam (see cats. 51, 55, 57, 58, 61). No doubt painted on the spot, the picture shows a view across a grassy, wildflower-filled foreground and over a small inlet toward a group of rustic fishermen's houses.[4] Whittredge had a special fondness for such scenes, admitting that what he found appealing in them was quite different from what drew fashionable people to the Rhode Island coast.[5] Obviously fully confident of his artistic powers and perfectly content to paint such a humble scene, Whittredge created in *Off Seconnet, Rhode Island* one of the gems of American plein-air painting. *Franklin Kelly*

1. "The Autobiography of Worthington Whittredge, 1820–1910," ed. John I. H. Baur, *The Brooklyn Museum Journal* (1942), 62–63.
2. "Autobiography," 63.
3. Sakonnet was sometimes spelled "Seconnet" in the nineteenth century. The title of the painting is derived from an inscription on the stretcher, which also records that Whittredge traded the work to a Dr. C. A. Nash in payment for dental services; see *American Paintings II* [exh. cat., Berry-Hill Galleries] (New York, 1983), 27.
4. The same group of houses appears in a small oil sketch entitled *The Fishermen's Homes at Sakonnet Point, Rhode Island* (private collection); see *Worthington Whittredge* [exh. cat., Munson-Williams-Proctor Institute] (Utica, New York, 1969), 61.
5. "Autobiography," 63. The modest homes and shacks in Whittredge's Rhode Island paintings make a striking contrast to the grand Newport mansions that were, even in Whittredge's day, monuments to conspicuous consumption.

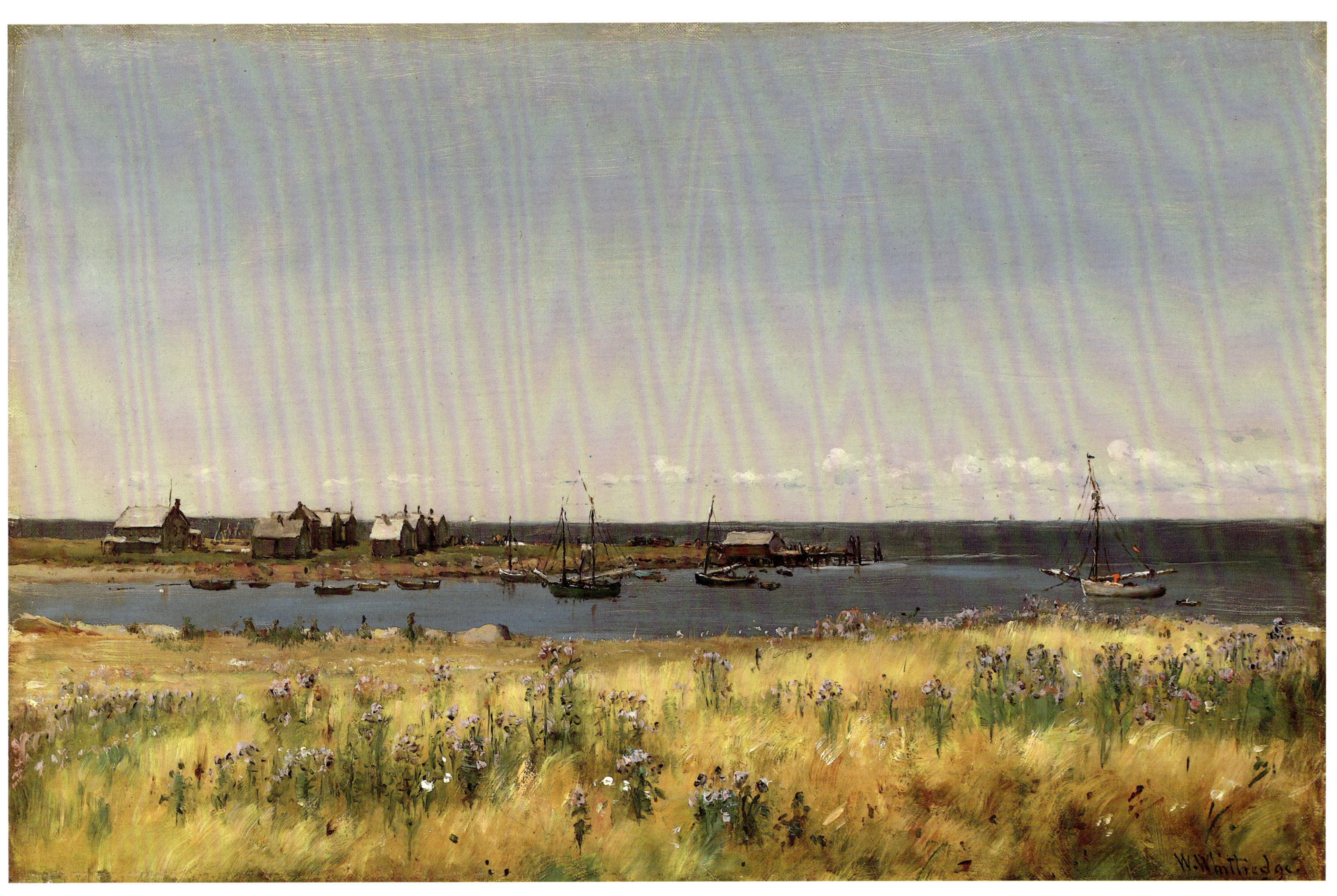

60

Willard Leroy Metcalf (1858–1925)
The Poppy Garden 1905
oil on canvas, 24⅛ x 24⅛ (61.3 x 61.3)

Willard Metcalf went to Old Lyme, Connecticut, in 1905, drawn there by his friendship with Childe Hassam and the summer colony of artists in residence at Miss Florence Griswold's boarding house. *Poppy Garden*, possibly painted in the Old Lyme garden of his colleague Clark Voorhees,[1] made its debut at the *Eighth Exhibition of the Ten Americans* the following spring.[2] Critics were impressed with the *lyrical lightness and charm*[3] of Metcalf's Old Lyme subjects, and in their reviews of this and a slightly earlier exhibition[4] pronounced them his best work to date.[5] *A capital river view with hedges, some billowy laurel bushes, and a gorgeous poppy garden*[6] was one of the works singled out for praise.

Metcalf had begun to incorporate the impressionist techniques of diffused light and broken color into his landscapes as early as 1895,[7] but he maintained a meticulous definition of form, and never completely abandoned the tonal values of color. This summer scene, with its high-key red and green palette, is one of his most animated improvisations on nature, the bright poppies and other blooms appearing as a magnificent blaze of color against the foil of the blue-gray water and the sun-bathed vista and pale blue sky.

Although Metcalf here took his primary inspiration from the example of Claude Monet, a more direct influence is found in the work of Childe Hassam, who painted informal garden scenes of this type at Appledore during the previous decade, some of lush beds of poppies offering a distant view of sea, sky, and the islands beyond.[8] At the same time, Metcalf impressed his own temperament on the subject, for it incorporates the square format and the ingratiating mix of brushwork—long and broken in the foreground, smooth in the river and sky—that characterizes his adaptation of the impressionist style. Most of these elements would appear again in the similarly structured *Purple, White and Gold*, a river view with a garden of flowers in the foreground, possibly also painted at Old Lyme.[9]

Nancy Rivard Shaw

1. William H. Gerdts, *American Impressionism* (New York, 1984), 218.
2. Metcalf sent six canvases to the exhibition, held at Montross Gallery, New York, March 1906. The other five were: *November Sunshine*, *The Misty Morn*, *On the River*, *Mountain Laurel*, and *Nocturne*.
3. Metcalf correspondence and papers, Archives of American Art, Smithsonian Institution, Washington, roll N70/13, frame 506. "Landscapes by Mr. Willard L. Metcalf," *New York Tribune*, 6 February 1906.
4. Held at Fishel, Adler and Schwartz Gallery, New York, February 1906.
5. Metcalf papers, Archives of American Art, roll N70/13, frames 505 and 506.
6. *Evening Post*, 16 March 1906, Metcalf papers, Archives of American Art, roll N70/13, frames 505 and 506.
7. For example, *Gloucester Harbor*. Illustrated in Gerdts, *American Impressionism*, 170.
8. William H. Gerdts and Russell Burke, *American Still-Life Painting* (New York, 1971), 210.
9. Illustrated in *Palette and Bench* (July 1909), color supplement.

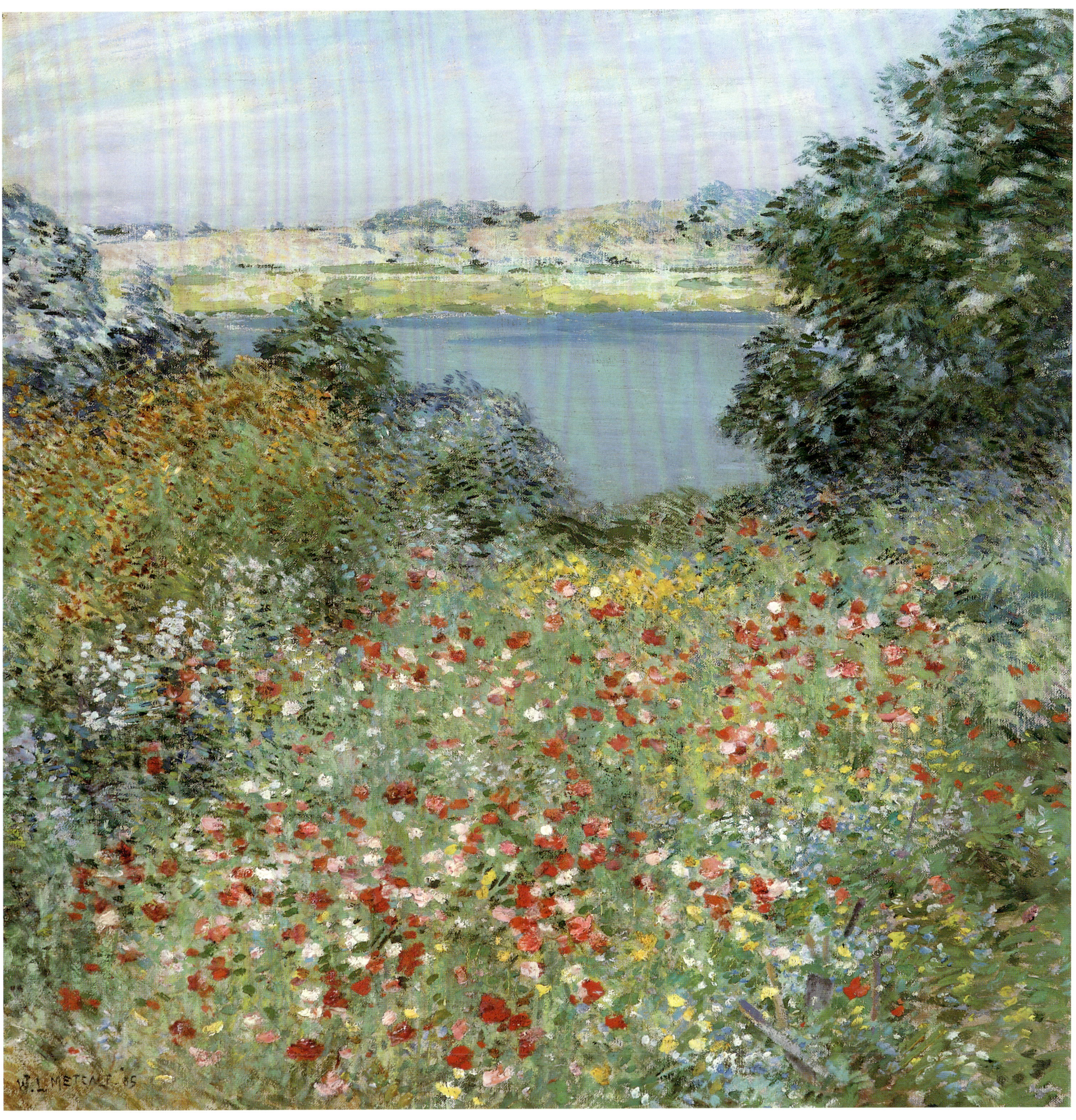
W.L. METCALF. 05

61

Childe Hassam (1859–1935)
County Fair, New England 1890
oil on canvas, 24¼ x 20⅛ (61.6 x 51.1)

Once exhibited under the title *Autumn Celebration in a New England Village*,[1] this painting is a wonderful example of Hassam's predilection for choosing as his subjects the most pleasant, picturesque aspects of contemporary life. One reviewer observed of the painting that no one could *refuse to appreciate heartily the holiday joyousness of color and the light touch.*[2] It is not known in which New England town Hassam painted this harvest festival, but its busy gaiety is typical of much of his imagery, particularly in these early years.

Throughout his career Hassam succeeded in capturing the most appealing aspects of any season, weather condition, or time of day. More than any other American impressionist, however, he preferred the drama of brilliant sunlight. The large swath of bright, blue sky, almost opaque and insistently flat, appears again and again in his paintings. In *County Fair*, he employed the warm autumn hues to best effect by energizing the foreground with the sparkle of golden leaves on the dark ground. His brushwork is lively and varied throughout the painting, and shows a much greater freedom than the careful, measured strokes that characterize much of his later work.

The white meetinghouse dominating the center of the canvas demonstrates Hassam's early concern with the pristine beauty of this architectural form so typical of New England. More than a decade after this painting was completed the artist painted a well-known group of images of the gleaming facade of the Congregational Church at Old Lyme, Connecticut (1903, private collection; 1905, Albright-Knox Art Gallery, Buffalo, New York; 1906, Parrish Art Museum, Southampton, New York). With its prominently placed flags, *County Fair* presages another central motif in Hassam's oeuvre. The banners decorating the meetinghouse, the flags among the crowd, and especially the Stars and Stripes isolated against the sky and framed by the tree branch are a preview of the great flag series Hassam would begin sixteen years later.

Deborah Chotner

1. The painting was shown with this title at the National Academy of Design in 1892, at Doll and Richards Gallery, Boston, in 1893, and at Milch Gallery, New York, in 1919. I am grateful to Kathleen Burnside for providing this information.
2. Anonymous review of an exhibition of Hassam's work at Doll and Richards Gallery, *The Boston Evening Transcript*, 28 January 1893, 4.

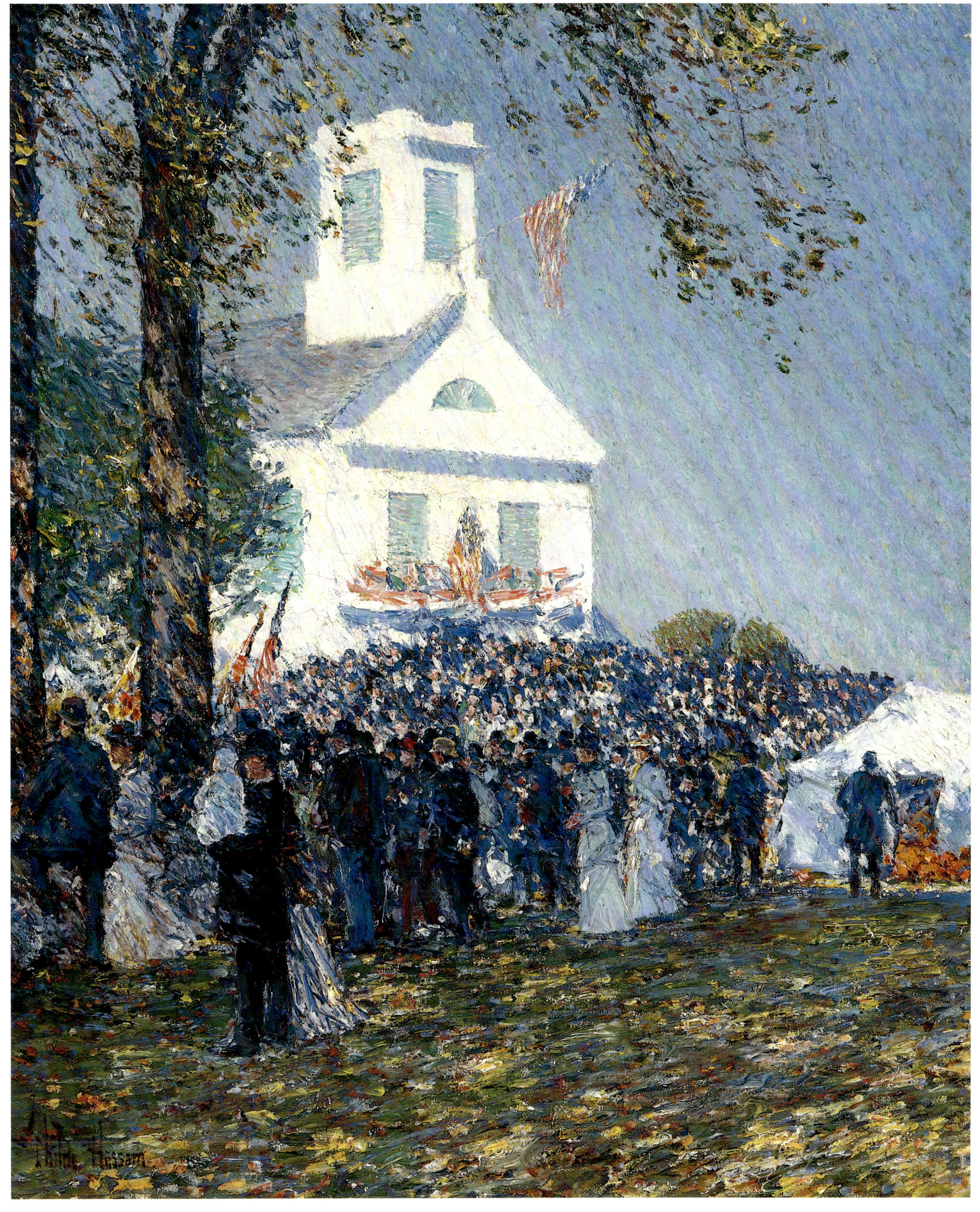

62

Frederick Carl Frieseke (1874–1939)
Venus in the Sunlight 1913
oil on canvas, 38⅜ x 51⅜ (97.5 x 130.5)

Between 1907 and 1913, the female nude was an overwhelmingly popular subject in French art—a trend reflected in the work of such masters as Bonnard, Cézanne, Matisse, and Renoir—and in Frieseke's art as well. His contributions to the Salons and other European exhibitions from 1907 through 1914 included a vast number of nudes, some in boudoirs, but most outdoors. The majority of these were painted at Giverny, near the stream that flowed past Frieseke's outdoor studio and on to Monet's. Others were executed at Corsica during the winter of 1912–1913. Frieseke's reason for choosing this subject appears to have been twofold: on the one hand, he was reacting to the favorable critical and commercial success his nudes received. On the other, he was responding to the freedom of expression he enjoyed in France as an expatriate: *Not only can I paint a nude here out of doors*, he explained, *but I can paint a nude in my garden or down by the fish pond and not be run out of town.*[1]

During this period Frieseke experimented with the technical and stylistic possibilities he had discovered in the work of the impressionists. In the late canvases of Monet, but more specifically Renoir, he found qualities to which he responded instinctively. Their use of pure color, for example, and their scintillating light effects held greater attraction for him than the tonalist schemes of his early career. Reveling in the play of sunlight over the nubile figures of his standing, seated, and reclining models, Frieseke created a dazzling atmosphere filled with shimmering light and luminous color.

Venus in the Sunlight is one of the culminating canvases of this series. Frieseke exhibited the painting with great success at the annual spring Salon of the Société Nationale des Beaux-Arts in 1914,[2] a success that may have inspired two additional reclining nudes, both dated 1914: *Summer* (fig. 1), and *Autumn* (fig. 2).

Decoration was primary even in Frieseke's early work, so there is a temptation to hypothesize that someone commissioned this trio of paintings as a seasons triptych,[3] although it is hard to imagine what a twentieth-century drawing room hung with three monumental nudes might have looked like. In any case, there is no evidence to support this hypothesis. Rather, they would appear to be three variations on a theme that preoccupied Frieseke over a sixteen-month period beginning in 1913. *Venus* was the first painting of the group. It is described by Clara MacChesney in the second of her often-quoted interviews with Frieseke at Giverny: *It was here that Frieseke produced one of his greatest pictures . . . It represents a life-sized woman, nude, lying on a mauve shawl, with the trees overhead and a glimpse of the stream seen in the upper left: in the upper right an open white parasol lies on the ground, making a white note in contrast to the glistening flesh tones. The sunlight flickers through the leaves and falls here and there on the satin skin. . . . For sheer beauty of flesh painting no other canvas equals it today. . . . The intermingling of mauve and of rose tones with the dazzling sheen of flesh, seen in sunlight, and all against a cool, green background, relieved on the grass by the shawl.*[4] MacChesney's precise description so closely conforms to the Manoogian *Venus* that it is almost certainly the painting she saw in Frieseke's Giverny studio, finished too late for the spring Salon.[5]

Frieseke would uncharacteristically title this work *Venus au Soleil*, but as Pierre Anthony put it, "*Nude*" *would have been sufficiently explicit. . . . It is simply a delicious nude.*[6] There is every reason to suppose that the work was inspired by Frieseke's admiration for Renoir's monumental bathers of the same period, but the composition more directly recalls Théodore Chassériau's *Sleeping Bather* (Musée Calvet, Avignon) of 1850. As in the Chassériau example, Frieseke evoked an Arcadian ideal of freedom and oneness with nature. And though the face of this fantasy creature is averted, we know by her closed eyelids that she is in a state of inward preoccupation, perhaps a daydream. Her upper torso exposed but her hips and thighs turned away from the viewer, she is both seductive and inaccessible—like a dream that seems real but is illusory.[7]

For all the memories of tradition Frieseke's composition evokes, *Venus* is emphatically modern. The frilly parasol and wide-brimmed hat proclaim the subject's contemporaneity, no less than does the gaily patterned garment that caresses her body and spills into the foreground. Frieseke has placed the figure in a brilliantly colored landscape setting, where foliage and flowers and dappled areas of sunshine and shadow create a strongly patterned decorative effect. The directness and lucidity of the paint application—dry-brushed in long varied strokes and bold patches of color—reveal Frieseke's original orientation as a watercolor painter.

It was the graceful lightness of his style, and the youthful beauty of his women—references were made to *delicate human flowers unfolded in the sun of life*[8]—that made Frieseke's nudes so popular. As is true of *Venus*, these figures are often presented in profile or three-quarter view, with the resultant outline separating them from their settings, yet Frieseke's concern for color and light and his dynamic brushwork reunite them with their environment. Unencumbered by any narrative, they become one with their setting formally and physically.

Frieseke's decorative approach to the nude was acknowledged by his critics. Pier Occhini wrote: *Here . . . there is no mind, no will, no passion. . . . Like the nature in which Frieseke usually places his figures, a nature without nights, winters, frosts and tempests, hardly alive and I would say almost unconsciously serene, his women do not palpitate, do not love, do not yearn, do not hope. . . . Like a pagan in love with perfect outside harmony of color and line, Frieseke paints woman; and if she evokes a memory, it is that of the divine youthfulness sung by Baudelaire, a young woman of simple appearance, with a limpid eye and serene brow, carefree as the blue sky, the birds and the flowers, spreading over all her perfume and her songs.*[9]

Although the decorative elements in Frieseke's work were noticed by the critics, the extent to which he planned his compositions has not been thoroughly studied. Frieseke claimed that he made no preliminary sketches but took *the inspiration for his picture straight to the canvas.*[10] In this case, the evidence suggests otherwise. There is at least one small sketch for *Venus*,[11] and a smaller oil version of the subject (fig. 3).[12] It has recently been noted that from time to time, Frieseke painted a small version of a completed painting of which he was especially fond,[13] but this one has the freshness and spontaneity of an immediate impression more likely to be found in a study than in a replica. Since Frieseke did not leave a record of his exact procedure, we can only surmise that because of the complexity of the composition, he painted the small version first, then used it as a study for the finished work. The composition is repeated in *Summer*, with minor alterations and the inclusion of a second, Monet-inspired figure.[14]

According to MacChesney, who reviewed the 1914 Salon for *The International Studio*, the directors of the Musée du Luxembourg negotiated to buy *Venus*, *but too late, for a French lady had just become the proud possessor.*[15] An explanation for Frieseke's second version of the composition was advanced by a representative of the owner in the 1960s. He wrote: *It* [Summer] *was intended for the Luxembourg Museum in Paris. The outbreak of World War I, however, closed the Museum. It was at that time that the French Government granted permission to send the painting to the 1915 Panama-Pacific Exposition . . . in San Francisco.*[16] Frieseke, who was both the official and the popular success of the exposition, was awarded the grand prize in the United States section because, in the opinion of the jury, his entries so clearly embodied the prevailing ideals of painting.[17]

Autumn, which is almost a pendant to *Venus*, did not make its first documented appearance until after the war, in 1918. It was exhibited at several American museums until 1923. Two years later it was acquired by its present owner. *Nancy Rivard Shaw*

Nicholas Kilmer, the artist's grandson, is compiling a catalogue raisonné of Frieseke's work, and has been helpful in the course of preparing this essay.

1. Clara MacChesney, "Frieseke Tells Some of the Secrets of His Art," *New York Times*, Sunday 7 June 1914, section 6, 7.
2. Salon of the Société Nationale des Beaux Art [exh. cat., Société Nationale des Beaux Arts] (Paris, 1914), no. 446, illus. 148.
3. *Venus* and *Autumn* share the same dimensions; *Summer* is seven inches higher and six inches wider than the other two. All three are painted on an unprimed coarsely woven brown canvas, and though each depicts a different season, they seem to represent the same time of day, and similar color combinations are repeated and varied throughout.
4. MacChesney, "Frieseke," 7.
5. MacChesney, "Frieseke," 7. Although this second interview did not appear in print until 1914, it is clear from MacChesney's comments on Frieseke's recent Salon contributions, which she had just reviewed in Paris, that the interview actually took place in the spring of 1913.

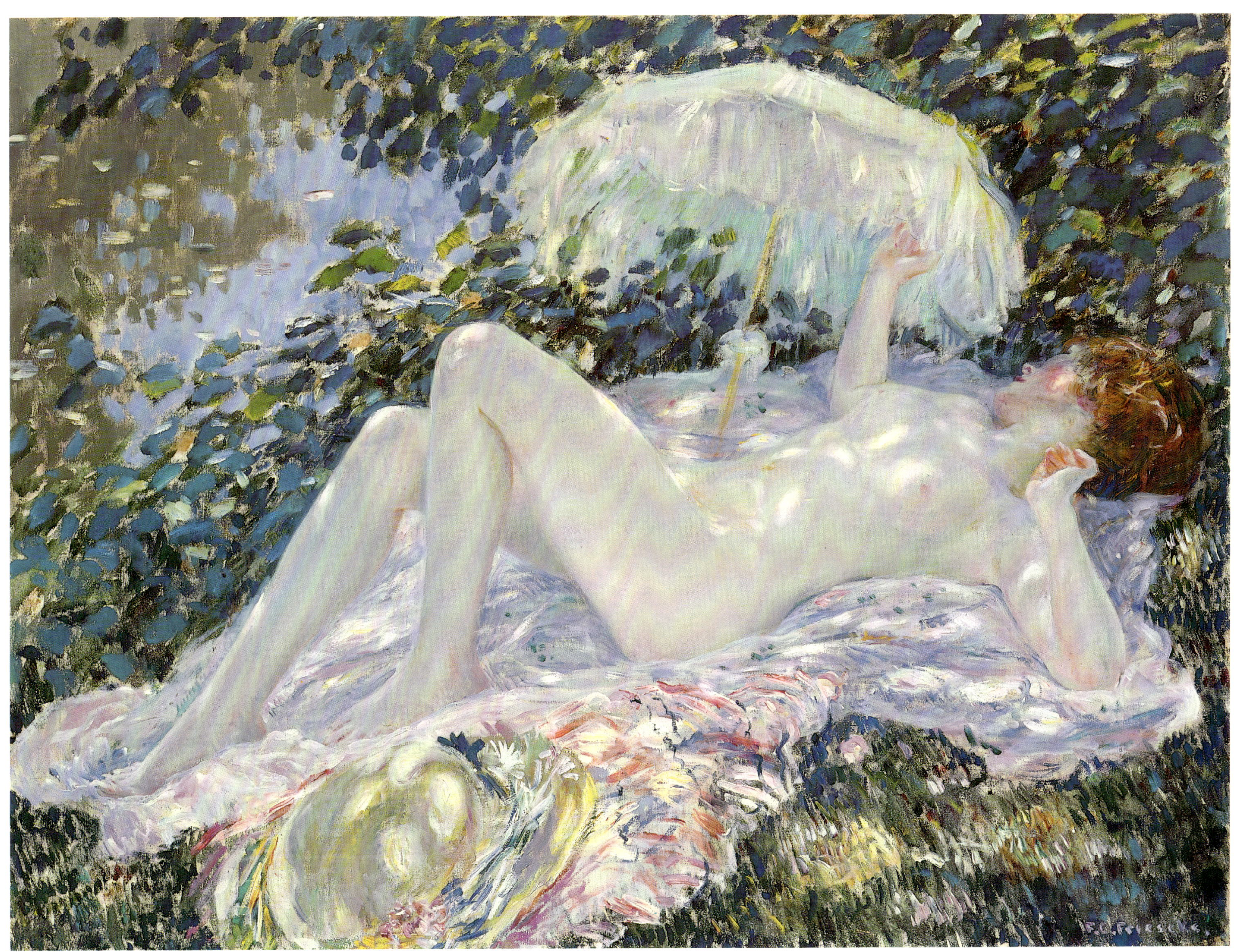

Fig. 1
Frederick Frieseke, *Summer*, 1914, oil on canvas, 45 x 57¾ (114.3 x 146.7), The Metropolitan Museum of Art, New York, George A. Hearn Fund, 1966

Fig. 2
Frederick Frieseke, *Autumn*, 1914, oil on canvas, 37¾ x 51 (95.9 x 129.6), Galleria Internazionale D'Arte Moderna, Venice

Fig. 3
Frederick Frieseke, *Venus Au Soleil*, oil on canvas, 16 x 20 (40.7 x 50.8), [Photo courtesy of Joan Michelman, New York]

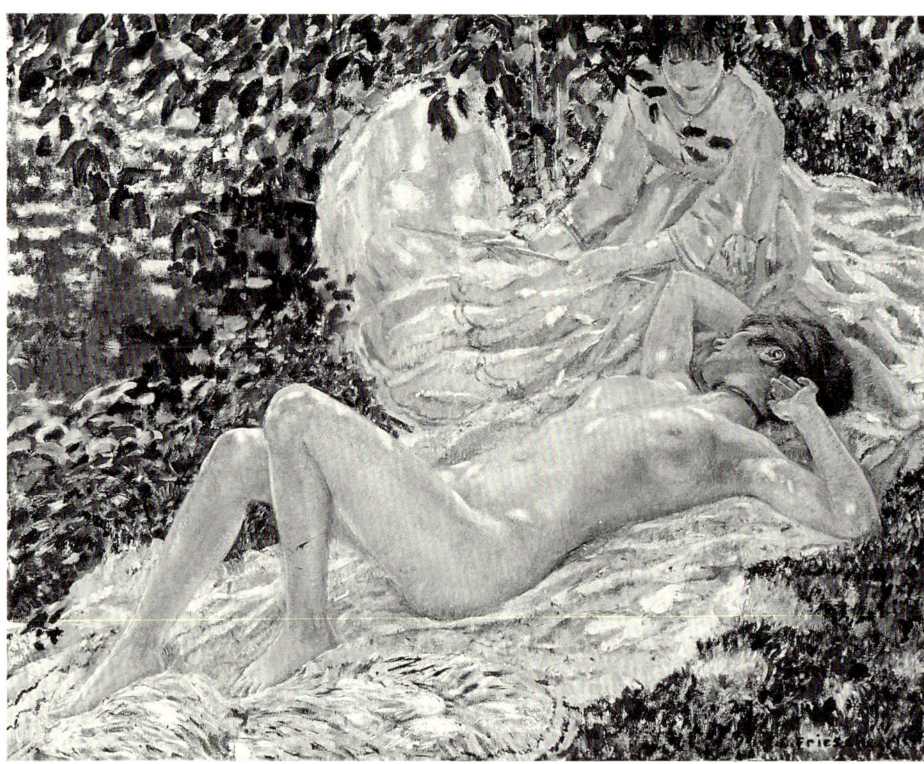

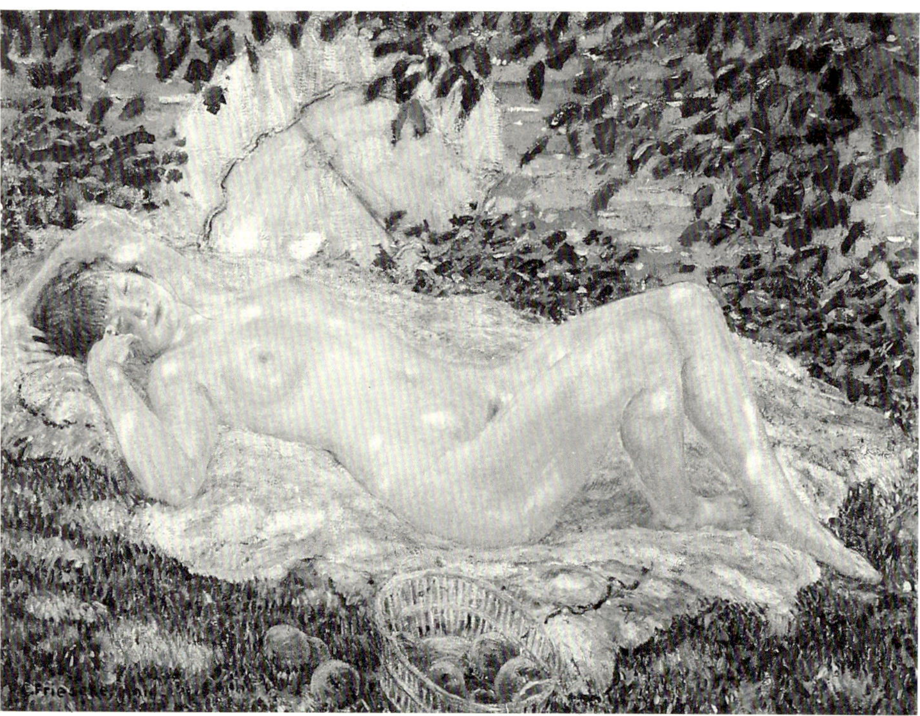

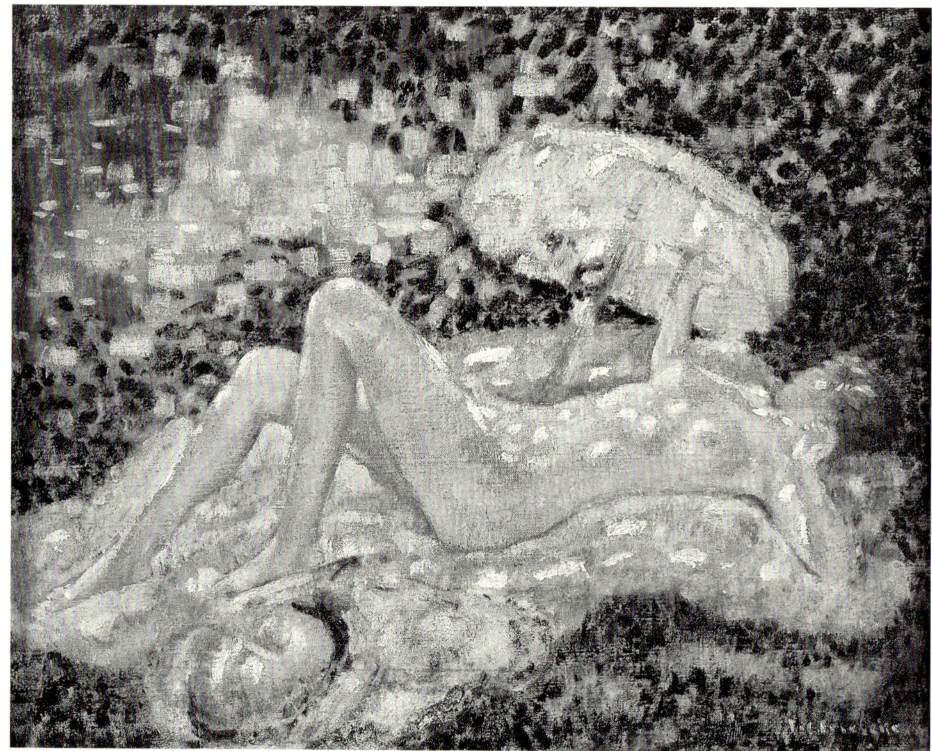

6. Pierre Anthony, "Salon de La Nationale (premier article)," *Revue de La vie mondaine* (20 May 1914), 180.
7. For an excellent discussion on the subject of the female nude in nineteenth-century French art, see Eldon N. Van Liere, "Solutions and Dissolutions: The Bather in Nineteenth-Century French Painting, *Arts Magazine* (May 1980), 104–114.
8. Pier Ludovico Occhini, "Karl Frédéric Frieseke," *Vita d'arte* 7 (February 1911), 66. I am indebted to Mary Grace Donnelly for translating this article for me.
9. Occhini, *Frieseke*, 59.
10. E. DeFestetics, "The Recent Exhibition of Mr. Frieseke's Paintings: Mr. Frieseke has Theories of His Own Which He is Bold Enough to Practise—His Problem, 'Light, Color and Sunshine,'" n.d. [probably 1912]. Detroit Institute of Arts, Reference Library, Clipping File.
11. This sketch has appeared twice at auction in the past six years. See *Sotheby's, American Impressionist and 20th Century Paintings, Drawings and Sculpture with a Selection of 19th Century Painting*, New York (2 December 1982), no. 8, illus. Also see *Sotheby's Important American Paintings, Drawings and Sculpture*, New York (28 May 1987), no. 177, illus.
12. See *Sotheby's. American Paintings, Drawings and Sculpture*, New York (25 May 1988), no. 164, color illus.
13. Nicholas Kilmer in *Sotheby's* 1988, no. 176.
14. There is a small oil sketch for this painting as well, titled *Sunbath* (present location unknown). See photograph in the Frieseke file at Hirschl and Adler, New York. Nicholas Kilmer also has a small oil sketch on wood, but with three figures instead of two.
15. Clara T. MacChesney, "American Artists in Paris," *The International Studio* 54, 213 (November 1914), xxiv. I am grateful to Kyra Curtis for bringing this article to my attention.
16. Ronald A. Hummel to Dear Sir, n.d. (probably 1966). Metropolitan Museum of Art, New York, American Paintings and Sculpture Department, Frederick Frieseke File.
17. Christian Brinton, *Impressions of the Art At the Panama-Pacific Exposition* (New York, 1916), 97.

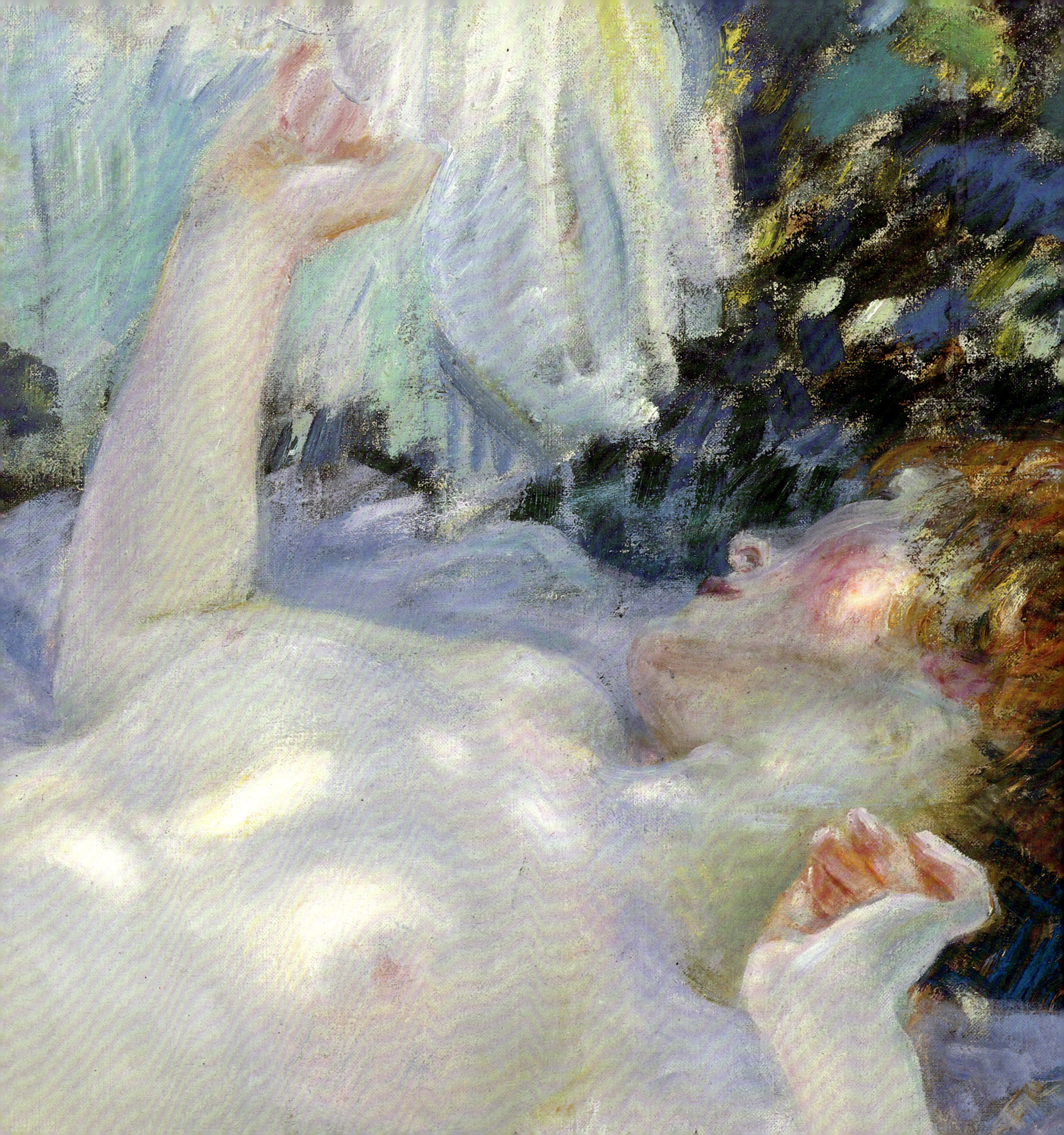

63

William McGregor Paxton (1869–1941)
1875, 1914
oil on canvas, 36 x 29⅛ (91.4 x 74)

When Paxton and his wife spent the summer of 1913 in a house built in the 1870s, Paxton was inspired to paint a few works on period themes, one of which was *1875*.[1] In the 1870s, the aesthetic-movement vogue for Japanese art reached America. Paxton has reminded us of this period with a humorous presentation of the meeting of East, represented by the porcelain figurine, and West, portrayed by Paxton's favorite model Lizzie Young. If it were not for the model's posture and the tense positions of her hands, Paxton's clever point would be overshadowed by the exquisite green dress Lizzie is wearing. Paxton had had the dress made in the style of the 1870s and had painted his wife wearing it in another work called *The Green Princess*. When *1875* was exhibited in 1916 at the Art Institute of Chicago, one critic rightly compared the brilliant handling of the gown to the work of Belgian painter Alfred Stevens.[2]

Illustrating Paxton's desire to raise the level of artistic appreciation by giving *the public what it wants, but to make the thing better than the public knows it is*,[3] the nostalgic appeal of *1875* belies the intricacy of its design. The rococo revival chair and table were chosen not as much for historical accuracy, since their style was old-fashioned by the 1870s, as for the compatibility of their forms to the model's position and to the dress. The single strong light source unifies the complicated rhythm of curves and at the same time focuses attention on the whimsical East-West cultural confrontation. *Sarah Towne Hufford*

1. Ellen Wardwell Lee, *William McGregor Paxton, 1869–1941* [exh. cat., Indianapolis Museum of Art] (Indianpolis, 1979), 114, 132, 133. *1875* was awarded the Lippincott prize for the best figure painting at the 1915 annual exhibition at the Pennsylvania Academy of the Fine Arts.
2. Indianapolis 1979, 133.
3. *Boston Herald*, 26 December 1920, as quoted in Indianapolis 1979, 112.

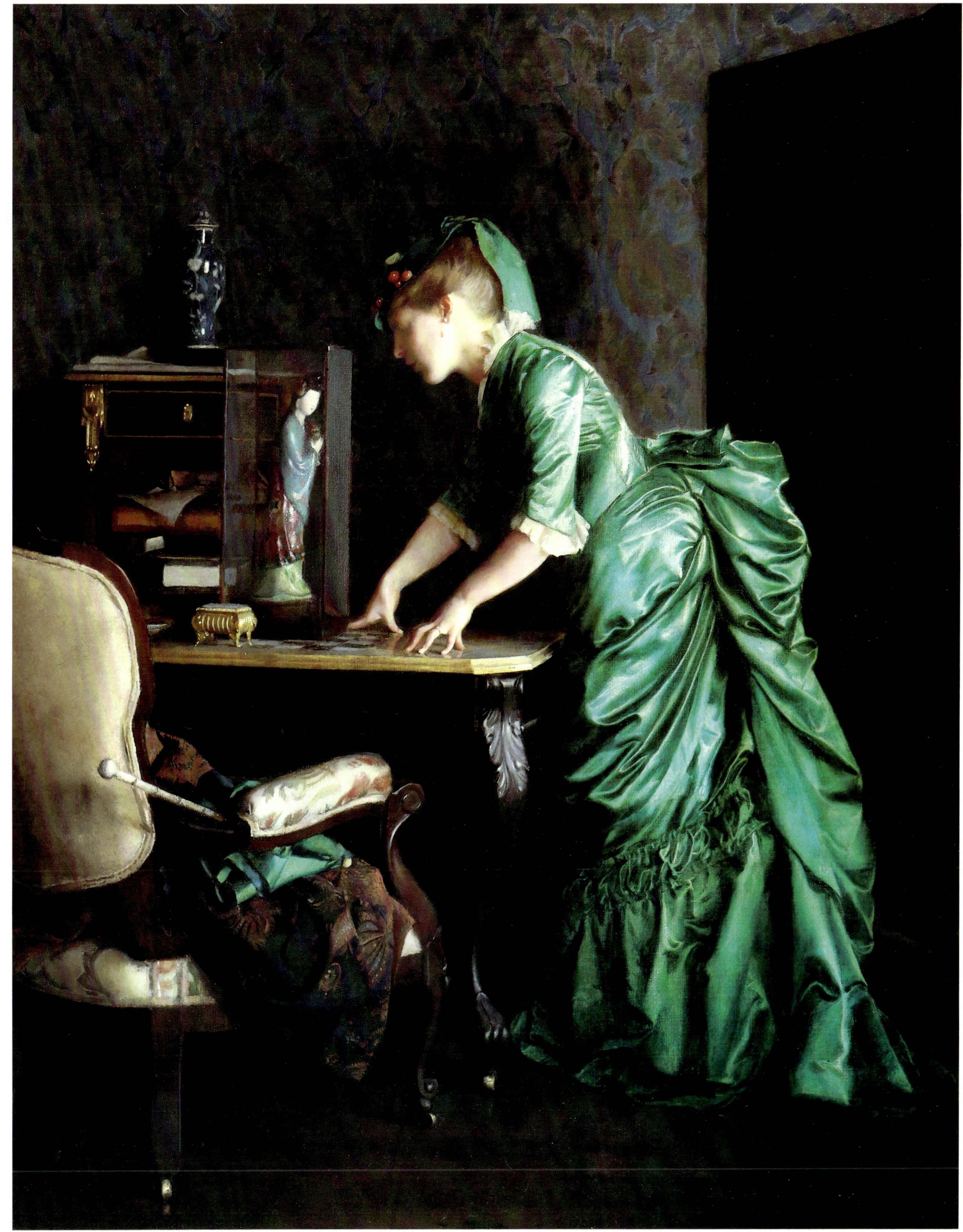

64

Robert Frederick Blum (1857–1903)
Flower Market, Tokyo c. 1892
oil on canvas, 31⅛ x 25¼ (79.1 x 63.8)

The two most elaborate and accomplished paintings of Blum's two-year visit to Japan were *Flower Market, Tokyo* and *The Ameya* ("Itinerent Candy Maker," now in the Metropolitan Museum of Art, New York).[1] These works are virtual pendents, occupying canvases of identical size, although the Manoogian work is vertical while the Metropolitan example is horizontal. Both paintings document a theme that occupied Blum in Japan as well as in his earlier European paintings, the craftsman or merchant engaged in his labor. In his illustrations for four articles for *Scribner's Magazine* accompanying Sir Edwin Arnold's text, Blum portrayed artisans practicing such picturesque trades as umbrella and lantern making.[2] Blum first depicted the subject of the flower peddler in Arnold's "Japonica," and then elaborated this image as an illustration in the second installment of his own three-part article for Scribner's entitled "An Artist in Japan" that began in April 1893 and ran for three consecutive issues.[3] Blum's illustration appeared as a photogravure over the title *Flower Market, Tokyo*, but was accompanied by no further description in the text.[4]

Blum is known to have collected photographs on his trip to Japan, and the unusual juxtaposition of the figures and sharply receding perspective suggest that he used these to construct *Flower Market, Tokyo*. However, it is evident from Blum's diary that for the pen and ink flower seller in "Japonica" he made figure sketches, and then arranged them until he captured a satisfactory, realistic compositional effect akin to a photograph. The model for the flower peddler was appropriately his gardner Fuyji, and the female model was his maid Sing.[5] The use of the anemone-like chrysanthemum, shimmering fabrics, and a foreground of variegated rutted earth provided a fruitful medium for Blum's facility in drawing and coloring.

On his return to New York, Blum exhibited *The Ameya* at the annual exhibition of the National Academy of Design in March of 1893, and the next month showed *Flower Market, Tokyo* at the Society of American Artists. Unfortunately, the New York critics were obsessed with the recent importation of neoimpressionism, as they imperfectly understood it, and focused their praise on the local proponents of the French movement such as Theodore Robinson and Robert W. Vonnoh. They saw Blum's *Flower Market, Tokyo* as outdated in style; *One reason why the extremely clever Japanese pictures of Mr. Robert Blum, like "Flower Market, Tokyo," leave us vaguely dissatisfied, spite of the nice color values and pleasing, crisp drawing, spite of the novel scene and excellent characterization of the people, is that Mr. Blum has not been through this practice of analyzing light and does not give us in his pictures the vivid sense of out of doors to which these Neo-Impressionists have accustomed us.*[6]

Regardless of the mixed reception at its debut at the Society of American Artists in 1893, *Flower Market, Tokyo* helped Blum achieve a bronze medal at the Exposition Universelle in Paris in 1900, and earned him a gold medal at the Pan-American Exposition in Buffalo in 1901. The work was purchased by his great patron of the Mendelssohn Hall murals, Alfred Corning Clark of New York City, and was subsequently owned by his son, the collector Stephen C. Clark of Cooperstown. *D. Dodge Thompson*

1. For a thorough description of *The Ameya* see Doreen Bolger Burke, "Robert Blum, 1857–1903," *American Paintings in the Metropolitan Museum of Art III* (New York, 1980), 301–304.
2. Sir Edwin Arnold, "Japonica," *Scribner's Magazine* 8, no. 6 (December 1890), 662–682; 9, no. 1 (January 1891), 17–30; 9, no. 2 (February 1891), 164–176; 9, no. 3 (March 1891), 321–340.
3. Blum's illustration of the "Flower-pedlers" appeared in Arnold's "Japonica," *Scribner's Magazine* 9, no. 2, 173.
4. Blum's illustration for the "Flower Market, Tokyo" in his "An Artist in Japan" appeared in *Scribner's Magazine* 13, no. 5 (May 1893), 629.
5. For a summary of this process as related in Blum's diary see Bruce Weber, "*Robert Frederick Blum (1857–1903) and His Milieu*," (Ph.D. diss., City University of New York), 371, n. 38.
6. "The Society of Artists: Shows the Effect of the Modern Study of Sunlight," *New York Times* 42, no. 13,000 (24 April 1893), 4, col. 6.

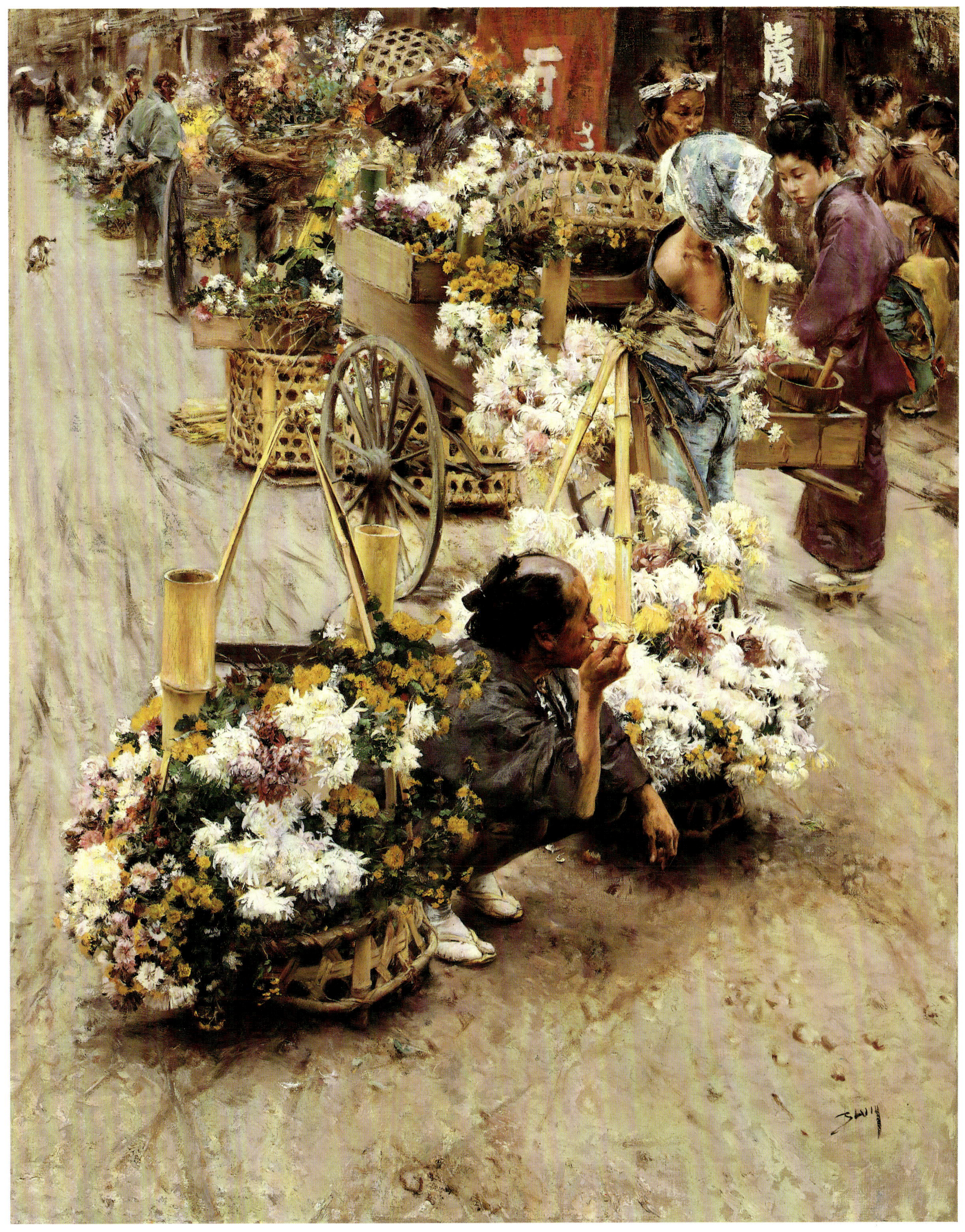

65

Frank Weston Benson
Summer Afternoon c. 1906–1908
oil on canvas, 30½ x 39½ (77.5 x 100.3)

Benson had begun to experiment with the impressionist techniques of diffused light and broken color as early as 1898, but he did not begin to work outdoors on a regular basis until 1901, when he bought a summer home on an island in Maine. The casual outdoor scenes he produced in this coastal area are as a group the best paintings he ever made.

Summer Afternoon, possibly painted in 1906,[1] confirms Benson's high level of achievement in this genre. The subject is the intense Maine light and its reflections on the blue coastal waters and on the white dresses of his daughters Elisabeth, Sylvia, and Eleanor, who are joined here by the family dog. The entire canvas is a carefully organized pattern of brushwork and light to achieve this effect. The whites of the costumes actually function to reflect the surrounding colors, and, more important, to emphasize them. The blues, browns, and reds are more intense because of the whites of the dresses, with their subtle quotations of the same colors. Eleanor holds a parasol; Elisabeth shades her eyes with her hand—a motif that occurs again in *Sunlight* (1909, Indianapolis Museum of Art) and *Summer* (1909, Museum of Art, Rhode Island School of Design).

Although all of the members of Benson's family served as models for these paintings, Benson's depictions of his daughters received the most critical attention. Caffin saw in them *a new type . . . something of the character of a fine-blooded racehorse, long in its lines, clean cut, spare of flesh . . . a product of intensive breeding—a cross between the exacting narrowness of Puritanism and the spiritual sensuousness and freedom of Emerson.*[2]

Even though recent research reveals that Benson used the camera in his working process, and that he idealized his subjects as he transferred them to canvas,[3] the images of his daughters in outdoor light remain the quintessential vision of American young womanhood at the turn of the century. *Nancy Rivard Shaw*

1. Family tradition dates this painting to 1906; however, it made its first documented appearance in *Second Exhibition, Oil Paintings by Contemporary American Artists*, at The Corcoran Gallery of Art, Washington, 8 December 1908 to 17 January 1909, cat. 229.
2. Charles H. Caffin, "The Art of Frank W. Benson," *Harper's Monthly Magazine* 119 (June 1909), 106.
3. Sheila Dugan, "Frank Benson: Outdoors," *Frank W. Benson: The Impressionist Years* [exh. cat., Spanierman Gallery] (New York, 1988), 24.

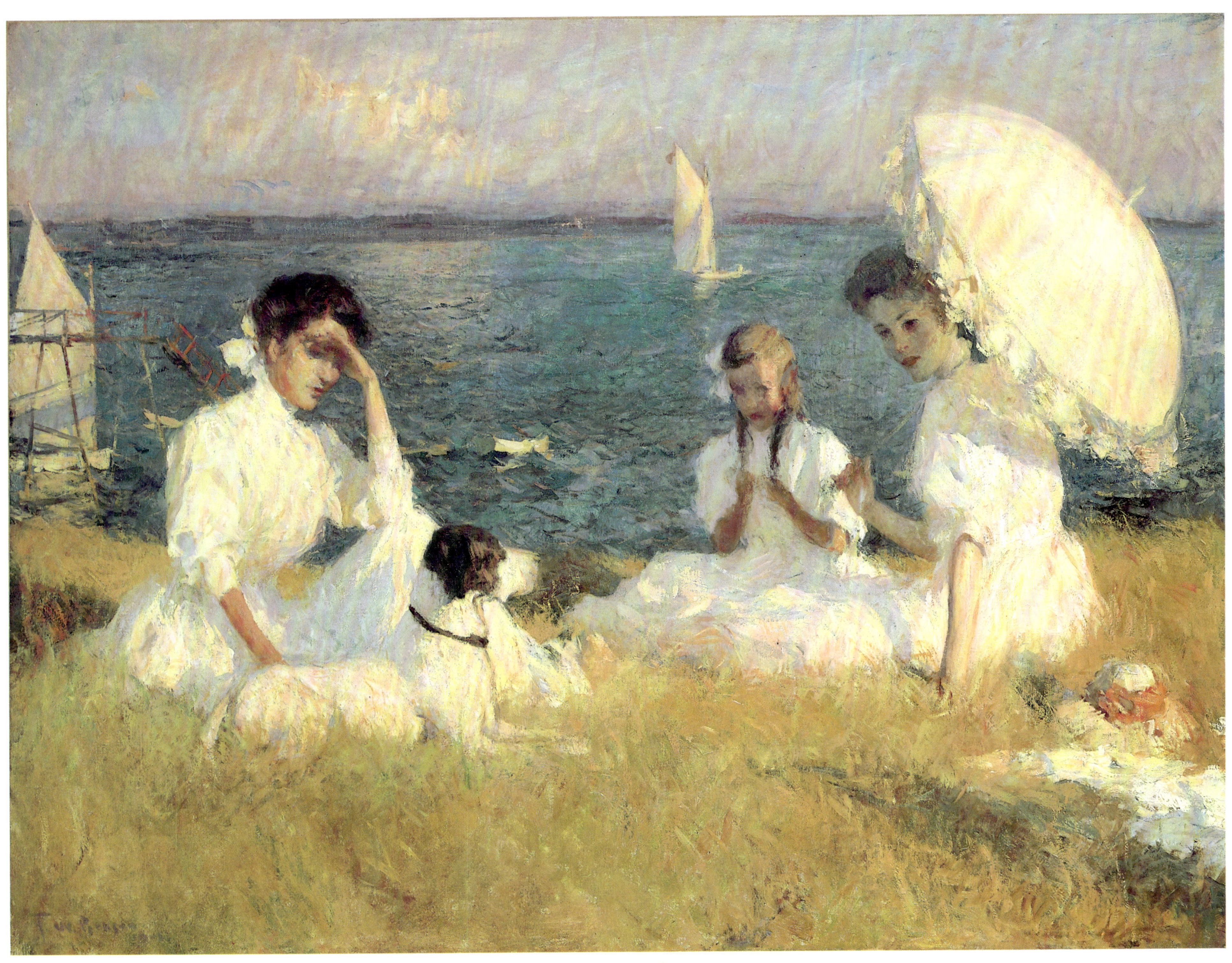

66

Maurice Prendergast (1858–1924)
Cove with Figures c. 1920
oil on canvas, 27¼ x 33¼ (69.2 x 84.5)

Cove with Figures, an extraordinary painting from the last phase of Maurice Prendergast's career, shows the results of a lifetime of exploration of modern art. In the 1890s, when the artist was first exhibiting, his tightly constructed watercolors of park scenes were well liked by Boston critics and collectors. But after the turn of the century, as Prendergast began to incorporate unusual colors and startlingly abstracted figures into his compositions, the admirers of the artist's early works were baffled and disappointed. More progressive critics and collectors, however, found his work to be an excellent example of exciting new developments in American art. As his career progressed, Prendergast, while remaining consistent in his choice of subject matter, experimented further in an effort to develop his own response to modernism. The results were eye-catching paintings, brilliant in design, with a lively surface pattern of color and line.

Between Prendergast's early and late works the contrast is dramatic. In the artist's first exhibited works, particularly the watercolors of Venice painted in 1898–1899, the exact location of the scene can be identified. Later watercolors and oil paintings have more generalized settings, often abstracted from the places used in earlier works. Narrative plays a role in the early works: people are conversing, children are playing, and sometimes there is a specific event, such as the launching of a hot-air balloon, in progress. But as the artist developed, the narrative quality disappeared as the figures became more abstract and more like shapes on a canvas rather than portrayals of people on holiday. Umbrellas and parasols, which were frequently pictured in the early works, evolved in the later pictures into arcs or half-circles of bright red suspended in space over the heads of the figures. The palette of the artist also changed from the elegant blues, reds, and greens in his light-filled watercolors to more intense color, sometimes very dark and, particularly in the paintings of Saint-Malo, France, very bright. But rarely could the colors Prendergast selected in his work after 1900 be considered realistic. The careful, painstaking handling of paint used in the early watercolors and oils to delineate each shadow on a building and fold of a dress was replaced by broader strokes of color in the later works, often applied in a lively pattern of line that gives simply a suggestion of the appearance of each object. In the final phase of the artist's career, the bright pattern of brushstrokes in his oil paintings evolved further into a technique of overlaying color upon color, which created an effect that was often compared by contemporary critics to tapestry weaving.

This evolution in style was not a smooth transition from an early to a mature style. Prendergast rarely dated his paintings, so exhibition and sales records provide the best evidence for the dates of specific works. He also repeated themes and compositions many times over, sometimes in the same style and sometimes in two or more different styles. An illustrated article written about Prendergast in 1910 by fellow artist Charles Hovey Pepper documents his wide range of techniques, confirming the fact that the artist's development was not linear with one distinct style following another.[1] The titles of Prendergast's work are often so general that one has the added confusion of determining which work of the many with similar names was actually in a given exhibition. It is only in the last few years that scholars have been able to amass enough information to unravel the complex history of Prendergast's development.[2]

Because *Cove with Figures* remained in the artist's estate after his death in 1924, there are no sales transactions documenting the life of the painting. There is also no record that the work was ever exhibited before it was sold to a collector in 1967. This is not unusual; many works by Prendergast were not seen by the public until years after his death. When *Cove with Figures* was exhibited for the first time at the Lyman Allyn Museum in New London, Connecticut, in 1968, it was given a date of c. 1914.[3] Subsequently, the painting has been published and exhibited many times, always with that date.[4]

A striking picture with bright blue water and sky, *Cove with Figures* includes a large tree in the foreground at the left that reaches almost to the top of the canvas, a high cliff in the middle ground at the right, a sailboat on the water, and a frieze of outlined figures in the foreground. These faceless figures, the majority of which are women in colorful dresses, sit, stand, and walk on the field of green with purple rocks. Two seated women face each other in the center of the foreground; the viewer's eye is led back from the space between them to three standing women and back still farther to the sailboat on the horizon. Yet the perspective in the painting is clearly askew. One does not know whether to read the foreground figures as standing on a bluff over the cove or on the same level as the shoreline; the boat also looms too large in the distance. Every inch of the canvas both in foreground and background is alive with small strokes of color.

In at least two other paintings by Prendergast, *Along the Shore* (fig. 1), an unsigned work now known only from a photograph,[5] and *Neponset Bay* (fig. 2), the same distinctive circular cove is portrayed, again with figures on the shore in the foreground, a large tree at the left, and a bluff in the middle ground in the right. If the title of the Nebraska painting is accurate (Prendergast's later titles are not completely reliable), it would mean that the basis for these paintings was the coastline of an area directly south of Boston. The degree to which the subject has been abstracted precludes any hope of identifying an exact location. The photograph of *Along the Shore* was found in an album of photographs of Prendergast paintings that has been dated c. 1915.[6] *Neponset Bay*, a well-documented painting, was exhibited at the Joseph Brummer Galleries in 1921 and presumably dates from that final period in the artist's career. In contrast to *Cove with Figures* and *Neponset Bay*, *Along the Shore* has long parallel paint strokes in the sea and sky, less-substantial figures in the foreground, and silhouetted people on the curved shoreline at the right. The paint surface seems to be less heavily built up than in the other paintings. This handling of paint is consistent with the style of the works Prendergast is known to have exhibited in an important one-man show at the Carroll Galleries in New York in 1915.[7]

In the last years of his life, Prendergast repeated many of the compositions from the era around 1915. Some late works with their heavily built-up surfaces actually hide earlier compositions below that have been reworked. The differences between the works from the earlier period with the late paintings are subtle, and so it is not surprising that *Cove with Figures* would have been mistakenly given a date of c. 1914. More correctly, however, the painting should be dated c. 1920. Unlike *Along the Shore* and the other paintings from the Carroll Galleries era, *Cove with Figures* and *Neponset Bay* have colorful abstracted figures (many of them now wearing the shorter skirts popular after World War I), which seem distinct from the background and more three-dimensional and solidly rooted to the foreground plane than the thinner figures that seem to melt into their surroundings in the earlier composition. A more complex pattern of textures is found throughout Prendergast's later works; *Cove with Figures* is alive with dabs of white in the ocean and a variety of greens in the trees. Colors and shapes echo across the canvas in a pattern that moves the eye, not only across the canvas but back and into the picture giving it the sense of solid form, rather than just an impression of a pleasing pattern on the picture's surface. To the viewer the arrangement of forms may appear random, but the placement of every shape was actually deliberate.

For Prendergast in the late phase of his career, a painting became the vehicle for creating a complex arrangement of colors, shapes, and textures. There was no story to tell, no specific people to portray. Everything in the painting, be it person, object, or setting, was simply part of the pattern. This is art about art, not a chronicle of an event or a record of the appearance of a particular place. One can interpret the people in later Prendergast paintings as dehumanized creatures, reduced to being simply shapes on the canvas. But the artist's sketchbooks record thousands of sketches of individual people that document that he was not averse to drawing people; in later paintings, such as *Cove with Figures*, the individual people were a point from which to begin, rather than end, a picture. In starting from a realistic scene, Prendergast sought to take his art a step further to create complex compositions where object, color, shape, texture, and design are all equally important components.

Gwendolyn Owens

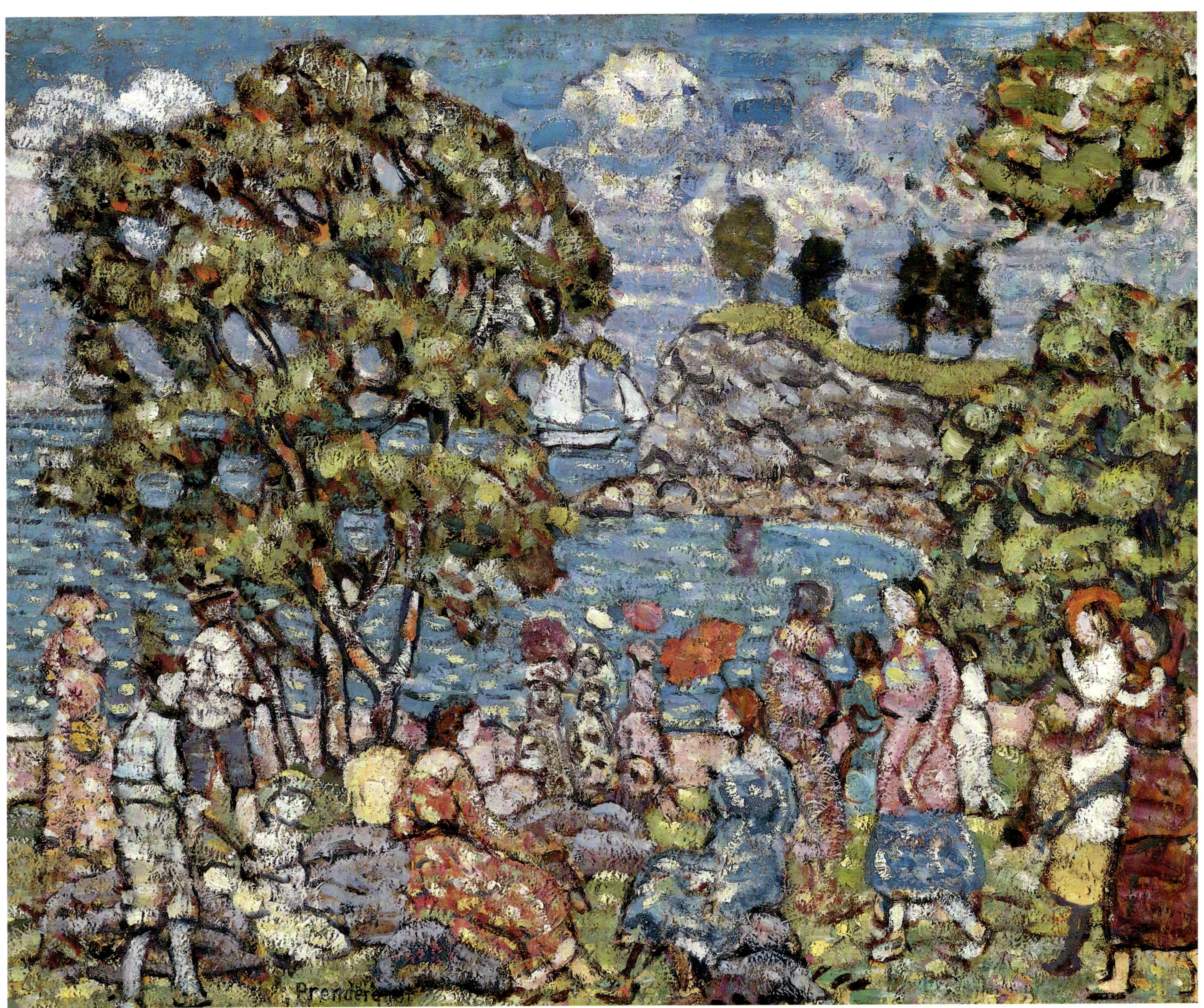

Fig. 1
Photograph of Maurice Prendergast's lost painting *Along the Shore*, Prendergast Archives, Willams College Museum of Art

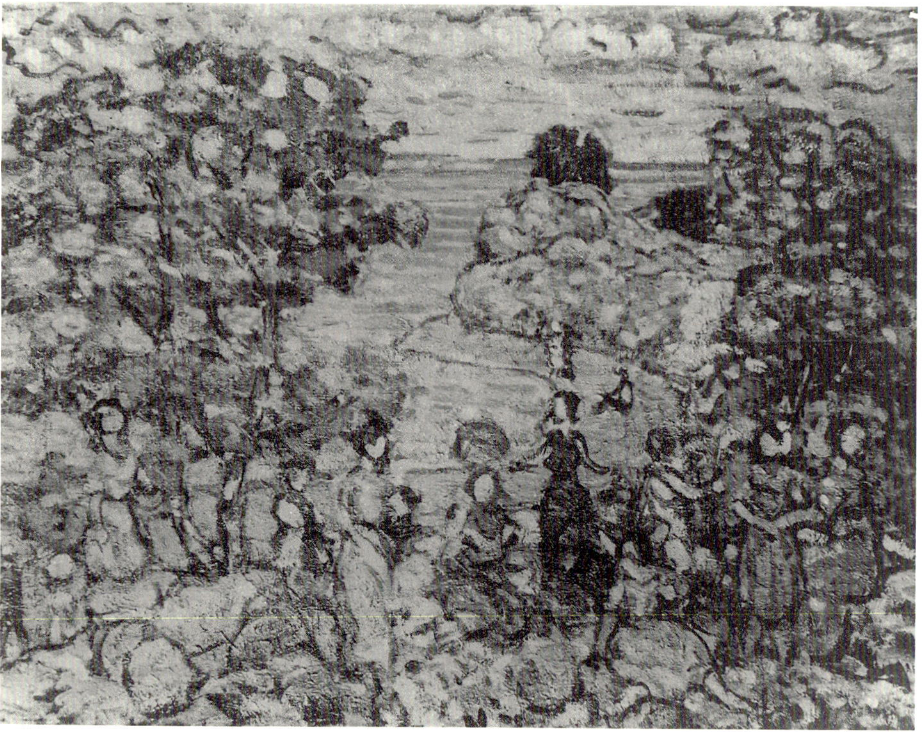

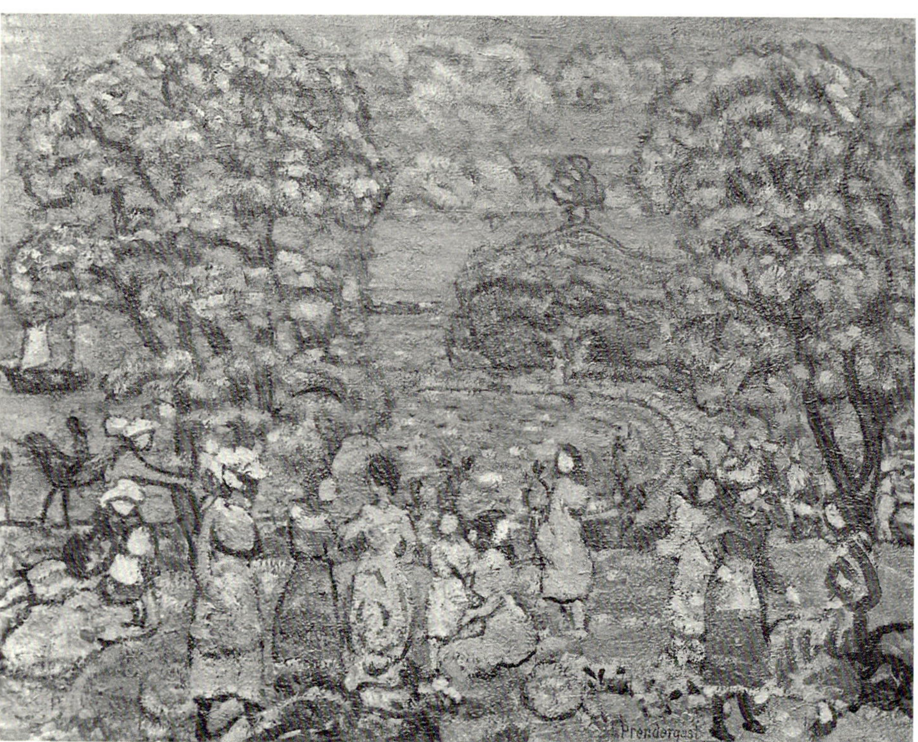

Fig. 2
Maurice Prendergast, *Neponset Bay*, c. 1914, oil on canvas, 24½ x 32¼ (62.2 x 81.9), Sheldon Memorial Art Gallery, F. M. Hall Collection, University of Nebraska-Lincoln

1. Charles Hovey Pepper, "Is Drawing to Disappear in Artistic Individuality?" *The World To-day* 19 (July 1910), 716–718. A larger group of photographs, which were later owned by Mrs. Charles Prendergast, were reportedly taken by or for Pepper at the same time. These photographs document an even broader range of technique. See Eleanor Green, Ellen Glavin, S.N.D., and Jeffrey R. Hayes, *Maurice Prendergast: Art of Impulse and Color* [exh. cat., University of Maryland Art Gallery] (College Park, 1976), 63.
2. A systematic catalogue of the works of Maurice and Charles Prendergast has been compiled by the Prendergast Project at the Williams College Museum of Art. The catalogue includes images of over 1,600 works by Maurice, with an additional 400 works known only from written records; it will be published in 1989 by Prestel Verlag, Munich.
3. *Painting and Sculpture from the Collection of Mr. and Mrs. Nathan Cummings* [exh. checklist, Lyman Allyn Museum] (New London, 1968).
4. *Cove with Figures* was later exhibited at the Elvehjem Art Center, University of Wisconsin in 1970; the Metropolitan Museum of Art in 1971; the Art Institute of Chicago in 1973; and the University of Maryland Art Gallery (and participating museums) 1976.
5. The photograph is now in the Prendergast Archives at the Williams College Museum of Art.
6. The dating for the album of photographs, which was until recently owned by Mrs. Charles Prendergast, is based on the fact that many of the works pictured were exhibited at the Carroll Galleries exhibition in 1915.
7. Paintings in this exhibition, such as *Bathers*, now also in the Manoogian Collection, were all given dates in the published checklist. This was the only time in the artist's lifetime that he had a one-person show in which the checklist included dates for the paintings; thus, the Carroll Galleries records are crucial in determining the development of the artist's style. See *Maurice B. Prendergast: Paintings in Oil and Watercolor* [exh. checklist, Carroll Galleries] (New York, 1915). John Quinn, the prominent lawyer and art collector, purchased many of the paintings in the exhibition; a catalogue documenting the collection was published after his death in 1924. Thus we know with certainty some of the works that were in this important exhibition and the style in which they were painted. See *John Quinn, 1870–1925* [sic]. *Collection of Paintings, Watercolors, Drawings and Sculpture* (Huntington, New York, 1926).

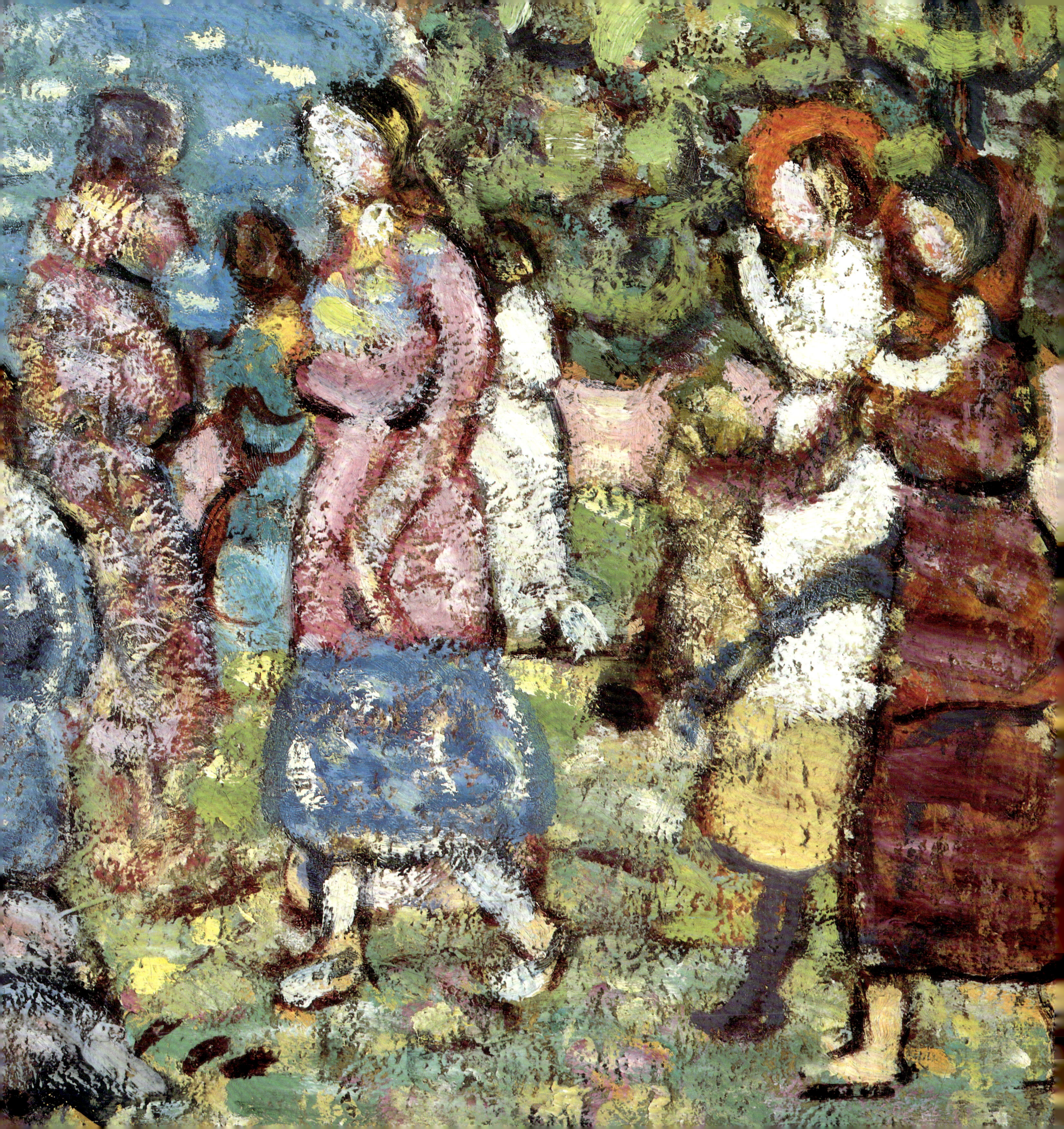

67

William Glackens (1870–1938)
Little May Day Procession c. 1905
oil on canvas, 25 x 30 (63.5 x 76.2)

Little May Day Procession is one of several views of New York's Central Park that Glackens painted around 1905.[1] It forms a pair with *May Day, Central Park* (c. 1905, The Fine Arts Museums of San Francisco), one painting showing the approach of a May Day procession, the other its rowdy aftermath. The urban park was a favored subject of Glackens' friend and colleague Maurice Prendergast (see cat. 66),[2] and would have been familiar to both artists from examples by Parisian painters of modern life such as Edouard Manet. Glackens also painted the Luxembourg Gardens in Paris during his 1906 visit, in works that are remarkably similar in composition and mood to his Central Park views.[3]

The first day of May was observed in turn-of-the-century New York as both the traditional moving day and an international labor holiday, but it was not always the date for organized May Day celebrations. These were held on an appointed day (usually Saturday) early in the month, when springlike weather could be assured. As Glackens' painting describes, certain festivities were reserved for children: [It] *was in Central Park that the biggest carnival was had. At Fifth avenue and Fifty-ninth street the parade of millionaires in their handsome coaches swept past one hundred little girls and boys marching toward the croquet grounds for a day of fun. . . . The park fairly bristled with youngsters. They came from far and from near. . . .* [P]*resently the grass was so strewn with white frocks that at a little distance it looked as if household linen laid out to bleach had suddenly taken to skipping about.*[4] Glackens described this festive event with the quick, facile lines that he commanded as an illustrator, and in the dark, rich colors that he learned from Henri and Manet. Everett Shinn noted the connection between Glackens' training as an illustrator and his style as a painter when he praised the *super achievement* of paintings such as this one in which *All color is mingled in his mighty draughtsmanship.*[5] The vivid, energetic paint handling and Glackens' sure execution yield an apt metaphor for the exuberant celebration of May Day in Central Park. *Sally Mills*

1. Others include *The Drive, Central Park* (c. 1905, The Cleveland Museum of Art) and *Central Park in Winter* (c. 1905, The Metropolitan Museum of Art, New York).
2. Prendergast painted several watercolors of Central Park, including a *May Day*, around 1901; see Patterson Sims, *Maurice B. Prendergast: A Concentration of Works from the Permanent Collection* [exh. cat., Whitney Museum of American Art] (New York, 1980), 15–16.
3. Glackens' paintings of the Luxembourg Gardens are in The Corcoran Gallery of Art, Washington, and The Wichita Art Museum, Kansas.
4. "May Queens Ruled Tiny Subjects in City Parks," *The World*, 8 May 1904; "Happy Youngsters Celebrate May Day," *The World*, 2 May 1903.
5. Everett Shinn, "Recollections of the Eight," in *The Eight* [exh. cat., The Brooklyn Museum] (Brooklyn, 1943), 19.

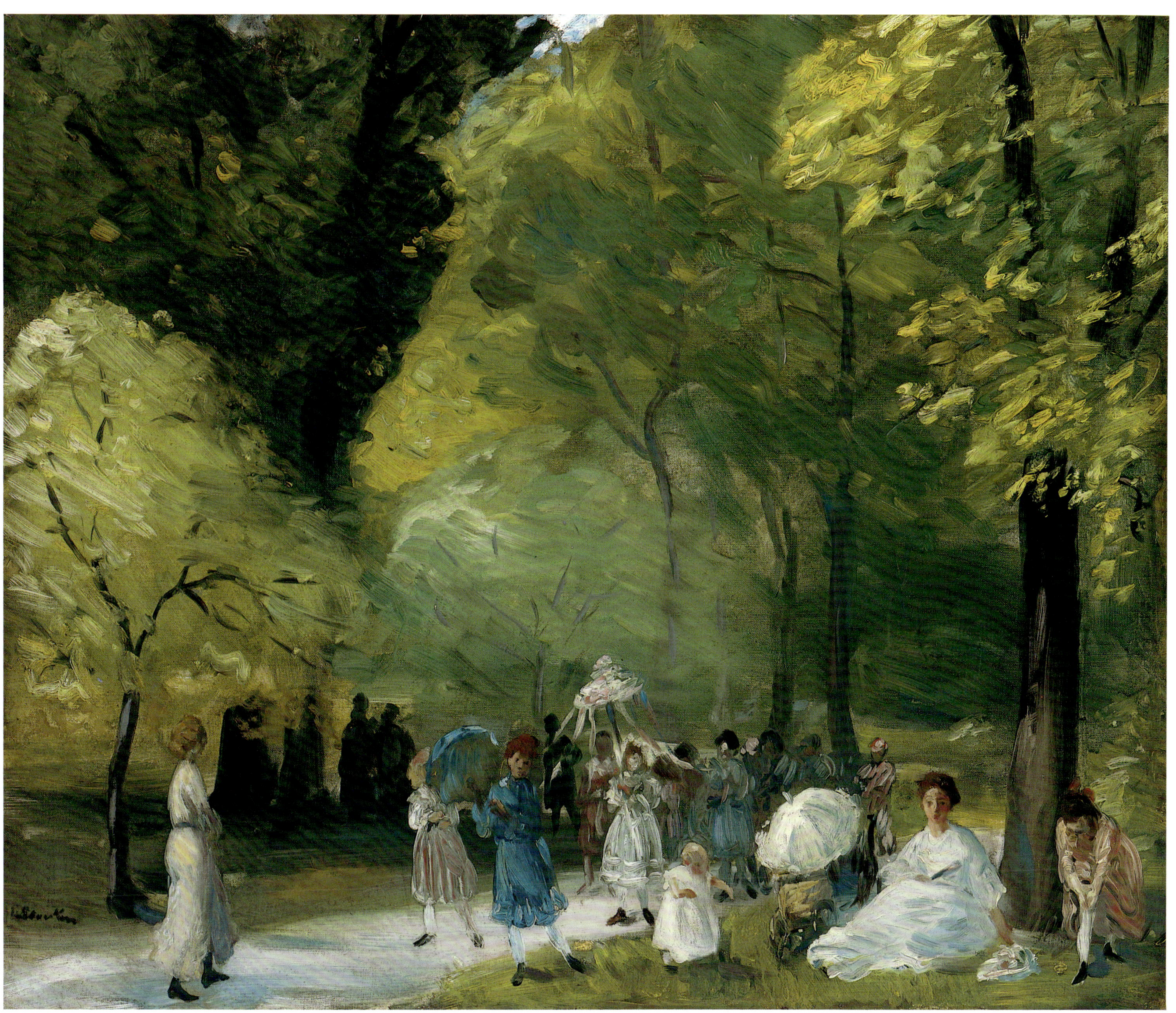

68

John Twachtman (1853–1902)
Last Touch of Sun c. 1893
oil on canvas, 25⅛ x 29⅞ (63.8 x 75.9)

In 1889 Twachtman and his family took up residence in a small Greenwich, Connecticut, farmhouse which he purchased soon thereafter, along with seventeen acres of land. Some of the artist's loveliest works were painted on this property on Round Hill Road. Like his French counterpart Claude Monet, Twachtman chose to depict the same humble sites again and again, in varied seasons and conditions of light. His intention, however, was not the deliberate creation of a series in order to precisely record optical phenomena; rather he sought to discover the beautiful in the familiar and to express the human sensibilities suggested by nature.

Unlike most of his colleagues, who spent their winters in the city and migrated to certain New England villages each summer, Twachtman lived year-round in the country.[1] He became especially well known as a painter of winter, excelling at evoking the subtle poetry of that season. *Last Touch of Sun* conveys the distinctive beauty of the hard light that falls when the sun is near the horizon and shadows are long. The work is somewhat atypical of the artist in that the solidity of the architecture, garden wall, and hillside are clearly conveyed. Often the forms in Twachtman's paintings are dissolved in a swirling confluence of the heavy impasto and dry, dragging brushstrokes that are characteristic of his work.

The building seen in *Last Touch of Sun* is Twachtman's own house, depicted in 1893 or earlier, before he built subsequent additions to accomodate his growing family. The subject was a significant one for the artist. The reviewer of Twachtman's important American Art Galleries exhibition with Monet, Besnard, and Weir, in which the painting was included, observed: *One of Monet's pictures is of his house in a garden of sunflowers; two are of haystacks; and Mr. Twachtman seems to have taken a hint from this preference for commonplace subjects made beautiful by light, and has given us several views of* his *house (more picturesquely situated, it is true) in summer and in winter. His snow scenes, with blue shadows of unseen trees lying across rocks and garden walls, are the most charming things he has done.*[2]

The same house, as shown in Twachtman's painting *Summer* (The Phillips Collection, Washington) was eventually expanded by another section with a dormer. By the turn of the century the home included a handsome neoclassical portico in front (*My House*, Yale University Art Gallery).[3] It continued to grow in an organic fashion, changing to fit the family's needs, yet cleaving to the landscape. Its appearance in its surroundings was not unlike that of Twachtman's paintings; strong, but restrained rather than strident; intricate and almost sculptural in texture. *Deborah Chotner*

1. While living in Connecticut, Twachtman taught two days a week at the Art Students League in New York, a short trip by train from Greenwich.
2. "French and American Impressionists," *The Art Amateur* 29 (June 1893), 4.
3. The house is discussed at length in Alfred Henry Goodwin's article "An Artist's Unspoiled Country Home," *Country Life in America* 8 (October 1905), 625–630.

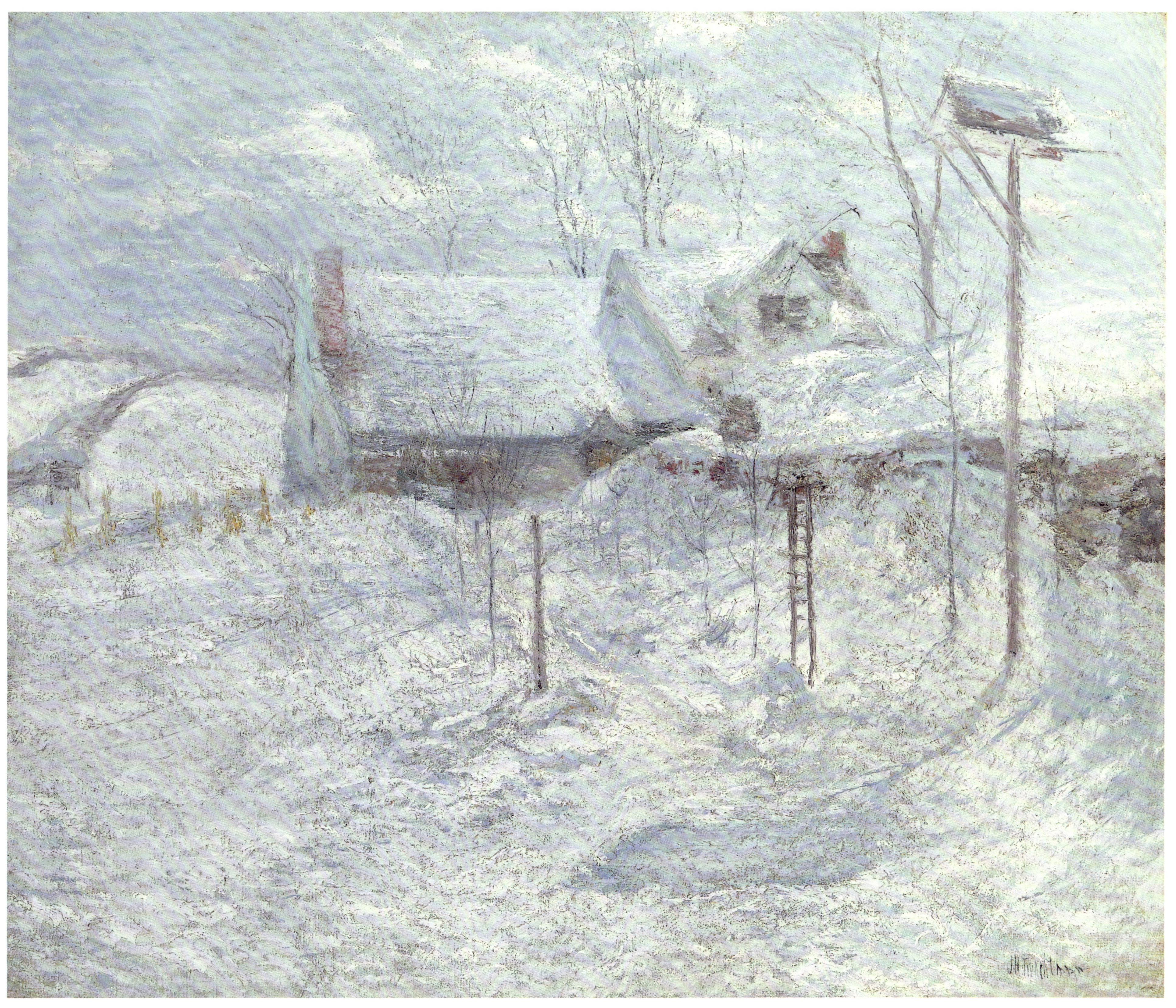

69

Ernest Lawson (1873–1939)
Harlem River c. 1913–1915
oil on canvas, 40⅛ x 50 (101.9 x 127)

In 1898 Ernest Lawson established a studio in northern Manhattan's Washington Heights. It was from this site that he produced the Harlem River scenes that are a staple of his oeuvre. Like Monet, who created a series of works examining haystacks and cathedrals under assorted light and weather conditions, Lawson turned toward the Harlem River to supply a similar subject for study. He chose the area around the High Bridge to examine the changes of season and time. *Harlem River* captures the river on an early spring morning, when the mist is begining to burn off and the atmosphere will soon provide a clear view of the opposite shore. Closely related is *Hospital Harlem River* (formerly in the John Quinn collection), which is similar in composition, but the season depicted is late fall.

Lawson almost sculpted his paintings, using his brush, palette knife, and thumb to create a plastic effect. He applied the pigment in a manner producing an air of spontaneity. *Harlem River* demonstrates this technique. The built-up pigment achieves a smooth plastic base upon which Lawson lightly sketched the skyline, thereby creating the hazy quality desired. He then depicted the river with thick paint; this culminated with the small tugboat, which actually projects from the plane of the canvas. The atmospheric effects are achieved through his great sense of color, which accents the mood of time and season. By selecting specific tones, he conveyed his desired sense of realism. In describing Lawson's work, a contemporary wrote, *Lawson's art is realistic, but he abhors the sordid and ugly (so many moderns wrongly think this is synonymous with character). He paints the prosaic but seen through the eyes of an artist not through the lens of a camera.*[1] *James W. Tottis*

1. A. E. Gallatin, "Ernest Lawson," *International Studio* 59 (July 1916), xv.

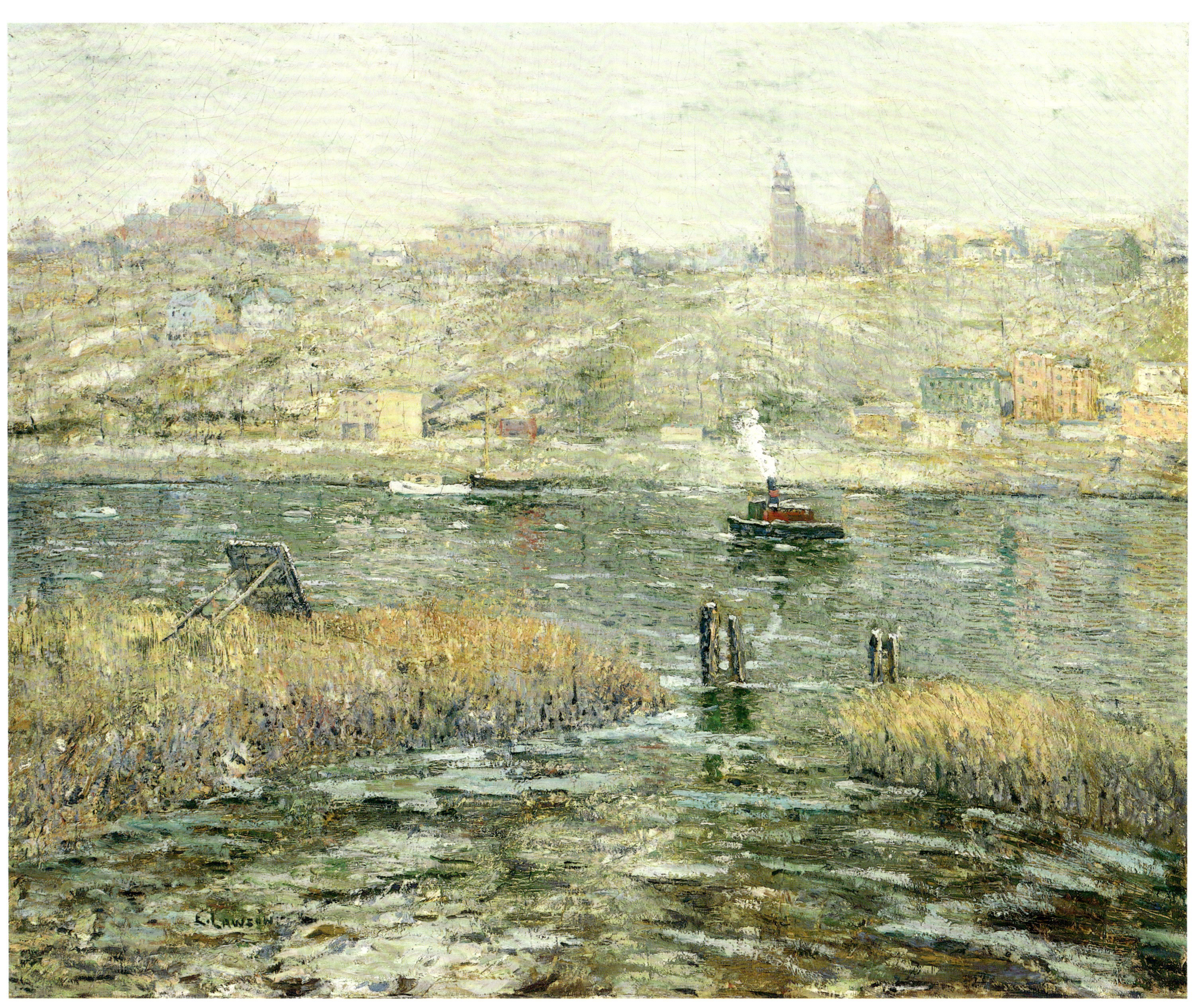
E. LAWSON

Artists' Biographies

FRANK WESTON BENSON (1862–1951)

Benson was born and raised in Salem, Massachusetts, and began his initial art training in 1880 at the School of the Museum of Fine Arts, Boston. He then went on to study between 1883 and 1885 at the Académie Julian, in Paris, under Jules-Joseph Lefebvre and Gustave Boulanger. During the summer months he painted at Concarneau in Brittany.

On his return to the United States in 1885, Benson joined the staff of the Portland (Maine) School of Art, and began exhibiting portraits and landscapes in Boston and elsewhere. In 1889 he secured a teaching position at the Museum School in Boston, where he remained for nearly thirty years.

Benson's paintings of the late 1880s and early 1890s, chiefly interior portraits and figure studies, reveal an interest in decorative design, especially evident in a mural cycle for the Library of Congress in Washington, which he completed in 1896. In 1898 he became a founding member of the Ten American Painters and turned his attention to outdoor subjects. After 1901, when he purchased a summer home on the Maine island of North Haven, Benson developed a mature impressionist style, frequently depicting his wife and children in bright sunlight. The paintings of the female members of the family, often dressed in white and silhouetted against a summer landscape, were lauded by critics as ideals of American young womanhood.

In the mid-teens Benson turned to sporting scenes, especially salmon fishing and duck hunting, painting them in oil and watercolor. About 1912 he began to work seriously as a printmaker, and participated in the revival of printmaking. Benson continued to exhibit both paintings and etchings of sporting subjects until about 1946, when failing health forced him into inactivity. *Nancy Rivard Shaw*

Fairbrother, Trevor J. *The Bostonians: Painters of an Elegant Age, 1870–1930*. Exh. cat., Museum of Fine Arts, Boston, 1986.

Dugan, Sheila. "Frank Benson Outdoors," *Frank W. Benson: The Impressionist Years*. Exh. cat., Spanierman Gallery, New York, 1988.

ALBERT BIERSTADT (1830–1902)

Albert Bierstadt was born in Solingen, Prussia, but spent his early years in New Bedford, Massachusetts, the son of immigrant parents. Although family members cautioned against a career as an artist, Bierstadt persevered and, after several lean years as a drawing teacher, journeyed to Düsseldorf in 1853 to seek formal instruction. The premature death of German artist Johann Peter Hasenclever, a distant relative with whom he had hoped to study, threatened his plans until American painters Emanuel Leutze and Worthington Whittredge, then working in Düsseldorf, came to his aid. In 1857, after four productive years of study and travel in Germany, Switzerland, and Italy, Bierstadt returned to New Bedford a technically mature painter.

In 1859 he joined Frederick W. Lander's survey expedition to the Rocky Mountains and in the alpine peaks of the Far West found the subject that made his career. Returning east, he moved to New York, took a studio in the Tenth Street Studio Building, and began producing the western landscapes that brought him early acclaim. Chief among these was *The Rocky Mountains, Lander's Peak* (1863, The Metropolitan Museum of Art, New York), a 6 by 10 foot canvas that rivaled Frederic Church's *Heart of the Andes* (1859, The Metropolitan Museum of Art, New York) in ambition and panoramic scope. In 1863, accompanied by well-known writer Fitz Hugh Ludlow, Bierstadt undertook a second western expedition, traveling overland to California and Oregon. Upon his return, he began a series of large pictures (*Mount Hood*, 1865, Southwest Museum, Los Angeles; *Looking Down Yosemite Valley*, 1865, Birmingham Museum of Art, Alabama; *A Storm in the Rocky Mountains, Mount Rosalie*, 1866, The Brooklyn Museum), which he exhibited in selected cities and eventually sold for substantial sums. With the rewards of such sales he built a lavish home, Malkasten, on the banks of the Hudson River and set off, in 1867, on a two-year working honeymoon in Europe. Celebrated abroad as well as at home, he exhibited paintings privately before Queen Victoria and was awarded the Legion of Honor by Napoleon III.

Between 1871 and 1873 he lived and worked in California, traveling again to Yosemite as well as other Sierra and coastal sites. Paintings from this period continued to celebrate the awesome beauty and spiritual power of America's wilderness landscape. In later years he journeyed to Yellowstone, the Canadian Rockies, the Pacific Northwest, Alaska, and the Bahamas. Beginning with his 1867 honeymoon and continuing into the 1890s, he also made numerous European tours as much for promotional purposes as for sketching.

Changing taste, evident as early as the mid-1870s, resulted in reduced sales and financial difficulties. In 1882 his home on the Hudson burned, and in 1889 a late masterwork, *The Last of the Buffalo* (1888, Corcoran Gallery of Art, Washington), was rejected by the American selection committee for the Paris Exposition. Declaring the canvas not representative of contemporary American art, the committee confirmed the view that Bierstadt was an outmoded master of an older generation. He died in New York on 18 February 1902. Interest in Bierstadt's work did not revive until the 1960s, when the abstract elements of his oil sketches caught the eye of a generation schooled on modernism. *Nancy Anderson*

Trump, Richard Shafer. Life and Works of Albert Bierstadt. Ph.D. diss., Ohio State University, 1963.

Hendricks, Gordon. *Albert Bierstadt: Painter of the American West*. New York, 1973.

Baigell, Matthew. *Albert Bierstadt*. New York, 1981.

GEORGE CALEB BINGHAM (1811–1879)

The life of George Caleb Bingham, the first major painter west of the Mississippi, exhibits the same spirit of restless westward movement that is celebrated in his paintings. Born in Virginia in 1811, he moved as a small child to Missouri, and spent his career in the new settlements that stretched along the pathway of commerce from Saint Louis to Kansas City, where he died in February of 1879.

Throughout his career he moved back and forth between two professions that are seldom combined, politics and art, and in both he achieved distinction. He served as a Missouri state representative and state treasurer. Politics, in fact, often provided the inspiration for his paintings.

Bingham supported himself chiefly by making likenesses of the frontier gentry. But with few exceptions, his portraits of local notables are boring, even by nineteenth-century standards. Bingham's renderings of lower-class characters, on the other hand, were handled with humorous affection, and have become the most valued of all nineteenth-century American genre paintings.

Bingham's artistic career can be divided into three phases. In the first, which extended from 1833 to 1845, he supported himself as an itinerant portraitist. His work of this period shows the linearity and flatness characteristic of the work of provincial, self-taught artists. In 1838 Bingham journeyed to Philadelphia, and spent several months of intensive study at the Pennsylvania Academy of the Fine Arts. It is not known if he had formal instruction, but during this period, probably mainly through copying paintings and plaster casts and consulting drawing manuals, he greatly improved his technical skills, particularly his mastery of three-dimensional treatment of form.

The second and most notable phase of Bingham's artistic career began in 1845, when Bingham returned to Missouri after several years in the East. Shortly afterward he submitted his first western scene, *Fur Traders Descending the Missouri* (The Metropolitan Museum of Art, New York), to the American Art-Union in New York. Bingham later offered other paintings to the Art-Union, depicting more conventional subject matter, but *Fur Traders* brought him nearly twice as much as they did. As a consequence he followed with a series of characteristically western subjects.

Bingham displayed these paintings widely in Missouri, where they attracted considerable attention. He made nearly all of his sales, however, through the American Art-Union. While Bingham's genre paintings were not numerous—he produced only about thirty—they provide a unique record of the American frontier, and have earned him a major place in every history of American painting.

Unfortunately, Bingham's activity as a genre painter virtually ended in the mid-1850s, largely because of the demise of the American Art-Union, which was disbanded in 1852. Without it, Bingham had difficulty in selling his more ambitious works, and was mainly a portraitist. Almost all of his genre paintings, at this point, were replicas of his most popular compositions, and he never equaled the emotional sincerity and artistic excellence of his first efforts. *Henry Adams*

Rollins, C. B., ed. "Letters of George Caleb Bingham to James S. Rollins." *The Missouri Historical Review* 32–33 (1937–1939).

Christ-Janer, Albert (with a preface by Thomas Hart Benton). *George Caleb Bingham of Missouri.* New York, 1940.

McDermott, John Francis. *George Caleb Bingham, River Portraiture.* Norman, Oklahoma, 1959.

Bloch, E. Maurice. *George Caleb Bingham: The Evolution of an Artist* and *A Catalogue Raisonne.* 2 vols. Berkeley and Los Angeles, 1967.

ROBERT FREDERICK BLUM (1857–1903)

Robert Frederick Blum was born in Cincinnati, the son of immigrants from the Rhenish Palatinate. He left school in 1874 to become an apprentice lithographer, studying drawing and painting in the evenings under Frank Duveneck at the Mechanics' Institute. The following year entered the McMicken School of Design (now the Art Academy of Cincinnati) where Alfred Brennen and Kenyon Cox were fellow students. At the urging of Cox the three aspiring artists enrolled briefly at the Pennsylvania Academy of the Fine Arts in Philadelphia in the autumn of 1876. Blum was dissatisfied with the teaching of the frail Christian Schussele, but was inspired by the exhibitions of the centennial in Fairmount Park, especially the contemporary painting of Mariano Fortuny and Giovanni Boldini, and began his lifelong enthusiasm for Japanese art after encountering the art, architecture, and crafts of that nation's extensive display at the fair.

Blum obtained a position as an illustrator at Charles Scribner's Sons in 1877, and in New York was befriended by Harry Humphrey Moore, William Merritt Chase, and other artists associated with the Society of American Artists. He was sent to Europe on assignment in 1880, and traveled to Paris, Rome, Geneva, Naples, and Venice where he became reacquainted with Frank Duveneck and met his spirited American students, as well as James McNeill Whistler. Following Whistler's example Blum took up etching and mastered the medium of pastel, becoming president of the Society of Painters in Pastel after his return to New York. Whistler also confirmed Blum's interest in Japanese art, and taught the younger artist the freedom of applying Japanese principles of design in his compositions and color arrangements.

In 1881 Blum returned to Europe with Chase and James Carroll Beckwith, and his illustrations of Venice from his trip were coupled with an article about the city by Henry James for *The Century Magazine.* The following year Blum returned to Europe with Chase, this time to Spain where the artists copied Velázquez and Ribera in the Prado; and in 1884 accompanied Chase to Holland, summering in Zandvoort where they produced landscapes in watercolor and pastel.

Blum returned to New York in 1885. There he occupied the former studio of J. Alden Weir, and completed his first important canvas, *Venetian Lace Makers* (1887, Cincinnati Art Museum), which he significantly chose to represent his work at the Exposition Universelle, Paris, 1889. This work demonstrated Blum's growth from facile illustration and the influence of the school of Fortuny toward a more mature style marked by an emphasis on immediate impressions created by light and atmosphere. The picturesque arrangement of figures and decorative objects in an interior setting with dramatic lighting shows the influence of Chase; while the subject matter itself, artisans at work, recalls the contemporary genre painting in Venice of John Singer Sargent and Charles Ulrich, and in turn a revival of interest in Velázquez.

Continuing his long association with *Scribner's*, in 1890 Blum was commissioned to illustrate a four-part article by Sir Edwin Arnold, *Japonica*, and departed for a two-year visit to Japan during which he completed a large number of ink sketches, pastels, as well as oils of genre subjects. On his return he exhibited *The Ameya* (The Metropolitan Museum of Art, New York) at the National Academy of Design, and was elected an academician for his efforts. That same year, 1893, he was commissioned to paint mural decorations, *The Vintage Festival* and *Mood to Music* (1893–c. 1898, Brooklyn Museum), for Mendelssohn Hall in New York. Thereafter he began a project for a mural decoration for the New Amsterdam Theater in New York, and was working on it at the time of his death in 1903. *D. Dodge Thompson*

Blum, Robert. "An Artist in Japan (with illustrations by the author)." *Schribner's Magazine* 13 (April–June 1893), 399–414, 624–636, 729–749.

Birnbaum, Martin. *Catalogue of a Memorial Loan Exhibition of the Works of Robert Frederick Blum.* New York, 1913.

Wickenden, Robert J. "Robert Frederick Blum." *Dictionary of American Biography.* New York, 1943, 2:395–397.

Boyle, Richard J. *A Retrospective Exhibition: Robert F. Blum, 1857–1903.* Exh. cat., Cincinnati Art Museum. Cincinnati, 1966.

Weber, Bruce. Robert Frederick Blum (1857–1903) and His Milieu. Ph.D. diss. City University of New York, 1985.

WILLIAM BRADFORD (1823–1892)

William Bradford was born at Fairhaven, Massachusetts, across the harbor from the port of New Bedford. His father, a ship's outfitter, owned a dry goods shop in New Bedford where the young Bradford clerked, drawing and painting at home in his spare time. After several unsuccessful attempts to establish a career in business, he abandoned his mercantile pursuits to become a painter of ship portraits. By 1855 he had studios in New Bedford and Fairhaven, and later spent several winters in Boston.

His early work is reminiscent of the style of Gloucester artist Fitz Hugh Lane (1804–1865), who is known to have visited New Bedford in 1845 and 1856. Bradford's precise draftsmanship, clear light, and cool palette were relatively unaffected by the more broadly painted, atmospheric manner of his only teacher, Dutch marine painter Albert van Beest (1820–1860). Van Beest came to Fairhaven from New York at Bradford's invitation in the fall of 1855; when he arrived he also became the instructor of the promising young artist R. Swain Gifford (1840–1905). Bradford and Van Beest summered together in Fairhaven, and over the next few years collaborated on several pictures of New Bedford whaling ships.

In this same period, inspired by the writings of Arctic explorer Elisha Kent Kane (1820–1857), Bradford made several trips to Labrador between 1854 and 1857 to sketch the frozen landscape. At the end of the decade, the patronage of New Bedford collector Benjamin Rotch brought increased attention to his work, and he moved to New York in 1860. Later he took rooms in the Tenth Street Studio Building, where fellow explorer-artists Frederic Church (see cat.3) and Albert Bierstadt (see cats. 18, 33), a friend from New Bedford, were also in residence.

Bradford made a series of ambitious expeditions to the Arctic in the 1860s, often accompanied by professional photographers. His large collection of photographs played an important role in the conception of his paintings. Despite the scientific nature of this medium and the voyages themselves, Bradford's paintings became more romantic, the massive icebergs set in richly painted vistas filled with warm, dramatic color.

He moved to London in 1872, where he became a respected lecturer on the Arctic. The fame of his celebrated voyage to Greenland in 1869 invited a commission from Queen Victoria, *The Panther off the Coast of Greenland under the Midnight Sun* (1873, Royal Collections, London); the expedition was also the subject of his 1873 book, *The Arctic Regions.* Returning to the United States in 1874, he was made an associate of the National Academy of Design. For seven years he maintained a studio in

San Francisco, from which he traveled to areas such as the Sierra Nevada and Yosemite, painting mountainous landscapes. He returned to Fairhaven, and died during a visit to New York City at the age of sixty-eight. *Debora Rindge*

Bradford, William. *The Arctic Regions.* London, 1873.
Wilmerding, John. *A History of American Marine Painting.* Boston, 1968.
—. *William Bradford, 1832–92.* Exh. cat., DeCordova and Dana Museum and Park. Lincoln, Massachusetts, 1969.
Horch, Frank. "Photographs and Paintings by William Bradford." *American Art Journal* 5 (November 1973), 61–70.
Wilmerding, John. *American Marine Painting.* 2nd ed., rev. New York, 1987.

ALFRED THOMPSON BRICHER (1837–1908)

Alfred Thompson Bricher was born in Portsmouth, New Hampshire, and spent his childhood in Newburyport, Massachusetts. He went to Boston in 1851, where he worked as a clerk in a dry goods store and painted in his spare time. While there he may have studied art at the Lowell Institute, although he is reported to have been mostly self-taught. In 1858, when he decided to become a professional artist, he established a studio in Newburyport. The following year he reestablished himself in Boston, working there until 1868.

Bricher began painting landscapes, but by the 1870s he had become a marine painter. This is not surprising, given that he had always lived by the sea, but Bricher's knowledge of contemporary renderings of coastal scenes must be considered as well. Perhaps the earliest such influence in the young artist's development occurred in the summer of 1858, when he met artists William Stanley Haseltine (1835–1900) and Charles Temple Dix (1840–1873) while sketching on Mount Desert Island, Maine, and was introduced to their seascapes. He is presumed to have known Martin Johnson Heade (cats. 20, 21, 44, 45) as well, as they had studios in the same building in Boston, and Heade worked in Newburyport in the 1860s. Bricher must also have been aware of the coastal views of John Frederick Kensett (cat. 4), for although his style is more painterly than Kensett's, it shares the emphasis on reflected surfaces, clear and bright light, and serene, spare, horizontal compositions.

There is no concrete evidence that Bricher ever went to Europe, but he traveled frequently in the eastern United States. He often summered on the coasts of Massachusetts and Rhode Island, and one of his favorite destinations was Grand Manan Island in New Brunswick, Maine, a subject he painted often. He traveled beyond the New England coast as well, sketching in the Catskills and White Mountains, and even ventured as far as the upper Mississippi River and Minnesota.

Bricher moved to New York in 1868, where he had a studio in the YMCA Building. His landscapes were sold widely in the form of popular chromolithographs published by L. Prang and Company of Boston from 1866 until the end of his career. An accomplished watercolorist, he was made a member of the American Water Color Society, and was also elected an associate of the National Academy of Design. In 1882 Bricher built a cottage in Southampton, Long Island, which became his summer home and studio. He moved from New York City in 1890 to New Dorp, Staten Island, where he lived until his death at the age of seventy-one. *Debora Rindge*

"Alfred T. Bricher," *Art Journal* 38 (November 1875), 340–341.
Sheldon, George W. *American Painters.* New York, 1879, 144–146.
Preston, John Duncan. "Alfred Thompson Bricher, 1837–1908." *Art Quarterly* 25 (Summer 1962), 149–157.
Brown, Jeffrey R., and Ellen W. Lee. *Alfred Thompson Bricher, 1837–1908.* Indianapolis, 1973.

JOHN GEORGE BROWN (1831–1913)

Brown, born in Durham, England, in 1831, was the son of a poor lawyer. At the age of fourteen, he began a seven-year apprenticeship in the glass-cutting trade in Newcastle upon Tyne. He also enrolled in drawing classes at the Newcastle upon Tyne School of Design. When his apprenticeship was over, Brown moved to Edinburgh. While working at the Holyrood Glass Works, he continued to study art with Robert Scott Lauder at the Royal Scottish Academy. In 1853 he moved to London and supported himself as an artist briefly before he emigrated to America.

While making designs for stained glass at a Brooklyn glass factory, Brown took night classes at the National Academy of Design. In 1855, with the financial backing of his employer and father-in-law, Brown opened a studio. He first exhibited at the National Academy in 1858. By 1863 he was elected a member of the academy for *Curling—A Scottish Game, at Central Park.* Although Brown painted landscapes, portraits, and rural genre scenes, his most popular subject was the city street urchin. Brown said he painted these children because of his own impoverished background, yet the well-scrubbed cheerful faces in his paintings bore little relationship to contemporary descriptions of these waifs. The *prompt sales* and *first-rate* prices for his works and the numerous copyrighted reproductions of them made Brown a relatively wealthy man. He died in New York City in 1913. *Sarah Towne Hufford*

John George Brown 1831–1913: A Reappraisal. Exh. cat., The Robert Hull Fleming Museum. Burlington, Vermont, 1975.
Ferber, Linda S. "Ripe for Revival: Forgotten American Artists." *Art News* 79 (December 1980), 68–73.
Wilmerding, John, Linda Ayres, and Earl A. Powell. *An American Perspective: Nineteenth Century Art From the Collection of JoAnn and Julian Ganz, Jr.* Exh. cat., National Gallery of Art. Washington, 1981.

GEORGE DE FOREST BRUSH (1855–1941)

George de Forest Brush was born on 28 September 1855 in Shelbyville, Tennessee, but he spent the majority of his childhood in Connecticut where his father captained a whaler. His father's absences provided ample opportunity for his mother, an amateur artist, to exert a great influence over Brush's early life. When the family moved to Ohio in 1871, Brush went to New York to study at the National Academy of Design. Four years later he traveled to France for a six-year sojourn at the Ecole des Beaux-Arts, studying with Jean-Léon Gérôme. While a student Brush spent a brief time in Florence. This visit, along with Gérôme's influence, provided a strong impact on his style and even later his choice of subject matter. Returning to the United States in 1880, he spent the next several years traveling among the various Indian tribes. Through studying, sketching, and living with the American Indians, he became familiar with their customs and lifestyle, and was an ardent advocate for the rights of the Native American.

In 1884 he moved to New York and established a studio, and two years later he married Mary Taylor Whelpley (Mittie), who became his primary model. For Brush 1888 was a paramount year. He was invited to teach at the Art Students League. He won the Hallgarten award for *The Sculptor and the King* at the National Academy of Design, and was elected an associate member; he became a full member in 1901. In 1888 Brush received the first of many varied awards and prizes. His attraction to Florence, which was developed during his student years in Europe, called him back in 1892 when he established a studio, returning each year through World War I. It was about this time that a change took place in his subject matter. The popularity of Indian paintings waned, and Brush turned to the "modern" Madonna and Child, using his wife and children as models. Beginning in 1901 through 1937, when he was not at his Florence studio, Brush worked at his farm studio in Dublin, New Hampshire. In 1922 he had his first major retrospective at the Century Club and the following year he was awarded an honorary degree from Yale. In 1937, after a studio fire, he moved to Hanover, New Hampshire, where he lived until his death on 24 August 1941. *James W. Tottis*

Merrick, Lula. "Brush's Indian Pictures." *The International Studio* 76 (December 1922).
Bowditch, Nancy D. *George De Forest Brush: Recollection of a Joyous Painter.* Peterborough, New Hampshire, 1970.

MARY CASSATT (1844–1926)

Mary Cassatt was born in Allegheny, Pennsylvania (now a suburb of Pittsburgh), to well-educated and socially prominent parents who took the family to live in Europe from 1851 to 1855. She spent four uninspiring years at the Pennsylvania Academy of the Fine Arts, then journeyed to Paris, where in 1866 she arranged for private instruction with the French academic master Jean-Léon Gérôme (1824–1904). Except for a brief return to Philadelphia at the outbreak of the Franco-Prussian war, Cassatt spent the years between 1867 and 1874 traveling throughout France and Italy, Spain, and the Low Countries, copying works by the Old Masters and studying with various artists. She finally settled in Paris in 1874.

Throughout this long apprenticeship, Cassatt submitted work to the official Salons, where it was occasionally shown, but more often rejected. Her entry in the Salon of 1874 was noticed by the French painter and printmaker Edgar Degas (1834–1917), who in 1877 invited Cassatt to exhibit with a group of independent artists known as impressionists. She later recalled that she accepted *with joy. At last I could work with absolute independence, without concern for the potential opinion of a jury! I had already recognized who were my true masters. I admired Manet, Courbet, and Degas. I hated conventional art. I began to live.* Cassatt showed in four of the eight exhibitions of "the new painting," the only

American formally allied with the French impressionist circle.

In the fall of 1877 Cassatt's parents and sister came to live with the artist in Paris. A new focus on her family as subject matter joined with a new confidence in her art, inspired and influenced by Degas. During the 1880s, Cassatt's favored themes—family members and young women, seen at the opera, drinking tea, reading newspapers—gradually gave way to the scenes of mothers and children for which she is especially remembered. Her achievements in oil painting were matched by those in pastels and printmaking; in 1891 Cassatt completed a set of ten innovative color aquatints inspired by Japanese woodblock prints. Cassatt sent works to occasional exhibitions in America, and in 1892 was commissioned to paint a mural for the Woman's Building of the World's Columbian Exposition in Chicago. If her own work was never so well received in America as in France, Cassatt played an influential role in promoting European art in the United States by advising American collectors, such as her brother Alexander Cassatt or her friends Mr. and Mrs. Horace O. Havemeyer, on the purchase of important French and Old Master paintings. Around 1910 Cassatt's eyesight began to fail; she was forced to give up painting in 1914. She died in her country home outside Paris in 1926. *Sally Mills*

Segard, Achille. *Mary Cassatt, Un Peintre des enfants et des mères*. Paris, 1913.
Sweet, Frederick A. *Miss Mary Cassatt, Impressionist from Philadelphia*. Norman, Oklahoma, 1966.
Breeskin, Adelyn Dohme. *Mary Cassatt: A Catalogue Raisonné of the Oils, Pastels, Watercolors, and Drawings*. Washington, 1970.
Mathews, Nancy Mowll, ed. *Cassatt and Her Circle: Selected Letters*. New York, 1984.

WILLIAM MERRITT CHASE (1849–1916)

William Merritt Chase was born in Williamsburg (later renamed Ninevah), Indiana, received his early training from a local painter, and began his formal study at the National Academy of Design in New York in 1869. His artistic sensibilities, however, were formed at the Royal Academy in Munich, where he studied under Alexander von Wagner and Karl von Piloty. In Munich he painted the first works (sent back to patrons in America) that heralded the presence of an artist who would soon become a major figure in the New York art world.

Upon his return to America in 1878, Chase acquired a huge studio space on Tenth Street in New York—a base he immortalized in a series of paintings. Crammed with exotic bric-a-brac, the studio was designed to publicize and promote his work, and to attract portrait commissions. In 1878, Chase was recruited as one of the first teachers at the newly formed Art Students League, where he taught from 1878 to 1885, from 1886 to 1896, and again from 1907 to 1912. Teaching was a vocation that would occupy him for the rest of his life, and led to the founding of two of his own schools: the Shinnecock Summer School of Art (1891–1902), America's first important school of plein-air painting, located on Long Island's east end, and the Chase School of Art, later renamed the New York School of Art (1896–1907). Other long-term teaching positions include the Brooklyn Art Association (1887, 1891–1895), the Pennsylvania Academy of the Fine Arts (1896–1909), and nine summer classes conducted in Europe 1903–1913.

While Chase completed a significant series of landscape paintings, and while these paintings are now recognized as a major contribution to what has become known as American impressionism, Chase rejected labels that tended to narrowly define his mature statement. If anything, he considered himself a realist, and the tremendous variety of his best work dates from the mid-1880s and extends through to the early years of the twentieth century. During those years he produced the landscapes for which he is so rightly celebrated, masterful still lifes, brilliant portraits, and loving images of his wife and children. He captured the idle hours of his family and other genteel Americans, creating a visual memoir of leisure life in this country at the end of the nineteenth century.

Chase played a prominent role in forging a new identity for American artists. He was a founder and longtime president of the Society of American Artists and helped form and was an important contributor to the exhibitions of the Society of Painters in Pastel. Through such organizations as these, Chase helped shape the course of American art at the end of the nineteenth century. His paintings and pastels were exhibited widely throughout this country and abroad, and won many coveted awards and medals. Chase was an artist of international stature as well as a much-loved teacher in his own country. In fact, his generosity, dynamic personality, and teaching principles inspired and prepared the next generation of American artists for their role in art. *Ronald G. Pisano*

Roof, Katherine Metcalf. *The Life and Art of William Merritt Chase*. New York, 1917; reprinted 1975.
Pisano, Ronald G. *William Merritt Chase*. New York, 1979.
Pisano, Ronald G. *A Leading Spirit in American Art: William Merritt Chase, 1849–1916*. Seattle, 1983.

FREDERIC EDWIN CHURCH (1826–1900)

Frederic Edwin Church was born in Hartford, Connecticut, the only son of a wealthy businessman. Although his father hoped he would become a physician or enter the world of business, Church persisted in his early desire to be a painter. In 1842–1843 he studied in Hartford with Alexander H. Emmons (1816–1879), a local landscape and portrait painter, and Benjamin H. Coe (1799–after 1883), a well-known drawing instructor. In 1844 his father, at last resigned to his son's choice of a career, financed two years of study with Thomas Cole, giving Church the distinction of being the first pupil accepted by America's leading landscape painter. From the first, Church showed a remarkable talent for drawing and a strong inclination to paint in a crisp, tightly focused style. In 1845 he made his debut at the annual exhibition of the National Academy of Design in New York, where he would continue to show throughout his career. Two years later four of his paintings were shown at the American Art-Union, and by that point he was established in New York as one of the most promising younger painters. In 1849, at the age of twenty-three, he was elected to full membership in the National Academy.

Church traveled widely in search of subject matter for his landscapes, first throughout the northern United States and then, in 1853, to South America. He was inspired by the writings of the great German naturalist Alexander von Humboldt, and traveled for five months in Colombia and Ecuador. Church created his first full-scale masterpiece, *The Andes of Ecuador* (Reynolda House Museum of American Art, Winston-Salem, North Carolina) in 1855. In 1857 Church's reputation as America's greatest landscape painter was secured with the exhibition of his *Niagara* (The Corcoran Gallery of Art, Washington) in New York. A second trip to South America took place that same year, and two years later he created his most famous painting of the tropics, *The Heart of the Andes* (The Metropolitan Museum of Art, New York).

Church continued to travel during the 1860s, with visits to Labrador, Jamaica, Europe, and the Near East, and painted several important works based on his experiences. By the early 1870s his reputation was already in decline, and Church more and more devoted himself to his family and to the construction of Olana, his palatial home set high on a hill overlooking the Hudson. After 1880 he painted relatively few important works, and when he died in 1900 he was largely forgotten. Interest in his works revived in the 1960s, and he is now once again considered the premier American landscape painter of the mid-nineteenth century. *Franklin Kelly*

Huntington, David. *The Landscapes of Frederic Edwin Church: Vision of an American Era*. New York, 1966.
Carr, Gerald L. *Frederic Edwin Church: The Icebergs*. Dallas, 1980.
Manthorne, Katherine. *Creation and Renewal: Views of Cotopaxi by Frederic Edwin Church*. Washington, 1985.
Kelly, Franklin, and Gerald L. Carr. *The Early Landscapes of Frederic Edwin Church, 1845–1854*. Fort Worth, 1987.
Kelly, Franklin. *Frederic Edwin Church and the National Landscape*. Washington, 1988.

JAMES GOODWYN CLONNEY (1812–1867)

James Goodwyn Clonney, who was born in Liverpool, England, painted genre scenes as typically American as those of his American-born contemporaries, William Sidney Mount and George Caleb Bingham. Clonney had apparently had some training by 1830, because he worked then for lithographic firms in Philadelphia and New York City. He also attended the antique school at the National Academy of Design and began exhibiting miniatures, portraits, and landscapes there by about 1833.

By 1841, Clonney had begun to specialize in genre subjects. Painting rural, primarily outdoor scenes, he first prepared outline and wash drawings of the whole composition and detailed drawings of individual figures or small groups. His subjects often seemed to follow those of William Sidney Mount. One of his most ambitious works, *Militia Training* (1841, The Pennsylvania Academy of the Fine Arts, Philadelphia) has affinities with *Pitlessie Fair* (1804, National Portrait Gallery, Edinburgh) by Sir David Wilkie, a British artist whose work influenced Mount and other Americans.

Between 1834 and 1852, Clonney lived in New York City, Peekskill, and New Rochelle, and exhibited regularly at the National Academy and the American Art-Union. In 1852, he moved to Cooperstown and stopped exhibiting in New York City. *Offering Baby a Rose* (1857, present whereabouts unknown), a painting of an upper middle class family in their parlor, represents a departure from Clonney's previous rustic characters and country scenes. Sometime after 1855 he moved to

Binghamton, New York, where he died in relative obscurity in 1867. *Sarah Towne Hufford*

M. and M. Karolik Collection of American Watercolors and Drawings, 1800–1875. Vol. 2. Exh. cat., Museum of Fine Arts. Boston, 1962.

American Narrative Painting. Exh. cat., Los Angeles County Museum of Art. Los Angeles, 1974.

Giese, Lucretia H. "James Goodwyn Clonney (1812–1867): American Genre Painter." *The American Art Journal* 11 (Autumn, 1979).

THOMAS COLE (1801–1848)

Born in Bolton-le-Moor, Lancashire, England, Thomas Cole was apprenticed to an engraver before he came with his family to the United States in 1818. Cole stayed in Philadelphia and then traveled to the West Indies before joining the family in Steubenville, Ohio. After learning the rudiments of oil painting from an itinerant artist named Stein, he followed his family to Pittsburgh in 1823. His first landscapes were scenes of the Pittsburgh area. Cole soon left Pittsburgh to return to Philadelphia. From 1823 to 1825 he took classes at the Pennsylvania Academy of the Fine Arts and studied the landscape paintings of Thomas Doughty (1793–1856) and Thomas Birch (1779–1851). He then followed his family to New York. A body of work that resulted from an 1825 summer sketching expedition up the Hudson River brought him recognition from New York's most important artists. In 1826, Cole became one of the founding members of the National Academy of Design. His often stormy, romantic conceptions of the Hudson River wilderness are credited with popularizing landscape painting in America.

Cole traveled in Europe from 1829 to 1832, where he was inspired by the elevating themes and powerful tradition of history painting. On his return, he painted classicizing Italianate landscapes and sought patrons for imaginative moral allegories such as the *Course of Empire* of 1836 (New-York Historical Society). He lived in the Catskills, where he also continued to paint American landscapes based on studies from nature for patrons who preferred an approach less didactic than the moral allegories. After traveling to Europe again in 1841–1842 he grew even more concerned with religious themes. At the same time he also produced American landscape scenes with a serenity of mood and richness of color and light that were quite different from the dramatic turbulence of his earlier work.

Cole had a profound influence on artists Asher B. Durand (cat. 5) and Frederic Church (cats. 3, 19), his student. A poet, writer, and lecturer, Cole was widely admired and much mourned after his death of pneumonia at the age of 47.

Debora Rindge

Noble, Louis L. *The Course of Empire, Voyage of Life, and Other Pictures of Thomas Cole, N.A.* . . . New York, 1853.

Merritt, Howard S. *Thomas Cole*. Rochester, New York, 1969.

Baigell, Matthew. *Thomas Cole*. New York, 1981.

Parry, Ellwood C. *The Art of Thomas Cole: Ambition and Imagination*. Dover, Delaware, 1988.

JASPER FRANCIS CROPSEY (1823–1900)

Jasper Cropsey was born at Rossville, Staten Island, New York. His father, who was a harbor captain and riverboat captain, was the son of a Dutch immigrant. Jasper's original intention was to become an architect, and he spent five years (1837–1843) as an architect's apprentice. During these years he studied watercolor and was encouraged to paint by William Ranney, William Sidney Mount, and Henry Inman. In 1843 Inman was instrumental in having his painting of Greenwood Lake exhibited at the National Academy of Design. Its positive reception enabled him to be elected an associate member and as a result he became determined to pursue a career as a painter. He attended the academy's life school in 1847 and married Maria Cooley of West Milford, New Jersey. They departed for Europe, where they remained for two years. In August, 1849, he made a sketching trip to the White Mountains, which provided the basis for much of his subject matter in succeeding years. Although Cropsey experimented with paintings of an allegorical nature such as *Spirit of War* (1851, National Gallery of Art, Washington), during the 1850s he became known for his colorful paintings of New England autumn. He was a prolific painter whose surviving works from his forty years as a painter number in the hundreds. His greatest autumnal ode is *Autumn on the Hudson River* (1860, National Gallery of Art), although he painted literally dozens of related canvases throughout his career. In 1856 he sailed for England where he maintained a studio for the next seven years. Two years later *The Crayon* reported (September 1860, 261) that Cropsey "says he has more to do and receives better prices than he ever did in America." Despite this his career always seems to have been on the verge of financial collapse. In 1863 he purchased forty-five acres of land in Warwick, New York, where he designed and built "Aladdin," a twenty-nine-room house and studio that led to his financial ruin. By 1885 creditors foreclosed on his house, and he was forced to move to Hastings-on-Hudson, New York, where he lived out his career. In no single year did he ever earn more than $9,000; his most successful year was 1865. When William H. Tuckerman wrote glowingly of Cropsey in the seven pages devoted to him in his *Book of the Artists* (1867), the painter was at the zenith of his career. Within ten years, however, Cropsey was in eclipse. Although he painted virtually until his death, he did so largely in obscurity and only in recent years, with the renewed admiration for mid-century American landscape painting, have the virtues of his work been appreciated once again. Even today Cropsey's largest work, *Richmond Hill in 1862* (114x72 inches), painted in London, has not been located. *Richard H. Saunders*

Talbot, William S. *Jasper F. Cropsey, 1823–1900*. New York, 1977.

Maddox, Kenneth W. *An Unprejudiced Eye: The Drawings of Jasper F. Cropsey*. Yonkers, New York, 1979.

Foshay, Ella M., and Barbara Finney. *Jasper F. Cropsey: Artist and Architect*. New York, 1987.

Hall-Duncan, Nancy. *A Man for All Seasons, Jasper Francis Cropsey*. Greenwich, Connecticut, 1988.

CHARLES DEAS (1818–1867)

During his creative life Charles Deas was recognized not only as a promising painter of genre and literary scenes, but more so as an artist devoted to a national subject matter in which he drew upon experiences in the Far West. Regrettably, only twenty-seven of his paintings are known today.

Failing in an attempt to secure admission to the U.S. Military Academy at West Point, Deas embarked upon a painting career for which he clearly possessed the necessary talents. Beginning in 1838, he earned recognition at successive annual exhibitions of the National Academy of Design, to which he was elected an associate in 1839, with subjects taken from James Fenimore Cooper, such as *The Turkey Shoot* (c. 1836, Virginia Museum of Fine Arts, Richmond) and from Washington Irving, such as *The Devil and Tom Walker* (1838, collection of Richard P. W. Williams).

Eager for adventure and perhaps inspired by George Catlin's travels, Deas journeyed west in 1840 and there discovered subjects of Indian and trapper life with which he would gain a reputation over the next eight years. During his first year in Wisconsin Territory he observed the colorful conjunction of the lives of trappers, *voyageurs*, and Indians who gathered at forts Crawford and Snelling. He even persuaded the Indians to sit for their portraits, none of which survive. He also traveled beyond the safety of the forts, especially to see the Winnebago, who that year were enduring another resettlement farther west.

By late 1841 Deas had settled in Saint Louis to continue his artistic career, but continued to venture beyond the city to see other Native Americans, notably with Major Clifton Wharton's 1844 expedition to the Pawnee. Among his major paintings drawn from his direct experience of frontier life were *Winnebagos Playing Checkers* (1842, Thyssen-Bornemisza Collection, Lugano, Switzerland); *A Group of Sioux* (1845, Amon Carter Museum, Fort Worth); *Long Jakes* (1844, Manoogian Collection); and *The Death Struggle* (1845, The Shelburne Museum, Shelburne, Vermont). They garnered critical praise and new patrons for the artist as they appeared in exhibitions in Saint Louis, Philadelphia, and New York.

Almost all of Deas' frontier paintings, whether taken from literary sources or from his own experience, express psychological tension, perceived danger, alarm, and flight. They may have reflected his own mental condition, for in 1848 the apparently deranged Deas was hospitalized in New York. He lived for almost twenty years after this, but painted in a new and bizarre manner. Deas' career, which had been characterized as of "early genius and bright promise" by the *Knickerbocker Magazine* in July 1840, had ended after less than a dozen years. *Carol Clark*

Tuckerman, Henry T. *Book of the Artists*. New York, 1867, 424–429.

McDermott, John Francis. "Charles Deas: Painter of the Frontier." *Art Quarterly* 13 (Autumn 1950), 293–311.

Glanz, Dawn. *How the West Was Drawn: American Art and the Settling of the Frontier*. Ann Arbor, Michigan, 1982, 44–50.

Clark, Carol. "Charles Deas." *American Frontier Life*. Exh. cat., Amon Carter Museum, Fort Worth, Texas. New York, 1987, 51–77.

ROBERT S. DUNCANSON (1821–1872)

Robert S. Duncanson was born into a free black family in Fayette, New York, and spent his early life in Monroe, Michigan, learning his father's trade of house painting. Aspiring to become an artist, Duncanson moved about 1840 to Cincinnati, Ohio. Duncanson painted still lifes, portraits, genre, and literary subjects while commuting between Cincinnati, Detroit, and Monroe in this decade.

In Cincinnati, Duncanson became associated with a regional group of second-generation artists of the Hudson River School of landscape painting. Two important landscape commissions around 1848 and exhibitions and sales of his work at the Western Art Union attest to Duncanson's rising reputation. Accompanied by artists William Sonntag and John R. Tait, Duncanson toured Europe in 1853–1854. His most ambitious work to survive, *Land of the Lotus Eaters* (1861, Collection of the King of Sweden, Stockholm) inspired by a poem by Alfred, Lord Tennyson, led a Cincinnati newspaper to hail Duncanson as being "the best landscape painter in the West."

Probably because of the Civil War, Duncanson moved to Canada in 1863. The realism in his Canadian landscapes would influence major later works such as *Ellen's Isle, Loch Katrine* (1870, The Detroit Institute of Arts). Duncanson and his paintings were enthusiastically received in England, Ireland, and Scotland from 1865 until his return to Cincinnati in 1867. Duncanson died in Detroit in 1872. *Sarah Towne Hufford*

McElroy, Guy. "Robert S. Duncanson (1821–1872): A Study of the Artist's Life and Work." *Robert S. Duncanson: A Centennial Exhibition*. Exh. cat., Cincinnati Art Museum. Cincinnati, 1972.

Hartigan, Lynda Roscoe. *Sharing Traditions, Five Black Artists in Nineteenth-Century America*. Exh. cat., The National Museum of American Art, Smithsonian Institution. Washington, 1985.

Ketner, Joseph D. II. "Robert Duncanson (1821–1872)." *Artists of Michigan from the Nineteenth Century*. Exh. cat., The Muskegon Museum of Art. Muskegon, Michigan, 1987.

Ketner, Joseph D. II. Untitled Monograph. Cambridge, England, 1989 (forthcoming).

ROBERT SPEAR DUNNING (1824–1905)

Robert S. Dunning was born in Brunswick, Maine, on 3 January 1829 and moved with his family to Fall River, Massachusetts, about 1834. There he displayed an interest in art at an early age while attending the public schools. As a teen he worked in the local cotton mill and then spent three years at sea. He studied briefly with James Roberts of Thomaston, Maine, prior to traveling to New York in 1849, where he attended the National Academy of Design and studied with Daniel Huntington. He remained in New York until 1853, when he returned to Fall River and established a studio.

Canvases depicting lush arrangements of fruit made up the majority of his oeuvre and established his reputation, though his early work consisted of portraits and seascapes, and it was not until 1865 that he began to use fruit as his primary subject matter. He married Mehitable Hill in December 1869. In 1880 he exhibited three paintings at the National Academy. Spending the majority of his life in Fall River, he died there on 19 August 1905 at the age of 96. At his death there were extensive obituaries addressing his commitment to Fall River and his myriad of still-life canvases. *James W. Tottis*

Fall River Evening Herald. 19 August 1905.

Gerdts, William H., and Russell Burke. *American Still Life Painting*. New York, 1971.

ASHER BROWN DURAND (1796–1886)

Asher B. Durand was born in Jefferson Village (now Maplewood), New Jersey, and learned the craft of engraving from his father, a watchmaker and silversmith. In 1812, he began an apprenticeship with engraver Peter Maverick (1780–1831) in Newark, which lasted five years. He became Maverick's business partner in 1817, and moved to New York to manage a branch of their firm. After enrolling in classes at the American Academy of Fine Arts, his work came to the attention of its president, artist John Trumbull (1756–1843). In 1820, Trumbull asked Durand to produce an engraving of his painting *The Declaration of Independence* (1786–1787, Yale University). When it was completed in 1823, this commission brought Durand to prominence and marked the beginning of his long and successful career.

In the 1820s and 1830s Durand owned a series of printmaking firms and was known primarily as an engraver of banknotes, illustrations, portraits, and contemporary paintings. It was not until about 1835 when, inspired by the landscape paintings of Thomas Cole (1801–1848) and encouraged by wealthy New York merchant and art patron Luman Reed (1785–1836), Durand turned from engraving to painting. He produced portraits, historical subjects, and increasingly, pastoral landscapes. Pursuing this interest, he visited Cole in the Catskills in 1836, and they traveled to Schroon Lake in the Adirondacks together in 1837.

In 1840, Durand left for Europe in the company of fellow artists John F. Kensett (see cat. 4), John Casilear (1811–1893), and Thomas P. Rossiter (1818–1871), where he studied the work of his contemporaries and the Old Masters, especially Claude Lorrain. By 1845, landscapes rendered directly from nature would become his specialty. Following Cole's death, Durand became the leader of the Hudson River School and one of the major painters of the American landscape in the mid-nineteenth century.

Durand became regarded a national authority on the subject with the publication of a series of nine "Letters on Landscape Painting" in 1855 in *The Crayon*, an art journal edited by his son, John, and William J. Stillman. Espousing theories similar to those of British critic John Ruskin (1819–1900), Durand advised American artists to work directly from nature rather than relying on compositional formulae. In summer and early fall, Durand would leave his New York City studio to take extensive sketching excursions to the Catskills, Adirondacks, White Mountains, Berkshires, and Green Mountains. Evoking the shadowed quiet of a wooded glade or the open expanses of rural countryside, Durand's paintings reveal the process of direct observation in their abundant and precise details.

Always an active and visible presence in the New York art community, Durand helped to organize the New York Drawing Association in 1825, and the following year was a founder of the National Academy of Design. He also helped to found the Sketch Club in 1827, the Century Association in 1847, and he served as president of the National Academy of Design from 1845 to 1861. In 1869 he retired to the family property in Maplewood, where he later died at the age of ninety. *Debora Rindge*

Durand, John. *The Life and Times of A. B. Durand*. New York, 1894.

Lawall, David B. *A. B. Durand: 1796–1886*. Montclair, New Jersey, 1971.

—. *Asher Brown Durand: His Art and Theory in Relation to His Times*. New York, 1977.

—. *Asher B. Durand: A Documentary Catalogue of the Narrative and Landscape Paintings*. New York, 1978.

GEORGE HENRY DURRIE (1820–1863)

Born in New Haven, Connecticut, George Henry Durrie was the son of a part owner of a local stationery, book, and printing shop. Along with his older brother John Jr., Durrie studied with the local portraitist Nathaniel Jocelyn (1796–1841) from 1839 to 1841. During the 1840s Durrie traveled throughout southern and central Connecticut, around New England, and to New York, New Jersey, Philadelphia, and Virginia in search of portrait commissions. In order to support his wife Sarah Perkins, whom he married in 1841, and their growing family, Durrie also painted signs and window shades and restored paintings.

After a decade primarily devoted to portraiture and a brief experiment with genre painting, it was clear by the early 1850s that Durrie's greatest interest was in painting views of the Connecticut countryside and its inhabitants engaged in their day-to-day activities. Unlike most other American artists of the nineteenth century, Durrie preferred to paint winter scenes, though he continued to paint landscapes with foliage throughout the rest of his career. His subject matter ranges from dense, wooded forests to broad vistas, but toward the end of his life his favored views became winter innyards and farmyards and their attendant activity. While some paintings depict actual views, in most Durrie composed romanticized scenes from a repertory of landscape, architecture, and genre elements.

Durrie's early works reflect his study of the works of his Hudson River School contemporaries, especially Cole and Church. By the mid-1850s, however, he had developed a distinctive style, especially in the winter scenes. A bright palette, pigmented surfaces, and atmospheric clarity characterize his style, as does the inclusion of somewhat stiff and generalized figures whose presence nonetheless offsets their gray, barren surroundings.

As Durrie himself recorded taking great pleasure from the rural surroundings and activities he depicted, it is not surprising that he spent most of his life working in the New Haven area, maintaining a studio in New York for only one year (1857). He did, however, exhibit in New York at the National Academy of Design in 1843 and 1845, and from 1857 until his death in 1863 except 1861. He also exhibited at the Pennsylvania Academy of the Fine Arts in 1862 and at the Boston Athenaeum in 1863. Locally he showed in his father's shop windows, in New Haven Horticultural Society exhibits at state fairs, and at the New Haven Art Union from 1848 through 1852. Durrie's works reached their widest audience through lithographs made by several companies; the best known, Currier and Ives, published ten between 1861 and 1867.

Durrie was only 43 when he died at his home on 15 October 1863 as a result of a sudden illness. During his lifetime, he was accorded little but local notice, since his unique style and his preference for winter scenes set him apart from his contemporaries. Soon forgotten after his death, Durrie was not rediscovered until the 1920s revival of interest in Currier and Ives. A 1947 retrospective of his work and recent scholarship have drawn more attention to Durrie's own works, which for so long had been eclipsed by the popular lithographs. *Sarah Cash*

Durrie, Mary Clarissa. "George Henry Durrie: Artist." *Antiques* 24 (July 1933), 13–15.

Cowdrey, M. Bartlett. *George Henry Durrie 1820–1863, Connecticut Painter of American Life*. Hartford, 1947.

George Henry Durrie, Connecticut Artist. Introduction by Colin Simkin. New Haven, 1966.

Hutson, Martha. "George Henry Durrie, an American Winter Landscape Painter." *Antiques* 103 (February 1973), 300–306.

—. *George Henry Durrie (1820–1863) American Winter Landscapist: Renowned Through Currier and Ives*. Santa Barbara, 1977.

THOMAS EAKINS (1844–1916)

Thomas Cowperthwait Eakins was born in Philadelphia, where he would spend most of his life. His father was a calligrapher and writing master whose influence is observable in the lettering in the artist's paintings. Eakins began taking courses at the Pennsylvania Academy of the Fine Arts in 1862. He attended anatomy lectures there as well as at the nearby Jefferson Medical College. In 1866 he went to Paris, where he attended the Ecole des Beaux-Arts and was a pupil of the celebrated French artist Jean-Léon Gérôme. Before he returned to the United States in 1870 he traveled through Europe and studied briefly again in Paris with portraitist Léon Bonnat and sculptor Augustin Alexandre Dumont. He also spent six months in Spain. His mature style would resonate with the influence of Velázquez, Ribera, and Rembrandt, evident in his rich chiaroscuro as well as his choice of subjects.

Upon his return he continued his anatomy studies at the Jefferson Medical College and taught life classes at the Philadelphia Sketch Club from 1874 to 1876. In 1878 he began teaching at the Pennsylvania Academy, and in the next year he was appointed professor of painting and drawing there. In his teaching Eakins stressed the study of anatomy and painting from the nude. To this end, he began to experiment with photography in 1880, and worked with photographer Eadweard Muybridge in 1884 and 1885 on motion studies. In 1886 Eakins was forced to resign his position at the Pennsylvania Academy over a controversy about his insistence on working from the nude. When he left the academy, a number of his pupils departed as well, and together they established the Philadelphia Art Students League, where Eakins taught for the next several years.

Though much admired by his students, Eakins was harshly criticized in Philadelphia, and he was not well known outside his birthplace for much of his career. He rarely left the city, though he did lecture in New York and Washington and even visited North Dakota in 1887. He received more recognition later in life, and in 1902 was elected an associate of the National Academy of Design. He died in Philadelphia at the age of seventy-one. *Debora Rindge*

Goodrich, Lloyd. *Thomas Eakins: His Life and Work*. New York, 1933.

Hendricks, Gordon. *The Life and Works of Thomas Eakins*. New York, 1974.

Goodrich, Lloyd. *Thomas Eakins*. Cambridge, Massachusetts, 1982.

Johns, Elizabeth. *Thomas Eakins: The Heroism of Modern Life*. Princeton, 1983.

FRANCIS WILLIAM EDMONDS (1806–1863)

Francis W. Edmonds, born in Hudson, New York, in 1806, successfully managed the double career of banker and artist throughout most of his life. Edmonds' childhood interest in art revived in 1826 when he took classes at the newly formed National Academy of Design. In 1829 he exhibited his first painting at the academy. Banking took precedence until 1835 when Edmonds began to relearn the mechanics of painting with the help of artist William Page. Although Edmonds painted portraits, landscapes, and genre and literary subjects, his genre paintings in the Anglo-Dutch tradition have become the work for which he is most remembered. Edmonds' paintings were compared very favorably to those of William Sidney Mount and Sir David Wilkie, whose work had influenced both Mount and Edmonds. He was elected associate member of the National Academy of Design in 1837. On the strength of *Sparking* and *The City and the Country Beaux* (both, Sterling and Francine Clark Art Institute, Williamstown, Massachusetts) exhibited in 1840, he was elected a full member of the National Academy.

Despondent after the death of his first wife in 1840, Edmonds traveled for eight months in Britain and Europe. As a result of his study of the Old Masters and contemporary British artists, his paintings, such as *The Bashful Cousin* (c. 1842, National Gallery of Art, Washington) and *The Image Peddler* (1844, The New-York Historical Society), immediately gained in the sophistication of their composition, lighting effects, and sense of atmosphere. Edmonds' later works, such as *The Scythe Grinder* (1856, The New-York Historical Society) and *Hard Times* (1861, Albrecht Art Museum, Saint Joseph, Missouri) often became less anecdotal, more realistic, and showed an even greater sensitivity to the human condition. Edmonds died unexpectedly of a heart attack in 1863 at his home, Crow's Nest, in Bronxville, New York. *Sarah Towne Hufford*

Mann, Maybelle. *Francis William Edmonds, Mammon and Art*. New York, 1977.

Edmonds, Francis W. "'The Leading Incidents and Dates of my Life': An Autobiographical Essay by Francis W. Edmonds." *American Art Journal* 13 (Autumn 1981), 5–10.

Clark, H. Nichols B. *Francis W. Edmonds, American Master in the Dutch Tradition*. Exh. cat., Amon Carter Museum, Fort Worth. Washington, 1988.

HENRY F. FARNY (1847–1916)

Born François Henri Farny in Ribeauville, Alsace, France, the artist came to America as a child when his family emigrated in 1853. They lived in western Pennsylvania for six years, where Farny's father ran a sawmill. In 1859 they moved to Cincinnati, which remained Farny's home for most of his life.

Shortly after graduating from high school, Farny began designing lithographs for a publishing firm. His first illustration for Harper Brothers was published in 1865, and he completed frequent assignments for them over the next thirty years, depending on commercial work for his livelihood. Farny became especially well known as one of the illustrators of the popular *McGuffey Readers*, first published in 1879.

From an early age he aspired to become a painter, however, and after moving to New York in 1866, he sailed abroad the following year. He traveled through Europe for four years, studying in Rome with Thomas Buchanan Read (1822–1872), a poet and artist from Cincinnati, and then in Germany with the landscape painter Hermann Herzog (1832–1932). He went to Europe again in 1873 and 1875. He studied briefly with Wilhelm von Diez (1839–1907) in Munich in 1873, where he met one of Diez's former students, Frank Duveneck (1848–1919) of Cincinnati, who was a celebrated young artist in Germany. Duveneck and Farny became close friends, often working together in Cincinnati over the next two years before they returned to Germany with two other Cincinnati artists, the sculptor Frank Dengler (1853–1879) and the painter John Twachtman (cat. 68).

In Cincinnati again in 1876, Farny was still forced to rely on commercial work. It was not until about 1893, when he had become a successful painter of Native American subjects, that he was able to give up illustration. He began collecting Indian artifacts about 1880, and made his first trip west to Dakota territory in 1881, perhaps hoping to illustrate Sitting Bull, who had just surrendered and was imprisoned at the Standing Rock Agency of the Sioux. Farny's first Indian illustrations, commissioned for Frank Cushing's account of his life among the Zuni in New Mexico in *Century Magazine* in 1882–1883, created popular demand for paintings of this subject.

Farny conceived his work in his Cincinnati studio, using sketches, photographs, and watercolors of Native Americans rendered on-site, as well as clippings from current periodicals. Farny traveled west several times to areas such as Montana and Oklahoma, making his last such journey in 1894. He died in Cincinnati at the age of seventy-nine. *Debora Rindge*

Taft, Robert. *Artists and Illustrators of the Old West, 1850–1900*. New York, 1953.

Henry F. Farny 1847–1916. Exh. cat., Cincinnati Art Museum. Cincinnati, 1965.

Carter, Denny T. *Henry Farny*. New York, 1978.

Henry Farny, 1847–1916. Exh. cat., Archer M. Huntington Art Gallery. Austin, 1983.

FREDERICK CARL FRIESEKE (1874–1939)

The American expatriate painter Frederick Frieseke was born in Owosso, Michigan, and studied briefly at the Art Institute of Chicago and the Art Students League in New York before going to the Académie Julian in Paris in 1898. Frieseke is also said to have had some instruction from Whistler, whose tonalist concerns influenced his early work.

In 1900 Frieseke began spending his summers at Giverny. This year also marked his debut at the American Art Association of Paris, whose president, Rodman Wanamaker, was Frieseke's early patron. Success came quickly; by 1904 the French government had purchased one of Frieseke's large Salon paintings, *Before the Mirror*, for the Musée du Luxembourg. That same year, Frieseke received a top prize at the Saint Louis International Exhibition, and another in 1905 at the Munich Exhibition. During this period Frieseke was also engaged in mural decoration, having been commissioned by Wanamaker to paint a large mural for his family's department store in New York City. In 1906 he installed murals in the Hotel Shelbourne in Atlantic City. Although Frieseke later disclaimed any real interest in this type of work, the favorable critical reviews for it in Europe and the United States helped establish his early reputation. Frieseke was a member of all of the important art societies in France and America, and exhibited in Italy at the Venice Biennales, and on occasion in London at the International Society shows.

In 1906 Frieseke rented Theodore Robinson's former residence at Giverny and became for the next thirteen years the summer neighbor of Claude Monet. Although Frieseke's contact with the French master appears to have been minimal, his early style now gave way to what has been termed his "high impressionist" period, in which the varied effects of sunlight became his principal concern. While Monet and Renoir were the major influences on his work—his nudes are clearly inspired by the example of Renoir—Frieseke's predilection for strongly patterned surfaces suggests the additional influence of Vuillard and Bonnard.

The pre-World War I period and through 1919 was the high point of Frieseke's fame. By 1920 public tastes had changed, and though Frieseke continued to receive awards well into the 1930s, he experienced a steady decline in sales. In 1919 he established a new residence in Normandy, at Le Mesnil-sur-Blangy, where he died in 1939. *Nancy Rivard Shaw*

Weller, Allen S. "Frederick Carl Frieseke: The Opinions of an American Impressionist." *Art Journal* 28 (Winter 1968), 160–165.
Gerdts, William. *American Impressionism.* New York, 1984, 262–267.
Panza, Arleen. "Frederick Carl Frieseke (1874–1939)." *Artists of Michigan from the Nineteenth Century.* Exh. cat., The Muskegon Museum of Art. Muskegon, 1987, 168–173.

SANFORD ROBINSON GIFFORD (1823–1880)

Sanford Robinson Gifford was born in Greenfield, New York, on 10 July 1823. As a youth he was raised in Hudson, New York, where his father owned an iron foundry. Gifford attended Brown University for two years but left in 1844 to study art in New York City with the drawing master John Reubens Smith. After additional study at the National Academy of Design and some sketching tours in the Catskills and Berkshires, Gifford turned from portraiture to landscape painting. Beginning in the late 1840s, he successfully exhibited his work at the National Academy of Design and the American Art-Union. In 1851, he was elected an associate member of the National Academy and three years later an academician. In 1855, after several years of sketching and painting in the Northeast, Gifford embarked on a two-year European tour.

After a lengthy sketching trip through Scotland and England where he met John Ruskin, Gifford traveled to the continent in September 1855. For the next year he toured France, Belgium, Holland, Germany, and Switzerland before arriving in Italy where he painted the landscape and antiquities of the Italian countryside. In May 1857 Gifford traveled to Naples and Capri with Albert Bierstadt before returning to England and departing for America. During his European sojourn under the influence of Turner and the Barbizon painters, Gifford turned away from the darker, balanced compositions of the Hudson River School to a new stylistic emphasis on light and atmospheric effects as seen in his paintings of *Lake Nemi* (1856, Toledo Museum of Art) and later in his American landscapes of *Mount Mansfield* (1859) and *Kauterskill Falls* (1862; both, The Metropolitan Museum of Art, New York).

After his return to New York, Gifford moved into the new Tenth Street Studio Building in 1858 and soon became one of its most popular tenants. With the outbreak of war in 1861, he joined the Seventh Regiment of the New York State National Guard, which he proudly served for the next three years as both soldier and artist. In 1868, after several successful years in New York, Gifford departed on a two-year tour of the Middle East, visiting Jerusalem, Egypt, Syria, Greece, and Turkey. The following summer he continued his travels touring the Colorado Rockies with John F. Kensett and Worthington Whittredge. Later that summer, Gifford joined the U.S. Geological Survey expedition in Wyoming under the direction of Ferdinand Hayden. During the summer of 1874, he visited California, Oregon, British Columbia, and Alaska. After concluding this lengthy tour, he told a friend that he made these extended journeys both to collect art material and to acquire "general knowledge of different countries and people." In 1880 during a trip to Lake Superior, Gifford contracted a fever and had to return to New York where he died of pneumonia on August 29. The next year, the Metropolitan Museum of Art honored Gifford by organizing an exhibition and publishing an extensive catalogue of his work. *Christopher Kent Wilson*

A Memorial Catalogue of the Paintings of Sanford Robinson Gifford, N.A. Biographical essay by John F. Weir. New York, 1881.
Cikovsky, Nicolai, Jr. *Sanford Robinson Gifford (1823–1880).* Exh. cat., University of Texas. Austin, 1971.
Weiss, Ila S. *Sanford Robinson Gifford. 1823–1880.* New York and London, 1977.
Weiss, Ila, and Steven Weiss. *Sanford R. Gifford.* Exh. cat., Alexander Gallery. New York, 1986.
Weiss, Ila S. *Poetic Landscape: The Art and Experience of Sanford R. Gifford.* Newark, Delaware, 1987.

WILLIAM GLACKENS (1870–1938)

Born in Philadelphia, William Glackens landed his first job in 1891 as a newspaper illustrator for *The Record.* He moved back and forth between *The Record* and *The Press*, growing friendly with a convivial group of artist-reporters including John Sloan (1871–1951), George Luks (1866–1933), and Everett Shinn (1876–1953), whom he joined at evening classes at the Pennsylvania Academy of the Fine Arts. By 1894 Glackens was sharing the studio of Robert Henri (1865–1929), who taught him to paint in oil. In 1895 Glackens traveled with Henri to Europe, where his appreciation of the Old Masters, especially Frans Hals (1580–1666), equaled his attraction to the more contemporary art of Edouard Manet (1832–1883). He settled in New York upon his return, as eventually did the rest of the Philadelphia group. Luks found Glackens a job with *The World*, and he was soon working for several newspapers and magazines, including *McClure's*, which sent him to Cuba on assignment to cover the Spanish-American War.

Glackens continued as a free-lance illustrator until 1915, but by the turn of the century was devoting his major energies to painting, finding subjects in the New York streets, parks, restaurants, and parlors. While he was attracted to the more genteel side of city life and urban recreation, as seen in his Manet-inspired canvas *Chez Mouquin* (1905, The Art Institute of Chicago), his early works burst with the vitality and immediacy that Henri promoted. Following a second trip abroad in 1906, Glackens participated with Henri, Sloan, Luks, Shinn, and three others in the landmark 1908 exhibition of The Eight, a non-juried exhibition that focused upon their predominantly realist, antiacademic approach to art. Shortly after this show, Glackens began to transform his style toward a lighter, more impressionistic mode. By the time he served as chairman of the selection committee for American entries to the 1913 Armory Show, he had shifted completely toward a bright, colorful approach especially reminiscent of, but not completely dependent upon, the French artist Pierre-Auguste Renoir (1841–1919). In 1912 Glackens' high school classmate, Dr. Albert C. Barnes, sent him to Europe to buy contemporary French art for him. Those purchases—Degas, Renoir, Matisse—remain the nucleus of the Barnes Foundation's collection in Merion, Pennsylvania. Glackens' later career was quietly successful; he traveled often to France, and was preparing work for the 1938 Carnegie International when he died suddenly at the age of 68. *Sally Mills*

Shinn, Everett. "William Glackens as an Illustrator." *American Artist* 9 (November 1945), 22–27.
Glackens, Ira. *William Glackens and the Ashcan Group: The Emergence of Realism in American Art.* New York, 1957.
Wattenmaker, Richard J. "The Art of William Glackens." *University Art Gallery Bulletin* [The State University, Rutgers] 1 (1967), 5–11.
Perlman, Bennard. *The Immortal Eight: American Painting from Eakins to the Armory Show.* Cincinnati, 1979.
Wattenmaker, Richard J. "William Glackens's Beach Scenes at Bellport." *Smithsonian Studies in American Art* 2 (Spring 1988), 75–94.

JOHN HABERLE (1856–1933)

Born to German immigrants in New Haven, Connecticut, John Haberle was apprenticed at about the age of 14 to the New Haven lithography and engraving company of Punderson and Crisand. He worked from roughly 1875 to 1880 as a lithographer, first in New Haven, then later in Montreal and possibly in Providence and New York City.

Returning to New Haven, Haberle worked for the Yale paleontologist Othniel Charles Marsh (1831–1899) cleaning fossils, making plaster casts, and possibly illustrating some of Marsh's books (Haberle probably had also worked briefly for Marsh in the 1870s). Haberle left Marsh's employment in 1884 for a year's study at the National Academy of Design and then returned again to the New Haven area where he spent the rest of his life. He established a studio in his home and entered into the artistic life of the community as a founding member, unpaid drawing instructor, and exhibitor at the New Haven Sketch Club.

He made his debut at the National Academy of Design in 1887 with *Imitation* (1887, Berry-Hill Galleries), which was purchased by the noted collector Thomas B. Clarke. During the next few years he painted some of the most illusionistic trompe l'oeil still-life paintings created in America.

Although his work did not receive extensive critical acclaim, Haberle was patronized by businessmen and saloon keepers, men who appreciated the subject matter of his paintings: pipes and tobacco, playing cards, photographs of young women, hunting paraphernalia, and money. Failing eyesight forced Haberle largely to abandon the meticulous still-life style in 1893. He continued to paint, though with the exception of certain works such as *A Bachelor's Drawer* (1890–1894, The Metropolitan Museum of Art, New York), it was in a more impressionistic style that dealt with themes such as flowers, dolls, and kittens. He also executed some small-scale sculpture and bas-reliefs, created decorations for interiors, and gave painting lessons. He spent his later years working as a custodian at a school in Morris Cove, twelve miles from New Haven, where he had moved in 1896. He died in New Haven. *Linda Ayres*

Marlin, Jane. "John Haberle, A Remarkable Contemporaneous Painter in Detail." *Illustrated American* 24 (30 December 1898), 516–517.

Frankenstein, Alfred. "Haberle: or the Illusion of the Real." *Magazine of Art* 41 (October 1948), 222–227.

—. *After the Hunt: William Harnett and Other American Still Life Painters, 1870–1900*. Berkeley and Los Angeles, 1953, rev. ed. 1969, 113–122.

Chirico, Robert F. "John Haberle and *Trompe L'Oeil*." *Marsyas* 19 (1977–1978), 37–43.

Sill, Gertrude Grace. *John Haberle: Master of Illusion*. Springfield, Massachusetts, 1985.

WILLIAM MICHAEL HARNETT (1848–1892)

Born on 10 August 1848 in Clonakilty, County Cork, Ireland, William Michael Harnett emigrated with his family to the United States in 1850, settling in Philadelphia. The young Harnett was forced to work to help support his mother and sister after his father's untimely death left them in near poverty. An apprenticeship in 1865 was the beginning of his career as an engraver, and two years later he attended classes at the Pennsylvania Academy of the Fine Arts. Shortly thereafter, in 1869, Harnett moved to New York where he worked as an engraver for several jewelry firms and attended classes at the National Academy of Design and the Cooper Union. He supported himself as an engraver until 1875, when he established a studio and turned to still-life subjects. Harnett later remarked that he was drawn to still lifes because as a student he could not afford to pay models and worked instead with objects such as pipes, books, and mugs. Returning to Philadelphia in 1876, he established a studio and resumed study at the Pennsylvania Academy of the Fine Arts. Over the next several years he exhibited at the National Academy in New York, and managed to sell enough work to travel to Europe in 1880.

This European study began with a brief stay in London. He was soon persuaded to visit Frankfurt, staying longer than planned due to the volume of commissions a wealthy patron, most likely Johann Conrad Cronau, provided. But his European success began in 1882 when he took a studio in Munich. He remained there until 1885, studying the seventeenth-century still-life masters and producing a great body of work. Early in 1885 Harnett moved to Paris to prepare his fourth version of *After the Hunt* for the upcoming Salon, where he received acclaim and notoriety. Returning approximately a year later to New York, Harnett again established a studio and entered his most lucrative period. It was at this point in his career that he painted the large exotic still lifes, such as *Music* (1886) and *My Gems* (1888), executing several variations of similar themes. Only six years after his return from Paris, Harnett died after a brief illness. Shortly after his death his work fell into obscurity, not to be rediscovered until 1939 by Edith Halpert of the Downtown Gallery. *James W. Tottis*

Frankenstein, Alfred. *After the Hunt: William Harnett and Other Still Life Painters 1870–1900*. Berkeley and Los Angeles, 1953.

Williams, Hermann W., Jr. "Notes on William M. Harnett." *Antiques* 43, no. 6, (1943), 260–262.

CHILDE HASSAM (1859–1935)

Childe Hassam was perhaps the best-known of the American impressionists, and had a long and extremely productive career. At the age of seventeen he was apprenticed to a Boston wood engraver and soon found work as a free-lance illustrator. As a young man determined to become an accomplished artist, he attended the evening life class at the Boston Art Club, studied anatomy with painter/doctor William Rimmer (see cat. 22) at the Lowell Institute, and took lessons from the popular German-born painter Ignaz Gaugengigl (1855–1932). By the age of twenty-two he had his first one-man exhibition and was establishing a professional reputation in Boston.

Hassam went to Europe for the first of several visits in 1883. The watercolors he produced in England, Holland, Italy, and Spain were exhibited in Boston later that year. From 1886 to 1889, the artist and his wife, the former Kathleen Maude Doane, lived in Paris, where Hassam exhibited at the Salons of 1887 and 1888 and continued to improve his skills at the Académie Julian. Exposure to French art was an important aspect of his training, but he did not slavishly follow any one school. Because of his descent from a seventeenth-century British immigrant to Massachusetts named William Horsham, Hassam liked to emphasize the importance to his work of such English painters as Turner and Constable.

After 1889 Hassam settled in New York, where he was active in the Pastel Society, the New York Watercolor Club, and the Society of American Artists. He became renowned for his atmospheric, optimistic views of the city in varied seasons and times of day. The culmination of his interest in this subject was the flag series of 1916–1919, in which Hassam explored the theme of Fifth Avenue and the adjoining streets colorfully swathed in the flags of the United States and her World War I allies.

While Hassam stayed in the city much of the year, his summers were spent in several idyllic New England retreats. Beginning in 1890 and for the next twenty years he painted on Appledore, one of the Isles of Shoals off the Maine/New Hampshire coast. With the bright palette and sharp, broken brushwork that characterized his style, he captured the fresh, unspoiled beauty of its rocky shore and the delicacy of the garden of his friend, the poet Celia Thaxter. Other favorite seasonal locations were Gloucester and Provincetown, Massachusetts; Newport, Rhode Island, and the Connecticut towns of Cos Cob and Old Lyme, which he frequented from the 1890s through 1916. A congenial and gregarious person, Hassam was as much attracted to these places by the pleasure of other artists' company as by the charming scenery.

After 1917 Hassam's summers were spent at East Hampton, Long Island, where he and his wife purchased a home. While the quality of his painting became somewhat uneven during this period, he was increasingly successful as a printmaker, producing many beautiful etchings of shadowy, tree-lined yards, as well as lithographs of busy New York streets.

By the time of his death in 1935, Hassam's work had been included in major exhibitions across the United States and had been acquired by many important private and public collections. His legacy also survived in the bequest of his works to the American Academy and Institute of Arts and Letters. In a final act of support for the art of his country, he directed these to be sold to establish a fund for the purchase of works by other American artists. *Deborah Chotner*

Adams, Adeline. *Childe Hassam*. New York, 1938.

Hoopes, Donelson F. *Childe Hassam*. New York, 1979.

Burnside, Kathleen M. *Childe Hassam in Connecticut*. Lyme, Connecticut, 1987.

MARTIN JOHNSON HEADE (1819–1904)

Martin Johnson Heade was born 11 August 1819 in Lumberville, a small town in Bucks County, Pennsylvania. At an early age he decided to become an artist, an ambition his father encouraged, and he subsequently trained with the painter Edward Hicks and possibly with Hicks' younger cousin Thomas, a portraitist. The influence of the two men is evident in Heade's earliest works; predominantly portraits, these paintings reflect both the stiffness of the elder Hicks' style and something of the greater sophistication of Thomas' works.

To further his artistic career, Heade traveled to Europe in 1838 and settled in Rome for two years. He made his professional debut in America in 1841, while he was still living abroad, when he submitted *Portrait of a Little Girl* (whereabouts unknown) to the Pennsylvania Academy of the Fine Arts. In 1843 he submitted another portrait to the National Academy of Design in New York. Heade eventually gave up portraiture entirely to focus on landscape and still-life painting.

Heade's interest in travel led him all over the United States, twice to Europe, three times to South America, and to Central America and British Columbia. In the coastal region around Narragansett Bay and in the salt marshes of Massachusetts, Rhode Island, Connecticut, and New Jersey, he painted the changing effects of light and atmosphere in landscapes and seascapes of considerable originality. Heade's friend Frederic Church encouraged him to visit South America in search of new subject matter, and in 1863 he made the first of his three trips there. Although Heade painted a number of important landscapes of South American and Jamaican scenery in the 1860s and 1870s, his experiences in the tropics were most important for having introduced him to a favorite subject, hummingbirds posed with orchids in natural settings.

Although Heade was friendly with a number of leading American artists of his day, he never gained full acceptance in the New York art world. The National Academy never made him an associate and he was denied membership in the Century Association. In 1883 he married and moved to Saint Augustine, Florida, where he for the first time in his life established a productive relationship with a patron, Henry Morrison Flagler. He continued to paint, executing a number of fine views of Florida marshlands and still lifes of magnolias and other cut flowers. In Saint Augustine Heade and his wife were the center of a small artists' colony, but when he died he had been largely forgotten by the rest of the American art world. It was only with the revival of interest in American art during the 1940s that his reputation was restored. *Patricia Burda*

McIntire, Robert G. *Martin Johnson Heade*. New York, 1948.
Stebbins, Theodore E., Jr. *Martin Johnson Heade*. Exh. cat., University of Maryland Art Gallery. College Park, 1969.
Stebbins, Theodore E., Jr. *The Life and Works of Martin Johnson Heade*. New Haven and London, 1975.

EDWARD LAMSON HENRY (1841–1919)

Born in Charleston, South Carolina, in 1841 and orphaned at seven years of age, Henry was taken to New York to be raised by his cousins, the Stows. His first instructor in art was landscape painter Walter M. Oddie. He was a pupil at the Pennsylvania Academy of Fine Arts before touring Europe from 1860–1862 and studying with Suisse, Gleyre, and Courbet in Paris. Back in New York, Henry painted scenes from his European travels and American genre scenes. Architecture, often of then-historic homes and churches, and modes of transportation, from horse and carriage to steamboats and locomotives, quickly became his favored subjects. His hobbies of photography and collecting antique furniture, carriages, and costumes provided him with visual aids for his paintings.

Henry quickly achieved financial success. Many of his paintings were sold before they were shown in the National Academy of Design exhibitions. His peers gave him early recognition by electing him an associate of the National Academy in 1867 and a full member in 1869 at the age of 28. Until 1885 he painted in the famous Tenth Street Studio Building.

In 1883, Henry built a house in Cragsmoor, New York, which became his principal residence about 1887. With Henry's help, Cragsmoor became a lively summer art colony. The residents and surroundings here and at nearby Ellenville appear in many of Henry's late genre scenes. Henry died in Ellenville in May 1919. *Sarah Towne Hufford*

McCausland, Elizabeth. *The Life and Work of Edward Lamson Henry, N.A., 1841–1919*. New York, 1970 (reprint of the *New York State Museum Bulletin* No. 339, 1945).
Buff, Barbara Ball. "Mr. Henry of Cragsmoor." *Archives of American Art Journal* 21, no. 3 (1981), 2–7.
Christman, Jan P., and Maureen Radl. *E. L. Henry's Country Life*. Exh. cat., the Cragsmoor Free Library. Cragsmoor, New York, 1981.

GEORGE INNESS (1825–1894)

Born in Newburgh, New York, George Inness spent his youth in Newark, New Jersey. He worked for his father, a grocer, and studied briefly with John Jesse Barker (active 1815–1856), an itinerant painter working in Newark. He then moved to New York, where he apprenticed two years with the engraving firm Sherman and Smith. His only other formal training was a brief period of study in 1846 with Regis François Gignoux (1816–1882), a French landscape painter working in Brooklyn. Inness first exhibited his paintings at the National Academy of Design in 1844, and came to be considered one of the finest landscape painters in America. He worked within the academic landscape formulas of Claude, Poussin, and the Dutch, but rather than painting careful transcriptions of nature as did many of his fellow American landscape painters in the second generation of the Hudson River school, his style became progressively more expressive and visionary.

Inness spent fifteen months in Italy from 1850 to 1852. In France from 1853 to 1854 he studied Barbizon painting, and as a result his own work became more painterly in technique and more poetic in subject. In the 1860s he moved from Medfield, Massachusetts, to Eagleswood, New Jersey. During this time he was introduced to the writings of the Swedish religious thinker Emanuel Swedenborg. Inness lived in Italy from 1870 to 1874 and visited France in 1875.

His late paintings, softly blurred, misty, and moody, evoke the concepts of Swedenborgianism, with vaguely defined forms suggesting the simultaneity of earthly and spiritual existence. Although he had been criticized early in his career for what was then an unusual approach to landscape, Inness became one of the few landscape painters of his generation whose work survived the change in taste in the last decades of the nineteenth century from strictly objective to more personal interpretations of the subject. Inness traveled to Virginia, Connecticut, Massachusetts, and California. He often wintered in Florida, and made his home in the last twenty years of his life in Montclair, New Jersey. He died on a trip to Scotland in 1894. *Debora Rindge*

Inness, George, Jr. *Life, Art, and Letters of George Inness*. New York, 1917.
McCausland, Elizabeth. *George Inness, An American Landscape Painter, 1825–94*. Springfield, Massachusetts, 1946.
Ireland, LeRoy. *The Paintings of George Inness*. Austin and London, 1965.
Cikovsky, Nicolai, Jr. *George Inness*. New York, 1971.
—. *The Life and Works of George Inness*. New York, 1977.
—, and Michael Quick. *George Inness*. Los Angeles, 1985.

JOHN FREDERICK KENSETT (1816–1872)

Born in Cheshire, Connecticut, John F. Kensett trained as an engraver in his youth. He worked with his father and his uncle in their printmaking shops in Cheshire and New Haven, and apprenticed with master engraver Peter Maverick (1780–1831) in New York before he was fourteen. Until 1840 he worked professionally as an engraver in New Haven, New York City, and Albany.

Aspiring to become a painter, Kensett exhibited a landscape subject at the National Academy of Design in 1838. Seeking study and travel abroad, he sailed to Europe in 1840 in the company of three other artists: the highly respected engraver Asher B. Durand (see cat. 5), who had recently become a painter, John Casilear (1811–1893), whom Kensett had known since his apprenticeship with Maverick, and Thomas P. Rossiter (1818–1871), a friend from New Haven. Kensett's extensive tour lasted seven years, including a residence of two years in England and several seasons in Paris and Rome. He sought engraving contracts to support himself until about 1845, at which point the proceeds of sales of a number of his paintings to the American Art-Union freed him to devote all his time to painting, and he began to produce landscapes for exhibition at the National Academy of Design.

When Kensett returned to the United States in 1847, he was recognized as a prominent artist. Active in New York art and literary circles, he became an associate of the National Academy of Design in 1848, and was made a full member the following year. He was invited to join the Century Association in 1849, and in 1854 was made a member of the Sketch Club. Kensett would leave his city studio in summer to paint in popular resort environs in the Northeast, at seaside locales such as Newport, Rhode Island, and inland to areas such as Lake George. His painting style, with its meticulous rendering of detail, evidences his background in printmaking. He was also influenced by Asher B. Durand and by the writings of British critic John Ruskin (1819–1900), both of whom advocated that artists make direct observations from nature. A leading member of the second generation of the Hudson River School, Kensett painted crisply rendered, brightly lit expanses of land and water that evoke a mood of tranquility.

Kensett traveled beyond the Hudson River area as well, trekking west as far as Montana and Colorado, and he returned to Europe in 1856, 1861, and 1867. A champion of the development of American art, Kensett was appointed a member of the Art Commission of the U.S. Capitol in 1859, chaired the Art Committee of the New York Metropolitan Fair in 1863–1864, and was a founding trustee of the Metropolitan Museum of Art in 1870. Much admired by his contemporaries and at the peak of his career, Kensett died in New York at the age of fifty-two. *Debora Rindge*

Johnson, Ellen H. "Kensett Revisited." *Art Quarterly* 20 (Spring 1957), 71–92.
Howat, John K. *John Frederick Kensett, 1816–1872*. New York, 1968.
Driscoll, John Paul. *John F. Kensett Drawings*. University Park, Pennsylvania, 1978.
Driscoll, John Paul, and John K. Howat. *John Frederick Kensett: An American Master*. New York, 1985.

ERNEST LAWSON (1873–1939)

Ernest Lawson was born in Halifax, Nova Scotia, on 22 March 1873, and spent the majority of his first fifteen years with relatives in Kingston, Ontario, before rejoining his parents in Kansas City. It was there that Lawson first studied painting at the Kansas City Art Institute with Ella Holman, whom he eventually married. A year later his family moved to Mexico City, where his father was a physician for an engineering firm, and Lawson worked as a draftsman while attending evening classes at the Santa Carlos Art School. Having saved enough money, at the age of eighteen he went to New York, studying with John Twachtman and J. Alden Weir at the Art Students League and then at their school at Cos Cob, Connecticut. The work of both formed a basis upon which Lawson drew throughout his career. Lawson traveled to Paris in 1893 to study with Jean-Paul Laurens at the Académie Julian, and once there shared a studio with the author Somerset Maugham. He later worked at Moret-sur-Loing where he met Alfred Sisley, who had a noticeable impact on his work while in France. He exhibited two works at the Salon of 1894, and returned to the United States briefly to marry Ella Holman. By 1898 Lawson had brought his young family to New York and settled in Washington Heights on the Harlem River, where they lived until 1927. It was from this location that his multitude of Harlem River scenes were inspired. In 1904 he met William Glackens, and through him other members of the soon-to-be "Eight." The acclaim the group received in 1908 caused the National Academy of Design to invite the artists to exhibit work at the spring exhibition, where Lawson won the Hallgarten prize and was made an associate member of the academy. In 1916 Lawson was able to take his family to Segovia, Spain, remaining there for about a year, and upon returning in 1917 was elected a full member of the academy. Throughout the late 1920s Lawson taught in Kansas City and Colorado Springs, eventually returning to New York in 1929. Through the 1930s Lawson suffered several setbacks, including a lack of funds, a decrease in sales, and deteriorating health. He spent the majority of the time in Florida. On 8 December 1939, Lawson's body was found floating off Miami. It was presumed that he died of a heart attack. *James W. Tottis*

Berry-Hill, Henry and Sidney. *Ernest Lawson—American Impressionist*. Leigh-on-Sea, 1968.
Young, Mahonri Sharp. *The Eight*. New York, 1973.

WILLARD LEROY METCALF (1858–1925)

Metcalf was born in Lowell, Massachusetts, and served a brief apprenticeship to a wood engraver. In 1876 he entered the studio of the landscape painter Charles Loring Brown while also attending life drawing classes at the Lowell Institute. He advanced his training at the Massachusetts Normal Art School and the School of Fine Arts, Boston.

To support his art education Metcalf turned to illustration, and in the early 1880s he traveled twice to the Southwest to sketch the Zuni tribe for popular periodicals. With his earnings as an illustrator and from the sale of some paintings he went to Europe in 1883, first visiting England and then Paris, where he studied at the Académie Julian under Gustave Boulanger and Jules-Joseph Lefebvre. During the summer months he sketched and painted in the countryside at Brittany, Grez-sur-Loing, and Giverny, the home of Claude Monet. An 1887 visit to Tunis and Morocco inspired the large painting *Arab Market*, which received an honorable mention at the Salon in 1888.

In 1889 Metcalf returned to Boston, and then moved to New York where he taught at the Art Students League and at the Cooper Institute. Metcalf was one of the first to sign the agreement of the Ten American Painters to secede from the Society of American Artists, and he exhibited with the group regularly after 1897. His work (chiefly portraits in the 1890s) did not receive satisfying critical attention until after 1903 when he underwent a personal crisis and turned anew to landscape painting. The success of what Metcalf termed his *first personal exhibition*, held at Fishel, Adler and Schwartz Gallery, New York, the following February, was immediate. Royal Cortissoz praised all twenty-one paintings as evidence of Metcalf's "new spirit" and "truth to the very soul of the American landscape." From that time on the artist devoted himself to recording the changing moods and seasons of the New England countryside.
Nancy Rivard Shaw

Cortissoz, Royal. "Willard L. Metcalf, An American Landscape Painter." *Appleton's Booklovers Magazine* 6 (October 1905), 509–511.
Teevan, Bernard. "A Painters Renaissance." *International Studio* 82, no. 341 (October 1925), 3–11.
De Veer, Elizabeth. *Willard Leroy Metcalf: A Retrospective*. Exh. cat., Museum of Fine Arts. Springfield, Massachusetts, 1976.

FRANCIS DAVIS MILLET (1846–1912)

Francis Davis Millet was born in Mattapoisett, Massachusetts. After service as a drummer in the Civil War and graduation from Harvard (class of 1869), Millet served as a reporter for Boston newspapers and studied lithography. From 1871 through March 1873 he was enrolled at Antwerp's Royal Academy, gaining an unprecedented number of prizes and medals. Millet spent another two years in Europe, the first principally in Austria as secretary to Charles Francis Adams at the Vienna Exposition, and the second traveling throughout Italy. Although in Rome he began his professional career as a portrait painter, as early as 1876 Millet submitted genre scenes to both the National Academy of Design and the Philadelphia Centennial Exhibition. Also during 1876 Millet reported on the centennial for a Boston newspaper and assisted John La Farge (1835–1910) in the decoration of Trinity Church, Boston. This juxtaposition of painting, decorative work, writing, and concern over the administration of major international expositions was characteristic of Millet's energies, and recurred throughout his career.

In 1877 Millet returned to Europe, settling briefly in Paris before serving as a war correspondent at the front in the Russo-Turkish War. In 1879 he returned to Boston, moving the next year to New York where he played an active role in professional organizations (Society of American Artists, 1880; associate of the National Academy of Design, 1881; promoted to academician, 1885; and elected vice president, 1891), social circles (he was a member of both the Tile Club and The Kinsmen, among many others), and taught classes in the history of costume at Harvard and the National Academy. His National Academy painting of 1883, *Reading the Story of Œnone* (Detroit Institute of Arts), modeled on the classicizing fantasies of Lawrence Alma-Tadema (1836–1912), was his first painting to enter a public museum collection (as well as being the first painting purchased by the Detroit Institute).

Although Millet had visited England several times previously, in 1884 he first visited the Worcestershire village of Broadway, where in the next year he established his principal family residence. An active exhibitor in both American and British annuals, Millet gained his greatest fame as a painter of historical genre scenes of the seventeenth through the early nineteenth centuries (*The Granddaughter*, 1885, Museum of Fine Arts, Boston; *Between Two Fires*, 1891, Tate Gallery, London). From 1892 onward, as director of decorations for the World's Columbian Exposition in Chicago, Millet's career as a designer and muralist took ever more of his time, although he continued his genre paintings, traveled extensively (Alaska, 1905; Japan, China, and Korea, 1908; Panama, 1911), served again as a war correspondent (in the Philippines in 1898/1899 during the Spanish-American War), and participated in many fine-arts planning commissions. It was in his capacity as the chief administrative officer of the American Academy in Rome that Millet sailed on the *Titanic* in 1912. He was among those who died on the night of 14 April after the ship struck an iceberg in the North Atlantic. *Marc Simpson*

Weinberg, H. Barbara. "The Career of Francis Davis Millet." *Archives of American Art Journal* 17, no. 1 (1977), 2–18.
Sharpey-Schafer, Joyce. *Soldier of Fortune: F. D. Millet*. Utica, New York, 1984.

THOMAS MORAN (1837–1926)

Thomas Moran was born in Bolton, Lancashire, England, the son of a weaver who later emigrated to the United States with his family. One of four brothers who eventually became artists, Moran attended public schools in Philadelphia until 1853 when he became an engraver's apprentice. Encouraged to pursue his interest in painting by his elder brother Edward (1829–1901), Moran gave up his apprenticeship after three years and began working in his brother's studio. There he met Edward's teacher, James Hamilton (1819–1878), a noted Philadelphia marine painter, who sparked his lifelong enthusiasm for the work of J. M. W. Turner (1775–1851).

In 1861, accompanied by his brother, Moran sailed for England where he spent months studying Turner watercolors and oils at the National Gallery in London. A second more extensive European trip (England, France, Italy) in 1866–1867 confirmed his allegiance to British landscape painting and Turner.

In 1870 Moran's career took a decisive turn when an editor at *Scribner's Monthly* asked him to rework several drawings that had been submitted with a manuscript describing the wonders of Yellowstone. Intrigued by the drawings and anxious to see the region for himself, Moran arranged to join Ferdinand Hayden's survey party bound for Yellowstone the following summer. In Yellowstone Moran found a land of breathtaking beauty and a display of natural color varied enough to challenge even the palette of Turner.

The chief result of Moran's first trip west was a large painting of the Grand Canyon of the Yellowstone, which was purchased by the federal government in 1872 for the Senate lobby. In 1873 Moran accompanied John Wesley Powell to the Grand Canyon and later produced a pendant to the earlier Yellowstone picture, which was also purchased by the government. Later trips to the Grand Tetons, the Mountain of the Holy Cross, Lake Tahoe, Donner Pass, and numerous other western sites resulted in drawings, watercolors, oils, engravings, and illustrations, all of which confirmed Moran's position as one of the chief interpreters of America's western landscape.

Although he continued to travel in the West during the 1880s and 1890s, Moran also made productive trips to Mexico and Europe. Captivated by Venice (again following Turner's example), he produced numerous views of the city. In 1884 he was elected a member of the National Academy of Design and in the same year completed construction of a studio at East Hampton, Long Island, where he and his wife, Mary Nimmo, a talented etcher, spent many summers.

Although his illustrations and etchings remained in demand, Moran's paintings fell out of favor with critics well before the turn of the century. The western landscapes, however, retained their power as promotional images and were reproduced extensively, often by railroad companies serving the growing national park system. In 1916 Moran moved to Santa Barbara, California, where he lived until his death in 1926.

Nancy Anderson

Wilkens, Thurman. *Thomas Moran: Artist of the Mountains.* Norman, Oklahoma, 1966.

Fryxell, Fritiof. *Home-Thoughts, From Afar: Letters of Thomas Moran to Mary Nimmo Moran.* East Hampton, New York, 1967.

Clark, Carol. *Thomas Moran: Watercolors of the American West.* Austin, 1980.

Morand, Anne, and Nancy Friese. *The Prints of Thomas Moran in the Thomas Gilcrease Institute of American History and Art.* Tulsa, 1986.

JOHANNES ADAM OERTEL (1823–1909)

Oertel was born in 1823 in Furth, Bavaria, and planned to become a Lutheran missionary. His pastor, who noticed his proclivity for drawing, urged Oertel to change his vocation. He became the pupil of J. M. Ensing Mueller, studying art and particularly engraving in Nuremberg and Munich.

After emigrating to Newark, New Jersey, in 1848, Oertel taught drawing, engraved bank notes, and painted portraits from daguerreotypes to earn a living. In 1850 he began to exhibit paintings, primarily of animals, at the American Art-Union and the National Academy of Design, and was elected an associate of the academy in 1856. In 1857–1858 he was in Washington to work on decorations for the Capitol. He continued exhibiting in New York, where his paintings on Civil War themes were especially well received. Reproductions of his religious painting known as *Rock of Ages* were extremely popular, but unfortunately for Oertel, the publisher received all of the royalties after the first few years.

Oertel was ordained a deacon in the Episcopal Church in 1867 and a priest in 1871. From 1869 to about 1894 he lived in various places painting, often serving as parish priest and carving reredoes and altars for churches. After 1894 his sons supported him while he executed four paintings on the redemption of man, a project he had first planned in 1851. He died in Vienna, Virginia, in 1909. *Sarah Towne Hufford*

Oertel, J. F. *A Vision Realized: The Life Story of Rev. J. A. Oertel, D. D., Artist, Priest, Missionary.* Milwaukee, 1917.

Malone, Dumas, ed. *Dictionary of American Biography* 13. New York, 1943.

Cosentino, Andrew J., and Henry H. Glassie. *The Capital Image, Painters in Washington, 1800–1915.* Washington, 1983.

WILLIAM MCGREGOR PAXTON (1869–1941)

Paxton grew up in the Boston area, the descendant of a New England seafaring family. After showing an early interest in art, Paxton won a scholarship in 1887 to study at the Cowles Art School with Dennis Miller Bunker. From 1889 to 1893, Paxton continued his training at the Ecole des Beaux-Arts with Jean-Léon Gérôme, Bunker's teacher, and at the Académie Julian. During a second trip to Europe in 1897, Paxton was particularly impressed with the works of Velázquez. The art of Velázquez and Vermeer provided the foundation for Paxton's mature style. Closely related to Vermeer's work were Paxton's artfully composed interior scenes, his concern with the effects of light, and his highly finished surfaces.

Paxton began his career primarily as a portrait painter. In 1904 the disclosure that his paintings reflected the theory of binocular vision, which meant that only objects in one's central vision are in focus and peripheral objects are slightly blurred, brought him national attention. After painting a highly successful portrait of former President Grover Cleveland in 1906, Paxton's reputation as a major artist was assured. From 1906 to 1913 he joined Edmund Tarbell and Frank Benson in teaching at the school of the Museum of Fine Arts, Boston. Although modernist styles began to dominate American art after the war, Paxton's paintings remained popular with the general public. His portrait commissions sustained him until his death in 1941. *Sarah Towne Hufford*

Lee, Ellen Wardwell. *William McGregor Paxton, 1869–1941.* Exh. cat., Indianapolis Museum of Art. Indianapolis, 1979.

Gerdts, William H. *American Impressionism.* New York, 1984.

Fairbrother, Trevor J. *The Bostonians: Painters of an Elegant Age, 1870–1930.* Exh. cat., Museum of Fine Arts. Boston, 1986.

RAPHAELLE PEALE (1774–1825)

Raphaelle Peale was the first major painter of still lifes in America, the initiator of a distinguished tradition in American art. He was also a painter of full-scale and miniature portraits, and with a physiognotrace cut innumerable silhouette portraits. Born in Annapolis on 17 February 1774, the oldest surviving son of Charles Willson and Rachel Brewer Peale was in many ways the son most like his father in character and talents. But he lacked the balance and good judgment of the elder Peale. Gifted in many arts—poetry, painting, and music—Raphaelle, of all the Peales, has been judged as probably the best artist in the family.

Reflecting aesthetic values evident in his harmonic still lifes, he propounded a theory that only those who could whistle, sing, or play some musical instrument could be artists. A convivial, good-humored man, he made frequent use of his talents as a story-teller, mimic, and ventriloquist: the Thanksgiving turkey would plead for mercy as he approached with a carving knife. In his humorous advertisements he solicited *painting from the corpse* under the heading *Still Life*, an association of the genre with mortality perhaps not unrelated to the theme of the exhibited still life (see cat. 37). The comic trickster side of his personality at times surfaced in painted *deceptions* that anticipated the efflorescence of trompe l'oeil painting in Philadelphia in the latter part of the nineteenth century.

Raphaelle shared his father's interest in science, assisting in the Peale Museum from the age of twelve. He was skilled in taxidermy, and undertook expeditions, including one to South America in 1792, to gather specimens. Later, in 1797, he ran the Peale Museum in Baltimore with his younger brother Rembrandt. He was active as an inventor, especially around the turn of the century, patenting bridges, a preservative for ship's timbers, a new plan for heating houses, and a method for purifying sea water.

In 1797, the year he began painting miniatures, probably instructed by his uncle James, Peale married Patty McGlathery, a red-haired woman whose sharp tongue matched her temper. In 1805 he began drinking heavily; four years later he was admitted to the Pennsylvania Hospital with "delerium," perhaps, Phoebe Lloyd argues, as much the victim of toxic doses of arsenic and mercury preservatives used in taxidermy at the Peale Museum as of alcohol; by 1812 his limbs were swollen with gout and at times he could not hold a brush. During his later years he turned increasingly to still-life painting, which permitted maximum artistic and intellectual content with minimal physical effort. At his death in 1825 he left behind a legacy of superb and profound still-life paintings that testify to the fact that beneath the comic and pathetic exterior—Charles Coleman Sellers said Raphaelle had become "a gentle, plaintive, friendly sot whom the world had left behind"—lurked a keen and thoughtful intelligence.

Jules David Prown

Raphaelle Peale. Exh. cat., Milwaukee Art Center. Milwaukee, 1959.

The Peale Family: Three Generations of American Artists. Exh. cat., Detroit Institute of Arts. Detroit, 1967.

Four Generations of Commissions: The Peale Collection of the Maryland Historical Society. Exh. cat., Maryland Historical Society. Baltimore, 1975.

Miller, Lillian B., ed. *The Collected Papers of Charles Willson Peale and His Family: A Guide and Index to the Microfiche Edition.* Millwood, New York, 1980.

Cikovsky, Nicolai, Jr. *Raphaelle Peale Still Lifes.* Exh. cat., National Gallery of Art. Washington, 1988.

Lloyd, Phoebe. "Philadelphia Story." *Art in America* (November 1988), 155–203.

CHARLES SPRAGUE PEARCE (1851–1914)

Charles Sprague Pearce was born in Boston, the son of China merchant Shadrach Houghton Pearce and grandson of the poet Charles Sprague. Following an education at the Brimmer and Boston Latin schools, he worked in his father's mercantile business for five years, painting as an amateur. On the advice of William Morris Hunt, Pearce chose Paris as the place to embark on a painting career, entering the atelier of Léon Bonnat in 1873.

A serious respiratory condition required that the artist seek a warmer climate, and during the winter of 1873 he traveled to Egypt with fellow artist Frederick A. Bridgman (1847–1927) for the first of several visits. His study with Bonnat, a leading orientalist and portrait painter, as well as his visits to Egypt and Algeria, directed Pearce's first significant efforts toward biblical subjects. After his debut at the Paris salon in 1876 with *A Portrait of Miss W*[alworth] (unlocated), Pearce submitted an Old Testament episode, *Lamentations over the Death of the First-born of Egypt* (National Museum of American Art, Smithsonian

Institution, Washington) in the realistic manner of Bonnat to the Salon of 1877. This initial success was followed by *The Sacrifice of Abraham* (unlocated) in 1879, and *The Beheading of Saint John the Baptist* (formerly The Art Institute of Chicago) in 1881. During these years he also produced portraits and orientalist genre paintings, including *The Arab Jeweler* (The Metropolitan Museum of Art, New York), exhibited at the Salon of 1882.

In the early 1880s Pearce turned to more sentimental contemporary subjects, especially the depiction of the French peasant popularized by Jean François Millet, Jules Breton, and Jules Bastien-Lepage. Pearce attracted critical attention as an author of peasant genre paintings with his submissions to the Salon of 1883, *Prélude!* (private collection, Boston) and *The Water Carrier* (private collection, Los Angeles). *A Shepherdess—Souvenir of Picardie* (unlocated), an ambitious, single-figure work of twelve by eight feet, was extolled and illustrated by the *Art Amateur* in its review of the Salon of 1886. This work was subsequently exhibited at the Exposition Universelle in Paris in 1889, where the *New York Times* critic proclaimed that *the real honors of the show will go . . . to Charles Sprague Pearce.*

The reviewer of the 1887 Paris Salon for the London *Magazine of Art* observed that Pearce's *Saint Genevieve* (private collection, Philadelphia) was indebted to the example of Bastien-Lepage, noting *The former master's well-known Joan of Arc* [now at The Metropolitan Museum of Art, New York] *has haunted his American admirer, though there is nothing approaching servile imitation in the picture*, and indeed Pearce's painting undeniably shows some influence of the French master. In contrast to many of his sympathetic, near-sentimental depictions of peasants, Pearce's *Village Funeral* (Joseph S. Waterman and Sons, Boston), which he exhibited at the Salon of 1891, is a harsher, more naturalistic view of French rural life.

Pearce was frequently compared with his countryman Daniel Ridgway Knight, who specialized in the genre, but any categorization of Pearce as a mere painter of French peasant scenes is too narrow. He made interesting essays in *japonisme* such as *Fantasie* (The Pennsylvania Academy of the Fine Arts, Philadelphia) and the more authentic *A Cup of Tea* (Smith College Museum of Art, Northampton, Massachusetts); sophisticated French costume portraits such as *La Dame de la Directoire* (Elvehjam Museum of Art, Madison, Wisconsin) and *The Mask* (The Armand Hammer Collection, Los Angeles); and suave *portraits d'apparat* such as the depiction of his friend, the sculptor *Paul Wayland Bartlett* (National Portrait Gallery, Smithsonian Institution, Washington).

Pearce was very active in American expatriate art circles, serving as a member of the juries of awards for the Paris exposition of 1889 and the Antwerp exposition of 1904, and chairman of Paris juries for the American expositions in Chicago in 1893 and Saint Louis in 1904. He remained in Auvers and Paris the rest of his life, visiting this country in the 1890s in relation to a series of six lunette mural decorations for the Library of Congress. *D. Dodge Thompson*

"Charles Sprague Pearce." *Art Amateur* 10, no. 1 (December, 1883), 5–6.
Quick, Michael. "Charles Sprague Pearce." *American Expatriates of the Late Nineteenth Century*. Exh. cat., Dayton Art Institute. Dayton, 1976, 122–123.
Burke, Doreen Bolger. "Charles Sprague Pearce 1851–1914." *American Paintings in the Metropolitan Museum of Art*. New York, 1980, 117–119.

ENOCH WOOD PERRY (1831–1915)

Enoch Wood Perry, Jr. was born in Boston, where his father had a grate and fender shop. The family moved to New Orleans, where Perry graduated from high school and worked as a clerk from 1848 to 1852, painting in his spare time. By then he had saved enough money to study in Europe. Sailing in 1852, he traveled through London and Paris before he enrolled at the Düsseldorf Academy for two years, where he was accepted into the studio of Emanuel Leutze (1816–1868). In Paris again in 1854, he joined the studio of Thomas Couture (1815–1879). He went on to Rome, then from 1856 to 1858 served as the United States Consul in Venice, a position his father helped him to secure, which permitted him to continue his studies in Italy. He returned to the United States in 1858, settling in Philadelphia for two years.

Perry traveled frequently, earning his livelihood in this early period by painting portraits of political leaders and prominent citizens in New Orleans from 1860 to 1862, Hawaii in 1864, and Salt Lake City in 1865. He also painted landscapes. From San Francisco, where he had arrived in 1862, he journeyed to the Yosemite Valley in the summer of 1863 with artists Albert Bierstadt (cats. 18, 33), whom he had met in Europe, and Virgil Williams (1830–1886), author Fitz Hugh Ludlow, and metallurgist Dr. John Hewston. Bierstadt's influence is evident in Perry's Yosemite subjects.

Perry moved to New York in 1866, and was in Bierstadt's former studio in the Tenth Street Studio Building by January of 1867. The success of the genre paintings he began to produce after the Civil War led to his election as an associate of the National Academy of Design in 1868; he was made a full member the following year. Although he maintained a studio in New York most of the rest of his life, he traveled frequently through the United States and Europe. He spent about three years in San Francisco before 1881, and after he married in 1899 he built a studio and summered in New Hampshire. He died in New York at the age of eighty-four. *Debora Rindge*

Sheldon, George W. *American Painters*. New York, 1879, 70–72.
Cowdrey, Bartlett. "The Discovery of Enoch Wood Perry." *Old Print Shop Portfolio* 4 (April 1945), 170–181.
Gibbs, Linda Mary Jones. Enoch Wood Perry, Jr.: A Biography and Analysis of His Thematic and Stylistic Development. M. A. thesis, University of Utah, 1981.

JOHN FREDERICK PETO (1854–1907)

Born in Philadelphia on 21 May 1854, Peto was one of four children of Thomas Hope and Catherine Ham Peto. The artist's father was a gilder and dealer in picture frames, and served as an honorary member of the Philadelphia Fire Department. Through the latter association the young man may have developed his love of playing the cornet, perhaps first learned while participating in parades and recreational band music. In any case, musical instruments were a familiar part of Peto's household and violins especially became a favorite subject in a number of his best canvases. For much of his youth Peto lived with his grandmother, Mrs. William Hoffman Ham, and early on he took an interest in drawing and sketching. Even before he enrolled for formal study at the Pennsylvania Academy of the Fine Arts in 1877, he had determined to be a professional artist, having completed his first accomplished canvas two years before and listed his occupation in the Philadelphia city directory in 1876 as a painter. During his two years at the academy, and for most of the 1880s in studios along Chestnut Street, Peto led an active career within the Philadelphia art environment: he struck up an association with William Michael Harnett, probably studied with Thomas Eakins, became acquainted with photography through William Bell who married into the family, and exhibited periodically at the academy. Eighteen eighty-seven was a major point in his life, for a painting commission took him to Cincinnati where he met his future wife, Christine Pearl Smith. Soon married, Peto began spending time on the New Jersey coast at Island Heights, where he built a house and moved permanently in 1889. The couple's only child, Helen, became the center of the artist's life, which otherwise was marred occasionally by difficult and senile maiden aunts who came to live with the family. Estate problems and Bright's disease brought increasing pain to Peto's later years and an early death in 1907. *John Wilmerding*

Frankenstein, Alfred. *John F. Peto*. Exh. cat., Brooklyn Institute of Arts and Sciences, The Brooklyn Museum. Brooklyn, 1950.
—. *After the Hunt: William Harnett and Other American Still Life Painters, 1870–1900*. Rev. ed. Berkeley and Los Angeles, 1969.
—. *The Reality of Appearance: The Trompe L'Oeil Tradition in American Painting*. Exh. cat., University Art Museum, Berkeley. Berkeley, 1970.
Gerdts, William H., and Russell Burke. *American Still-Life Painting*. New York, 1971.
Gerdts, William H. *Painters of the Humble Truth: Masterpieces of American Still Life, 1801–1939*. Exh. cat., Philbrook Art Center, Tulsa, Oklahoma. Columbia, Missouri, 1981.
Wilmerding, John. *Important Information Inside: The Art of John F. Peto and the Idea of Still-Life Painting in Nineteenth-Century America*. Washington, D.C. and New York, 1983.

MAURICE PRENDERGAST (1858–1924)

Maurice Prendergast was born in Newfoundland in 1858. Sometime in the 1860s the Prendergast family moved to Boston where the artist and his younger brother, Charles, attended grammar school. After the eighth grade Maurice went to work, reportedly beginning by wrapping packages at a dry goods store. His brother Charles, a craftsman of fine carved picture frames and later an artist in his own right, recalled that Maurice always wanted to be an artist and spent every available moment sketching. When he was able to save enough to begin formal study of art, Maurice Prendergast elected not to study in Boston but instead traveled to Paris where he became a student at the Académie Julian in 1892.

Returning to Boston in 1895, Prendergast began a lifelong career as an artist. His primary interest was portraying people at leisure: strolling in parks, on the beach, or city streets. Prendergast documented a elegant world of ladies who sit shaded from the sun by parasols, children who walk with balloons, and couples who stroll down fashionable boulevards. He worked in watercolor and oil as well as monotype, the unusual print process that results in single (or occasionally double) editions. In 1898 he went to Venice; he returned the next year with watercolors that recorded the city in precise detail. Word of his mastery of the watercolor medium led Macbeth Galleries in New York to give the artist a one-man exhibition in 1900. Prendergast, however, was not content to simply repeat the format and style of his successful works; having established his reputation as a painter of delicate light-filled watercolors, Prendergast went on to experiment with darker, more abstract oil paintings that were not as well received by reviewers. Feeling himself to be in need of new inspiration, he traveled to France again in 1907, where he saw the new hot-colored fauve paintings and the complex compositions of Paul Cézanne. Integrating the lessons from the trip to France into his work, Prendergast painted more forceful works of art, still of the same subject matter, but with startling bright colors and staccato brushstrokes. As one of the eight "Men of the Rebellion" who staged an exhibition at the Macbeth Galleries in 1908, which was held as a challenge to the more conservative leaders in the art world, Prendergast was sharply criticized for paintings that seemed to be too abstract and brightly colored.

After another trip to Venice in 1911–1912, Prendergast returned to serve on the committee of artists who organized the Armory Show, the famous 1913 international exhibition of modern art in New York. In 1914 Maurice and Charles Prendergast, disappointed in the lack of interest in Boston for modern painting, together moved to New York City. There in 1915 Prendergast had another one-person show, this time at the newly established Carroll Galleries. Although the critical reaction to Prendergast's work continued to be mixed, he developed several important patrons in this period, among them John Quinn, Lillie B. Bliss, and Dr. Albert Barnes. In the last years of his life, he continued to paint the same subjects (often repainting the same canvases), but with figures that were even more a part of the decorative pattern of the composition and less convincing as actual bodies. By the time of his death in 1924, artistic taste was beginning to catch up with Prendergast; he was widely regarded, both by artists and critics, as the first American artist to be a modernist and as the artist who really understood the concepts of structure and form found in Paul Cézanne's work. Since that time, Prendergast's reputation as an important American artist in the crucial turn-of-the-century period has continued to grow. His work is today widely exhibited and found in many public and private collections.

Gwendolyn Owens

Basso, Hamilton. "A Glimpse of Heaven." *The New Yorker* 22 (27 July 1946), 24–30; (3 August 1946), 28–35.

Rhys, Hedley Howell. *Maurice Prendergast 1859–1924*. Cambridge, Massachusetts, 1960.

Green, Eleanor, Ellen Glavin, S.N.D., and Jeffrey Hayes. *Maurice Prendergast: Art of Impulse and Color*. Exh. cat., University of Maryland Art Gallery. College Park, 1976.

Owens, Gwendolyn. *Watercolors by Maurice Prendergast from New England Collections*. Exh. cat., Clark Art Institute. Williamstown, Massachusetts, 1978.

Langdale, Cecily. *Monotypes by Maurice Prendergast in the Terra Museum of American Art*. Exh. cat., Terra Museum of American Art. Chicago, 1984.

WILLIAM TYLEE RANNEY (1813–1857)

William Ranney was born in Middletown, Connecticut, the son of a ship's captain. In 1826 he was sent to live with an uncle in Fayetteville, North Carolina. He began to draw during his six-year apprenticeship to a smith there. When he returned to the north in 1833 or 1834, he found employment in an architect's office in New York, and studied painting and drawing.

In the early years of his career, Ranney's work consisted primarily of portraits and historical subjects, but later he became better known as a genre painter who specialized in scenes depicting hunters, trappers, and frontier settlers in the southwest. Although these paintings were produced in his studio in the east, they feature outdoor settings peopled with regional types inspired by Ranney's eight-month stint in the army of the Republic of Texas. In response to the call for volunteers after the battle of the Alamo in 1836, Ranney went to New Orleans to enlist in the fight for Texas independence. The sketches he made during this period became the sources for his later western paintings.

Returning east in 1837, Ranney lived in Brooklyn. The following year he received his first commission for a *Portrait of Mr. Thompson* (whereabouts unknown), which was exhibited at the National Academy of Design. Working primarily in portraiture, he established a studio in New York City in 1843. About 1845, however, scenes of frontier life began to dominate his work. In a decade when national attention was drawn to the West, with the admission of Texas to the Republic, the outbreak of the Mexican War, and the onset of the California gold rush, Ranney's evocations of incidents witnessed ten years earlier were a timely response to current events.

The appeal of Ranney's work can be measured in part by the frequent patronage of the American Art-Union in New York and the Western Art-Union in Cincinnati. At the middle of the century, genre subjects were tremendously popular with the American audience. Unlike the domestic interiors and often humorous narratives painted by his contemporaries, Ranney's subjects are heroicized, cast in static poses, and set in stark, open landscapes. Although he occasionally rendered such dramatic incidents as prairie fires, scenes with Indians are rare, and there are no subjects depicting events related to the Texas fight for independence. Ranney's paintings instead are moody expressions of the quiet isolation that characterizes the vastness of the West.

Held in high esteem by his colleagues as well as by the popular audience, he was elected an associate of the National Academy of Design in 1850. In 1853, Ranney moved to rural West Hoboken, New Jersey, where a studio filled with saddles and other frontier paraphernalia furthered his identity as a painter of western subjects. After a lingering illness, his career was cut short when he died of consumption at the age of fourty-four. *Debora Rindge*

Grubar, Francis S. *William Ranney: Painter of the Early West*. Exh. cat., Corcoran Gallery of Art. Washington, 1962.

Ayres, Linda. "William Ranney." *American Frontier Life: Early Western Painting and Prints*. Exh. cat., Amon Carter Museum. Fort Worth, 1987.

ROBERT REID (1862–1929)

Born in Stockbridge, Massachusetts, Reid began to study art in 1880 at the Boston Museum of Fine Arts School under Otto Grundman (1848–1890) and Frederick Crowninshield (1845–1918). Among his classmates were Edmund Tarbell (1862–1938) and Frank Benson (1862–1951), artists with whom he would be associated throughout his life. Reid served as assistant instructor for three years, while founding and later contributing to the school's journal, *Art Student*. He studied briefly at New York's Art Students League in 1884–1885; by the fall of 1885 he had traveled to France and enrolled in the Académie Julian. He spent three summers in Etaples on the Normandy coast, the site of an artists' colony and inspiration for sentimental and religious narrative works such as *Death of the First Born* (1888, The Brooklyn Museum). He exhibited in the Paris Salons of 1887, 1888, and 1889 and the Exposition Universelle of 1889.

Returning to New York in July of 1889, Reid taught at the Art Students League and the Cooper Union, and soon became active in mural decoration. His first murals were painted for the Liberal Arts Building of the 1893 World's Columbian Exposition; later commissions included churches, hotels, and court houses in Boston and New York, as well as the Library of Congress in Washington, and the Fine Arts Building of the Panama-Pacific Exposition in San Francisco. For the decoration of a church in Fairhaven, Massachusetts, Reid executed a scheme in stained glass.

Despite his accomplishments in mural decoration, Reid continued to paint easel pictures throughout his life, works such as *Fleur de Lis* (c. 1899, The Metropolitan Museum of Art, New York) that are notable for their bold design and glowing color. He was a founding member of The Ten, a group of artists who withdrew from the Society of American Artists in 1897 in protest over their policies for selecting and displaying work, and he exhibited with that body from 1898 to 1919. His lyrical, highly decorative paintings of the late 1890s and after favor the theme of elegant women, often dressed in exotic costumes or surrounded by flowers, painted with broad strokes and organized around a dominant hue. In his later career Reid created "portrait impressions," brief descriptions of his sitter captured with only a few energetic strokes. In 1917 Reid moved to Colorado Springs, helping found the Broadmoor Academy there. Stricken with polio at the age of 63, his final years were marred by paralysis, and he died in 1929. *Sally Mills*

Goodrich, Henry W. "Robert Reid and his Work." *International Studio* 36 (February 1909), 113–122.

Hoeber, Arthur. "Robert Reid." *The Century Magazine* 77 (March 1909), 799.

Brinton, Christian. "Robert Reid: Decorative Impressionist." *Arts and Decoration* 2 (November 1911), 13–15.

Weinberg, H. Barbara. "Robert Reid: Academic 'Impressionist.'" *Archives of American Art Journal* 15 (January 1975), 2–11.

Gerdts, William H. *American Impressionism*. New York, 1984, 181–185.

MARTIN ANDREAS REISSNER (1798–1862)

Few details are known about the life of this German expatriate artist, and only two of his paintings have been located in America to date (*The Delaware Water Gap, Pennsylvania*, 1854, private collection). Almost certainly born in Germany, by 1819 Reissner had settled in Riga, then the second most important Baltic port in Russia, now the largest city in Latvia. Reissner may have had some artistic training or affiliation in Riga, long a cultural center, since shortly before his death he donated a landscape of Niagara Falls to the city's art academy. Between 1819 and about 1848, when he arrived in America, Reissner traveled from Riga to Switzerland and Italy, where he painted landscapes (some of which he later exhibited in America). At some point during this period he journeyed north to Saint Petersburg, where for a number of years he oversaw scene painting at the Imperial theater.

Reissner is first recorded as living in America in 1849, when he appeared in the New York city directory and exhibited at the American Art-Union. He must have arrived from Riga at least a year earlier, however, since by the fall of 1848 he had already executed and in New York exhibited an enormous panorama of General Zachary Taylor's campaign in the Mexican War. According to newspaper accounts, the panorama was executed from life sketches made by one of General Taylor's officers, covering 10,000 feet of canvas, and containing figures of 350,000 men and animals. A commission well suited to his scene and landscape painting experience, the panorama was subsequently exhibited in Philadelphia's Franklin Hall from November 1848 to January 1849.

In 1850 Reissner exhibited at the National Academy of Design for the first and only time, and had moved to Brooklyn. He then moved frequently within Brooklyn, as he is listed in city directories at five different addresses between 1852 and 1861. However, absences from three directories coincide with his documented presence elsewhere during these years, suggesting at least two brief periods of itinerancy: the first to the midwest where he painted *The Forest Queen in Winter* (cat. 31) in 1857, and the second to the Philadelphia area in 1859, when he exhibited from Germantown at the Pennsylvania Academy of the Fine Arts (again for the first and only time). Though listed as an artist in most of the city directories, he seems to have specialized during certain periods: in 1852–1853 he is shown as a printer, and in the 1853–1854 and 1854–1855 directories as a portrait painter.

The titles of the works Reissner painted in America—the two aforementioned as well as *Scene near Canaan, New York*, and *The Devil's Whirlpool, Cresham Creek, near Germantown (Moonlight)*, both of which were exhibited at the Pennsylvania Academy of the Fine Arts in 1859—suggest that he traveled widely in America, as he had in Europe, in search of subject matter. How prolific he was and how his artistic career progressed, however, will remain unknown until more works or more details about his life come to light. Reissner returned to Riga in 1861, and died a year later in Dorpat (then in Russian-controlled Livonia, now Tartu, Estonia) at the age of 64. *Sarah Cash*

Public Ledger [Philadelphia], 27 November 1848, 2; 2 December 1848, 3,4; 18 January 1849, 3.

Neumann, Wilhelm. *Lexikon Baltischer Künstler*. Riga, 1908.

Groce, George C., and David H. Wallace. *The New-York Historical Society's Dictionary of Artists in America 1564–1860*. New Haven and London, 1957.

WILLIAM RIMMER (1816–1879)

Sculptor, painter, lithographer, physician, and shoemaker. This was William Rimmer. Born on 20 February 1816 in Liverpool, England, Rimmer spent most of his life in America. His father, Thomas, believed himself to be the dauphin of France and, perceiving that his family was in danger, emigrated to Nova Scotia in 1818. By 1825 the Rimmers had settled in South Boston, where Thomas eventually would establish himself as a shoemaker. Nonetheless, Thomas instructed the younger Rimmer in the classics, music, art, and other teachings befitting an heir to the French throne.

Rimmer began to display an artistic affinity in his early teens, producing small sculptures and drawings. While in his early twenties he secured a position with a lithographer and shortly thereafter he and Elbridge Harris formed a partnership as sign painters.

In December of 1840 he married Mary Peabody, which was approximately when he began to study medicine. Through most of the next decade he worked as an itinerant artist, with a few commissions coming from local churches, while continuing his study of medicine. About 1848 he began to practice medicine in South Boston. From late in the 1850s through the early 1860s, while still working as a physician, Rimmer devoted more of his artistic efforts toward sculpture, producing *Saint Stephen*, *Falling Gladiator*, and *Hawk-Headed Osiris*. Then in 1866, after meeting Peter Cooper, he moved to New York and became the director of the Cooper Union School of Design for Women. He remained there four years, leaving in 1870 after a controversy arose concerning his teaching methods. During the last decade of his life Rimmer concentrated on painting, and lectured and exhibited as well. It was during these final years that he produced many of his most intriguing paintings. In August 1879 he died at the age of sixty-three. *James W. Tottis*

Bartlett, Truman H. *The Art Life of William Rimmer*. Cambridge, 1890.

Weidman, Jeffrey, Neil Harris, and Philip Cash. *William Rimmer; A Yankee Michelangelo*. Hanover, New Hampshire, 1985.

THEODORE ROBINSON (1852–1896)

Born in Irasburg, Vermont, in 1852, Theodore Robinson grew up in the Midwest, where his clergyman father brought the family in 1855. Although he briefly studied art in Chicago in 1869, Robinson's chronic and, in the end, fatal asthma soon forced him to retreat to Denver and then home again to Evansville, Wisconsin. In 1874 Robinson moved to New York, enrolling at the National Academy of Design; while there he was instrumental in founding the Art Students League. From 1876 to 1879 Robinson was in Paris where he studied first with Carolus-Duran (1837–1917) and soon thereafter at the Ecole des Beaux-Arts with Jean-Léon Gérôme (1824–1904). During the summer of 1877, the young artist participated in the Anglo-American art colony at Grez; late the next year he traveled throughout northern Italy. In 1879 Robinson returned to the United States, eventually settling in New York where he taught, worked at decorative projects for, among others, John La Farge (1835–1910), and in 1881 joined the Society of American Artists.

In 1884 Robinson journeyed again to Europe. With the exception of occasional trips home he remained there for the next eight years. Although he stopped in Paris and Barbizon (and, during the winter of 1890/1891, Italy), the principal locale of Robinson's development was the village of Giverny, which he visited in 1887 and where he settled from 1888 to 1892. There, working closely with Claude Monet (1840–1926), the young American practiced plein-air light effects and broken brushwork in both his landscape and figural works, such as *A Bird's Eye View* (The Metropolitan Museum of Art, New York) and *The Wedding March* (Daniel J. Terra Collection, Terra Museum of American Art, Chicago). He established in the best of his paintings a strong sense of design, a distinctive and delicate color sense, and a lack of sentimentality apparently inspired by Monet, but maintained a solidity of form not found in the works of his French colleague.

On his return to the United States in 1892, Robinson taught summer classes at Napanoch, New York, and Princeton, New Jersey, as well as in 1895 the spring term at the Pennsylvania Academy of the Fine Arts. In his own work the artist sought to use his cosmopolitan technique to capture the recognizably American scenery of Connecticut and Vermont. Critical response to these American works in his first one-man exhibition (Macbeth Gallery, February 1895) was favorable, and the artist himself in late 1895 felt on the verge of a new and deeply felt emotional response to the land. Before he was able to realize this emotive depth, however, Robinson succumbed to the asthma that had plagued him all his life. *Marc Simpson*

Low, Will. *A Chronicle of Friendships*. New York, 1908.

Baur, John I. H. *Theodore Robinson, 1852–1896*. Brooklyn, 1946.

Johnston, Sona. *Theodore Robinson, 1852–1896*. Baltimore, 1973.

Clark, Eliot C. *Theodore Robinson: His Life and Art*. Chicago, 1979.

Burke, Doreen Bolger. *American Paintings in the Metropolitan Museum of Art*. New York, 1980, 3:125–129.

Gerdts, William H. *American Impressionism*. New York, 1984, 66–75, 151–154.

JOHN SINGER SARGENT (1856–1925)

John Singer Sargent was born in Florence, Italy, to an American expatriate family. Thanks to a small independent income, the Sargents continually moved across Europe, from spa to spa, shifting locale with the seasons. As a result, much of Sargent's education was gained through travel and sight-seeing. He was formally (albeit briefly) schooled in Italy and Germany, early manifesting a talent for drawing. Although he worked with a variety of artists in Italy, his first significant training began in May 1874 when he entered the Paris atelier of Carolus-Duran. Gifted with a natural facility, the next fall Sargent entered the Ecole des Beaux-Arts; he was to work in both settings for three years.

Sargent exhibited at the Salon first in 1877 and in New York the next year. In 1879 his Salon entry, *Carolus-Duran* (Sterling and Francine Clark Art Institute, Williamstown, Massachusetts), successfully launched his career. Although Sargent during the 1870s and 1880s painted genre works and incredibly vivid watercolors (in part based on his continuing travels, particularly to Spain and Venice), he gained his greatest reputation for his portraits. His Salon painting of 1884, *Madame X (Madame Pierre Gautreau)* (The Metropolitan Museum of Art, New York) climaxed his Parisian career, creating tremendous notoriety for both painter and sitter.

During the early 1880s Sargent visited England regularly, painting the families of wealthy industrialists and importing a style of working that was seen as peculiarly French. In 1885 he joined Francis Davis Millet (1846–1912) in the Worcestershire village of Broadway, where he began his masterpiece of English impressionism, *Carnation, Lily, Lily, Rose* (1887, Tate Gallery, London). In 1886 he moved permanently to London.

In 1887 Sargent traveled to the United States. The demand there for his portraits among the leaders of society altered the shape of his career, prompting a two-decades-long concentration in England and America on society portraiture that made Sargent the best-known portraitist of his generation. Although he continued to paint genre and landscape works, and undertook major mural cycles for the Boston Public Library, the Museum of Fine Arts, Boston, and others, it was as a portraitist that he was most frequently honored. A friend of some of the greatest writers, actors, and artists of his time, Sargent's later life was yet an outwardly uneventful one. As his friend Vernon Lee wrote in 1926: *More and more it has seemed to me that Sargent's life was absorbed in his painting; and the summing up of the would-be biographer must, I think, be:* he painted. *To some of us he seemed occasionally to paint to the exclusion of living.* *Marc Simpson*

Charteris, Evan. *John Sargent*. New York, 1927.
Ormond, Richard. *John Singer Sargent: Paintings, Drawings, Watercolors*. New York, 1970.
Ratcliff, Carter. *John Singer Sargent*. New York, 1982.
Hills, Patricia. *John Singer Sargent*. Exh. cat., Whitney Museum of American Art. New York, 1986.
Olson, Stanley. *John Singer Sargent: His Portrait*. New York, 1986.

FRANCIS AUGUSTUS SILVA (1835–1886)

The eldest son of an immigrant barber, Francis Silva was born in New York City and grew up near the East River docks, a telling proximity for his eventual choice of career as a marine painter. He showed artistic talent even at the age of thirteen, when he was one of three students to exhibit pen drawings at the twenty-first Annual Fair of the American Institute of the City of New York. Though he worked as a sign and ornamental painter before opening his first studio in 1858, Silva's mature artistic career did not get underway until after he had served in the New York State Militia and, in 1868, married Margaret A. Watts of Keyport, New Jersey. In that year he established himself as a painter in New York City, where he lived on the Lower East Side for most of the 1870s. He then relocated to New Jersey about 1880, but maintained his studio in New York City, which from 1882 until his death was located in the famous Tenth Street Studio Building.

Despite his lack of formal training, Silva quickly developed a crisp, polished style in both oil and watercolor, honed on his frequent painting trips throughout the 1870s in search of marine subjects. Painting titles and sketchbook notations indicate that he traveled along the East Coast from Delaware to Maine, and to Venice at least once, probably around 1879. Though he painted typically luminist subjects such as Boston Harbor, Cape Ann, Narragansett Bay, and the Hudson River, in the 1870s Silva was most prolific as a chronicler of marine views around his native New York City. After 1880, it was the New Jersey coast that occupied Silva's artistic efforts almost exclusively until the end of his life, during which time he traveled considerably less than in the previous decade.

Silva exhibited his first works at the National Academy of Design in 1868, where he continued to show almost yearly until his death. From 1869 to 1885 he was also a regular exhibitor at the Brooklyn Art Association, where he chose to show subjects of local interest such as marine and shipwreck views of Brooklyn and Long Island. In 1872 he was elected to the American Watercolor Society, and in 1873 to the Artists' Fund Society. Silva died suddenly of double pneumonia on 31 March 1886 while at the home of a friend in New York City.

Contemporary criticism of Silva's work was mixed, and after his death he was largely forgotten. He has received some attention in recent years, but little relative to his fellow luminists. Unlike the major figures such as Heade and Lane, he maintained a remarkably consistent style throughout his life, albeit highly accomplished for a self-taught artist. His repetition of subjects and compositional formulae and his intense study of light and atmospheric effects reflect a relentless pursuit of perfection. *Sarah Cash*

Werner, Charles J. F. A. Silva. Unpaginated, 1949. Charles J. Werner misc. ms., New-York Historical Society.
DeCosta, William. F. A. Silva: Painter of the Shore. Unpublished typescript, 1975. William DeCosta Papers, Archives of American Art, Smithsonian Institution.
Baur, John I. H. "Francis A. Silva: Beyond Luminism." *Antiques* 118 (November 1980), 1018–1031.

JULIUS L. STEWART (1855–1919)

Julius LeBlanc Stewart was born in Philadelphia, son of the prodigious collector William Hood Stewart (1820–1897). At the end of the Civil War the Stewarts moved to Paris, where the family continued to be supported by prosperous Cuban sugar plantations. The elder Stewart collected the contemporary works of Alma-Tadema, Baudry, Boldini, Bonnat, Corot, Fortuny, Gérôme, Madrazo, Meissonier, Rico, Stevens, Troyon, and Zamacoïs, and the younger Stewart was acquainted from an early age with many of these artists. J. L. Stewart described himself as a student of Zamacoïs, Gérôme, and Madrazo, and since the first of these painters died in 1871 when Julius was only sixteen, his art training apparently began at an early age. He entered Gérôme's atelier on 15 May 1873, and the latter's biographer Fanny Hering noted that he was one of the master's *beloved pupils*. Stewart accompanied the Frenchman to Egypt for a few months in 1874. In the mid-1870s he moved into a studio adjacent to Madrazo's on the rue Copernic. The influence of the popular Spaniard immediately became evident in Stewart's work such as the ambitious A. J. Drexel family portrait, *After the Wedding* (Drexel University, Philadelphia) of 1880.

Stewart made his debut at the Paris Salon in 1878 with two paintings, and for the next three decades exhibited continuously there as well as throughout Europe and America. His *Portrait of a Lady* (unlocated) in the 1883 Salon was called by the *Art Amateur the most sensational American picture of all*. He continued his success at the Salon in 1884 with *Five O'Clock Tea* (private collection, Philadelphia). The artist's greatest success at the Salon was the *Hunt Ball* (Essex Club, Newark) of 1885, the acclaim for which occasioned a pendent, *The Hunt Supper* (Buffalo Club) of 1889.

In the early 1880s the critics noted that Stewart was one of the principal proponents of a hybrid form of painting, a cross between portraiture and genre invariably depicting friends from the world of high society or theater in their milieus. While this form is indebted in part to the drawing-room genre compositions of his friend Jean Béraud as well as to works of contemporaries such as Albert Aubert and J. J. Tissot, Stewart brought it to the public attention at the Salon with large-scale works like *The Hunt Ball*. Much of the fascination of these works derived from the identification of the sitters. His female subjects included Lillie Langtry, Sarah Bernhardt, Christine Nilsson, Laure Hayman, the countess of Essex, the vicomtesse de Gouy d'Arcy, Baronne Rothschild, Baronne Benoist-Mechin, Baronne Bethmann, and Madame Bischoffsheim. Portraits of men included duc de Morny, Baron Nathaniel de Rothschild, vicomte de Jange, Anthony J. Drexel, and James Gordon Bennett.

Bennett, the greatest international sportsman of the era, was Stewart's most loyal patron, and was portrayed in two of the artists's most accomplished works, *On the Banks of the Seine at Bougival* (1885, Manoogian Collection), and *The Yacht Namouna in Venetian Waters* (1890, Wadsworth Atheneum).

In the late 1890s Stewart painted nudes in landscapes and views of Venice, as well as society portraits. Like Béraud he also began to paint religious subjects in contemporary costume in the early 1900s. Stewart's reputation was in eclipse until the mid-1970s, when it was revived by inclusion in a series of exhibitions (Dayton 1976, Detroit 1983). *D. Dodge Thompson*

Mendenhall, Loella B. [pseud. Laura McProud]. "Julius L. Stewart." *American Students' Census, Paris, 1903*. Paris, 1903, 110–112.
Quick, Michael. *American Expatriate Painters of the Late Nineteenth Century*. Exh. cat., Dayton Art Institute. Dayton, 1976, 135–136.
Joyner, Sue Carson. Julius L. Stewart, Life and Works. Master's thesis, Hunter College, New York, 1982.
Pyne, Kathleen, and others. *The Quest for Unity*. Exh. cat., Detroit Institute of Arts. Detroit, 1983, 243–245.
Thompson, D. Dodge. "Julius L. Stewart, a Parisian from Philadelphia." *Antiques* 130, no. 5 (November 1986), 1046–1058.

ARTHUR FITZWILLIAM TAIT (1819–1905)

When his father's prosperous mercantile business in Liverpool, England, was wiped out by the Napoleonic Wars, Arthur Fitzwilliam Tait was compelled to fend for himself. At twelve he became a clerk in Thomas Agnew's gallery in Manchester and discovered his aptitude for art. To learn a practical trade, he taught himself the fundamentals of draftsmanship, then acquired the skills of the new technology of lithography. In the 1840s he published two folios of views of the stations, viaducts, and scenery of the newly built passenger railways. Disillusioned when railways shares suddenly dropped on the stock market, Tait turned to painting in oils, producing a few creditable canvases of horses and highland hunting scenes and a portrait of a black Newfoundland dog.

To test his options and find more promising opportunities as a professional artist, Tait sailed to Manhattan in 1850 and within a few years was elected an associate of the National Academy of Design. Some of his earliest successes included canvases commissioned by the printmakers Currier & Ives. Nearly forty in all, several were dramatic episodes of life on the western prairies—a region he never visited.

But Tait discovered his true métier as a painter of the bear, deer, grouse, and trout in the Adirondack woods and waters of upstate New York, where as an enthusiastic sportsman he spent several months of each year from 1851 to 1882. On visiting the Chateaugay Lakes he became fascinated with depicting the native black bear, an animal he had not seen before in the wild.

In his later years when the patronage for sporting art all but disappeared, Tait deftly shifted to pastoral canvases of chicks, sheep, and cows in fancy gilt frames to embellish American parlors and dining rooms. He kept a careful record of his lifetime work of some 1,700 paintings. He was busy at his easel until his death at the age of eighty-five, content with the belief that in his chosen specialties he had few peers. *Warder H. Cadbury*

Cadbury, Warder H., and Henry F. Marsh. *Arthur Fitzwilliam Tait, Artist in the Adirondacks. An Account of His Career* [and] *A Checklist of His Works*. Newark, Delaware, 1986.

Cadbury, Warder H. "Arthur F. Tait." *American Frontier Life. Early Western Painting and Prints*. Ed. Ronnie C. Tyler. New York, 1987, 109–129.

JOHN TWACHTMAN (1853–1902)

John Twachtman was born in Cincinnati, Ohio, the son of German immigrants. At the age of fourteen he began working as a decorator of window shades, a trade which his father also practiced. Concurrently, he attended the Ohio Mechanics Institute and by 1871 had enrolled part-time at the McMicken School, later the Art Academy of Cincinnati. It was there, in 1874, that he met the influential American painter Frank Duveneck, who had just returned to his hometown after three years of fruitful study in Munich.

A year later Twachtman joined Duveneck in Europe, enrolling at the Royal Academy of Fine Arts in Munich where he learned the rich, dark palette and broad brushwork of that school. The artists traveled together often and it was during their second visit to Venice, in 1880, that they and other young Americans met the expatriate James McNeill Whistler. The subtle tonalities, so-called *harmonies*, of Whistler's art later had a substantial influence on Twachtman.

Briefly in the United States in 1881 for his wedding to Martha Scudder of Cincinnati, Twachtman sailed with his bride for Europe soon thereafter. They traveled through England, Belgium, and through Holland, where Twachtman painted and sketched with his friend J. Alden Weir (1852–1919). After another stay in America in 1882 for the birth of his son, Twachtman again headed for Europe.

From 1883 to 1885 he was enrolled at the Académie Julian in Paris, spending his summers in the French countryside. One of the most hauntingly beautiful paintings of this period of his career is *Arques-la-Bataille* (1885, The Metropolitan Museum of Art, New York), which depicts an expanse of silvery greens and grays, pierced in the foreground by the deep green spikes of reeds growing by the river's edge. By this time, as a result of his exposure to the art of France, Twachtman's sensitivity to the effects of natural light was heightened, yet he would not adopt his more impressionist approach to the canvas until a few years later.

After 1886 Twachtman and his family lived in Connecticut. There, Twachtman painted and etched extensively with J. Alden Weir. He also experimented with pastels, exhibiting regularly with the Society of Painters in Pastel. The delicacy and understatement of Twachtman's style is particularly evident in this medium.

In Greenwich, Connecticut, where Twachtman and his family lived after 1888, he produced perhaps his best-known, most impressionist paintings. Using as his subjects the brook, woods, and hills of his land, he displayed an extraordinary ability to capture the subtle poetry of the varied moods of nature. Although Twachtman was never very successful commercially, he was very much admired by colleagues and critics. He won a silver medal at the World's Columbian Exposition in Chicago, 1893, and a gold medal at the Pennsylvania Academy of the Fine Arts the following year. During the same decade Twachtman and his friends Childe Hassam (see cats. 55, 61) and J. Alden Weir organized The Ten, a group of painters who withdrew together from the Society of American Artists in order to exhibit their work in smaller, more personalized shows.

About 1900, Twachtman's palette became bolder and his brushwork more open, expressive, and calligraphic. Some of the most successful paintings of this period were created in the scenic fishing town of Gloucester, Massachusetts. Twachtman died there suddenly in the summer of 1902 at the age of forty-nine. *Deborah Chotner*

Hale, John Douglass. The Life and Creative Development of John H. Twachtman. Ph.D diss. Ohio State University, 1957.

Boyle, Richard J. *John Twachtman*. New York, 1979.

THOMAS WORTHINGTON WHITTREDGE (1820–1910)

Worthington Whittredge was born near Springfield, Ohio, on 22 May 1820, the son of a Massachusetts sea captain turned frontier farmer. At the age of seventeen, the younger Whittredge moved to Cincinnati to pursue a career as an artist. He began as a house and sign painter but within a year was painting portraits and landscapes. By 1844 Whittredge was established as a landscape painter in Cincinnati; two years later his *View on the Kanawha River, Morning* (location unknown) was accepted for exhibition at the prestigious National Academy of Design in New York. The academy's president, Asher B. Durand, admired the painting and sent the young artist a letter of praise and encouragement. In April 1849, secure with numerous commissions from Cincinnati patrons, Whittredge sailed for Europe, where he would spend the next decade traveling and working. While in Düsseldorf (1849–1856) he befriended Emanuel Leutze and subsequently posed for two figures in the famous *Washington Crossing the Delaware* (1851, The Metropolitan Museum of Art, New York). Whittredge also lived for a time in Düsseldorf in the attic of the landscape painter Andreas Achenbach, but apparently received no direct instruction from the German artist. Whittredge moved to Rome in 1857, where he spent much of his time with his close friends Albert Bierstadt and Sanford Gifford. The three artists toured and sketched together in Italy and Switzerland.

Upon his return to the United States in 1859, Whittredge spent a few months traveling but soon settled in the Tenth Street Studio Building in New York. He was elected an associate member of the National Academy of Design in 1860, made an academician the following year, and served as president in 1875 and 1876. He was also a member of the Century Association and became well known in New York artistic and cultural circles.

Whittredge married in 1867 and eventually moved with his family from New York to Summit, New Jersey. Throughout his life Whittredge continued to travel. He made several trips to the American West (1866, 1870, and probably 1871), often visited the Catskill Mountains of New York State, and spent many summers in Newport, Rhode Island. In 1896 (and probably earlier in 1893) he journeyed to Mexico. In 1905 Whittredge completed his autobiography, which is of considerable importance for its information about the Hudson River School of landscape painting. He died on 25 February 1910, just three months before his ninetieth birthday. *Patricia Burda*

"The Autobiography of Worthington Whittredge." John I. H. Baur, ed. *Brooklyn Museum Journal* (1942), 3–66.

Janson, Anthony F. The Paintings of Worthington Whittredge. Ph.D. diss. Harvard University, 1975.

Cibulka, Cheryl A. *Quiet Places: The American Landscapes of Worthington Whittredge*. Exh. cat., Adams Davidson Galleries. Washington, 1982.

Index of Artists Represented in the Exhibition